"*A Course Called America* is an unequivocal pleasure. Tom Coyne gives a fresh perspective on many places I've been, and I had to pause a number of times to relish the way he reflects on what he encounters—the people, the history, and the humor. Here is a soulful and thoroughly entertaining journey that will give people a sense of what golf means to so many of our friends who love the game."

—Ben Crenshaw, two-time Masters champion

"In *A Course Called America*, Tom Coyne sets out to discover what makes a great American golf course. Well, I'll tell you what makes a great American golf book—Coyne, an ambitious itinerary, and his eye for what's special on and off the course. This result is exceptional—a big, sweeping adventure, as endearing as it is sprawling, and a fitting tribute to American golf."

—Phil Landes, aka "Big Randy" from *No Laying Up*

"*A Course Called America* is a discovery of our country, our culture, our people, and the diverse ways we come to the game of golf. Tom Coyne is a wonderful storyteller, and the stories that unfold across this vast landscape called America—some laugh-out-loud funny, and some stirringly poignant—get to the soul of our game and the heart of our nation."

—Gil Hanse, renowned golf course architect

"As Tom uses his gift for storytelling to chronicle his journey through some of America's best golf courses, you'll find yourself remembering why you first fell in love with the game. *A Course Called America* is a beautifully woven-together story that is somehow hilarious and moving all at once, and paints a vivid picture of all that golf in America has to offer."

—Stacy Lewis, two-time major champion

"An entertaining blend of travelogue, memoir, and sports writing . . . Golf nuts will be tantalized by the glimpses of America's premier courses, while those looking to book an epic post-pandemic golf trip will find plenty of inspiration."

—*Publishers Weekly*

"Besides oozing with rich golf history and lore, Coyne's heartfelt anecdotes about people he meets and the joys of companionship are appealing. . . . This is a delightful, entertaining book even nongolfers can enjoy."

—*Kirkus Reviews*

A COURSE CALLED

AMERICA

FIFTY STATES, FIVE THOUSAND FAIRWAYS, AND THE SEARCH FOR THE GREAT AMERICAN GOLF COURSE

TOM COYNE

AVID READER PRESS

NEW YORK   LONDON   TORONTO   SYDNEY   NEW DELHI

AVID READER PRESS
An Imprint of Simon & Schuster, Inc.
1230 Avenue of the Americas
New York, NY 10020

First Avid Reader Press trade paperback edition May 2022

AVID READER PRESS and colophon are trademarks of Simon & Schuster, Inc.

For information about special discounts for bulk purchases,
please contact Simon & Schuster Special Sales
at 1-866-506-1949 or business@simonandschuster.com.

The Simon & Schuster Speakers Bureau can bring authors to your live event.
For more information or to book an event contact the
Simon & Schuster Speakers Bureau at 1-866-248-3049
or visit our website at www.simonspeakers.com.

Interior design by Ruth Lee-Mui
Opening map by Thomas Young/Ballpark Blueprints

Manufactured in the United States of America

3   5   7   9   10   8   6   4

Library of Congress Cataloging-in-Publication Data has been applied for.

ISBN 978-1-9821-2805-0
ISBN 978-1-9821-2806-7 (pbk)
ISBN 978-1-9821-2807-4 (ebook)

For Jim and Alice Coyne,
who crossed this country
in a Ford Fairlane

Centre of equal daughters, equal sons,
All, all alike endear'd, grown, ungrown, young or old,
Strong, ample, fair, enduring, capable, rich,
Perennial with the Earth, with Freedom, Law and Love,
A grand, sane, towering, seated Mother,
Chair'd in the adamant of Time.

—Walt Whitman, "America"

Continue on I-90 for 351 miles.

—Google Maps

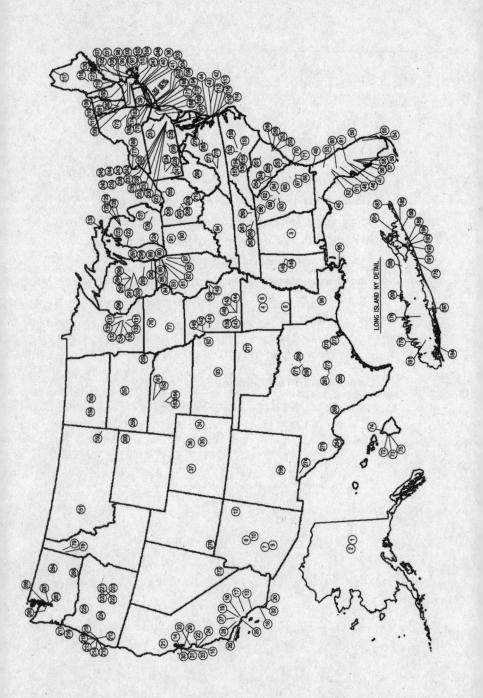

LONG ISLAND NY DETAIL

300 rounds
294 courses

*Nine-hole layout
**Par-three course
(p) denotes public, semiprivate, or resort accessible

VIDALIA, GEORGIA

The soil was perfect for onions and for golf. It wasn't a place people visited unless they were interested in one or the other, and as I didn't care for onions on anything, I was in Vidalia for one reason: to give my buddy a haircut.

Brendan was a former college player with a legit scratch handicap, and our regular matches were the benchmark against which I measured the health of my game. (It wasn't very healthy, if you asked him—he denied my ever beating him, though I had eyewitness accounts to the contrary.) He was ten inches shorter than me, with a ponytail he'd been cultivating for the last five years, and I couldn't decide which of those details frustrated me more when it came to his closing me out on the seventeenth hole.

We were the same age, raised in suburbs on opposite sides of Philadelphia.

My side left my accent flat, while Brendan possessed a regional twang that less charitable folks might call hoagie mouth. His idiosyncrasies were widespread: A former Deadhead turned therapist, he golfed in obnoxiously tinted pants and proudly slept in the nude, aside from a scrunchie that kept his hair out of his face (yet he often wondered aloud why I refused to share a hotel room with him). His texts typically included a phallic vegetable emoji, and the signature line in his emails read *By the power of Grayskull!* At one point, he had programmed the keyboard on his wife's phone to change the word *she* to *nipples* and to convert his name to *balls.* He cherished the small joys in life, but I don't think anything gave him more joy than saying, in simple terms, "Tom, you cannot beat me."

I was playing well, and had certainly been playing enough—two hundred rounds over the last four months—yet our match in Georgia felt like the only one that mattered. Our ongoing debate was tired; it was time to put proof on the record and teach balls a lesson.

Brendan was so confident that he wagered his hair; if I won, he would submit to the clippers, terms that immediately placed his wife on my team. If I lost, I had to get us a game at the course of Brendan's choosing, anywhere in America. When it came time to pick a date and place for our showdown, I zeroed in on the week I would be in Georgia and invited him to thirty-six holes at the Ohoopee Match Club, the only venue suited to such a contest.

It was a course built specifically for grudges: No real pars on the scorecard, no set tee markers, holes designed for risk-taking and one-upmanship. The winner of the previous hole picked the teeing ground for the next one, and if your dustup wasn't finished by eighteen, or if the loser wanted quick vengeance, there were four extra holes to settle all grievances. Forget your tally of total strokes—all that counted was winning golf holes, and without a course rating, you couldn't post your score if you wanted to. The only news of consequence at Ohoopee was in the club's motto, a question embroidered on belts and hats in the shop, and one we had both traveled a long way to answer: WHO WON THE MATCH?

• • •

Though I had met this Brendan at a golf outing in Pennsylvania farm country seven years before, I had been battling Brendans for decades. They were those voices in my mind's outer rim, put there to remind me that I couldn't make this putt, or miss that pond, or win this match. They hammered down hope, turned the possible into the unlikely, and replaced my potential with my shortcomings. The idea that someday I might not hear them kept me sticking tees into the ground. After all, there had been a time before the Brendans; maybe there could be a time after them. I believe it was Lao Tzu who said, "A journey of a thousand golf courses begins with a single hole." And mine began beside warm blue waters.

My dad had let me tag along on an excursion to the Dominican Republic, an annual reward trip for stockbrokers who'd made their numbers, where he and his colleagues skipped meetings for tee times and smoked cigarettes by the fistful, the collective stress of a week away from the stock ticker hanging thick around the resort.

I was fourteen and headed into my first high school golf season that spring, ready to make, or get cut from, the varsity team. I had spent the winter clipping balls off the mats at an indoor range under the tutelage of a leather-skinned golf pro determined to get me swinging harder. *Faster, harder*, he would say. *You've got muscles—use them.* He could always teach me to back off, but I had height and needed to use it. And he was right. I was flexible enough to figure out a straightish trajectory, and the balls were bouncing past flags I hadn't noticed before.

I stepped up to the first at Casa de Campo's Teeth of the Dog, undaunted by its name and reputation as a ball filcher. So much grass. No more rubber tees. It all looked friendly and simple. I pushed my tee into the ground and swung faster, harder. Fairway. I reached for a 9 iron and spun a divot out of the turf like a dealer tossing playing cards. Ten feet from the pin. Up on the green, my ball turned for the hole not with effort but with inevitability. I'm pretty sure I smiled, but I didn't feel the need for much more. Golf, after all, was easy.

I dumped a few in the ocean that afternoon, but mixed in six birdies as well, tempting my dad to find his boss in the foursome behind us and tell him he was quitting to ride his son's coattails to the Tour. I didn't make any birdies the next day, and though I did make the team that spring, I struggled as fifth man while golf reality set in, a reality I would wrestle with for the next thirty years of my life.

They were years of trophies and shanks; days of junior club championships followed by being cut from the college golf roster; moments of minuscule handicaps followed by a tournament where I ran out of balls and a letter from the USGA placing me on competitive probation for carding such a robust number. Golf took more than it gave as I labored to prove I was better than I was, because for one day in the Dominican Republic, I had been. Golf was easy once, and like an addict chasing the feeling of his first high, I searched the world over for the day when it would be again. I hoped it would be this day, here in Georgia, with a friend I was playing for his hair.

When we finished our morning eighteen at Ohoopee, I was up two holes at the halfway point. As we walked off the green and approached two elegantly prepared lunch plates—we were the only golfers on the property, as if they knew to clear the stage—I asked Brendan how he was feeling about the match.

"Great. Not worried at all."

But for some damn reason—the same reason behind my life's every missed cut, shredded scorecard, and three-putt on the last—I was.

ROCHESTER, NEW YORK

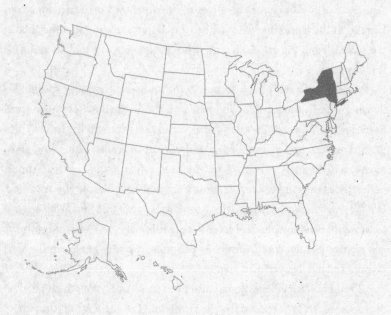

I was somewhere near Rochester, or Harrisburg, or Atlanta, perhaps, when the next two years of my life exploded into an American golf odyssey of unreasonable proportions.

It was one of my regular road show affairs—when the karaoke guy was unavailable, golf clubs would invite me to come talk about my travels and sign books that I would request they buy in hardcover, and in bulk. Sometimes there were bagpipers or Irish dancers; often there were whiskey tastings or a keg of Guinness procured in my honor. I no longer partook in either, which was an easy way to peg whether folks had read the book I was there to talk about. Being told how wonderful my Scotland book was (where I discuss getting sober) before being offered a shot was always an awkward juxtaposition of hospitality, but I was accustomed to the patrons of the golf speaking circuit: the close-talker explaining Royal Dornoch to me as if he were the only surviving golfer to have played it; the member seeking a blessing on his upcoming Ireland itinerary; the spouse unable to drag her husband to a book signing but who needed a signed copy for him anyway; the semicircle of cocktail hour executives wondering how I made a living and if I could get them on Pine Valley (the first question sank any shot they had at the second); and the guy asking me who the speaker was tonight and if he was any good.

My former strategy for overcoming the uneasiness of public speaking—dousing myself like a coach who had won the Super Bowl of booze—had been replaced by a calm born of perspective. I wasn't testifying before Congress. The stakes of a dinner party address are, in reality, rather low, and I already had the answers to oft-asked questions: *Are you still married?* Almost definitely. *Have you been to Old Head?* Yes, and now I know you have, too. *What's your handicap?* Gout. *My sister wrote a book—can you help her get it published?* Sorry, my phone, I have to take this call . . . *What's your favorite golf course?* Carne. *What?* Carne. In Belmullet, County Mayo, on the west coast of Ireland. *Never heard of it.*

But there was one question that stopped me, a query for which I had no rehearsed reply: *What's your favorite course that I've heard of? In America?*

And just that quickly, tonight's expert had been exposed; a charlatan was in our midst. I could talk the British Isles as if I'd been born in a Liverpool jersey, rattling off obscure and tongue-cramping course names, but when it came to my own country, my meek résumé could slide neatly into the shredder. Sure, I had the Philly courses covered, but push me out of my zip code—*Bandon? Chicago Golf? Shinnecock? Pebble Beach?*—and I was lost. I could only shake my head like a dunce and try to steer the conversation back to left-lane driving and blood sausage. "Hey, does anyone know what the *craic* is?" I would whimper, the American golf writer entirely ignorant of American golf.

For years I wore my aversion to my native courses as a badge of honor, a marker of evolved sensibilities and a broader worldview. No American course could match the genius, the rigor, the authenticity of links golf *over there*; our version was but a manicured imitation of Scotland's gift. But my badge was just a cover for a shortcoming, as I belittled my backyard courses for the same reason I rebuked cucumbers and CrossFit—I had never tried them. So, on one of those evenings in front of a fireplace, answering inquiries about the best brand of rain pants and why I had played hardly any golf west of the Mississippi, I heard my future fall out of my mouth and plop onto the podium:

"I'm doing America next," I said. It was a promise that caught the room off guard—myself included—and it might have been easily forgotten or dismissed in the brighter light of day if it wasn't for Dad and his emails.

I wasn't sure who showed Dad how to forward electronic mail. Retirement orientation apparently included some sort of tutorial on the dissemination of chain messages, missives that itemized the sundry ways our country was going to hell or romanticized the days of untreated schoolyard injuries. My father's forwards seemed a nuisance I would have to suffer in silence, but I kept opening his FWs, because within them was a dad I had never known.

My father—the erstwhile stalwart of stocks and bonds, the man of a thousand collar stays, the retired Naval officer—LOL'd and enjoyed the occasional boob joke. He was not averse to the political musings of Russian bots or manifestos written in ALL CAPS with flamboyant punctuation. But the topics Dad found most irresistible for distribution were paragraphs that touched on TROOPS or THE FLAG or AMERICA! I knew him to be a patriot, but I hadn't understood how deep his love of our country ran, or how readily it could be captured in a GIF.

I was born during Watergate. This sounds like the opening of a keynote address at a flag burners' convention, but I offer it as oversimplified evidence of the two Americas in which my dad and I came of age. While his youth involved stockpiling bacon grease to make glycerin bombs for the war effort, my 1980s childhood involved longing for Lamborghinis and caddying for guys I was sure drove them. America, to my father, was something we earned, and an ideal paid for with sacrifice. To me, it was something I already had, an aspiring but imperfect playing field that I had been placed on at birth presided over by dubious referees. I understood that his generation's single-mindedness was what made my generation's cynicism possible; we took for granted our right to moan. The line was thin between whether that made us spoiled brats or brave thinkers, but as I watched my father's fealty to his country stiffen with age, I felt like he revered an Old Testament America—an absolute to which we offered alms and adhered to its dogma—while I was at the altar of a New Testament USA, where forgiveness reigned and the rabbis were refutable. Where, if we tried our best, we'd all be saved.

Dad and I would agree that America was big enough for both takes, but still, there was something in his voice when he sang the anthem at a ball game or in his eyes when he watched *The Bridge on the River Kwai* or on his face when he shook the hand of another veteran. I was never asked to serve as he had been, and I wondered if that precluded me from appreciating our country as he did. It very well might, but I wanted to try. I wanted to love America the way my father did. He earned that affection by packing for war. That wasn't my particular path or skill set; I hoped packing for golf might be good enough.

So, I set my sights on the country beyond my driveway, a place more foreign to me than the Highlands of Scotland or the cliffs of Donegal. I would go and find the Great American Golf Course, and by doing so, settle two matters of contrasting significance.

The first—figuring out what makes a golf course *great*—mattered to a good many of us: the seekers and rankers and debaters who reacted with outrage or approval when a particular course was notched above or below another. With this trip, I might finally manufacture a rubric for a course's worthiness, a takeaway that would at least buy me some bona fides on Twitter. But more interesting and important seemed to be an attempt to define the other adjective of my mission—*American*. What did it mean in 2019? What did it mean ever? If I could figure that out, then I would have done more service for my spirit than any of my previous wanderings abroad.

How to go about accomplishing any of the above confounded me, not only in theory but in execution. Experiencing the United States was no simple summer holiday. It became clear that my search for America should begin within my smallest slice of it: in a house, in a kitchen, over a sink on an evening where I had offered to do the dishes, until death do us part.

DEVON, PENNSYLVANIA

I imagined myself high atop a mountain road in Colorado or West Virginia or Alaska, low on fuel and all out of trail mix, peering over the guardrails to places where helicopters would never find me. Almost as soon as I decided to take on America, the visions came at night, and they placed me on a redwood-choked road of no discernible end, stepping out of a smoking car that I had rented with my kids' college money, with no cell signal to connect me to the lifelines of modernity. Or I was curled into a ball beneath see-through sheets on a mattress in Montana where the bedbugs had scooched over to make room, wiping tears with my last pair of clean socks and muttering to myself, "The corkboard told me this would happen."

The opening rite of planning a cross-country golf trip, for me, has always been digging a four-foot-by-six-foot board out of the basement and covering it with a map of my destination. Right-size road maps for Scotland and Ireland were easily procured and filled with pins, but America, I quickly learned, was not built for corkboards. I would have to wallpaper my office with pages torn from a road atlas to visualize my ocean-to-ocean route, so I abandoned the pinboard and turned to planning via Google Maps. In that surrender, there were clear and obvious signals: *America is huge. And that bare board is an omen—you are not fit for the task.*

I was looking at a year, not a few weeks, and it didn't feel safe—not just the miles and the routes through a canyon America I had seen only in cartoons but the very suggestion of doing it at all. After Scotland, I had promised my uncommonly understanding wife, Allyson, *never again.* But like the golfer whose mind doesn't hear the *don't go* part and only hears *left*, I suspected Allyson knew that *never* was negotiable, while *again* was a sad certainty.

As I scraped the meals from our daughters' untouched plates into the garbage disposal, both of them opting for microwaved mac and cheese as they sat in front of the television, victorious over dinner yet again, Allyson sat across the counter from me with tired eyes. She looked the way my mother had when I slid her a detention slip for signature at the end of the evening, saving the worst news for last.

"I saw you took the board out of the basement," she said in a tone lacking any lilt of enthusiasm. I flinched at her foresight; she'd noticed and preempted my rehearsed opening statement. "Where?" she asked.

"America."

"Huh." She looked across the kitchen, her eyes casting a long glance as if our refrigerator were in Oregon. "That makes sense."

"It's better than my being out of the country," I offered, a lame technicality through which she saw clearly, and lifted an eyebrow.

"America is enormous."

"It is," I agreed. "But I would break it up into pieces. It would be easy to get back whenever you need me. I would be home every month."

"Months?" she said, as if *months* was an ex-girlfriend I wanted to invite over for dinner. "How many?"

It seemed a good time for a distraction, like stuffing a potato or a dinner knife or my hand down the disposal, but instead I called over our two redheads, Maggie and Caroline. The latter was five and loved pretty much any proposition that didn't involve flash cards. Maggie was nine and quickly growing bored of her parents, but she still embraced the suggestion of a trip for the inflight hours of iPad it promised.

"What would you guys think about traveling around America next summer with Mommy and Daddy?" I asked.

Caroline hopped with excitement, her orange curls bouncing. Maggie tilted her head and nearly smiled. Allyson stuck to her line of questioning: "I have to work, Tom. We can't go with you all summer. How long is it going to take?"

"I'm not sure yet," I said. It was the truth. On a legal pad upstairs I had scratched dozens of failed iterations of an American golf trip. Where to start, end, and roam in between? What were the must-plays and the maybe-skips? I promised Allyson I would soon have a timeline for us to consider; I was about to fire a paragraph out into the social media universe, crowdsourcing the most essential American golf experiences. I was sure a few helpful, anonymous souls could lend clarity to my endeavor.

Three weeks later, I reached the bottom of my inbox, eyes weary and fingers bent. Next to me was a list of over nine hundred golf courses that, if I were to miss a single one of them, I risked being roasted on Twitter by the golf itinerary illuminati.

I plugged every name into a spreadsheet and plotted them on my virtual map, color-coding each course red, yellow, or green according to priority. Red was reserved for the must-gos, the anchors around which the rest of the trip would revolve. After 890 of the entries came up red, I switched strategies and decided my tentpoles would be the fifty-one courses still in existence to ever host a US Open. I wanted to learn the history of golf in America during my travels, and by visiting every US Open venue, I would be literally walking much of that path. Green labels denoted strong leans for visiting, mainly applied to courses of architectural significance or rare history, or really nice places where someone had offered to host me for free. Curiosities and places that had been campaigned for via emails of more than four paragraphs were shaded yellow, and void of any coloring were the courses where someone wrote *If you can get me on that course, it would be sick* or *You have to come play it—it's a Ross*, referring to immortal architect Donald Ross, whose work spread so wide that I imagined him to be America's great golf pollinator.

One fall evening, Allyson popped into the Golffice, my sanctuary above the garage where the walls sag with souvenirs, and where I'd cut a practice hole into green carpet that rolled at a precise 11 on the Stimp, to see where her husband was hiding as bath times approached. I didn't notice her over my shoulder as I scrolled through the Christmas-colored list.

"What is that?" she said, and I shot up in my seat at the sound of her voice. Some husbands feared being caught peeping at thongs on their laptops. Others of us had golf to hide.

"Are those the courses?" Allyson asked. "There's hundreds."

"It's a working list. I'm not going to play all of them."

"Still," she said, grabbing the mouse and spinning down the list. "This doesn't end. You're going to be gone forever."

"I'm working on cutting it down."

"Tom. Leaving me here with a job and kids with you gone for five months—that's not fair."

She was right. It wasn't fair. And if five months wasn't fair, I thought I'd better get this part over with. "I think it's going to be more like eight."

I didn't relish the fact that I had heard from dozens of husbands who had successfully invoked my name when having the Golf Talk with their spouses, my monthslong road trips getting them off the hook for wanting to go to Punta Cana for a week. My behavior had become a handy benchmark for spousal negligence, and it made me cringe to imagine that somewhere, on some couch in some office, a guy might be referencing my boondoggles, winning nods from both his wife and their therapist as they all acknowledged that, yes, it could be worse.

I'm asked about Allyson more than any other subject when I speak at golf clubs. I tell the audience that she's a saint and a parenting virtuoso whom I clearly don't deserve, and explain that the key to great golf trips is not playing well but marrying well, which sometimes gets a chuckle. What I don't try to convey through a microphone is that I would not be standing there if, many years before, a young woman who wrote poetry and wore tie-dye hadn't said yes to a college dance and, as we crossed campus through an Indiana tundra in search of the soiree, stopped to kiss me in the snow. The pre-dance swigs of Mad Dog might have had something to do with the affection, but I'd rather trace the roots of our life together back to providence.

Allyson isn't the woman behind the man—she's way out in front of me in pretty much every category aside from golf, but she's a tennis player anyway. From the start, she believed in my own aspirations more than I did, and through her saying yes—to a dance, a ring, a walk around Ireland—her trust has launched these stories, and this adventure on which I was about to embark. I say all of this because if you're thinking about asking out that person you're afraid is out of your league, you're probably right, and you should ask anyway.

Still, eight months was insane. I considered the scapegoats I might invoke—my publisher, my social media, my juvenile sense of self that required golf to remind me who I was—but instead I settled on a gang of friends who went by the collective moniker No Laying Up.

While the rest of the golf-news world was drowning in unread bylines, five best friends had started a golf text thread that morphed into a mini-empire of podcasts, videos, and merchandise, accidentally reshaping golf media in the process. No Laying Up struck upon a winning formula of informed wit, modern takes, and savvy social posts to energize a younger, less tradition-bound demographic. They were cool, and by way of being informed and unapologetic golf fans, they inadvertently became pillars of a new golf revolution. They were scoring interviews with Rory and Tiger and Phil and had built a vibrant new base of followers who shunned country-club memberships and their fathers' golf brands. Five ball-busting dudes who now bunked together in a golf cave in Jacksonville had become, at least in my eyes, bright symbols of golf's future. They went by the names Tron, Soly, Neil, DJ, and Big Randy. Soly was the stick of the team, Tron the grinder and contrarian, DJ the pro journalist, Neil the brainy jester, and Big Randy the gentle giant whose charming nihilism carried their self-deprecating videos. So, when they asked me if I wanted to come to Ireland with them in early 2019, of course I had said yes, and it was at one of our dinners during that recent Irish sojourn, I now explained to Allyson, where my America trip had spilled over into its present state of unmanageability.

We had been tucked into the corner of a pub one evening in County Mayo, recalling that day's round at Carne and playing a game in which you compared the golf course to a rock band. Neil paired Carne with Pearl Jam for its rugged unpredictability, while Randy matched it with Pink Floyd, a trippy dark side of the moon that you could probably play backward. Soly knew about the American expedition that was spinning in my head, and he asked about my plan for covering so much ground. Before I could contrive an outline I might share, a new game was suggested: best state, worst state. I listened closely for clues. They had all traveled far more of the country than I had.

I might have slotted the Buckeye State toward the bottom half of my fifty, but it was a top pick among our table of Ohioans. Texas ranked as both the best and worst, for reasons everyone agreed were obvious. Louisiana was beloved; Missouri was penalized for poor performance when it came to matters of race. North Carolina, Neil claimed, was unwelcoming, because he had visited his college roommates there once and their friends were all weird to him. Colorado was a winner, but the golf season was too short. Same for Michigan and Vermont. Arizona should not exist, Tron explained, because it was created by air-conditioning. California was brilliant—aside from LA, of course—and Montana fascinated Neil; he wanted to explore it deeply. Iowa was good people. Virginia made Tron nervous (the DC overflow was rife with contemptible phonies), and Oregon seemed to top most of their lists as the most tempting region for relocation, but its libertarian vibe cut both ways—a chill outdoor playground of microbrews and legal pot, but also a cradle for separatist militias with armories up in the woods.

As the food arrived and the conversation turned to how many shepherd's pies in one week was too many, America had finally taken form for me. It was that conversation in Ireland, I told Allyson, that convinced me I needed to plant a tee in each of the fifty states. I couldn't guess what life was like in New Mexico or accept that North Carolina was inhospitable or agree that Arizona was expendable if I didn't travel there myself. It was a consequential and confusing time in America, and the compulsion to go make better sense of my country by knowing it from one end to the other, by sharing that safe space of universal accord—a tee box—with people I wanted to understand: It was worth the months, I contended, and Allyson agreed. Once again, she said yes, which meant at least one of us believed I was up to the task.

GLENSIDE, PENNSYLVANIA

I expected Mom and Dad to disapprove, but instead they threw me a party. Hearing their son was going to be on the road for eight months while his wife juggled a job and two young girls meant an opportunity for Mom to help with the babysitting and laundry. For Dad, it was an excuse to set a date for a send-off round. I had either cultivated a clan of golf enablers or they trusted that my ambitions were worthwhile. The pressure to prove the latter weighed heavily as I packed up my bags and prepared for my bon voyage.

We played Dad's home course of LuLu, a curiously named and under-rated Donald Ross outside of Philadelphia that was founded by a group of Shriners back in 1912. Dad assembled a group of fifteen golfers to join us:

some cousins plus guys from the club to whom he had given my books over the years, whether they'd asked for them or not.

Dad put me in a foursome of Scranton cousins while he shared a cart with Dr. B, a dear family friend who had taken up the game at age seventy, and as a result brought all the agonizing golf habits of a very late bloomer. He was athletic for his age and still worked on his bench press, and though he was a genius in the operating room, the customs of a round of golf somehow eluded him. Or he was just old enough to not really care. Inspired by the look of the pros on TV, he once showed up for golf with my dad wearing a gardening glove. He brought out a stash of yellow balls and dumped them into their cart, and when my dad picked one up, it was heavy as musket shot.

"Where the hell did you get these?" Dad asked.

"My basement," Dr. B replied. Apparently, he had found some old Dunlops, and to make them easier to spot, had coated them with a few layers of leftover house paint. It was soon clear that he'd have to paint more for next week; Dr. B didn't care much for watching his drives or looking for balls, preferring to toss another one out onto the fairway—or to just go ahead and play the ball he'd found, which was usually my dad's. I was happy to see him pull up at LuLu, but also happy enough to see his bag in the foursome behind ours.

I went around in 73 strokes, which seemed a good start to my venture. As with every round I played with Dad, I wanted to post a number not that *I* could brag about but that *he* could. Now eighty-five, his drives were fighting to reach the fairway, and breaking 100 was probably a goal he'd abandoned. Some people feared the days when their parents took to canes and wheelchairs, but for a golfing son, it was the forward tees that were hard to watch. So, I played my ass off when we got out together, knowing he would tell my mom and his friends what I shot, grateful that on those days my score would be his.

Mom was waiting for us at the end of eighteen with a spread of cheesesteaks to bid her Philadelphia son goodbye. The pro posted our scores on the wall, and I could hear Dad casually telling his buddies, "There's a seventy-three on there. Anyone beat a seventy-three?" I'd won both net and gross, though I wasn't allowed to collect the prizes—which was fine, because Dad's prize table was three of my books.

I wasn't sure how much, if any, of the trip Dad would be able to join me for. His back had been acting up, and long travel days spent finding me in some corner of the world were probably stories already written in those books on the table. He walked me out to my car and hugged me goodbye: "Be safe, Tom boy." It was never *play well* or *go low* or *make birdies* but *be safe*. And it was always *Tom boy*. He was the only person who ever called me that. Whether we teed it up together during the next year or not, I knew Dad would be following. This trip was as much his as mine. He didn't travel the world looking for hallowed golf holes, but he was a chaser, still hooked on finding the round, the hole, the shot that went right.

People who don't play golf grow to envy their golfing neighbors, admiring it as a nifty game you can play to a ripe old age. What they don't understand is that we don't keep playing because we can; we play because we don't know how to stop. It lands in our hands for just a moment before slipping through our fingers, and we grab for it again and again. It's a shell game, a music man, a three-card monte from which we can't walk away. Once in a while it glances back at us, and it's achingly beautiful. A siren? Perhaps. But those sailors at least got the closure of wrecking on the rocks. Golfers find the rocks and just drop another ball.

NEWPORT, RHODE ISLAND

"I probably wasn't getting past Tiger," Bill conceded with a smile. "But it was nice to see my name in the brackets with him."

We were loosening up on the first tee at Newport Country Club, home to the pinnacle of Bill's accomplished golf career. He had seven New Jersey club championships under his belt (four of which he won at Pine Valley, which was reason to keep Bill on the check-in-often list), and in 1995 he qualified for the US Amateur. Just getting to the US Am is to reach a rare stratosphere of golf, but hovering above it is making it through the thirty-six holes of stroke play and into the final sixty-four matches, which Bill did at Newport by bending a twenty-footer into his last hole. No matter that he was knocked out in the first round by future Tour player Mathew Goggin; busting through to match play was the rarest of achievements in amateur golf, and doing so was a memory Bill was eager to relive. So, when he heard that I was beginning my American crusade at Newport CC, my friend asked to come along and revisit his memories of Newport's eighteenth green.

The rest of the world likely remembers it as the spot where Tiger stuffed his approach on the final hole to win his second consecutive US Amateur, coming back from two down to best Buddy Marucci. But for us, this was the place where my friend Bill, at the not-so-young age of forty-three, earned his ultimate prize: proof that he could play stick. Most of us spent our lives seeking that unmarred moment of our absolute best, but twenty-four years ago, Bill had watched his moment trickle over the edge of the cup. Now, he walked me over to the right side of the eighteenth green, ready to roll it home once again.

He missed by three feet, but no matter—his 1995 could never be spoiled. I expected the completion of my first round of the trip to be a more celebratory affair, but three hours of cold May rain was plenty. Bill and I both scooped up our balls and hurried for the clubhouse.

That morning, we were met before our round by George Peper, which was the best way I knew to begin any round, or day, or trip. The former editor of *GOLF Magazine* and a prolific author himself, his uncommon golf life had earned George a variety of rewards: He had once played eighteen holes on eighteen courses between dawn and dusk with Ben Crenshaw. Another publicity stunt allowed him to play the Old Course, Winged Foot, and Pebble Beach *in one day*. He'd spent years in St. Andrews in a home beside the eighteenth hole, and was a member of that club behind the tee on the first.

George had recently tallied his life's golf courses in an article and had arrived at a number of 750. My total hung around 550, so when I read his number, I recalled thinking: *I could overtake one of my golf-quantity heroes this very year.* I didn't mention this when rationalizing with Allyson—*Don't you want me to pass George Peper?*—but I did consider it a welcome consequence of the travels ahead.

He showed us around the Newport clubhouse, which may have simultaneously been the most majestic and impractical building in golf. It resembled a fine French château sitting alone on the horizon, and approaching it via the long gravel driveway was like pulling up in a horse-drawn carriage, wondering if your princess was awaiting you inside. Its founders (establishment types who summered in Rhode Island in the 1890s, including John Jacob Astor IV, the wealthiest person to die on the *Titanic* and the second half of Waldorf-Astoria) had apparently forgotten to add a kitchen, so the large marble non-dining rooms felt somewhat superfluous. The locker room upstairs, however, did not, and George led us to the doors next to the lockers, which led onto a rainy balcony overlooking most of the course. Its subtle contours were still dark with winter, but its treeless spread against distant waters hinted at a links-like morning for the two of us.

George would not be joining our twosome for golf; he had to run home and help his wife pack for their annual month in Scotland, an excuse I envied for both its destination and its convenience, saving him from a morning of muddy pants and pruned fingers. As we changed our shoes by his locker, I gave George the broad strokes of my cross-country itinerary, and I watched his brow twist with a disapproving sort of confusion. My spirits dropped. If my golf-wandering hero thought I had planned too big, I was in rare and lonely territory.

"How long did it take you to arrange all of this?" George asked, and I admitted that I'd been staring at a mix of maps, spreadsheets, and emails canvassed across two screens in my Golffice for the better part of a year. Though I gave the impression that the planning was complete and all the tee times arranged, the best I'd been able to lock down were the next six weeks. The rest of my year was a timeline dotted with question marks.

Paring down the course list had been an act of agonizing editing, as well as an indicator of how entitled and inconsequential my life had become. My daily struggles involved gauging guest feedback on Airbnb or finding a way to squeeze Shoreacres into my itinerary (it still burns that I couldn't).

With pins on my Google map denoting courses that made the final cut, I drew shapes around chunks of America that seemed manageable over two- to three-week stretches, breaking the country up into twelve segments. Three consecutive missed weekends at home seemed our max family tolerance, though two-day returns to do laundry and remind Allyson that I was leaving yet again probably brought more injury to her routine than help. Clustering the states effectively was a brain teaser I consistently flubbed: *Damn, I missed Kentucky. And Hawaii. Again.* But wrestling the map turned out to be a soft introduction to the planning.

Turning each chunk into an itinerary with tee times and accommodations and flights and rental cars—each piece contingent on whether a course allowed guests on Saturday mornings or was open on Mondays or didn't have a member-guest on its calendar—was like playing Jenga with a broomstick. One email about a course closing for aeration and *crash*: start over. And that was assuming I could actually get on the courses. Over half of them were private. I might be able to ping some friends in New York or New Jersey for help, but Oklahoma? In my Irish and Scottish travels, I had never come so close to quitting the trip before it began, and there were very good Irish and Scottish reasons for that.

In both countries, I could dream up a map and go play, as visitors were welcome at nearly every club in the British Isles. Their clubs could be exclusive, but they didn't claim sole dominion over the courses on which they played. Golf's oldest societies often shared holes with a handful of other groups, their rivals' clubhouses erected directly beside their own. Golf was originally a game of separation between club and course; not everyone was invited into the former, but go ahead and play the latter—and that practice continued in the UK and Ireland with a scheme of visitor greens fees that kept the courses in good shape without gouging the members.

That line between club and course was never drawn when golf came to America, and while golf thrived among American Anglophiles eager to imitate this British game, the fact that Yankee practitioners blended golf with the country-club movement of the late nineteenth century seemed one of the roots of golf's struggles in the twenty-first.

George White's "History of Golf" articles describe some version of golf being played in America as far back as the Revolutionary War. Golf historians point to a 1743 shipping receipt for ninety-six clubs and 432 balls sent from Scotland to Charleston as the first record of the game landing in the States. Going to war with Britain twice in forty years didn't help a British game's cause in the former colonies, however, and it wasn't until the end of the nineteenth century that golf in America gained momentum, thanks to an industrial and economic boom that provided Americans with expendable money and time. In *Golf and the American Country Club*, Richard J. Moss highlights how this era of prosperity cut both ways when it came to golf, affording it new playing grounds but planting them behind fences.

It was a time of social change and economic mobility in America, and the old guard holding on to America's puritanical roots felt the threat. They reacted with reform movements aimed at drinking, prostitution, and working conditions in the cities. While their efforts were well-intentioned, they were, in some ways, the last gasps of a Victorian elite in America—unless, of course, said elite could find safe havens to keep practicing their old modes of propriety among their peers. Coming together to enjoy the classically British arts of horse riding, cricket, foxhunting, and, eventually, golf was a restoration of order and Anglican civility in an America turned unruly by immigrants and new money.

As a result, the country club was born, in places like Boston and Philadelphia and New York. Prohibition played its part as well (the number of private clubs in America swelled during the 1920s, thanks in part to their capacity as safe drinking spaces), but even before booze was banned, the clubs were well-established bastions of high-born standards in America. By cornering the market on golf, British-loving American country clubs spawned a golf innovation that was not very British at all: no trespassing. This nineteenth-century country-club hangover made getting tee times in the twenty-first a genuine pain in the ass, and by keeping out visitors and favoring elaborate clubhouses with meticulously maintained grounds, we sure showed those Scots how to make golf cost a whole lot more.

In order to overcome this American golf problem, I employed the American golf strategy of begging for the benevolence of a member. I searched my emails and my contacts and my overflowing drawer of business cards, desperate to recall forgotten faces who once suggested over drinks on a patio: *If you're ever in Chicago* . . .

It quickly became evident that every regional golf scene had a guy or gal who knew someone at every club in his or her section, and if that guy or gal had happened to receive one of your books for Christmas, then he or she could do a month's worth of work for you in the space of an afternoon.

I found a few such willing accomplices, unlocking Chicago, Minnesota, San Francisco, Long Island, and Boston. But there remained a golden goose course where all my leads fizzled into the oblivion of unanswered email. I had been fortunate enough to once play Augusta, and living in Philadelphia meant I got the call to Pine Valley every few years, but the last member of the triumvirate of coveted American courses remained ever distant, an abandoned dream on a faraway coast.

Some people said they knew a guy at Cypress Point, but some people apparently lost their phones along the way. The thing that got me invited to most of the courses—the words on these pages—was actually a hindrance when it came to Cypress. They weren't seeking publicity, and the writer label pinned me as a guest who might arrive with untoward motives. No matter— I had three hundred other courses to distract me from my one Monterey shortcoming. If Cypress was meant to happen, it would happen, I told myself before firing off another email to some-guy's-cousin-in-California-who-knew-a-guy-who-played-Cypress-with-his-boss-once, and set my sights on Newport.

Recent tree removal had opened up long water views around the holes at Newport Country Club, and the place had the subtlety and quiet resolve of an old classic, not overly adorned or bunkered, a sort of archetype for seaside New England golf. Its proximity to an idyllic town helped raise my enthusiasm above the rain; my dad had been stationed there after the Korean War, so the evening before we played, I strolled past the cedar-shingled storefronts and cruised streets with yachting inspired names. The town was packed with toney beach clubs and nineteenth-century mansions and sleeping fishing boats. It seemed a place where you spent July pruning the garden or going to tea—so unlike my Jersey boardwalk summers, where the days were for sunburns and the nights were for throwing up in the cool ocean breeze. A gang of tourists gathered around the entrance of the church where Jackie and JFK had been married. On the tenth tee down at the golf course, the play was to aim for Jackie's window, her childhood home looming large on the horizon.

I dined on clear broth chowder and a buttery lobster roll in a corner restaurant, feeling a new awareness about the wealth of my country, both old and new. I had never before visited the summer retreats of America's East Coast dynasties, and now, having experienced one where a tech CEO was putting in a pool beside a Vanderbilt estate, I felt a bit dazed by this epiphany of money. Forget the 1 percent, those deadbeats; here were the .001 percent, a species with their own language and rituals who measured their wealth not by the money they had but by how little they thought about it.

I would discover that other stops on my map, like the Hamptons and Cape Cod and the Carolinas, all possessed pockets of hushed billionaire retreats (where nobody ever seemed to be home), and while I didn't abide conspiracy theories, I did feel like a very small participant in a world moved by forces with which I was unfamiliar. I didn't resent them for their wealth, and took solace in knowing that most of them probably couldn't break 90, and might give a chunk of their portfolio to do so. This assumption wasn't a dig—a friend had actually been there on a driving range when someone asked Mike Bloomberg how much he would pay to shoot par. He considered it for a moment, then replied, "Five billion."

George never asked why my journey was beginning in Newport. He knew the history behind the choice—I had read about it in one of *his* books, after all. Newport was not just a founding club of the USGA (along with Shinnecock, Saint Andrew's, Chicago Golf, and Brookline) but also the site of the first US Open and first US Amateur, depending on whose history you read. While today the USGA celebrates Newport's 1895 Open as the original, when I later visited Texas, I found a venue list in the program from the 1941 Open at Colonial that began with an 1894 US Open at Saint Andrew's in New York. Somewhere along the way, the narrative shifted, much to Saint Andrew's chagrin. I imagined that this rivalry over US Open provenance stemmed from a broader divide about who should be called the patriarch of golf in America—Saint Andrew's John Reid or the force that was Charles Blair Macdonald.

Both American businessmen of Scottish roots—Reid born in Scotland, Macdonald in Canada but educated in Scotland—Reid got the nod as golf's granddad for his pioneering initiative, after asking a friend headed overseas to bring back some clubs from Old Tom's shop in St. Andrews. When the sticks arrived, Reid took his friends to a field across the street from his home, where someone achieved American golf's first whiff in February of 1888. Their group would grow and move up the street to an apple orchard (I struggle to imagine Yonkers being full of fields and orchards, but I take Saint Andrew's club history as truth), where onlookers labeled them the Apple Tree Gang for their meeting spot by the first tee. They officially dubbed themselves the Saint Andrew's Golf Club so as to stake their claim as the American home of golf.

Charles Blair Macdonald would likely have balked at the notion of golf in an apple orchard. Raised on the Old Course and introduced to the game by Old Tom himself, he was a renowned bellyacher, but golf owes a debt to his stubbornness. It was his rancor regarding the pedestrian state of American courses that gave birth to some of the country's greatest venues in the early 1900s, when he and his partner Seth Raynor set out to remedy America's shortage of interesting holes. Macdonald's protests over the results of the 1894 Amateur at Saint Andrew's, where he lost in the finals to one of Saint Andrew's own members, led to the formation of the USGA as a governing body to oversee national championships. Macdonald got his do-over in 1895 when the first USGA-sanctioned championships took place at Newport. He prevailed and became America's first US Amateur champion, or perhaps its third.

There had been an even earlier version of a national championship at Newport a month prior to the 1894 Saint Andrew's tournament, where Macdonald shot 100 and lost before declaring the event illegitimate for its stroke play format, and for a bad ruling he received when his ball got snookered by a stone wall. Lost in all these theatrics was poor Willie Dunn Jr., the pro who should have gone down as the first US Open champion for his win at Saint Andrew's (the Open and Am tournaments were originally played on consecutive days), but his victory was expunged for being pre-USGA; Horace Rawlins took his spot in the record books when he won the Open at Newport the following year, where Dunn came in second.

While it's said that Macdonald's own friends dodged him to avoid another discourse on the state of the game, he should get credit for giving American golf confidence and an identity, and for pushing it out from under Scotland's shadow. His National Golf Links on Long Island took the best hole designs of the British Isles and recast them with American ambition and vigor, stringing together a symphony to rival any eighteen in the world. National was my Cypress substitute for the best course I was going to see this year, though in the meantime, the courses of Rhode Island didn't feel too far off the pace.

LITTLE COMPTON, RHODE ISLAND

George took a break from his packing to reconvene with us at Newport. With his US Am memories revived, Bill headed home to New Jersey while I followed George's car over to his regular summer hang, a course called Sakonnet. A hand-painted placard hanging by the entrance showed its name along with a depiction of fields and stone walls and, curiously, a large red heart. By the time I passed that sign again, I would deem it an appropriate symbol. While Newport owned the history and the prestige, Sakonnet had all the love and charm of a valentine.

As at our previous stop, its topography was mild seaside terrain, a gently rippled layout ruled by wind and water. While Newport was a Tillinghast, little Sakonnet (and it was little in the coziest sense, with a wee locker room off the pro shop that felt like a closet with shelves for your shoes) had design chops, too. A sign announced Donald Ross as both "Architect and Member," and I was told his summer cottage was just around the corner. I thought to myself that Sakonnet had to be good if Ross chose to play his own golf here, and I soon learned it was—a tidy routing of crowned par 4s divided by old rock walls, greens that butted up against the bay, and an effortless vibe showcasing that most brilliant tool in any architect or artist's bag: restraint. Ross gave the waterside setting top billing, and rightly so.

Gil Hanse had come in a few years before to restore the Ross features and build two new holes, and he added tight chipping areas that flowed into the next tee, a Hanse calling card I adored. It was a tiny touch, not using any rough to separate a green complex from a tee box, but for me it provided a course with unity and momentum, giving one's movement from green to tee the feeling of a plot unfolding. It felt like golf's version of an infinity pool, and it subtly nodded to golf's first rule, codified in 1744: "You must Tee your Ball, within a Club's length of the Hole." The next time you watch a birdie putt get pushed offline by a ball mark, consider the gashes that golf's forefathers were putting through.

It was a shame to catch my day-one courses in conditions that hid their personality. These were bump-and-bounce courses, with seaside winds forcing you to engage the tilts of firm fairways, but that day they were mostly splat courses, with mud seeping into my shoes. I did the math in my head as I hiked up the last fairway; 78 and 76 were respectable starts, I figured, for golf in the slop. I had told myself the scores wouldn't matter on this journey, even though they *always* mattered, a barometer whereby I judged my station as a golfer, and thus a metric for my self-image, for better and often worse. But there by the Sakonnet clubhouse, a reminder to try to do otherwise waved to me. The Rhode Island state flag snapped white against gray clouds, showing a golden anchor circled by stars, with one word emblazoned underneath. Its four letters pulled my feet forward. I had thought I was beginning in Rhode Island because of headstrong Macdonald, whose protests anointed Newport as the birthplace of the US Open, but I preferred this new vision as to why I was starting here. Two courses down and too many left to fathom, but as the rain poured off my fingers, I saw *HOPE*, quite literally, on my horizon.

GROTON, CONNECTICUT

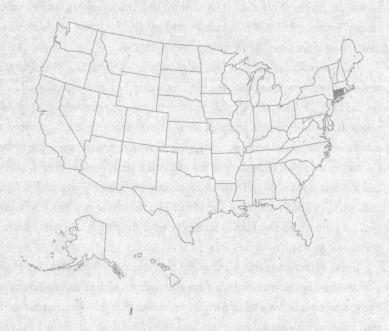

The one-story clubhouse showcased beer-branded banners announcing Sunday brunch specials, and I found six strangers milling about the putting green at Shennecossett. It was early on a Wednesday, and they were all too young for retirement, so I wondered if I'd arrived in the midst of a tournament. Discovering that they were here to put their stamp on my map was strange and humbling; they had learned my whereabouts on social media and were ready to become the first new citizens of *A Course Called America*. I patriated them with grateful handshakes. The road ahead was long, but now it didn't feel so lonely.

Shenny is a rare Donald Ross public, and a very good one at that. While some of his holes had been lost to commercial incursion, the course's routing tilted toward a waterside meeting point of the Thames River and Long Island Sound (if you find yourself lucky enough to be boated out to the Fishers Island Club, look left, and you'll see a green sliver of Shenny). We played in two foursomes of New Englanders and golfers from farther afield. One attendee had joined us from Delaware, which made me want to reimburse him for gas, or to apologize for not being as interesting as Instagram might make me seem.

A young man named Nathan hadn't traveled as far; he was a clean-cut thirtysomething with a country-club swing, but his No Laying Up towel revealed him to be *woke*, a label of honor among golf's new breed of informed practitioners uninterested in the game's fusty status quo. Speaking with him reminded me that while the game as we knew it was languishing, golf as we might not yet know it was brimming with enthusiasm and possibility.

"I really got burned out with the competitive side of it, and for me, all I cared about was score," Nathan explained as we wandered toward our tee balls. "If I was playing on this course where I knew I needed to birdie the first hole and didn't, I was basically ruined for the day—literally one bad shot and I felt like I was done. I needed to walk away, so I gave up the game for about a year and a half, and what really got me back into it was the community. Not necessarily the golf community locally but actually online. All these guys left messages on Instagram and were doing new and interesting things with golf and new brands and new ideas—it drew me back to the game. The little things about golf were what I really loved about it, and if it was hitting persimmons or using old clubs or any way to kind of have fun with it as opposed to trying to make a score and play for the best shot of my life—that got me playing again. Playing nine holes or eighteen holes, or walking nine after work, that's the small swing. That's the small bit of time. The rest of it is the fun part that lasts longer. It's thinking about my bag, thinking about clubs, thinking about where to go next, seeing photos online, learning architecture, getting ideas from podcasts—that's the incredible community part of golf. That's what helped me get back into it."

Nathan's perspective was woke indeed. I had spent plenty of hours following my ball across a field, but what about the time I'd spent replaying that walk? Planning the next one? Strategizing my gear, or planning this trip?

They were all happy hours, and most had been spent in socks instead of spikes. Testimonies from the front lines of golf would tell you tee times were down and courses were closing in 2019, but industry reports couldn't quantify the new ways in which golf was being consumed. Such metrics didn't account for Nathan and his peers, who didn't belong to country clubs or play five days a week, who spent most of their nonworking hours in the conversation but not on the course. In Dad's playing era, there was golf time, work time, home time; technology now stirred that all together, and instead of showing up on Saturday morning for a regular game at the club, golf's next generation was tuned in to a broad community where a tweet about some wanderer who was playing Shennecossett tomorrow was reason to call in sick and come meet fellow members of a global golf club that required nothing more than a username to join.

At the end of our morning round, as I dropped my clubs into the trunk and waved to that morning's playing partners passing by as their cars left the lot, it occurred to me that this trip was already reorganizing my emotional constitution. We had just spent four hours talking about matters of minor importance, laughing at our on-course inadequacies, and cheering our small triumphs, and ended it with an exchange of phone numbers and email addresses. There was no pretension to any of it, and I wondered if I had just effortlessly acquired a few of those things men so famously failed to collect: friends.

It's well-documented sociology that men struggle with genuine friendships. Many call it a crisis, and studies have deemed adult male loneliness a greater threat to their health than smoking or obesity. Loners live with an increased risk of cancer, stroke, and heart disease, while their friend-healthy female counterparts reap the rewards of community and connection. But it wasn't always that way. In early adolescence, boys bond as well as girls do, but somewhere around the age of fifteen—the same age depression begins to spike—dudes start shutting down. They stop needing or seeking friends, describing it as a sign of weakness or femininity. And thus begins the lonely road of the American male.

The distractions of modernity have only made retreat easier, and when men do converse with other men, scholars describe them as "shoulder to shoulder" interactions, while women excel at face-to-face friendships. (Take a look around your next cocktail party, and watch women speak to one another while guys lip their drinks and eye a blank television.) Whatever the root cause, I perused the studies and came to a happy conclusion: Thank you, golf. You are saving my life.

My golf friendships aren't bonds of psychotherapeutic perfection; I'm more interested in beating my playing partners than having a chat, a pastime I never really mastered or valued. Trish, Brendan's wife, would inquire for updates after our rounds: *How are Tom's kids? How's Allyson? How was their trip to Florida?* His weekly response: *I don't know.* This always confused her. *Didn't you just spend half the day with him? What did you talk about?*

What *did* we talk about? Golf, I guess. And stuff.

But sometimes, I realized, that stuff really did matter. In not asking for information, it was offered. It was on the golf course that another friend once confided that his marriage had dissolved into an acrimonious mess, that he was losing his kids and was holding on by a very thin thread. I'd heard confessions of infidelity, of financial jeopardy, of teens who hated their fathers' guts with heartbreaking and inscrutable intensity. Waiting to hit on a par 3 could become a mini-confessional, because golf friendships possessed some of those vital elements that therapists would approve of: trust and genuine vulnerability.

I had seen scores of alpha males turn fragile on the first tee and witnessed bulls of the business world sink into meek apologizers, humbled by our game. The trials of a round of golf could break us down to the point where, by the sixteenth hole, four quiet acquaintances had become comrades rowing a lifeboat. I had no plans to call any of my new friends for an afternoon chat—*chatting* was a concept that made me wince—but at least I had the golf course, where walking shoulder to shoulder was better than walking alone.

I had spent more hours walking beside my dad than any other partner. Thanks to our shared pastime, Dad was both father and friend, and though it trickled out slowly, so many evenings spent together in the grill room revealed his story, with details he wouldn't have shared in another setting. He grew up in the coal-cracking corner of Pennsylvania, where one of his earliest childhood memories was running home from a friend's house after the bombing of Pearl Harbor, looking up at a plane in the sky and thinking Scranton was under attack. He played basketball and football at Central High and later attended Penn because my grandfather had, back when Bs and a legacy could get you into the Ivy League. With the Korean War well underway, he found a draft card waiting for him by the door when he returned home after graduation, and was soon following his older brother's footsteps into the navy.

He married my mother while on leave, and for their honeymoon, the new officer and his bride traveled from Scranton to San Diego in a white Ford Fairlane convertible, two kids who had never left the Northeast heading for a new post. He shipped off soon after arrival, so Mom knocked on doors in their apartment complex and introduced herself: "My name is Alice Coyne. I don't know anyone here, and my husband just left for the war." She made a quick circle of close friends, in a former America where you opened the door to strangers, or opened your front door at all.

After the war, Mom and Dad settled back in Philadelphia, where another officer from Dad's destroyer (his hearing never quite recovered from the cannon blasts) said he could get him a job with a brokerage firm. He built his business while they had two daughters and three sons. I was well at the back of the pack, a rhythm-method surprise who ended up being closer in age to my nieces than to my siblings.

Dad returned to Philadelphia in the 1960s not just with a job waiting for him but with golf clubs. Scranton Irish didn't play a lot of golf, so it wasn't until he was back from deployment and working a navy desk in California that he took his first swing. He and his officer buddies would walk across the street at lunchtime to the naval base nine-holer and hack away on their break. The golf bug dug in quickly; he started playing Torrey Pines on the weekends (its military rate was so cheap that he couldn't afford *not* to golf), and eventually joined Rolling Green outside Philadelphia, a Quaker club that was friendly to Catholics, where many years later I would learn to golf, caddie, bullshit, drink, and smoke, the five primary pastimes of my youth.

For fifteen years I lived my summer months at Rolling Green, writing or caddying in the morning, then heading to the course or the range. Mom spent the summers down the Jersey Shore while Dad stayed up home to watch the market, so every weekday afternoon I waited for him to come around the corner toward the pro shop, his tie already loosened, ready to tee it up.

We'd play until dark and then eat dinner in the grill—the same holes, the same menu every night—and it never got old. They were the best summers of my life. In my memory it all feels like a sun paused on the horizon, the air light and cool, the only sound our golf cart racing for home, its engine echoing through the trees at dusk. I don't recall what Dad and I talked about; I don't think we talked about very much at all. We usually watched the Phillies and complained about their hitting, then went home and slept in rooms on opposite ends of the house, nothing on the calendar but the same day tomorrow.

I didn't know any other twentysomethings who spent as much time with their fathers, and more than anything else golf has given me—and its gifts have been abundant—I'm grateful to it for that. I'm grateful that Dad decided to follow one of his navy buddies across the street to that nine-holer. I hoped to one day visit that San Diegan ground zero for golf in our family; I owed it a lot. Who knows what life would look like if Dad hadn't found it— where I'd be, or what I'd be looking for. But because he had, I pulled out of the parking lot at Shenny with clear purpose and destination. I'm sure he'd been pleased and maybe even impressed by what I'd found in the British Isles, but for a retired United States serviceman, I imagined this quest meant a little bit more. Two days in and I was already looking forward to returning home safe and well and telling Dad that I'd played this country, and yes, I had found it: the Great American Golf Course.

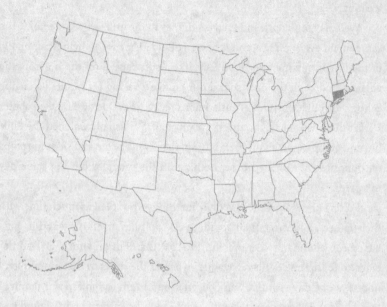

I felt a chip growing on my shoulder as I approached the gray walls of Yale. *Notre Dame was in the top twenty*, I told myself. *The Catholic Ivy, people say.* Granted, those people mostly went to Notre Dame, but no matter—I wasn't here to give a lecture. I was here to see if the course lived up to the lore.

I had heard the Course at Yale described by some architecture wonks as their favorite day of golf. It was a C. B. Macdonald/Seth Raynor design of wide acclaim carved out of forest and rock and swamp, a vast canvas where Raynor re-created Macdonald's template holes in grand scale. It was also a walk I had been warned about—the climbs were apparently knee-breakers.

Of course, I was excited about Yale because I actually knew what template holes were, and who Seth Raynor was. Along with Charlie Banks and

Charles Macdonald, he was part of the National School of design, not to be confused with the Ross School or the Philadelphia School. If one preferred the alternative grouping of golf architecture schools—the Penal, the Heroic, and the Strategic—he or she might be inclined to place Raynor within the third (credit to Geoff Shackelford, whose writings elucidate these design taxonomies). And if all of the above sounds superfluous, like a wine-tasting lecture when all you want to know is if it's a twist-off, you're not alone.

There was a time, not very long ago, when names like Hogan, Watson, Nicklaus, and Woods were all you needed to know to sound informed around the clubhouse. But now the names of the sketchers and earth movers outshine the players: Tillinghast, Flynn, Crump, Thomas, MacKenzie, and Macdonald. I grew up at a William Flynn course, but if someone had mentioned him to me back in my caddie days, I would have gone looking for his clubs in the bag room, hoping he was a good tipper. His name wasn't even on the scorecard in the 1980s and '90s. Now it's emblazoned in bronze beside the first tee: ROLLING GREEN GOLF CLUB—WILLIAM S. FLYNN ARCHITECT.

In the last ten years, designers have become heroes and celebrities of the game, at least to those of us on golf Twitter. I credit Andy Johnson's *The Fried Egg* podcast as the wellspring of the woke architecture age, though the modern Golf Course Architecture (GCA) movement can likely trace its roots to the discussion boards of another GCA, the Golf Club Atlas. The Internet gave golfers a new space to geek out, and those geeks multiplied into legions and became one of the most significant developments in golf in the last twenty years: the proliferation of pseudo-golf-architecture experts, a rank to which I aspired.

You could now become a golf authority of significance from the comfort of your office and see your voice heeded on message threads, regardless of whether you played once a week or month or year. Architecture punditry was a pastime within the pastime, one of those new and appealing entry points Nathan had referred to: it cost little, was less frustrating than the actual game, and lasted longer than eighteen holes. Its effects have been largely beneficial—more information makes for better choices in course alterations and restorations, and more knowledgeable consumers have, no doubt, led to more noteworthy designs—but I resisted anything more than a passing glance at the websites where somehow people had enough time to pen multichapter treatises on the properties of a true Redan hole or complain about a wrongly attributed design in *A Course Called Ireland*.

I couldn't remain on the GCA sidelines for much longer. I had found myself cowering in corners at golf cocktail parties the way I did at my English department functions, where I tried to dodge my colleagues' indecipherable punchlines about Derrida and Melville. To now find a strange new vernacular being spoken in my world of comfortable expertise sent me to the history books, where I discovered that Harry Colt was not the gun guy, that MacRaynor was not an actual person, and that someone named Perry Maxwell was.

These books were rarely published in paperback and never in large runs, so I was forced to scour the used markets for heavy tomes I would display on my bookshelf, awaiting a home visit from a design pundit who would see that of course I had read *Scotland's Gift* and had dog-eared the pages of *The Spirit of St. Andrews*. But as I labored through all the bygone prose and descriptions of yet another dogleg, I wished someone had just written a GCA cheat sheet, something I could slip into my pocket before exchanging quips in the grill about MacKenzie's ninth hole at Crystal Downs. So, with the help of Keith Cutten's invaluable *The Evolution of Golf Course Design*, I wrote one myself, and placed it in the back of this book (see Appendix C).

Now, as I climbed the mounds at Yale, its fairways still thin and soft in May, I felt gratitude for the haughty voices of GCA. What I might have dismissed as a thigh-burning ascent toward an invisible pin on number twelve was, upon reflection, a genuine Alps hole and a peak of architectural genius inspired by Scotland's Prestwick links. On the next hole, it was clear that Raynor had re-created North Berwick's Redan par 3 with its signature angled green, but his was a beefier American version, with a muscular right-side kicker to toss your Titleist toward the pin. And the Biarritz hole, borrowed from the Biarritz Golf Club in France, might have been dismissed as golf curiosity if I hadn't known the origins and effects of the green's trademark swale. I could stand in the dip in the middle of the ninth green and nearly disappear.

Macdonald's templates were no silent subtext at Yale—they were fists banging for attention, his model holes swollen with American aspiration. If I hadn't understood the careful purpose and the distinguished lineage of each offering, I would have walked off knowing Yale was good, but not understanding why. Golf Course Architecture, it turned out, was not just about showing off on social media. It was about grasping the picture, pausing to consider, and more deeply appreciating the eighteen paths you had been given that day. Had the rolled eyes and condescending emails of the golf-net not pushed me over to the research table, I would have only half appreciated the walk.

I left Yale feeling as if my GCA badge had been earned; I could take it home and have Mom iron it onto my uniform. I would be more discreet about my new belief that the best thing about New Haven wasn't golf but round dough smothered in cheese and tomato. The Course at Yale met the hype, but New Haven pizza (or *apizza*, as it's known) existed beyond the realm of accolades in some enlightened universe of celestial pizza archetypes. Off to New York I went, not tempted to even look at a Ray's but very curious to see what might be for lunch in the Hamptons.

EAST SETAUKET, NEW YORK

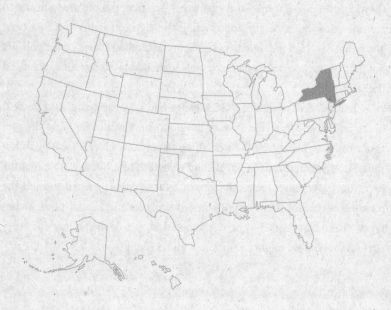

We talked about Jimmy as if I knew him. Bill, my playing partner from New-port, actually did; they were buddies from Pine Valley, bonded as Notre Dame grads and top-flight amateurs. Given our shared alma mater, I had lumped myself into an imaginary threesome with them, despite the fact that I'd never met or spoken to Jimmy, and that he was a very different sort of Irish. While I pretended my annual donation plea went missing in the mail again (truthfully, I opened it for the free Notre Dame sticker, then dumped it in the recycling), Jimmy served on the board of trustees, and had a new dorm named after his family.

In any case, I *felt* like I knew him. I had seen him on TV and heard the legends of his course records and his Rolodex of club memberships, including

Shinnecock and National Golf Links—which made him my lone dream shot at visiting either. Bill put us together on a text thread, and while I was shocked when a man of Jimmy's unwieldy schedule found time to reply, I was more floored to find my request for golf's great two-banger met with a yellow thumbs-up.

Don't forget a jacket, I was told, for the legendary lunch at National (I did forget, but was able to procure one at a nearby fashion boutique called Target). With the apex of Long Island golf secured on my calendar, I spent a week coming to grips with the inadequacies of my previous voyages. I would never regret so many pilgrimages to Scotland and Ireland—the bowls of unspecific soups, the scraped quarter panels, the feet turned to porridge had all changed my life for the better. But to think, there was a golf island like this just a few hours from my home? It was a right-under-my-nose revelation that started with St. George's.

Located around the midpoint of Long Island on its northern shore, St. George's was quiet on the morning I arrived; they squeezed me in on a Monday when the holes were closed for maintenance. An affable club historian named John came out to walk with me and point to where a recent Gil Hanse restoration had brought the best out of Devereux Emmet's routing.

John was soft-spoken, with the mustache and broad spectacles to befit the academic he was (a law professor at the nearby SUNY campus), and our shared vocation sparked a connection. You could eye much of the course from the clubhouse, though the expanse had once been crowded by conifers, their saplings cheap to buy and quick to grow, framing holes that needed no framing during the tree-planting splurges of the 1950s and '60s. John told me that he had discovered in the club's yellowing minutes that his own father had purchased and planted all the pines. *Sorry, Dad*, he'd thought as they were turned into firewood under his watch as club president. It was the right move. What he and Gil Hanse created was a golf landscape that called to you from every corner—*Come play with me.*

Gil had brought John over to National early in the restoration process for inspiration, showing him that they had the same bold terrain at St. George's, but the overgrowth was hiding it. It was land chosen for a course versus consigned to it—Devereux saw Macdonald's creation at National and wanted his own playground, so he searched the island for these precise 125 acres that, for their compactness, were a routing achievement. Gil wanted that routing to shine again, so he grew the place from twenty-three acres of fairway to thirty-five, leading members to think their course had gotten easier. But in reality, scores hadn't improved all that much.

"Gil created a bigger playing field to enjoy golf," John explained after the round, as we sat on a porch admiring an empty span of green ebbs and flows. "You have better playing angles into the holes. You're not chipping out from rough. You're not chipping out from trees. You're having a better time enjoying the game. And it really doesn't make the course easier, because all the new fairway brings a lot of bunkering into play. It brings in a lot of hills. It brings in a lot of ground movement that otherwise wasn't there, that *is* there now. We just brought back what Devereux Emmet saw in 1915."

John had articulated why we called this golf's second Golden Age— Hanse and his contemporaries were building courses we would label classics by the end of our lives, because they were looking back and taking cues from the old standards. They were making amends for an era when American architecture had been drunk on heavy machinery and flowerbeds and real estate plays. The time and imagination required to uncover a landscape's inconspicuous offerings were often abandoned in favor of dump-truck drama stamped onto landscapes by design corporations hired to sell not just golf holes but the adjoining timeshares. Design had now returned to the principles of Macdonald and Emmet and their contemporaries: great golf came from great land, wherever it might be.

As Bandon Dunes architect David McLay Kidd had explained to me, the real estate bust was one of the best things to happen to American architecture, freeing designers from having to consider access roads for condos or where the community center was going to go. The Masters showing up on color TV hadn't helped American architecture's cause, either, as consumers equated lush and blooming with good and worthy—thus ushering in golf's gardening age, when greens committees spent more time sourcing trees and perennials than they did considering the strategic qualities of their property. We all believed that pretty equaled good for a while, until enough people got back over to Scotland and Ireland, I imagined, and realized what pretty in golf really meant.

I'd approached the Long Island private clubs tenderly, anxious about breaching unwritten codes at these aged enclaves of the golf establishment, but being shepherded around by a wise prof like John settled my nerves. And while I knew Long Island would unveil itself as a buffet of great American golf experiences, I'd already decided that if I could choose a course to call home, it was here. So many soft crests, so many wide expanses of tight grass, so many tilted approaches down to wide-mouthed greens; it was a walk where you didn't quite feel your steps. Its low, white clubhouse resembling an idyllic summer cottage, its logo of an armored St. George slaying a dragon with a 5 iron, its more modestly moneyed membership—add it all to the welcome and the rolling terrain, and this was the place I would have summered, had I been born into a family that used *summer* as a verb.

That St. George's rarely ranked among Long Island's must-plays had me feeling both elated and suspicious about what I would find as I golfed my way toward its eastern edge. That afternoon, I headed to semiprivate Bellport with local legend Tommy Draycott and my friend Michael Bamberger, a fellow writer and Philadelphian (you should read his books, after this one). Tommy had been emailing with me for months—as the club historian at nearby Southward Ho, he had a friend of a friend at every club on Long Island. His son had been a golf pro in the area, and he took my itinerary under his wing like a benevolent uncle, planning my days down to the hour.

With his thick Irish build, thinning white hair, and heavy handshake, Tommy smiled through every shot at Bellport, a local golf institution of modest terrain. It was a Raynor design, but that didn't seem to be the draw here—it was a thoughtful community course, a place to knock your ball, not take notes. Bellport was a perfect foil to the gated golf around the rest of Long Island (sixty dollars for a seaside Raynor was a steal), with a clubhouse restaurant crowded with guys in sneakers and untucked shirts downing longnecks and crab-cake sandwiches. And Tommy knew everyone—the pro, the bag guy, the foursome coming off eighteen, the waitresses next door. The exception was Michael, even though he had grown up caddying at Bellport, a course he still considered a nostalgic favorite. As we got out into the holes bent along the water, I started to feel some nostalgia myself.

Though we had exchanged dozens of emails and shared the stage at a few speaking events, it was my first time teeing it up with Michael, and while he had been a generous friend to both me and my books, I wanted to outplay my hometown golf-writing rival with all the zeal of a forgotten underdog. He had spent most of his career at *Sports Illustrated*, a glossy with expense accounts and interview access and easy media passes, while Augusta's annual rejection of my credential request was one of the few constants in my professional life. It was a rivalry in my imagination only, but as we played, I kept careful tally of our shots. I knew Michael played for the love of the walk, and often ventured out alone at Philadelphia Cricket Club's St. Martins nine-hole course, so baiting him into a real match was out of the question. Disclosing the results of our hypothetical showdown would be similarly ungenerous, so I tried to forget the numbers and sought his input on what qualities I should be looking for in my Great American Golf Course.

"A great course, to me, is a course you walk. Where you can find your golf ball. Where you can go to the pro shop and take out your wallet and get on the first tee. Those would be my first three requirements. A golf course that's welcoming. If it has grass, that's nice, but it's not the most important thing," he explained. "Now, once you have all those things, if you've got even a hint of brackish breath to the course, like this one does, that adds immeasurably to the experience. As the old Scots say, 'If you've got wind, well, then your day is made.' Then you really are in heaven."

He used words like *brackish* and *immeasurably* in passing sentences, and they sounded effortlessly appropriate. I quickly got back to counting strokes; I was two-up, and consoled myself by believing that driving stats trumped elocution in most circles.

From Bellport I visited another New York public, state-owned course called Montauk Downs, that, had it not been set on the far eastern tip of Long Island, would have been a US Open candidate à la its state park cousin, Bethpage Black. The Robert Trent Jones design was a burly beast spread over a wide property, with deep swales and plateaued greens and holes that went on for weeks in the wind.

I went around Montauk Downs with a local turned golf vagabond, a kindred wandering spirit named Matt Cardis. Born and raised in East Hampton, Matt had set off a year ago with his camera and his sticks, sleeping in a tent atop his station wagon, photographing courses and meeting up with social media followers along the way. He caddied when money got tight and showcased cool new golf brands on his Instagram feed. Tall and bearded with a flat-brim cap, Matt had the slim build of a guy who ate ramen on the road, and he proved to me that there was something cooler than golf traveler: golf hobo.

On the golf media and marketing scenes, people like Matt were the new disrupters, the emerging conduits whose savvy and self-made voices reached a younger, phone-gazing audience, whether by juggling balls with their wedges or plotting out trick shots in their backyard or doing impressions of Sergio García. It was a new Wild West in golf marketing, as brands struggled to figure out how much some guy with a drone and a hundred thousand followers was worth, and as a result, many of these amateur tastemakers had turned pro, earning steady YouTube revenue and endorsement deals. It was great to have Mickelson wearing your hat if you were an accounting firm, but if you wanted to be cool, Matt Cardis was your guy. I listened to him describe how he had monetized his shoes, golf bag, van, sunglasses, and hats; he wasn't getting rich, but he'd figured out a way to golf and travel for a living without breaking par. In just a year he'd accomplished what it had taken me decades to achieve. And he didn't even have to write a book.

"When people talk about growing the game, the focus is always on the youth," Matt explained as we hoofed the hills of Montauk. "It's all about getting kids involved and bringing them into the game. And that's great. But I think about growing the game more as a cultural thing. This isn't our fathers' game anymore. It's our game. It's about the modern golfer now. It's about bringing the current-day lifestyle—the music, culture, art, fashion—bringing it all into golf. This stuffy game of pleated pants isn't going to cut it anymore. But what's going up behind it is exciting and young and alive."

I checked my pants—no pleats—and felt a little bit cooler for having spent a round with a golfer of the moment. That afternoon, we headed off to a place that might be a little less current in its aesthetics, but who cared: Maidstone was a course neither of us was going to miss.

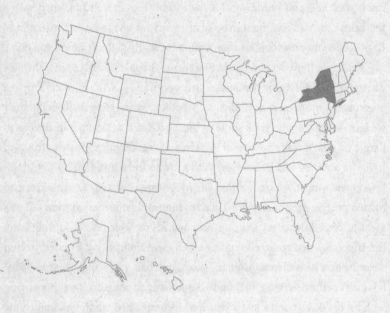

As a teenager, Matt Cardis had ridden his bike past Maidstone's fairways on his way back and forth to school. Today he was going to have the first chance to walk them himself, and we did so with a generous member named Andrew, a teacher at a boarding school in New England whose family legacy had won him one of the more coveted memberships in the Hamptons. In the sacred triad of Shinnecock, National, and Maidstone, the last was a family spot, thanks to a bustling beach club directly behind the clubhouse. It was an active club versus a museum piece, Andrew explained, with paddle sports and boating, where the most prized position was on the wine committee. (Its members took annual trips around the world in search of rare vintages that were supposedly stored beneath the tennis courts.) But we weren't here for cabanas and cabernet—we were headed for the dunes, to find ourselves a piece of Ireland.

Willie Dunn and Seth Raynor had taken stabs at laying out Maidstone, but it wasn't until the club acquired nearby Gardiner's Peninsula that Willie Park Jr. was able to shape a miracle of sand and swamp and beach grasses in 1924, its hues and textures as vivid as any I'd found on the most rugged foreign links. Just as interesting as its layout was the family who had once owned the property. The Gardiners' money was as old as old money got in America—in 1639, they had purchased nearby Gardiners Island from the Montaukett tribe. There they built America's longest-running family estate. Today, should you sail too close to the island in the bay between Long Island's forks, you'll be summarily turned back by guards on jet skis (colonial tidal rights are still the law in New York, where you own the water around your property up to a cow's height). Captain Kidd supposedly buried treasure there, which Robert Gardiner, the island's sixteenth Lord of the Manor, hinted at having found by way of his mysterious diamond pinky ring. In the 1990s, Gardiner was quoted as proclaiming: "The Fords, the du Ponts, the Rockefellers, they are nouveaux riches!" Thankfully, his ancestors weren't riche enough to avoid selling some of their huge cache of Long Island property. Maidstone's added acres gave Willie Park enough room to shape eighteen holes that wandered from ponds and marsh holes to beachside gigglers.

An easy favorite was the eighth, a par 3 with a green obscured by a sandy ridge. I was a sucker for the hit-and-hope whimsy of blind par 3s, but I enjoyed this one mostly for the controversy its veil had once concocted. As it was told to me by a club pro from the Midwest, two Maidstone members had been engaged in a tight club championship match when they arrived at the eighth. Both men hit their tee shots toward the pin, but with tall, thick grasses backing the green, outcomes were unknown until they climbed past the dune. They found one ball on the green, with no sight of the other. They went searching the grasses, picking through the reeds until one announced, "Found it! Titleist with a black dot. Got it right here." He proceeded to wedge his ball close enough for the putt to be conceded, but as his opponent bent over to pick it up, he noticed something curious in the hole: A ball, already there. The player lifted it out and inspected the markings.

"Titleist with a black dot?" he asked before tossing the cheater his original ball, and walking directly toward the clubhouse. By the time the fraud collected his jaw off the eighth green and made it back to the pro shop, his locker had already been cleared out. He had managed to spoil both his ace and his membership in one fell swoop.

There was no such chicanery in our threesome, though Andrew's ball did bear a curious customization. In knocking a putt back to him, I noticed that this dad and high school teacher was rolling a TaylorMade with a surprising number.

"You're playing a sixty-nine?" I asked him. "Seriously?"

Andrew laughed and explained that he was also the golf coach at his prep school, and one of his freshmen had won an important local tournament that year. As his prize, he got four dozen new balls with the number of his choosing, and naturally he selected his winning score. The young man so proudly and earnestly presented his coach with a dozen 69 golf balls; all Andrew could do was smile and pat him on the back. He wasn't about to explain the connotations to a thirteen-year-old. *Well, Bobby, sometimes when a Mom and Dad get bored . . .* No chance, he decided. His friends would tell him soon enough.

Maidstone had made its case for the Great American Golf Course; its blend of bog and dune and ocean and pasture ticked every box one could ask for in a golf landscape. But I was most transfixed by those striped beach tents behind the eighteenth green—a day of this golf and that surf was the dreamiest weekend retreat. Matt and I agreed that we might never find Maidstone's equal, but as he started up his van and left the parking lot for parts unknown, I wondered how long that opinion would linger. Just down the road were courses that had redefined American golf architecture, and in the case of one of them, had literally created it.

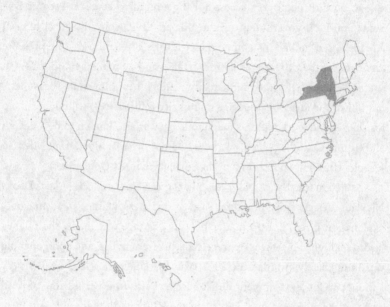

The rest of the week passed in a Gatsby-esque daze, spring afternoons spent drunk on the charms and luxuries of New York society. I imagined myself in a linen suit mingling with robber barons, taking in the views from the Sebonack clubhouse or the patio at Sleepy Hollow as I caught my breath from another evening of blue-blood small talk, trading stock tips and techniques for tacking a jib. In reality, I didn't own any linen, and I didn't get to laugh with any socialites—though I did get to sleep in one of the cottages at Sebonack. While most on-property accommodations skewed toward the utilitarian in my experience, Sebonack's quarters were ready for a state visit.

Sebonack was neighbor to National Golf Links, and though the latter once had a chance to purchase the adjacent property, they had passed, allowing the Electrical Workers Union to come in and buy it as a summer retreat in 1949. Fifty years later, when the union was ready to sell, a developer named Donald Trump backed out of the deal when he couldn't get the planning permissions for a course. In stepped a man named Michael Pascucci, a car and cable TV magnate, who took a chance on the belief that he would be able to push through permissions for three hundred acres on Peconic Bay. Some 250 local government meetings later, all of which Pascucci himself attended, and he had his golf course, with the stipulation that he preserve a portion of the property as natural habitat and an agreement to throw in some golf outings for the municipality. I didn't meet him while I was there, but I liked the idea of Pascucci, a millionaire (billionaire?) willing to roll up his sleeves and work with his neighbors. He was also known to be a devout and tithing Catholic, which was how I scored my free night's stay when St. Joseph's University popped up in my email signature. (Go Hawks.)

At Sebonack, I was told I was playing the first, and likely last, Doak-Nicklaus design collaboration. "Two strong personalities" was the only explanation given, but no matter how the sausage was made, the billowy layout set high above the water received exuberant praise, and upon opening was immediately awarded the 2013 Women's US Open. *Good for Pascucci*, I thought. Golf development didn't have to be a strong-arm game of push and win, or push and quit. He put in the hours and got himself an Open, on a course that deserved one. The codesigners might not send each other Christmas cards, but Nicklaus's bias for player experience had combined with Doak's naturalism to produce a visually stunning result. I walked its first through its last with an unshakable grin.

I left my cottage at Sebonack with an immediate wistfulness for our night together and headed for Southward Ho and Southampton, both first-rate courses for folks who actually live and work on Long Island. Southward Ho, named after the twelfth hole at Carnoustie, took its tower logo from the windmills that dot the property. It's a Tillinghast that showcases one of Tillie's favorite templates, a Reef hole, where the direct path to the green is guarded by a storm of trouble, but safe passage is offered around the side. He was a sailor himself, so a hole that mimicked a ship navigating a reef seemed to fit his repertoire. My favorite thing about Southward Ho was its pace—if you chose to tee off before nine a.m. on a weekend, you had to play in three hours, forty-five minutes. One minute more and a sternly worded letter was headed your way.

Southampton was a Raynor design and the fourth corner of the great golf intersection of Shinnecock, National Golf Links, and Sebonack. Of the group, it was the one where you were most likely to bump into the guy who was fixing your roof, an authentically Southampton hangout. It certainly existed in the shadows of its neighbors, but its location did have its advantages. The pro told me how, a few years before, a Southampton member bladed an approach through the green, through the fence, and onto the highway, where it dinged a passing car. Up to the fence came an irate driver, jabbing fingers and demanding his car be repaired.

"Calm down, don't worry. The club has insurance," the pro explained. "Just go up the road to the clubhouse and they'll get it all taken care of for you."

Unbeknownst to the aggrieved motorist but very well known to the Southampton foursome, the clubhouse up the road wasn't Southampton's. It was Shinnecock's.

Back in the Southampton clubhouse, the pro waited for his phone to ring. It did.

"What the hell are you doing down there?" came a voice from up the road. They shared a laugh and took care of the driver, no harm done. No matter where they find themselves stationed, the connection between club pros is sincere.

I kept my ball off the road as I battled my new buddy Keith, a local defense attorney I'd met somewhere among the circles of golfers who went to No Laying Up events or followed Tour player turned Instagram star Zac Blair online. Keith was of a physique I would describe as British pub: modest height and not actually fat; his weight was just poorly distributed à la the round-bellied, skinny-legged pint drinkers from my London days. But the guy could hit it—a scratch player, we played even-up for high stakes. If I won, the lifetime Giants fan would have to wear a Giants jersey to an Eagles game. If he won, I'd have to say he was good-looking on camera.

Rarely had I pegged it with so much on the line—Keith was risking his life, and I was bargaining my journalistic integrity. Bruises would heal, I told him, but my reputation as a forger of the facts would remain with me forever.

"Play hard, then, smart-ass," he said. And I did. He got me down two holes early, but I battled back to a final-hole eight-footer that would see Keith spending a long and beer-soaked drive back up the turnpike that fall. The ball caught most of the cup before ripping out and sitting on the edge. We both exhaled, freed from the weight of uncomfortable stakes.

That afternoon, I drove deep into the woods to find a driveway that wound beneath the faded paint of a starting-line bridge, a holdover from the property's former function as a road-racing track. I passed a Phillips 66 billboard planted in the trees, not far from what looked like a lunar landing module. I was not convinced I was heading toward a golf course, until the head pro met me in the parking lot at The Bridge. Jeff Warne had won most of the PGA events in his section and had his own morning show on PGA Tour Radio, but his pleated khakis and loose-sleeved shirt didn't quite match the avant-garde clubhouse. He was tall and laid-back with a soft southern drawl, an old-school pro at a place that seemed anything but.

Maybe it was the Formula 1 car in the men's locker room that made The Bridge feel a little different, or the 360-degree race simulator in a room beneath the restaurant, or that the spaceship I had spotted by the entrance was actually a padded playroom replete with a stocked martini bar; a great hangout if you knew the guy with the key. Perhaps it was the signs and stickers that turned the Gulf Oil logo into Golf, or the Richard Price art installations that dotted the course (a wooden prison cell, a tapestry of torn tires, shrubs made of vintage clubs), or the sculpture by Charles McGill depicting his alter ego Arthur Negro, the Black militant linksman with a golf bag and an Uzi, that made it feel like I wasn't at Maidstone anymore. The Bridge had been developed by a Wall Street trader who was keen to style the place more after Manhattan than the Hamptons (hence the million-dollar mosaics in the lunchroom) and erase any hints of country-club stuffiness. It was a fresh ethos that the membership embraced: last year's club champion had won playing in flip-flops and a Mickey Mouse T-shirt, and the trophy he'd earned was a painted car transmission on which his name was scratched in pencil.

As I changed my pants beside a race car, I watched couples enjoy their lunches on the other side of a tall glass wall that I assumed was tinted from the other side. I was later relieved that I opted against taking a shower when I found that the panes were perfectly transparent, the patio separated from the locker room by the clearest glass in the Hamptons. For all its idiosyncrasies, I figured the place had to be a money-losing vanity project for its owner, but when I learned there was a healthy waiting list of would-be members ready to pay the seven-figure entrance fee, I conceded that Manhattan art scene meets golf was a winning formula.

I expected those on the waiting list prized their art more than their golf, because as good as the course was—and it was its own sprawling canvas of immaculate green brushstrokes through brown sand and bramble—it was the toughest test I'd faced in years, with hefty carries to banked fairways leading to greens that, perhaps appropriately, ran at road-racing speeds. I found their pace unplayable, though Jeff claimed the members all loved it— they didn't take themselves too seriously at The Bridge, so greens running at 16 was all part of the fun. I suppose it *was* fun, but my brand of golf bliss, it turned out, was just across the water.

When I finished eighteen, Jeff grabbed my bag and threw it in his truck. "I'll show you a different place now," he said, and we drove back out the long driveway past another work of modern art, this one a large metal sign proclaiming THERE WILL BE NO MIRACLES HERE.

The Goat was a four-minute ferry ride across the Peconic River to Shelter Island, and though its real name was the Shelter Island Country Club, nothing about it resembled a country club save the nine flags planted around the property; everyone referred to it by the name of its restaurant and island hub, the Flying Goat. Jeff had stopped for a six-pack on the way (oh, how many rides had I taken with golf pros driving with a beer between their knees) and piloted us down to the ferry like a seasoned visitor. This was clearly his post-work routine, a place of restorative simplicity after a day of making golf go well for art and bond traders.

They were chaining up the golf carts when we arrived, but there was one set aside, as if they knew to leave it out for Jeff. We went inside and paid our fifteen-dollar greens fees at the bar, and on the first tee, Jeff decided our wager. The loser would pay the dinner tab, which meant I was buying, since Jeff had been around the Goat's 2,500 yards roughly five hundred times. He knew its every bend and bounce, and as the course lacked any real irrigation, the bounces were mighty. I loved its compact quirk and nonchalant nature, but Jeff lamented that I wasn't getting the true Goat experience.

"It's better when it's completely brown," he explained. "The ball does crazy things out here. Irish links have nothing on these fairways when they're cooked."

My ball still managed to do crazy things pretty well. I found myself playing over benches and picking my ball out of the fence line; there was no stopping your shots at the Goat, and seeing Jeff go around with four birdies and five pars was like watching some sort of golf voodoo. I gladly paid for our steaks that came smothered in a piquant pepper gravy. For what looked like a bar where you dropped your peanut shells on the floor, the food at the Goat might have been its best surprise.

"This is where I go to find golf again when I'm playing bad," Jeff explained as he waited for his next Budweiser at the bar. "I can shoot eighty-one in a section event, then come out here and find my swing again. It's never about mechanics here. You just play. You just play and swing away and chase it, and that's always how I can get my game back."

Coming from a guy who worked on one of the most gorgeous driving ranges in New York, designed with swanky hitting bays and TrackMan monitors aplenty, it was wisdom I wanted to remember. *Just play.*

As we headed back across on the last ferry, I wondered why a place so simple had felt so special, realizing the answer was in the question. Perhaps my course search had been too centered on architectural nuance and historical significance. Maybe I was giving too much credence to the magazine rankings, or too easily equating exclusivity with quality. I thanked Jeff for a day that had taken me to the polar extremes of the golfing spectrum, newly aware that the course I was chasing might exist at either end of it. I wasn't looking for America's greatest layout anymore, I decided. I was searching for a playground from which I couldn't pull myself away.

RIVERHEAD, NEW YORK

The next morning, golf changed its colors yet again, and Long Island continued its campaign to shame every region left on my map. In twenty-four hours, I'd gone from an art gallery racetrack to an island of hardpan to the place Harry Potter went to school.

It was hard to eye the dark gables of Friar's Head and not imagine Hogwarts, both for its architecture and for its inaccessibility. It was regarded as one of the more elusive invites in golf, and I drove past its entrance twice—no sign—before daring to buzz my way in. A North Shore newcomer founded in 2003, the clubhouse had the feeling of a restored castle perched above the sea, with stone arches like imposing brows that set a very different tone from the race car golf carts at The Bridge. It felt like a hideout for golf Jedi, with no yardages or hole handicaps on the scorecard—a haven for pure golf.

My friend Joel joined me from New York City, and as we slowly crept up on the clubhouse, first lurking about the parking lot, then the bag drop, then the pro shop, we waited for someone to acknowledge our presence and confirm that we were indeed going to golf today. Once we found a friendly face in the caddie master, the conversation quickly turned into a tutorial on how not to mess up this opportunity. My primary takeaways: no phones or photos or laser rangefinders; our caddies didn't carry them, either. We wouldn't find any rakes in the bunkers, and we were twice told not to repair our ball marks. Instead, we were to inform our caddies of any indentations, and they would fix them by a Friar's Head–patented technique of squirted water and tee-lifted turf.

As for how to allocate strokes for a match given the minimalism of the scorecard, our caddies told us it wasn't that kind of place. Play even-up— real golf—or don't play a match. There was only one tee per hole, no tips or senior tee boxes. It was a place of singular vision—even the pins were unique, each holding two flags (the nautical flags for *F* and *H*). This should have been no surprise, as the course had been built by a former US Mid-Am champion who obviously wanted a no-bullshit golf experience. He achieved much more than that; the Coore-Crenshaw routing left both Joel and me gobsmacked.

We played a match that day, but I doubt either of us would recall the result (I checked; we tied). Our stroll through dunes and farmland and sand and meadows was topographical gluttony that overshadowed our contest. The course wandered between hulking sandhills that gave the place its name (long before it was a golf course, sailors in Long Island Sound decided one of its sand-topped dunes looked like a friar's noggin) to the more sedate spreads of a former potato farm, but in either setting, Bill Coore and Ben Crenshaw had highlighted every last drop of drama. If I never got to play Cypress, I figured this was a pretty grand substitute, as far as rugged and audacious golf holes beside the beach went. And I was certain it had one feature Cypress couldn't match: the most dramatic green-to-tee walk in golf. The trek from the fifteenth green to the sixteenth tee took us across a wooden bridge hanging off the side of a cliff, with waves splitting upon rocks far below our feet.

After some shopping in a quiet and carefully curated pro shop—no sale racks at Friar's Head—Joel and I left the property as silently as we had arrived. As I passed through the gate, I felt a tangle in my heartstrings. I loved everything about our day at Friar's Head, yet I lamented that such quality was shared with so few. It wasn't a sensation unique to this club but one I was bumping into at so many premier courses that hosted less than a dozen rounds a day. I was no golf class warrior, but I was making an uneasy daily bargain, and would be doing so for months without a clear conscience to guide me. I was begging my way onto places I didn't belong and courses I couldn't afford, attesting to their greatness like some door-knocking bootlicker. I had seen golf done otherwise, in villages across the British Isles where every tee was open to a visiting player, but here I was playing the game of networks and flattery to score myself a game. Was I a hypocrite? Or was I just a golfer who wanted to play?

I didn't write the rules over here, but I suspected that those who did had missed something essential about the game. When King James IV lifted the ban on golf in Scotland in 1502, he was reversing a rule that had been put in place to keep soldiers—that is, common people—from spending too much time on the links, away from their archery practice. It wasn't a sport of kings, at least not until we got hold of it. In my search for the Great American Golf Course, I feared we might be excelling at course but losing at golf. If I could reconcile my misgivings and see past the gates, I might remember that much of the jolt of playing this golf came from the rarity of the chance. Exclusivity certainly bred excitement. Maybe that was more cop-out than conscience, but I was going with it for now. Especially with the courses on my calendar for tomorrow.

SOUTHAMPTON, NEW YORK

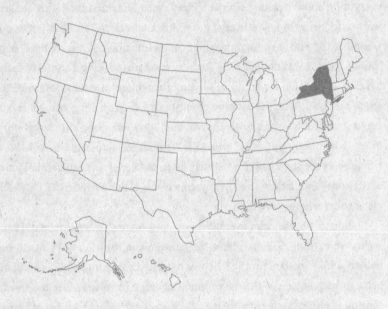

I was awake and dressed for golf by five a.m., leaving me four hours to scrub my grooves and second-guess a dozen belt/hat combinations. When I arrived at Shinnecock later that morning, I found US-Am Bill was already on the putting green—he had traveled back up from New Jersey to join us, and had brought new Fighting Irish caps for our foursome. Bill was the mutual friend who had helped arrange what others might have called Shinnecock-National Day, perhaps the most coveted back-to-back in golf, but because I'd read and watched so much about our host, I nervously knocked putts back and forth across the green, waiting for Jimmy Dunne Day to start.

I'd first learned of him through a Golf Channel piece sent by a friend: "How Golf Saved the Life of Jimmy Dunne." It told the story of Jimmy's record-setting day at Shinnecock in 2010, describing perhaps his best day on the golf course, and then detailing his most painful. Back in 2001, he had been planning on taking a run at the US Mid-Am when his longtime best friend and business partner, Chris Quackenbush, walked into his office at Sandler O'Neill, the investment firm where Jimmy was a partner and founder. Quackenbush was also an avid golfer and had accompanied Jimmy on his first playing experience at Shinnecock—as teenagers, they had been painting the house of a member when he invited them out for an afternoon round. As he perused the Mid-Am application on Jimmy's desk and studied the list of qualifying sites, Quack (as Jimmy called him) asked where his friend was planning to play. Jimmy had eyed up the qualifier on September 10 in Connecticut, but Quack told him he should go to Bedford the day after instead. It was a course where he could break par, Quack explained.

Jimmy took the advice, and was one under through four holes at the qualifier when an official approached his foursome on the morning of September 11, urging him to call his office.

Sandler O'Neill lost 66 of its 171 employees, Quack included, when the Towers collapsed that day. As the helplessness of the post-9/11 world set in, Jimmy went to work identifying what his firm's families needed. They needed benefits, so he asked the CFO what the firm could afford, and then doubled it. They would also need an income, so Jimmy decided every family would stay on the payroll and receive larger bonuses than they had ever received before. He also set up a foundation that would pay for the tuitions of all seventy-six children who lost a parent in the attacks. Today, Jimmy still plays every round with a Q on his ball in memory of his friend.

As I puttered around the practice green with Bill, I felt the nerves in my fingertips. I wasn't just about to play beside a great golfer; I was going to spend the day with a man who had faced days I could not fathom, and had done so with a strength and an integrity that, to me, seemed larger than life. The nerves softened when Jimmy arrived and greeted us. He was a guy of modest height and thick gray hair; he had an easy smile and a tan from a winter spent at Seminole, I surmised. With his Long Island accent, Jimmy said he didn't need to hit balls, and led Bill and me to the first tee, where he told us today's match was a five-dollar closeout "on the flat." (No strokes given.)

We talked about the courses I'd been visiting, and Jimmy knew all of them well. I asked how many clubs he belonged to—my guess was around thirty—and his response was, he explained, the same answer he gave his wife when she asked: "Is that something you really need to know?"

I thought about it. *Want?* Absolutely. *Need?* I paused. "No, it isn't."

"Good. Because that information is on a need-to-know basis," he said with a smile.

For a moment, I wondered if it was possible he'd forgotten the number. I knew he was president at Seminole, and further research had linked him to Chicago Golf, Shinnecock, National, Sebonack, Ohoopee, Pine Valley, Augusta, and Cypress. Judging by the fact that the desk in his Hamptons home office was formerly the desk of the secretary at Muirfield, I guessed he was a member of the Honourable Company as well. Probably the R & A, too. I soon learned that he certainly remembered his every membership, every championship, and every round, because the secret sauce behind Jimmy's success was his elephantine memory.

"Not necessarily for names," he explained, "but if I have a conversation with someone, I can recall it verbatim. When I was trading on the bond desk, I was a mediocre trader, but there's an expression in that business, if there's a question on a trade—can you re-create the trade? And I could. *You said take the offering, I said give me ten, he said he can sell you twenty, I said I'll take twenty-five if he's got them.* I could re-create the dialogue. I remember when I left Bear Stearns, they thought I took all my records. But my assistant told them, 'No, Jimmy doesn't write anything down. He can remember every trade.' That's really the only skill I have. In terms of intellect, the rest is pretty marginal, but I do have an unusual memory."

Jimmy was being modest—he had abundant skills to share, and golf was one of them. He'd qualified for the US Senior Amateur at age sixty-two, and had set a course record of 63 at Shinnecock (he humbly conceded the record to Tommy Fleetwood, who had posted his 63 in a US Open). There were plenty of recall savants out there, but they didn't count Rory McIlroy or President Obama or Justin Thomas or Phil Mickelson or Tom Brady as playing partners. How he had achieved such a network of friendships without playing on the Tour or working as an agent or the CEO of a golf company I was not endeavoring to find out on this trip, but I was sure I had identified the most interesting man in golf.

As seemed to be his practice, Jimmy invited Kyle, a Shinnecock assistant pro, to be our fourth that morning, and discussed job openings with the young man as we went. He had not only placed kids from the 9/11 families in jobs with his firm, I came to understand, but looked out for the assistant pros and caddies at his clubs as well, helping them find work when they needed it. For all his successes, Jimmy the Wall Street mogul was still Jimmy from Long Island, a caddie from Southward Ho who used to paint houses and tend bar with his buddy Quack, a young boy who was amazed when his father finally joined a golf club and told him that there were no tee times—they just brought out your bag and you could go play. Jimmy marveled at the thought of that, and decided he needed to get into one of those golf clubs someday.

"My father said there were three really important things other than your health and your faith," Jimmy explained. "Marry the right woman; go to the best college you can get into; and get good enough at golf so that you're not scared to death on the first tee." He told me that his dad had started him in golf around the age of eight, hitting balls in the backyard and heading out to the public course near their home in Babylon, Long Island. He'd wake Jimmy at four a.m. on Saturdays so they could sign in for a tee time at the pro shop, and then they would go have breakfast, hit some balls, have some more breakfast, and get on the course by nine a.m., where they'd put in four hours of patience to play nine holes. Jimmy loved it. By age eleven, he was telling the caddie master at Southward Ho that he was fourteen so he could get a job carrying bags, and it was in the caddie room where he earned his stripes. "By twelve I was somewhat seasoned, both as a golfer and certainly as a gin rummy player. They didn't treat you like you were a little kid if you could break eighty, and if you knew what the count was in the gin game."

Jimmy's caddie friendships remained with him through his entire life, even as his stock was (quite literally) skyrocketing. Many years later, when word began to spread that Jimmy had been invited to join Augusta National, one of his first callers was his former gin and golf partner from Southward Ho.

"I was in the office and my assistant, she looked over and she wasn't annoyed, but I could tell she was a little irked by the guy on the phone. She basically said, 'Jimmy, there's this guy on the phone—Leroy Brown, I'm not sure who he is. I can just tell him to get lost, but he's insisting to talk to you.' I gave her the one finger up, and I got off my other call and took the phone.

"He always called me kid, and he said, 'Kid, is this true?' I said, 'What's that, Roy?' He says, 'True about Augusta.' I told him, 'Well, yes, believe it or not, it is.' He said, 'When are we going?' I said, 'Listen, Roy, I promise you I will take you—you have my word. I just got in; I haven't been down there yet myself. I've got to feel my way out. I'm not sure how things are done down there.' And Roy said, 'No, no, no, no, we're not waiting! They haven't gotten to know you yet. You won't be in there long. You got to take me now!'" Jimmy laughed. "And so I did. We had a great time. It was really good."

That sort of loyalty lined up with the stories I'd heard. I'd been told an unsubstantiated anecdote in which Jimmy had invited Justin Thomas and Jordan Spieth out to Shinnecock and asked that they bring their caddies as well—not to carry bags but to play. When the round was over, he pointed the pros toward a restaurant in town and invited the caddies over to his home for dinner. Jimmy wasn't one who was always looking out for the little guy, because he didn't judge anyone as little. His life was guided by a belief that he wasn't better than anyone else, or worse than anyone else. It was a great way to live, and I tried to think that about myself as we headed out into the hills, quieting those voices that said the guy next to me was better than me in pretty much every measurable way.

Jimmy explained that day's courses by way of a useful Irish comparison: National was like Royal County Down, a cerebral test of blind shots and a trial of angles that took multiple loops before you began to feel swept away by its genius. It was a course that hid from you a bit. Shinnecock, though, was more like Royal Portrush—as subtle as a punch in the jaw, a wide-shouldered, in-front-of-you golf course that was easy to fall for at first glance. Jimmy also contended that Shinnecock was "the finest golf course in the world," and since he belonged to most of them, I deferred to his opinion. He had traveled the globe playing the planet's top one hundred, and his astonishing recall allowed him to identify the characteristics of every hole on every course of note. He liked to test his assessments by playing a grillroom game in which you pitted courses against one another in a hole-by-hole match.

Which course had a better first hole? Okay, they were one-up. Now, compare their second holes—and so he went through all eighteen until a winner was declared. It was a dizzying and fantastic endeavor to listen to, where Jimmy was able to re-create and contrast the seventh holes at Garden City and Royal Melbourne without pause. In all the times he'd played the hole-by-hole showdown, there was only one course that remained undefeated: Shinnecock. As we wound our way through the fescue-lined fairways, over rolling property that felt peaceful yet perilous with golf shots I wanted to hit for the rest of my life, I suspected Jimmy's game had gotten it right.

It also didn't hurt that the early sun was warmer at Shinnecock than the afternoon rainclouds, and that our foursome was still bright with energy and breezy conversation when we played it. We were leg-weary as we headed for National, and pulling on our rain gear wasn't likely to fill our sails. I'd seen it happen on this trip before, when a second eighteen declined into a schlep of fatigued introverts. As Bill later noted, "There's nothing as quiet as a foursome walking up their thirty-sixth hole."

I had arrived at National Golf Links of America well-versed in the mythology surrounding its founder, C. B. Macdonald, a man so modest he installed a life-size statue of himself in the library, where it still holds court today. NGLA was more than Macdonald's passion; it was his life's collective wisdom and experience, all pressed into the soil beside the bay. He had originally wanted to buy and redesign Shinnecock, but instead opted for the ground next door, where he applied his study of the top-rated holes in Great Britain and re-created them—his much-tweeted-about templates—in the sandbanks of Long Island.

Macdonald was the first designer to refer to himself as a *golf course architect*, and it was a label he earned. The scholarship he put into National evolved course-building from afterthought to art form. As George Bahto notes in his history *The Evangelist of Golf*, Macdonald was also a forefather of American golf agronomy; his search for the best blend of seeds and soils at NGLA changed the way courses planned their planting, and by installing America's first irrigation system at National, he reset the bar for course conditioning, making clear he would not allow American golf to be a shaggy rendition of the British game—not in its look, nor in its practice. His push for proper championships gave birth to the US Open, the second of which was held on the course we had played that morning. It was during that event in 1896 when Macdonald witnessed the moment golf in America came into its own.

In the field that year was a sixteen-year-old named John Shippen, an African American caddie who had learned the game from Shinnecock's pro, Willie Dunne. According to Lane Demas, author of *Game of Privilege*, Shippen's father was a freed Virginia slave who had come to Long Island to do missionary work on the native Shinnecock reservation. His son quickly took to the game being played next door, giving lessons, making clubs, and nearly breaking Dunne's own course record. Shippen's talent inspired the Shinnecock members to enter his name for the Open tournament, along with his caddie friend Oscar Bunn, who was of Shinnecock descent. By playing for a purse, one Black and one Native American golfer made history by becoming the first two American golf professionals—but when the old guard got word of Shippen's entry, it was a history that almost didn't happen.

Macdonald entered the Open that year as an amateur and found himself paired with Shippen, who was already being celebrated in newspapers across the country as the American teenage phenom who might topple the foreign talents. But the tournament was nearly upended when a group of British professionals protested the inclusion of a Black golfer, threatening to boycott the event. As English and Scottish players made up almost all of the professional field, the new USGA faced a pivotal choice—bow to the golf establishment or pursue a different path. USGA president Theodore Havemeyer was resolute in telling the dissenters that play would go on with Shippen included, even if he and Bunn were the only two players on the course. The Brits capitulated, and Shippen went on to fight for the lead in the US Open, ultimately undone by an 11 on the thirteenth hole in his final round, landing him in a respectable fifth place.

Macdonald's temper got the best of him in the Open—he posted an opening 83 and quit the tournament. Some accounts claim his withdrawal had to do with being partnered with a Black player; more reliable sources attest to his admiring Shippen's talents and choosing to walk with him and keep his score during the final round. Macdonald might have been a curmudgeon, but perhaps not a bigot; the fact that he founded the Links Club in Manhattan after his son-in-law was denied entry into another city social club for being Catholic might offer evidence that his intolerance has been overstated.

As we made the short drive over to National Golf Links, an undisputed bit of Macdonald history appeared on my horizon. I slowed down and soaked it in: the grand and iconic windmill set beside National's sixteenth green. It was built when Daniel Pomeroy, an early member, suggested to Macdonald that a windmill would enhance the look of the property. Macdonald agreed. He had the structure built to hide the club's water tower and sent the bill for it to Pomeroy.

Just as evocative as the windmill was National's curious logo. Macdonald had collected forty or so Delft tiles during his travels that depicted stick-holding figures—likely players of the Dutch game *colf* rather than golf—and had the blue-and-white shingles installed on the walls around the library. One tile portraying two face-to-face club-holders became the National logo, with golf clubs and balls added to the picture. I bought myself a full ensemble emblazoned with the two little Dutch dudes before heading into the clubhouse for the event that rivaled its course in reputation and nearly unseated Shinnecock from my top spot on Long Island.

We put on our blazers in the locker room, then headed upstairs, where we were seated by the windows. Almost immediately, a waiter in formal attire dropped a cleaved lobster onto my plate, with an accompanying side of piquant yellow sauce. Jimmy smiled. "Welcome to lunch at National," he said. A handful of M&Ms was my typical midday meal, so I tried to eat slowly; the hills outside looked mighty, and I didn't want to play them with an angry stomach. But I was powerless against the crustacean before me—in minutes its shell was picked clean, and I was sucking the juice from its tentacles. Again, the waiter approached our table. I expected him to hand me an extra napkin. Instead, he pulled out a notepad and asked us what we wanted for lunch.

Jimmy said he'd take the soup and the crab cake, and the rice cakes for dessert. *Wait a second*, I thought to myself. *We just had lunch*. And then it struck me: That football-sized lobster was an amuse-bouche. The lobster was *snacks*.

I proceeded to amuse my bouche with everything the waiter placed in front of me. After dessert, I waddled out to the fifth hole, as an outing had clogged the opening holes with players. Not playing National in its intended sequence may have had something to do with my slim preference for Shinnecock, or maybe it was because I didn't see the tenth hole at National at all—when I spotted what might have been a bathroom at the edge of the woods, I darted for its door as if running across cracking ice. "Don't wait!" was the only explanation I left in my wake, and for the next nine minutes I swore to myself that, from this day to my last, lunch would stop at lobster.

I knew Jimmy's gift of Shinnecock and National Golf Links of America meant that I would be asked one question by golfers I knew and many I didn't: Which is better? I played them both with senses tuned for a favorite, and while it was a coin-flip call, I feared my GCA badge would be revoked when I settled on Shinnecock. Perhaps I was exposing myself as an amateur course evaluator, but I couldn't dismiss performance as a factor, and I played well at Shinnecock, carding ten consecutive 4s with Jimmy as my partner and pocketing those five dollars.

The online architecture gurus pretty much swore by National as the greatest collection of golf holes in America, as many rightly worshipped at the altar of C. B. Macdonald. It was easy to appreciate its holes as perhaps golf's most fascinating ensemble, in both shape and style. In all my golf, I had never pondered an approach like I had on its third hole, Alps, where we looked right toward an angled fairway before tacking left toward a green hoisted atop a fescue-filled ridge. The drive on its Hog's Back hole was a giddy showdown of arching fairway split by a yawning bunker, and the punchbowl green beside the windmill on sixteen was one of the rare golf moments when you feel wistful before you're even finished, grieving its passing before it's gone. Eighteen was the best risk-reward finisher I'd ever faced—lay up for a tricky uphill second, or take it deep over a bunker and up to a second sliver of fairway. I walked off National feeling grateful that I'd taken a quick detour that morning. It meant more now.

• • •

A friend had texted me directions to where both Macdonald and Raynor were buried in Southampton. I didn't think I'd have time to visit, but waking before dawn had left me a few hours to decipher his imprecise instructions— *It's the cemetery after the first cemetery; their graves are near a bench.* As I walked through a graveyard of a thousand benches, I nearly abandoned my search, but I was glad that I didn't. I turned a corner and felt my breath stop for just a moment. There were the letters, tall on a dark and simple tombstone: RAYNOR. Seth J., deceased 1926, buried with his wife, Araminta. I turned around from Raynor's modest marker and found CHARLES BLAIR MACDONALD directly across from him. Macdonald's resting place was covered with a long granite slab; even in death, Macdonald spoke more loudly than his partner. Born in Canada, deceased 1939. Admirers had left small stones atop their tombstones and placed golf balls beside them, and I considered leaving one myself. I didn't, but after playing National, I understood why a token of gratitude was warranted. I stood there for a quiet moment between their names, between two friends sharing a burial plot, and I felt a shiver of awareness about what friendship could actually mean.

At day's end, we all drove back to the pro shop at Shinnecock—Bill needed one more sweatshirt for his kids—and as we waited for him, I walked over to find Jimmy in his front seat and on his phone. How many messages a day of no-cell-phone policies left him with I could only guess.

"My wife teases me about it," he later told me. "I called her once after playing Pine Valley, and she said, 'Just tell me where I was on your list of people to call.' I said, 'You don't really want to know.' She said, 'No, I do. Just give me the exact number.' So I told her—she was twenty-one. She said, 'Well, who was twenty?' I said the locker room guy at Seminole." He laughed. "And she goes, 'Well, that's not too bad.'"

Jimmy was probably not very far into his list when he put the phone down, and I asked if it might be possible to do a proper interview with him. I typically fished for answers during a round of golf, but I had so many more questions about how Jimmy Dunne had become Jimmy Dunne. He said no problem—he had a few more calls to make, but he'd meet me in half an hour, and he handed me an address.

SOMEWHERE IN THE HAMPTONS

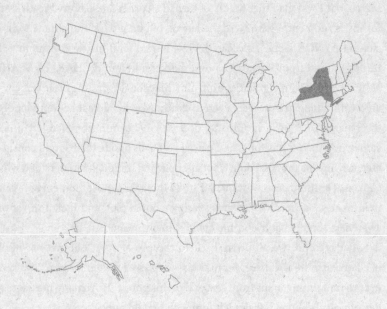

As my tires crunched across a driveway of tidy brown pebbles, the sprawling property I was approaching made me reach for my phone and check the address. It was not the sort of place you wanted to knock on the door without absolute confidence. Allyson would have wept at the sight of the gray-shingled Hamptons abode of manicured gardens and a wraparound porch, I thought. When I spotted a stone sculpture of a fighting leprechaun in the garden, I knew I was in the right spot.

Jimmy's wife welcomed me inside—she was cutting and arranging flowers in the kitchen, which seemed the most Hamptons thing I would see in the Hamptons. It was a detail I would have to keep from Allyson. She was convinced Martha Stewart and Ina Garten were living lives for which she was intended, and the image would have been too much for her to process. Mrs. Dunne asked me if I would be able to stay for burgers. I thanked her and said I couldn't (of course I could; I was just too nervous to say yes), as I peeked through French doors to where a handsome helper was cooking patties on a grill, and a long pool framed by fairway-height grass led to a pool house that would have fit my family comfortably.

Jimmy soon arrived and took me up to his sanctuary. Jon Rahm called it "the Shrine" when he visited Jimmy on Long Island, and it encompassed the entire third floor. The middle of the room was open to a winding staircase, and all around it were corners and crannies, each nook and wall dedicated to one of his golf clubs or life events. There was a model of the dorm he'd donated to Notre Dame, and above the door to the bathroom hung a saber he'd been given after addressing the cadets at West Point. Trophies spilled off tables too short to hold them, and the walls were covered with his most notable scorecards, blown up to billboard size. A giant Seminole rug stretched out from under the desk he'd bought from Muirfield. This was no man cave. This was the room you hoped you saw when the lights finally went out.

As I looked around Jimmy's room, I wondered how it was possible to cram so much into sixty years. To not just belong to these clubs but to actually have time to play at them and compete; to not just have so many connections but to cultivate and maintain them as genuine friendships; to not just work but to reach the top of your field; and to not just have a family but to care for the families of so many others—I had to ask him: When did he sleep?

"I sleep a little more than I used to," he admitted. "I'm trying to, anyway. There were times in my life when I lived on two hours of sleep, and it wasn't a big deal."

As he walked me through the memories on the walls, we talked of his golf with Tom Brady ("I never want to be his partner. I want to beat the GOAT's brain in every chance I get. People really don't understand how competitive he is. There's really no one quite like him"), playing with Patrick Reed at the AT&T ("When he makes a bogey, it goes through the whole foursome"), and Rory calling him up to come play with Bill Clinton. But what was more surprising than any of the circumstances of his stories was that none of it felt immodest. He wasn't interested in impressing anybody; he was genuinely himself, which is probably why these names gravitated toward him in the first place. He was generous with his blessings, so generous that he was giving me another hour of his time at the end of a very long day. I wanted to ask him why, but then he explained it.

"My buddy Chris Quackenbush, he used to say, when we worked at a bar together, how it bothered him that all these guys we worked with, these hard-nosed guys, bouncers and bartenders and tough guys, how he was so much nicer to all of them than I was, but they all liked me better than him," Jimmy said. "I said, 'Well, there's a reason for that, Quack. Look, you're the son of a doctor, you got sixteen hundred on your SATs, you're going to go on to be unbelievably successful. You know it, and they know it. With me, I don't know what's going to happen. I don't think like I'm going to do much better than these guys. I look at them like they're equals, and in the nicest way, you don't.' I can remember vividly when I was first starting in the investment business, when I found out that caddies could play at Cypress, and I remember thinking to myself, 'If I don't stop drinking at some point in time, I could be back here. This would not be a bad place to work.' I wasn't kidding; I was thinking that could happen," he said, and I felt myself beginning to nod as his story bumped into my own. "I've never viewed success as if it was a foregone conclusion. I do think that it could go away tomorrow, and if it goes away tomorrow, what do you got? I think my father was very good that way. He instilled that in me."

I noted that I had gotten sober as well, and since we both understood how that path went—lots of pain, lots of humility, then lots of hope—Jimmy knew I wasn't sharing it to score points. Years of shared experience passed between us without another word being said. Funny, I had already pegged him as a nondrinker before he mentioned it. No one who closed their day with cocktails could get as much done as he did.

A few of the walls in Jimmy's third floor were dedicated to memorializing his friends lost in 9/11, with conspicuous remembrances of his buddy Quack. We didn't discuss that side of the room. There are experiences to which a podcast or pages can't quite do justice, so we stuck to the experiences we shared. And for Jimmy, just as it was for me, the thing we shared was more than a pastime.

"I always laugh, because in Scotland, when you ask somebody about someone, they'll say, 'Oh, well, Frank so and so, he's John and Mary's son, he works down at the butcher shop and he carries a four.' So his handicap is integral to his persona, and I kind of feel like golf is that way with me. The game is integral to who I am."

The next afternoon, I was reminded how my relationship with golf was exactly the same. Nothing will confirm your addiction to something like going searching for it in the Bronx.

THE BRONX, NEW YORK

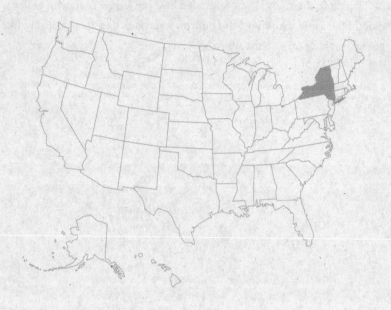

One of my earliest sports memories was a Flyers-Islanders brawl at the Spectrum, where I screamed for our goalie to bloody theirs, my sports innocence lost at the ripe age of eight. I had amassed a lifetime of Philadelphian assumptions about crude and condescending New Yorkers, but on my first trip to Long Island and the boroughs, I had yet to see the stereotypes come to life. I anticipated a landscape of stone-faced men with gold hoop earrings standing watch at every corner, guys running numbers from one dark doorway to the next, a New York of tank tops and Yankees caps where the hustle was on. My world thus far had been cedar-shingled clubhouses in the Hamptons, populated by Manhattan bankers and executives from Tokyo. But finally, as we set off in our carts for eighteen holes at Split Rock in the Bronx, I found the New York attitude for which I was searching—and it arrived in the form of a course ranger in cutoff jeans.

A gentleman named Jim had been following my itinerary on social media, and he reached out via email to invite me for golf in the Bronx. I was eager to play authentic New York golf—not the retreats out on the island but the people's courses within our most populated city. Jim—soon to be another Jimmy—wrote short missives of loose punctuation, assuring me he had spots for us at Split Rock and Vanny (Van Cortlandt Park). He also told me to invite a fourth to join him and his buddy Lenny.

I sent out an invite by Twitter and connected with an Irishman named Colm who could join us, and in a few days I met Jimmy by the Split Rock clubhouse, a pillared brick mansion left behind by some baron, I imagined, when the Bronx was small farms and summer homes in the 1800s. Jimmy had the thick build and tight haircut of a New York City doorman, which he was, and on the backsides of both his calves I found markers of hostility: large tattoos of the NY Rangers and Giants logos to welcome me to his corner of the world.

I suggested we play for fight songs captured on video—Eagles for him, Giants for me. Jimmy negotiated himself a few more strokes for such stakes, and we loaded up the carts he had arranged for us (I preferred to walk, but I wasn't talking back to my hosts today) and rolled over rumpled asphalt toward the opening hole. As Jimmy drove, I used a tee to dislodge smashed cigarette butts from the drink holders.

Split Rock seemed straightforward enough, and it was greener than I expected. If I could keep it out of the forests guarding its edges, I thought, its modest length could produce a respectable card. We were halfway down the first fairway when that ranger in jorts made a beeline for our group.

First tees no longer made me nervous, but somehow rangers still did, and I wondered what he could want as he slammed on his brakes beside us. I readied some placating remarks about the weather or the fine condition of the course. We were one shot into our day, and he couldn't be after us for slow play already.

A cigarette bisected a mustache that otherwise concealed his lips, and his T-shirt had lost its sleeves somewhere out there on the cart paths. He was whisper thin, and beneath wide glasses his tan cheeks were dented with thick lines from so many Split Rock summers. Strands of gray hair snuck out from under a floppy baseball cap and touched the top of his shoulders.

"Beautiful day," I said from the passenger's seat in our cart.

"Keep the carts on the fucking paths," the ranger said without a smile. "The fucking fairways are fucked up."

"Will do!" I said. *This* was the New York golf I had been looking for. We sped ahead to our golf balls, and I couldn't help but note to Jimmy: "You don't hear that at Shinnecock."

What I had heard that previous week was "Welcome to [insert course of international acclaim and rare architectural significance]. Who are you playing with?" It had been nine days of places whose architectural renderings hung in elegant clubhouses and on the walls of single men. In the pissing match between the Philadelphia and New York sections for golf supremacy, I was worried that I might soon be singing a New York fight song, and meaning it. But as perspective-shifting as New York golf was, it wasn't the courses that stuck with me half as much as New York's two Jimmys.

I could imagine them enjoying a round together, two adroit storytellers hewn from the same slab of genuine city grit. Jimmy's door job in Midtown was a good one "for a guy with no college education," he explained, with union benefits and solid pay—the Christmas tips alone made it one of the more coveted blue-collar gigs in Manhattan. It gave him plenty of downtime to plan golf trips for him and Lenny, a nearby town manager with whom he had been best friends since the age of ten.

As a doorman, Jimmy's influence flipped the pecking order between Manhattan workers and elites. Want to get that million-dollar kitchen job done upstairs? It was Jimmy who decided whether the crew got the keys to the service elevator. Want your wife to remain unaware of that acquaintance whose heels just went clicking through the lobby? It was important to be good to the doorman. He had shuffled girlfriends and boyfriends out back doors while husbands and wives came in the front; when investment bankers or their college kids needed recreational substances, the doorman was their connection. Jimmy knew in which penthouses the skeletons were hiding, and more essential to his job than pulling a door handle was keeping them there. He also knew which golf clubs his tenants belonged to, which came in handy when he and Lenny felt like teeing it up out on Long Island.

Split Rock showcased the tight corridors of an overgrown muni (municipal course), and when one of our drives bounced back out of the trees, Lenny was quick to ask: "Hey, were you cupping the leprechaun's balls last night?" Every good golf break in the Bronx thus became referred to as cuppage. *Damn, you got some cuppage there, my man!* The Dubliner in our group, Colm, loved this new expression, and though it had cost him a day off from his banking job, he thanked me for the best golf day he'd had in a while. I assured Colm it was he who deserved the thanks. The harmonious blend of a European financier with a Philly guy and two buddies from the neighborhood reminded me how wonderful this game was. We had little in common that morning, but after eighteen holes, I would have trusted Jimmy with my kids, and I was already imagining spots where we could all rendezvous again on my travels. Golf never failed at making accidental foursomes feel like providence. It was indifferent to our scoring ambitions, but when it came to connecting people, golf had a generous sense of cuppage.

From Split Rock, we hustled over to Van Cortlandt Park in the North Bronx. It was America's first public golf course and a regular hangout for the likes of Babe Ruth, Willie Mays, and the Three Stooges. Its upstairs locker room had been featured in *Wall Street* as the post-racquetball spot where Gordon Gekko transforms his hair in three quick brushstrokes, though now it looked nothing like the movie—just a dusty firetrap of dark wood and boxes of soda cups. The lockers had been neglected, but the course was in great nick; considering the place was absolutely stuffed with golfers (I had to pay a guy two dollars to park, a golf first for me), the greens were immaculate, and the pace moved along pleasantly.

How the routing at Vanny functioned in the days before golf carts I wasn't sure—the tee-to-green distances were substantial, winding around ponds and forest—but for its modest yardages, it was a tricky test of hard-packed turf. On most every hole, we were kicking around in the weeds for balls that had bounded through the green. A few of those were mine, which had Jimmy liking his chances in our match. He hummed the Giants fight song down sixteen and seventeen, leading me by a hole, but Lenny continued to remind his best friend that he'd never made a putt on the eighteenth to win.

I squared things up on seventeen, then bogied eighteen to leave the door open for Jimmy. His par putt scooted past the hole, which Lenny seemed to enjoy—"I told you! He can't do it!"—but when he missed the eighteen-incher coming back that would have halved the match, I couldn't say a word. Lenny could: "Ha! I have *never* seen you make a putt on eighteen!"

I put my camera away—there would be no recording of any Eagles fight song. Not only did I hate winning that way but I'd been there, and the empathy was real. Jimmy's face was pale with shock as we shook hands. On a Giants fan, such dead-eyed bewilderment was beautiful, but on my new friend Jimmy, it was sad to see.

Sort of. A win was a win. Fly, Eagles, fly.

It wasn't until two weeks later that I learned how meaningful our day in the Bronx had been. Irish Colm texted to wish me well on my travels and said he and Jimmy and Lenny were getting together Saturday for more golf in the city. I was in the middle of a lonely five-hour drive to play some golf holes in Oregon, and it was a well-timed reminder: I wasn't out here alone.

My every-Open-venue crusade pointed me back toward a few courses on the west end of Long Island—Inwood, Garden City, Fresh Meadow, Bethpage—plus New Jersey's Baltusrol before heading home. On the way I squeezed in a visit to the Skyway Golf Course in Jersey City, a new nine-holer where a white-haired gentleman whose name tag read Edmund Burke was working the desk in a trailer turned pro shop. (I resisted asking him to reflect on the French Revolution—prof humor.) Ed had the enthusiasm of a proper course greeter, and he knew Jersey City inside and out.

"This was all a garbage dump when I was a kid," he explained. The county had since reclaimed the land beside the Hackensack River, cleaned up the dump, restored the wetlands, and built a community golf hub—three par 5s, three 4s, three 3s—that was an oasis of green and fescue against a backdrop of steel bridges and jagged skyline. Ed walked me over to an aquarium in the pro shop where the course mascot was having lunch. He had found Jojo the Turtle in the parking lot when he (she?) could fit in his palm; now the size of a saucer, Jojo hopped up against the glass like a puppy as Ed approached. "Jojo's been good luck for this place," Ed said. As I looked around, it seemed to be true. Skyway Golf was busy. The pro told me he ran three beginners' clinics each week, and they sold out in twenty-four hours. When I asked him to describe the golf scene in Jersey City, "Hungry" was the word he used.

Joining me on the first tee was Scott, a graphic designer who zipped around Skyway's nine holes daily, after dropping his kids at school and before heading into the city to lay out the *New York Times*. A teaching pro named Chris and another Skyway regular named Mark filled out the foursome. Chris had tattooed biceps that stretched the seams of his sleeves, and Mark played in a T-shirt and jeans, encouraging me to go untucked. For a recovering country-club kid, a shirt blowing in the wind felt irresistibly mischievous, so I obliged. *Damn*, I thought as the breeze brushed my waist, *it does feel good to be a gangster.*

"We've got inner-city kids here, county residents who can play for cheap. They haven't had access to golf before, and they want to learn," Chris explained. First impressions had left me judging Chris by his muscles and shaved head—Jersey gym rat, I assumed—but he turned out to be an intellectual who collected rare books and whose partner designed Broadway productions. He didn't hit the ball as straight as the compact property required, but he pounded it with a barbell fury. He was longer than any rare book collector I'd ever met.

I also learned that it was Mark's first day back at Skyway after a long layoff. He was just returning from having a brain tumor removed, and as I watched him knock down pins across an immaculately maintained model for interesting golf in limited space (on two, he missed an ace by inches), I wondered what brain surgery might do for my own game. As we walked, I asked him how he was doing.

"Oh, I'm fine," he said, glancing down as we marched ahead to our balls. Then he stopped and looked up. "Wait. Where am I?"

I froze and looked over at Chris for help. Then they all laughed at me.

Skyway's undersized yardage on the scorecard belied its challenge; water, water everywhere, with wild green complexes to boot. Every buzzword we toss around when plotting the golf of tomorrow—*community, public, unfussy, affordable, quick, accessible, nine holes, playable, diversity, underrepresented, youth*—they had them all right here. I left with spirits buoyed for golf's future and headed for another look into its past.

LAKE SUCCESS, NEW YORK

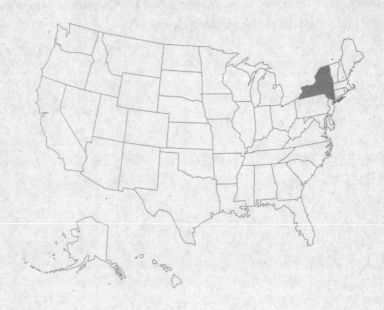

Lake Success, indeed. The lineup of Maseratis in the parking lot identified the place as a coveted status club, and while its course was handsome, it was an uneven design, with a plain front nine and a rowdy back, all of it squeezed in a way that felt like golf in handcuffs.

Fresh Meadow's original Tillinghast design had resided in Queens, where its former pro Gene Sarazen won the US Open in 1932. A traditionally Jewish club, it counted Bernie Madoff as one of its members, and his schemes nearly sank the place; my host told me Bernie bilked $2 billion out of the Fresh Meadow members. "It wiped out the waiting list and a good chunk of our membership," he explained. "But hey, that's how I got in." Fresh Meadow's relocation to Lake Success also meant that I was now attempting to play every golf *club* to host a US Open versus golf *course*; it had sold the former course to developers and moved to Nassau County in the 1940s.

After my stop at Fresh Meadow, I rolled down to Rockaway and found a Long Island world of my favorite childhood movie—*The Flamingo Kid*—a coastline of cabana-boy beach clubs and golf courses, one of them called Inwood. Another historically Jewish club, its windswept layout hosted the PGA in 1921 won by Walter Hagen, and the US Open in 1923 where Bobby Jones won his first major after golf's original "shot heard 'round the world" (195 yards on the eighteenth, off a bare lie and over a pond to six feet). Outside of Royal Liverpool, Inwood was the only course where Jones and Hagen both won majors, and "Hagen's Willow" by the eleventh tee recalled some historic groundskeeping: After Hagen used the eighteenth fairway as a shortcut in early rounds of the championship, some of the pros paid to have a willow installed overnight, blocking his improvised route on eleven. Hagen won anyway.

I had to give the USGA its due—during a time when clubs were firmly segregated along religious lines and Jewish players were denied membership at the establishment courses, hosting two early Opens at Inwood and Fresh Meadow was a progressive gesture, and a nod to the legacy of Havemeyer's defense of Shippen at Shinnecock.

It wasn't far from Inwood to Garden City, a club that did not specialize in progressive gestures. Its guys-only reputation preceded it in most conversations (it was right there in its name, often referred to as "Garden City Men's Club"), which was a shame. Its Devereux Emmet–Walter Travis–Tom Doak routing was a dandy—I'd never played a flat course that was more compelling—and had been home to the US Open in 1902 and the 1924 Walker Cup. Those credentials rarely got mentioned in the stories surrounding its dudes-only ethos, tales that had grown in magnitude and inaccuracy over the decades. I had expected to be met at the gate by gender-sniffing dogs, but the rumors had misled me: Women weren't entirely barred from the property (from the clubhouse, perhaps), and no member I spoke to had ever played in their boxers (a popular Garden City legend). Female sightings were somewhat rare, but there were two days every week when wives and daughters were welcome to join their husbands and fathers on the course (it wasn't quite a sit-in at Berkeley, but it was something).

The only alarms that might sound at Garden City were tuned to the club's strict jackets-in-the-clubhouse policy—leave the locker room without one, and you'd know it quickly. It was a throwback statute I rather appreciated; there was a time and place for hoodies and flops, but with a blazer now rolled up in my trunk, I was ready for a little formality. I embraced all of golf's wardrobes; I also embraced all its genders, colors, and creeds, so while I felt comfortable in my jacket, I felt less so about being a guest at a club where my daughters couldn't be.

My hosts met me with three tall silver tumblers bearing the Garden City thistle logo, the kind of vessels most people used for coffee, but here they carried transfusions (a blend of grape juice, vodka, and ginger ale that, like snapper soup and Clubman aftershave, existed only in the country-club universe). I politely declined mine, and nobody seemed to mind being burdened with a backup. This was clearly a guy's hang where I doubted most of the women I knew would want to spend much time (the clubhouse had a dark and aged vibe; not unkempt, but confidently unfussy). People were entitled to organize into clubs according to any parameters they wished, and gender solidarity was an old golf theme that historically worked both ways. At the Home of Golf, two of the Saint Andrews links' five clubs remain ladies-only (the Saint Rule and Saint Regulus), and both enjoy the same playing privileges as the clubs next door. But this Scottish arrangement succeeds according to an understanding that never informed the American game, namely that exclusivity is for golf clubs, not golf courses. If you can get it around, you should go around. Citing tradition as justification for doing otherwise was a lame dodge: Mary Queen of Scots was draining bombs at Saint Andrews back in the 1550s, and their clubs and courses have somehow managed to scrape by.

Garden City didn't deserve to be pedestaled in the exclusivity debate; there were other male-only golf retreats out there, but few possessed the same quality or historical significance. Its members didn't deserve to be singled out, either, as misogynists or villains; the ones I met were quality people—hospitable, generous, and crazy about our game. But the fact that I felt I needed to point that out—it made one wonder if old rules were worth the trouble.

I decided to take a Scottish view of Garden City—let the club be a club, and enjoy the course as an independent entity—and by doing so, I could appreciate the blissful rhythm of its routing, and the magic of its inverted sand traps (they were like turned-out pants pockets, the pits flipped into peaks of gravity-defying sand). With tees set just a short shuffle from the previous pin, and with bunkers so naturally nestled against small, firm greens—no matter the style or setting of golf you preferred, Garden City had a moment of it waiting for you somewhere.

I didn't berate myself for having so much fun. The club was, frankly, a cultural novelty at this point, and I wasn't terribly worried that my daughters' futures were threatened because a men's club existed on Long Island. Perhaps I was making another self-serving bargain, but if two hundred guys wanted to have their own golf course, so be it. The sun would come up tomorrow.

And it did, this time over a redbrick clubhouse in New Jersey.

SPRINGFIELD, NEW JERSEY

My GPS route to Baltusrol took me straight through the nucleus of Newark. I decided against popping into the Newark Knights Motorcycle Club to capture some local flavor, and as I drove its main drag, I noticed how boarded-up storefronts were occasionally interrupted by check-cashing places or Chinese food take-out counters or beauty supply shops. At nearly every intersection someone was begging for change, and at a stoplight, a man in heavy layers knocked on my window, seeking money for a meal. And then, suddenly, in just a few more blocks, I was behind the gates at Baltusrol, rolling my bag into a clubhouse where I was shown to a cozy bedroom upstairs as, out my window, the sun was setting across two of the world's most prized layouts.

This notion of two distinct Americas wasn't new or surprising to me, but to find them so close together and yet so impossibly remote—we were a country of islands, it seemed, and the aspirational bridges that might have once connected them had been neglected to the point of collapse. We Americans liked to talk about resiliency and ambition and bootstraps, but those were easy things for people like me to say. I'd been born with pretty nice boots.

Baltusrol had hosted myriad majors—nine at last count—and with its two Tillinghast courses, it owned the rare distinction of being the only club to host the men's and women's US Opens on two different courses: its Upper and its Lower. The Upper was the course members tended to prefer for a casual game, a more secluded walk back in the woods, while the Lower was the less forgiving track where Baltusrol's more recent majors were played. Both were beauties, though I had a hard time recalling specific holes after our thirty-six-hole day, which seemed a requirement for any course I might deem America's greatest. The quality was consistent and abundant, but perhaps not as soul-stirring as I wanted in my top track. Where it did top all other clubs, however, was in the story behind its name. I found its origin described by Marshall Lewis in Baltusrol's centennial history.

On February 22, 1831, two men broke into a local farmer's home, beating him and dragging him out of the house as his wife watched in hiding, eventually fleeing the scene and running for help. She returned with three men, only to find her husband's body strangled and bound by the front gate, and their home ransacked. Two suspects quickly emerged: The widow fingered one Peter Davis as an assailant, while his accomplice killed himself on hearing the news that Davis had been arrested.

The macabre details of the case gripped the New York press. The story of murder on a peaceful Jersey farm filled national headlines and became the subject of a popular book. Inadmissible evidence helped Davis beat the murder rap, but he was charged with other crimes while in custody and would die in prison while serving a twenty-four-year sentence. Today, the slain farmer's body rests in a cemetery in nearby Westfield, New Jersey. His name? Baltus Roll.

Given the notoriety of the crimes committed there, the farm and surrounding area became known as Baltusrol, and when publisher Louis Keller decided to build nine holes on the farm in 1894, he gave his club the same name.

We played our back-to-back rounds at Baltusrol on Memorial Day, which one of my playing partners described as a double-loser weekend for golfers. If you were golfing on Memorial Day, it meant you didn't have a beach house (loser). It also meant that you didn't have any friends willing to invite you to theirs (double loser).

Either way, it was hard to feel like a loser at Baltusrol. After our rounds, I wandered the labyrinthian clubhouse and studied its long hall of history, where placards highlighted majors that stretched from 1903 to 2016. I eventually found the all-day buffet of salmon and filet medallions, and we tucked into a table that featured the house special: orange cheese spread and Ritz crackers. I had been learning the inverse relationship between a course's reputation and the extravagance of its table snacks. The holes, the decor, the membership might all have changed, but it was golf club noshes that were immune to the whims of trends and taste. You knew you were somewhere special when cheese and crackers were the only thing available at the halfway house, and somewhere elite if the menu was ginger snaps and peanut butter.

On my drive from Baltusrol that evening, I called my family—first Dad, to thank him for his time in the navy. I'd never picked up the phone to call him on Memorial Day before, but three weeks on the road had me eager to reach out. Then I called Allyson, who had spent the last three days with the girls at my in-laws' going to the community pool.

"I wish you were here. They wanted to go in the deep end," Allyson told me, and though she meant nothing by it, the image of that scene stung. *A dad should be home on a holiday weekend*, I thought, *ready for when his daughters called to come pull them across the water*. I had a few days ahead to make up for lost weeks, and swore I'd spoil them with fun-dad outings.

I used the rest of the drive to return a call from my coach, Mike Dynda, who was caddying for another of his clients in sectional US Open qualifying at Streamsong. He knew I'd been there and was looking for tips on playing the Black course.

"The greens are huge. I don't know what else I can tell you," I said. "Fairways and greens, right?"

"Nope," Dynda said. "Not anymore. Smash it, find it, and make a bunch of putts."

Damn. I hadn't even figured out fairways and greens yet, and now they'd rewritten the rules. Golf was changing, indeed. I had smash it and find it down pretty well; I just hoped the third part would reveal itself tomorrow at the people's country club.

FARMINGDALE, NEW YORK

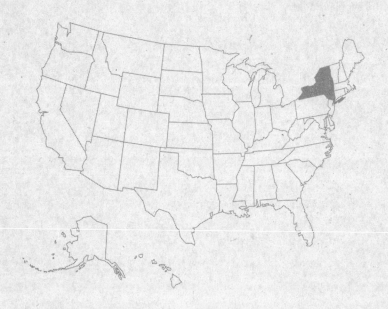

It was hosting the PGA Championship when I passed it last week, so my final round before a respite at home required a U-turn back to Long Island, to stand and be judged at Bethpage Black.

Brendan was traveling from Philly to meet me for a match at Bethpage, and was gung-ho for a night in the front seat. Such was the tradition at Bethpage State Park, where you parked your car in a numbered slot the day before and awaited a predawn knock on your window, when you were handed a wristband that granted you a spot in the queue for a tee time on the Black course when the clubhouse opened up.

A nightlong tailgate was part of the Bethpage experience, I was told, passing footballs and flasks between new friends who had traveled to one of the nastiest tests in championship golf. I had once slept in my car for U2 tickets in high school, so I had checked that rite of passage off my list, and decided it kind of sucked. So, when a friend from the greens crew said he could save us a night in the parking lot, I told Brendan to shoot for seven a.m. and booked myself a room at a nearby Hilton, where I shared a Garden Inn with most of the guests from Robby and Jenny's wedding. I didn't think people without kids used the pools at these turnpike hotels, but the wedding-goers certainly did. Johnny brought out his Bluetooth speaker and kept the party hopping. From my window above the festivities, I could see the bottles and cigarettes passing back and forth between women in too-tight cocktail dresses and men in suit pants who had traded their jackets for long T-shirts. All the guys went to the same barber, it seemed—some stylist whose repertoire had been reduced to clippers and gel.

I'd encountered plenty of such merrymaking in my day, and had been the instigator of most of it—the post-post-party was always the best party. I watched a ring of twelve people hold six entirely different conversations over one another, using their waving arms as some sort of Long Island sign language. I couldn't make out a word of it, though once in a while I'd hear "Eli Manning!" over the sound of my television. The noise didn't bother me. Sleeping tonight was a bit of a cheat anyway, as I should have been keeping vigil in a parking lot down the road. When I arrived promptly at seven the next morning, it was clear that hundreds of golfers had done precisely that.

The parking lot was already packed to capacity, and I found Brendan on the putting green. He'd been here since 5:30, he said, and complained that he'd watched the other golfers already collect their wristbands. I told him to relax and called my friend from the greens crew. He answered in a hushed tone and told me to meet him by the pro shop entrance. We went inside the clubhouse, and our contact greeted us in the hallway. He looked left and right, then nodded for us to follow him. He ushered us into an empty room and asked us for our credit cards.

"Are any of you New York residents?" I told him no, but that I was in a New York state of mind. He didn't smile. This was serious backroom business. Fifteen nervous minutes later, he returned with credit card receipts and wristbands that we were told the starter would remove when it was our time to go. We had an hour to putt and shop, which for me was a clear and present danger. I'd told myself the only things I would collect on this trip were free pencils and ball markers, but I was being defeated daily by stacks of neatly folded shirts and mesh-backed hats. I had so many of both at home that my closet already spilled into golf drawers and golf boxes, to the point that selecting a shirt and hat was a paralyzing decision. I opted for a T-shirt featuring Bethpage's warning sign—one could never have too many T-shirts—and headed off to have my wristband removed by the starter's scissors.

We paused by the sign outside the clubhouse for obligatory pictures of the most photographed caution in golf: "—WARNING—The Black Course Is An Extremely Difficult Course Which We Recommend Only For Highly Skilled Golfers." Take your picture and then ignore the words seemed to be the practice at Bethpage, as lowly skilled golfers lined up for six hours of penance. These morning crowds were clear evidence that golfers were masochists; ours was the rare pastime in which we somehow had fun having no fun at all. It also spoke to one of golf's irresistible peculiarities: fans never got the chance to play nine innings at Fenway, but golfers had the opportunity to walk the same holes as their heroes and hit the shots Brooks Koepka had hit here two weeks ago—or try, at least.

As talk of bifurcation buzzed through the golf world, suggesting pros should play different gear than us amateurs, I feared that such a move would dampen that intoxicating feature of the game, that rousing notion that Tiger and I were playing the same sport. It was obviously an illusion, but damn if it wasn't a fun one—and this parking lot was proof. For at least one moment today, we all hoped we might be them, and I doubt anyone here would have opted for a juicier ball than Brooks had. Just like the sign said: bring on the pain.

The starter snipped off our bracelets, and Brendan's games began: "How many strokes do I have to give you?" he asked. I hadn't taken strokes from him in five years, but he still offered, prodding my mental soft spots before our opening drives. The first at Bethpage Black seemed rather benign. Its perched tee box begged us to cut off the dogleg far below, and both of us did, though my line proved more prudent, leaving me with an 8 iron to a birdie putt while Brendan buried his approach in the rough. As we reached the green, I learned that today might very well be my day, because Brendan looked in his bag and dropped his shoulders.

"I left my putter on the practice green." We looked back up the hill, where the clubhouse looked like some distant estate floating in the clouds. Given Bethpage's tight tee times, the group behind us was already waiting in the fairway, so jogging back was out of the question. I smiled and made four while Brendan putted with his wedge. One-up.

On our walk to two, I couldn't help but show mercy. He'd gotten up at three a.m. and arrived two hours early for a shot at one of his last remaining must-play courses; he had bought two shirts and hit a hundred practice chips, and then went and forgot his putter. I called my friend on the greens crew and asked if someone could bring it out to us. It arrived by the third green, which was handy for Brendan, as he had a long look at birdie. As did I. We walked to four, me still one-up, where our match took on a different tenor.

I was already two-up in my mind as I watched my birdie putt curl past the hole. Brendan was in for six on the par 5, and as I approached my par putt of two feet (maybe three), a conspicuous silence settled across the green.

I knew exactly what he was doing, and that knowledge crowded my head with thoughts of the wry smile no doubt boring into my back. I countered these thoughts with a wishful technique called quick-putting: Take a careless swipe at your ball to suggest the hole is over, conceding yourself the putt by way of improvised indifference. Force him to tell you it wasn't good, which, as my ball rolled past the edge of the cup, Brendan had no problem doing.

"That was good," I said as I scooped my ball, unable to look Brendan in the eye.

"No it wasn't!" He laughed. "No way was that good. You wanted that putt so bad there was no way I was giving it to you."

Though I remained one-up, the rest of our match was a fait accompli; we turned at all square, and Brendan closed me out on sixteen. I consoled myself by thinking he hadn't outplayed me—I hit the ball well, and had a putt for 79 in front of two guys in the leftover PGA grandstands. They sat there amid a sea of empty benches with Bud Light pounders, and I could hear their whispers echoing down to us: "Ten bucks he misses." I made one of them ten bucks richer and carded an 80.

It was a respectable number, considering the rough was still standing at major championship height, and though Brendan beat me handily by holes, his stroke tally was the same. Where he had bested me was in my head, as he tended to do. He had a skill for keeping golf breezy and simple, while I bullied it into a corner and tried to slap it into submission. Brendan used a large Bill Murray ball marker that read "The more relaxed you are, the better you are at everything," and damn if that fortune-cookie wisdom wasn't the truth. His grip got lighter as the stakes got higher, while mine turned into a vise, like I was trying to wring water out of black rubber.

I could blame our six-hour pace for my mental collapse, but Brendan was playing in the same slog. We were stuck behind a foursome of Asian gentlemen who were well out of position with the foursome ahead (after customers had waited so long and paid so much, the rangers at Bethpage were lenient). They were playing the tips and wearing long pants and rain layers in 90-degree heat, and took desperate amounts of time over each chop in the rough. They pushed heavy tour bags, and my suspicion was confirmed when we found one dropped on a cart path: iron covers.

As we laid on the tee boxes and waited our turn, I couldn't help but wonder if I was actually having any fun, especially after Brendan closed me out. It was the best of golf, and the worst of golf. The property was preposterously good, with breath-stealing climbs over plunging hills, and the routing was packed with robust imagination. But when Rees Jones came in to stiffen up the design prior to its first major, he may have sucked much of the imagination out of it. By turning the fairways into ribbons, holes that once may have presented myriad strategies now presented one: straight or die.

The place deserved credit; signs advertised it as "The People's Country Club," and insofar as it gave the four guys ahead of us the chance to hang around a vintage clubhouse and play a major venue in immaculate shape, it was indeed that—a rare golf treat. But how much more of a treat would it have been, I wondered, if the golf had been fun, too? I could have been sour from my defeat, or bleary from the closing climbs; the finishing holes should have come with a towline. Golfers loved a beating, after all, even if I didn't love mine.

Despite these small grievances, there was one thing about Bethpage

I unequivocally appreciated: that its history had been rewritten to give its original designer his due. As detailed in a *Golf Digest* article by Ron Whitten, the attribution was a contentious matter. While the oldest available drawings bore no name, the plaque by the clubhouse credited A. W. Tillinghast with designing Bethpage Black, plus its Red and Blue courses. But more recent research revealed that an unknown architect had laid out the courses before Tillinghast ever set foot on the property.

When New York's master builder Robert Moses—the titan immortalized in *The Power Broker* and one of the most powerful unelected men in American history—went on a parks and highway building binge, golf at Bethpage State Park became part of his public works vision. Moses tasked an employee named Joseph Burbeck with overseeing the development of a golf complex that would eventually hold five courses. During the same period, Tillinghast had fallen on hard times: Work had dried up after the Depression, and heavy drinking wasn't helping his fortunes. His home was foreclosed upon, and he took on work with the PGA of America that would once have been beneath his station, traveling the country and consulting on courses where PGA pros were employed. He was hired as a consultant on the Bethpage courses, but not until the Red, Black, and Blue had already been laid out.

Tillie's name being attached to Bethpage (even though his contract lasted all of fifteen days) likely inspired its caretakers to give top billing to an eminent architect, but he wasn't there when the drawings were made, and when the courses were being constructed he was out touring America for the PGA. In his own writing about Bethpage, Tillinghast credits Burbeck with dreaming up the strategy for Black, and in a later note to Donald Ross, the devoted Republican described his antipathy for WPA projects (of which Bethpage's construction was one), noting his relief at never having participated in such a waste of public funds. He may have seen the course sketches at some point, but his role at Bethpage State Park seemed to have been primarily promotional.

Burbeck passed away in a retirement home in 1987 after serving as the Bethpage park superintendent for thirty years, never living to see his name attached to his own layouts. His son fought for and eventually won that recognition, at least in Whitten's 2002 article, but even after sixty years,

Burbeck's son recalled how his mother told him, "We don't ever mention the name Tillinghast in this house."

It was a strange feeling to place my clubs in the trunk without thought of what my ball count was, or if I needed to save today's socks for tomorrow. I set off for home cooking, and Brendan texted to say thanks for the invitation. He didn't mention the margin of victory, or victory at all—he said it was worth the drive to hang out with me for a day, and that if I was ever feeling squirrely or lonely on the road, I should give him a call and he'd hop on a plane. Not only was Brendan more comfortable when it came to close-out putts but he was at ease telling another man that he mattered to him. It was not a tool that yet resided in my emotional toolbox, so I texted back a thumbs-up. Baby steps.

Four days, I learned, was not quite enough time to feel like I'd come home. I got busy paying bills and taking the dog to be groomed and changing that light bulb that required a ladder; save for those three errands, I was proving to be entirely expendable as a partner and parent.

I chauffeured the girls from the pool to the movies, the mall, and McDonald's; there was no fatherly guilt that a trip to Claire's couldn't soften. Whatever Allyson asked of me, I promised her, the answer would be yes. So, when a new putter showed up in the mail from Titleist and she asked, "Are you seriously going golfing today?" I kept to my word.

I couldn't leave for Seattle with an untested wand—a quick morning eighteen at Waynesborough and I'd be home before the kids had finished their Saturday cereal. Through sheer quantity of golf, my scores were improving and my handicap had dipped below 2, so I was excited to unleash my road-hardened game on a course I knew as well as my own bed, had I actually seen either in a month. But the showcase I planned for my regular golf buddies was stalled by a front-nine 43 as I bashed my new mallet from one edge of the green to the other.

I finally dropped a bomb for par on nine and told my caddie I'd figured it out, and that I was going to shoot 75. And for the first time in my golfing life, I actually called my shot—four birdies and five pars later my putter had cemented its spot on the team, and I went from golf weary to golf craving in the space of two hours. The allure of the next hole—I'd once loved myself a cocktail, but there was nothing as irresistible as another pin when the putter was glowing.

I sent Brendan a picture of the scorecard, careful to leave the front nine out of the frame. He did the math anyway.

43 on the front, he texted. *I'd have closed you out before the birdies.*

We would see about that. I told him to keep his September open, and asked him if he'd ever heard of Ohoopee.

TACOMA, WASHINGTON

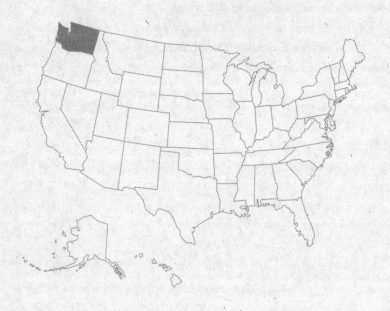

It was June in America's northwestern corner, but on the practice green at Meadow Park, the players were dressed for Halloween. My feet slowed as I approached a crowd of knickers and caps and buttoned-up shirts, bearded men in vests and long sleeves and bow ties. And just as Halloween wasn't all that fun anymore unless you really bought into it, I wondered if I could summon the necessary enthusiasm for my first round of hickory golf. It was seven a.m. Chances were sleepy.

Dave was milling among the crowd of period dressers; he had become my accidental Seattle chaperone after reaching out with a charitable email, inviting this stranger to Chambers Bay, where he worked as a host and cad-die. He'd hoped I would have time to meet his hickory friends at Meadow

Park. Hickory golf at dawn for an afternoon at Chambers Bay—I'd made worse bargains.

Dave had retired from the army and then law enforcement and now worked the fairways, where his good humor earned him free golf as a greeter. I found it hard to imagine Dave ever arresting anyone; too much positivity fit within his condensed frame. Whomever he did apprehend, I was sure they left the experience feeling pretty good about it. Judging by the size of the group he'd brought out to greet me, he'd oversold me as a playing partner, especially when I secretly believed hickory golf to be kind of dumb.

For years, I'd dodged similar invitations from hickory devotees, mainly because I was uninterested in pretending it was still 1908 and was turned off by the silliness and sanctimoniousness of it all. A wood-shafter once asked me, "If you would like to play a historically accurate round of golf during your travels, I can arrange eighteen holes with our hickory society," and I wanted to write back that he had arranged for me to barf. I demanded every ounce of game improvement that technology could afford me. Golf was hard enough; I didn't want yesteryear's golf clubs in my bag. I wanted *next* year's clubs, and I wanted them now. My putters and drivers had shelf-lives that were only slightly longer than those of cheese, and my irons seldom outlived their grips. But the bags over there—I had to admit, the leather satchels did look pretty cool, especially the ones propped up on those homemade two-stick trestles. As I wandered over toward the green, Dave met me with an ear-to-ear smile and a "There he is!"

I shook hands with his crew, a contingent from the Northwest Hickory Players, an association of a few hundred golfers dedicated to a pre-1935 version of the game. Meadow Park was a favorite muni of theirs for its reasonable distances and open-mouthed greens that could be accessed via low runners. The place dated to 1915—pretty old by West Coast standards—and was one of the first Northwest courses to welcome players of color. Today, they catered to the hickory scene and rented sets of rusty clubs in the pro shop.

I wouldn't have to rent mine, I was told. The group's cofounder and clubmaker, Rob Ahlschwede, whose name I believe translated to *huge white beard*, had curated a bag for me, and as I listened to him describe each club's name and vintage and the work he'd put into restoring it, I began to think that this floppy-capped guy in the knee-high socks might be onto something. I wasn't sure if hickory was fun to play, but tinkering with old golf clubs sounded liked a winter well spent.

Rob handed me three golf balls with a mesh pattern on them, replicas manufactured by a company in Nebraska for the growing lost-in-time golf market. His advice on the first tee: "Swing slower. Smoother is better." I liked the look of the brassie he put in my hand—Rob called it a 2 wood—though it felt like someone had stuck a cantaloupe on the end of a broomstick. Its weight forced me to swing it slow, and when I did, a little miracle happened: The ball went forward, and straight, and up into the sky. The proof I'd made contact wasn't in my hands—I'd felt only the gentlest click in my fingers—but out there on the fairway. These things actually worked.

The irons weren't so supple; the mashie and niblick dug like trowels, but when I clipped the ball first, they knocked pleasant head-high stingers in a remarkably direct fashion. The mashie-niblick, a 7 iron, became a quick favorite, along with the center-shafted brass blade Rob gave me to putt with. I played eighteen holes without reaching for anything but the three aforementioned sticks, and didn't lose a ball.

Knock by knock, the appeal of hickory revealed itself. Given that the ball didn't go very far and traveled with minimal spin, it eliminated the big miss—no more drives drifting away on the wings of indifference. It also encouraged golf as a ground game, which immediately jibed with my links-loving outlook. The gap between good and bad shots wasn't as dramatic as I'd found with modern equipment—solid contact or otherwise, the ball tended to dribble itself toward the target. It required you to reset par in your mind, but I'd like to think I was close to hickory par with my 82. I was shocked to have been so thoroughly converted in three hours' time (hickory golf was quicker, too). The company certainly had something to do with it.

I paired up with Dave and Rob and Billy, who won best-dressed for his vest, tie, tall argyles, and saddle shoes. Billy was the youngest of our group and didn't hear Rob's swing-slow advice; rather, he mashed his mashies and twirled his niblicks. When I asked why a player of his modern swing and swagger would want to play old-timey golf, he explained: "When you're playing hickory, it's just you and the ball. With modern golf, it's you and five hundred scientists and a hundred years of technology. But with this, your good shots are all yours. Your bad shots, too. If you can play well with these things, it's satisfying in a really deep way."

Billy was African American, and playing hickory had pushed him to start researching the game's roots, where he found his golfing life's inspiration: that dauntless sixteen-year-old from Shinnecock, John Shippen. Shippen's story had been lost in the history books, but before Tiger Woods, before Charlie Sifford and Lee Elder, he had been a pioneer and a virtuoso, and Billy played hickory in his honor.

As with all the best travel days, this one had veered far away from expectations. I wasn't sure about the outfits, but I was sure I wanted to play with these happy relics again. (The clubs, not the people.) I thanked Rob with genuine gratitude, and as I walked to my car, he called me back and handed me the wooden-shafted putter I had borrowed. "That's yours. Keep it," he said. "You got better results out of it than I do."

"No, no, I couldn't keep this," I said, though my fingers didn't budge from its grip. I feigned protest for another moment, then gave Rob a two-handed shake of thanks.

Rob asked where I was headed next. I knew I had Chambers Bay in the afternoon, and then tomorrow—was it Gamble Sands? Coeur d'Alene? My memory struggled to reach beyond the day I was in. I think it was a defense mechanism; America was too big and the trip too young for me to grasp the scope of the golf remaining. Just play the next hole until the next hole was my last.

I told him I couldn't remember, but I was playing somewhere.

"Well, where'd you play yesterday?" he asked.

The look on people's faces when I described my wanderings—it never got old.

"Buffalo," I said. "Where else?"

BUFFALO, NEW YORK

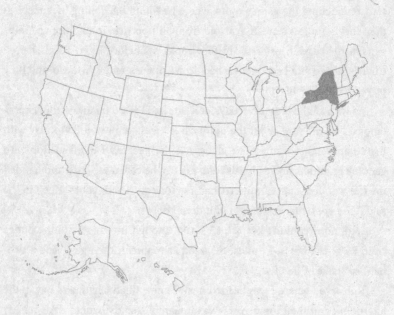

The bad news came back in March. I was sitting at the head of a long table in Rochester, where I'd just finished explaining the characteristics of a true links course to a hundred people, four of whom cared. My host, Rich, had taken me back to the grill for a post-speech snack at a golf club called Monroe, and while it was my second speaking gig up here, I'd yet to see the golf course. Winters lingered in Rochester, and the course was covered, smooth and white, like fondant on a wedding cake.

I was explaining my upcoming travels to some nightcappers, and how I would be back soon—nearby Oak Hill had hosted just about everything, including three US Opens, and Rich was confident he could score me a tee time. As long as I didn't wait.

"You know it's closing in July," he said.

"Say what?" In that moment, I saw nine months of planning crumbling into the peanut bowl before me. I had slotted my western New York swing for September, and moving it now would mean rearranging some 250 tee times, some of which were written in cement.

I drove back to my hotel in defeat. A friend had hand-painted a poster for me with the logos of every existing US Open course; I was going to gift a print to each club when I visited, and now, I was going to fall one short. The gentlemen of the game would say that's how it goes, rub of the green, it's a fickle and maddening endeavor. But I preferred a simpler lament: golf hurts.

I scoured the calendar and found a slim ray of hope. I could cut a few courses and wedge in forty-eight hours in Rochester before flying off to Seattle. Rich locked in the dates and gave me a thumbs-up for golf at Monroe, Oak Hill, Buffalo CC, and Grover Cleveland. Buffalo CC had also hosted a US Open, but the course they played was now a muni named after our twenty-second and twenty-fourth president. I had to play them both, and now had just enough hours to do so.

So, on an early June morning, I met Rich in a Rochester diner. I'd met Rich, a gregarious peddler of stocks and bonds, the way I met most people these days—he emailed about my escapades and invited me to golf. We'd become close friends since, and had played together in Scotland. His dry sense of humor made him easy company.

"Let's sit by the fire and make grand statements," he said as we grabbed two seats in a booth, and he caught me up on his latest golf travels. "So, enough about me," he said. "Let's talk about you. What do you think about me?"

Rich was the reddest of Republicans, with a proud picture of himself and Trump saved as the background on his phone. It had become standard practice to purge our friend lists of those who didn't watch the same news we did, but Rich reminded me to practice a little of that tolerance I liked to preach. While he had the pressed cuffs and parted coiffure of a CPAC volunteer, he was also headed to a fundraiser that evening for local kids with incarcerated parents. He was chairman of a nearly shuttered Catholic city high school that was now thriving under his leadership; when city kids couldn't afford the tuition, Rich often paid it himself, and he had become a surrogate father to an African refugee, whom he shepherded through high school and college, getting him a finance job and a place to live in New York. He'd even spent a few evenings there when the young man was afraid to be alone in the city. It was easy to paint our country in blocks of red and blue, but our shades were more interesting than I'd expected.

We made a quick loop around Monroe, a damn good Donald Ross that was thoroughly overshadowed by his two other courses at nearby Oak Hill. Oak Hill was the only club in the country to have hosted the Ryder Cup, PGA Championship, US Open, US Amateur, US Senior Open, and the US Senior PGA Championship—its trophy case was a trophy room—though wee Monroe had some tournament chops of its own. Its annual invitational was one of the most prestigious events in amateur golf, where the likes of Dustin Johnson, Tiger Woods, and Fred Ridley (future Augusta National chairman) had competed.

Rochester was a Kodak town, so when George Eastman decided in 1921 that the university needed an expansion—and that he would be willing to fund it—Oak Hill was given the chance to swap its tight quarters along the river for a spread that could accommodate two courses. Donald Ross laid out the holes, and a Dr. John Williams put the *oak* in Oak Hill by personally planting more than seventy-five thousand seedlings around the property. It was because of Tom Fazio that I arrived there four months ahead of schedule. Fazio had done extensive updates on the East Course, even replacing some of the original Ross holes (one of which, the par 3 sixth, left the members' faces red when it yielded four aces in ninety minutes during the 1989 US Open, thanks to a punchbowl pin). Design pundits had slammed the changes as painting over a Picasso, so they were shutting down the course to let Andrew Green, a hot name in course restoration, return the Ross. I could see the logic in it—the Fazio routing had a few obvious kinks—but plowing under such silky greens seemed a small tragedy.

Following our round, we met the faces of legends within Oak Hill's Tudor castle of a clubhouse: Jack Nicklaus. Lee Trevino. Curtis Strange. Shaun Micheel. Rich wondered aloud whatever happened to that guy. Doesn't matter, I told him. Just like Bill at Newport and Jimmy's 63 at Shinnecock, Micheel had had his moment. He had felt golf shine gently upon him, while the rest of us wandered a purgatory of rounds that could have been.

We drove to the Country Club of Buffalo, where Rich had booked us rooms upstairs. The CC of Buffalo had bounced around a few times but had been settled in its current site since 1927. Donald Ross must have left western New York a wealthy man; he had drawn the holes at Buffalo as well.

While clubhouse accommodations were typically convenient and modest, at Buffalo we had two-room suites with flatscreens and jars of soft molasses cookies. The clubhouse was canvased with French wallpaper and Impressionist art, and room after room was lined with wide-plank flooring. (Such luxury shifted my expectations about Buffalo, birthplace of the hot chicken wing.) The members' lockers occupied the best of its rooms, with high beamed ceilings over cubbies organized into rectangular nooks, each with fat leather chairs and wide televisions. I'd seen grander post-golf hangouts, but Buffalo's setup won for coziness and hospitality. A young locker room attendant in a green barber's jacket and glasses came over to welcome us and check if we needed anything, anything at all.

"I think we're set," Rich said. "Man, this place is nice. We didn't expect a locker room like this at a muni."

I looked down and stared at the floor. Rich couldn't help himself. The young man was still smiling, but he tilted an ear in our direction. "Sorry?"

"This is Grover Cleveland, right?" Rich said, invoking the place that was CC of Buffalo a hundred years ago but today is an eighteen-dollar county course with a cinder-block clubhouse and a toilet stall for changing your pants.

Rich sat down to tie his shoes. "My friend here is playing every US Open course. We're in the right place, right? Where do we pay our greens fees?"

Then the locker room guy wasn't smiling. I watched his eyes swell with panic.

"This is—well, it's not, it used to be . . ." He looked over his shoulder, presumably for security or his boss, ready to be fired for giving lockers to two guys off the street.

"We're messing with you," Rich said, and the color returned to our friend's face. He was still laughing as we passed through the exit and headed for the first tee.

The course had a quiet quality to it; its old bones were meticulously maintained, and its flat holes were made interesting by bold bunkering and thoughtful angles. The sixth, Pulpit, was more than a signature hole; a volcano-top green birthed from the belly of a limestone quarry, its drama rendered the rest of the holes somewhat tame in comparison.

Raindrops joined us on the drive over to Grover Cleveland, where we were met by Mark, the county commissioner who oversaw the operations at GC. BuffaloGolfer.com's own Ron Montesano was waiting for us as well, a Golf Club Atlas regular in glasses and a floppy bucket hat. It would take a keen GCA eye to appreciate the nuances at Grover Cleveland, or to see them at all—the course was flat and encroached upon by tall, bland buildings. Its most memorable feature was an open-air halfway shack with a BEER sign you could see four holes away. "We sell a lot of that here," Mark told me. As a six-pack-in-the-pushcart course, Grover Cleveland served its purpose well, a place to get in your cuts on an effortless walk. It was named after Buffalo's former mayor turned president, who, as Ron explained, was the only American president to personally execute a man, which he did while working here as county sheriff.

Ron had grown up on these holes—he pointed out his childhood street on the other side of the fence—and showed me which were Walter Travis, which were Donald Ross, and which had been lost when they built the VA hospital next door. It was a straightforward layout, but it was theirs, a course for and of Buffalonians, and a home for the septuagenarians who sipped their coffee from Styrofoam cups on folding chairs in the clubhouse.

At many private clubs, the members literally owned the place as shareholders, but nowhere did a sense of ownership feel more immediate than among the patrons of an eighteen-dollar muni. Most private-club golfers could always join somewhere else, but when you'd budgeted eighteen dollars a day for the rest of your retirement, you cherished your place with a fealty the country clubbers would never know. Hell hath no fury like an old muni golfer who's heard they want to bring in some fancy architect to spruce up the joint, and tick up greens fees, too.

Grover Cleveland was a visit long circled on my calendar. It didn't just host a US Open; from my perspective, it crowned the most tragic champion in golf.

Born the son of a postman in West Philadelphia, Johnny McDermott grew up caddying and learning the game at Aronimink (before Aronimink left Philadelphia for the suburbs). He dedicated himself to his training with a zeal we take for granted today—no booze, no cigarettes, no girls, just golf from sunup to sundown. Such dedication forged a golf prodigy; at the age of nineteen, McDermott won the 1911 US Open at the Chicago Golf Club, becoming the first American to win our national championship. He repeated that feat in 1912, right here at what was then Country Club of Buffalo. He remains the youngest golfer to ever win the US Open, but his name is not in the World Golf Hall of Fame, nor can most golfers claim to have ever heard of him. I probably wouldn't know his name, either, if I didn't know John Burnes.

John and I grew up not far from where McDermott was born, and through mutual caddie friends we had shared golf and beers over the years (not necessarily in that order). On one of those afternoons, he told me he was researching a local golfer who had grown up playing and caddying at the same places we did, a forgotten Philly boy who had won US Opens and topped the golfing planet for a while (Harry Vardon had described McDermott as "perhaps as great as any in the world"). John dedicated his hours to McDermott's cause, successfully campaigning for the state to place a historical marker in front of his birthplace and lobbying for McDermott to be inducted into the World Golf Hall of Fame. His being excluded seemed a tragic oversight, but tragedy was the theme when it came to McDermott's story.

By the age of twenty-four, he was diagnosed with paranoia and schizophrenia, and to go from US Open champ to institutionalized in the space of four years remains one of the most baffling declines in sports. The root of his breakdown might be traced to an event in 1914, when, after missing his tee time in the Open at Prestwick due to travel snafus, his return voyage to the States was interrupted by a foggy collision in the English Channel. The passengers survived, but being shuttled into a lifeboat two years after the sinking of the *Titanic* may have had a disastrous impact on McDermott's psyche.

A year later, he would collapse in panic at the Atlantic City Country Club, and when treatments proved unable to stem his breakdowns, his mother had him committed as an option of last resort, and he remained in the hospital for fifty-five years, until his death in 1971.

John described to me how McDermott had continued to golf in some capacity for the rest of his life. He was allowed to leave the hospital on the weekends, and his sisters would take him out to nearby Whitemarsh or Overbrook for a few holes. Dressed in a wool suit and swinging hickories, his playing partners often knew nothing about the old man with whom they had been paired. The State Hospital for the Insane also had a six-hole course that he played, and his peers would visit from time to time. Walter Hagen played the asylum course with McDermott, and he and other celebrities of the time—Gene Sarazen and Al Jolson among them—donated to fund his treatment.

Popular history left McDermott behind, but some pros never did. His sisters brought him to the US Open at Merion in 1971, a few months before his death, where, at seventy-nine years of age and unrecognizable in shabby attire, he was escorted out of the clubhouse where he'd been hoping to speak with some of the players. But one of the players did recognize him. As the story goes, this pro was mid-waggle when he spotted McDermott watching from the edge of a tee box and stopped to tell the crowd, "Ladies and gentlemen, there is Johnny McDermott, the first American to win the US Open." The crowd erupted with applause as Arnold Palmer walked over to shake McDermott's hand and thank him for being there.

As we walked Grover Cleveland in a downpour, I imagined myself following McDermott's path as he stalked his ball and bested the Brits. It gave the place an air of both triumph and sadness, and the rain felt appropriate. I had battled bouts of panic, and the idea that, for some, the terror never went away left me frightened, and grateful. I loved golf for allowing me to get lost in my head, but I could get stuck there, too. I needed friends like Rich to pull me out once in a while and take me to go get wings.

We rode down the street to an uncrowded mall with a Duff's Famous Wings and dried off at a table in the corner. I wanted to investigate the Anchor Bar, where the Buffalo wing was said to have been born, but Rich insisted that true Buffalonians ate their wings at this local chain. I ordered a sampling of wings of varying temperatures, while Rich confused the waitress by ordering a salad. We seemed to have found the last open business in the derelict shopping center—industry had fled western New York, but people still needed to eat, and the bar stools were full at five p.m. with men who were no strangers to the menu at Duff's.

"This was a good night to come," Rich said, nodding toward the bar, where wide frames shadowed steaming piles of bone and meat. "We have a meeting of the local chapter of the Buffalo Three Hundred Club tonight. Larry over there finally got his membership card after eating fifty wings for lunch last week. George there, he's got to watch out. He's been getting way too much exercise."

I smiled and licked fire sauce from my fingers, and wondered if this was a wise preflight meal. Rich took out a soggy scorecard and claimed he had beaten me two-up. I conceded defeat. I wasn't there to make a number, anyway.

"Have you ever heard of Johnny McDermott?" I asked.

Rich said no. But after a salad and two dozen wings that were indeed better than anything we could find in Philadelphia, I made sure he had.

UNIVERSITY PLACE, WASHINGTON

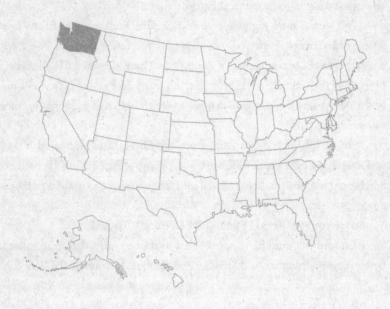

I was grinding over a birdie putt on a course where I didn't expect to make any, so I called in my caddie, Dave, and asked him for a read. He gave it a thoughtful look, then turned to me and said, "You're a much better golfer than me. I'd go with whatever you think."

I thanked him for the candor—I'd take it over guesswork every time. My Titleist tumbled off the left edge and into the cup, and Dave slapped my hand in triumph, an ideal team tuned to each other's strengths and short-comings.

I was expecting a patchy field of perdition at Chambers Bay, where the putts would bounce like bingo balls and asphalt fairways would funnel my ball into pits of fescue. What I found were resurfaced greens that were smooth as poker tables and an impeccable, uproarious layout beside Puget Sound that, to me, felt like golf rock 'n' roll.

Its controversial 2015 US Open had stamped Chambers Bay with an unfortunate reputation, after four days of bumpy greens and burnt fairways and uneven routes for spectators who twisted their ankles in the dunes. The Open may have come to Chambers too early, but the place certainly deserved one. Its transformation from an abandoned gravel mine to a lush links hillside where heroic holes raced toward the water was a feat of vision and engineering, and I hoped the rumors that the Open might return were true. There was magic going on here. As if by spell, the manufactured had been made natural, and the coast of Washington had been sculpted into the wildest edges of the British Isles.

My hickory-playing buddy Dave had offered to loop for me at Chambers, and as he was well connected at his new retirement hang, he paired me with the GM and caddie master, the latter of whom had a wide lexicon for drives gone wrong: "That one's in the shwing shwong"; "Going left—Snapagawea"; "There's a weed head"; and "That's in the Teddy Ruffspin." When my drives found the shwing shwong, Dave rescued every last one. While Chambers revealed a contender for best American golf tree—its only tree, the Lone Fir, had survived both vandals and course architects, and poignantly punctuated the horizon from the fifteenth tee—I notched the course as a surprise hopeful on my best-of list. Then I headed east to seek the counsel of someone who could tell me what *best* in a golf course might mean.

A friend's warning that everything in the Pacific Northwest is four hours away from everything else quickly proved itself true. It took precisely four hours to haul from Tacoma up to Brewster, through green hills covered with sheets of sliding rock, through a national forest and past one-room cafes, their dirt parking lots crowded with motorcycles at nine a.m.

Placards of Smokey the Bear waved to me from the side of the road, where Smokey described today's forest fire risk as MODERATE. I wasn't sure if that was good or bad for these parts, but nobody seemed too worried. For a hundred miles on a single-lane highway, I followed a green truck with a dreamcatcher dangling from the rearview and a bumper sticker with *Terrorizing Native Americans Since 1492* over the face of Christopher Columbus. So much for the nursery rhyme about him sailing the ocean blue.

Pine trees gave way to desert and caverns and roadside shops selling sparkly rocks by the handful. That Washington was so dusty surprised me; more surprising was how the desert turned to lush apple orchards every few miles. When I finally reached Brewster and found the man I'd come to meet, he explained that it was the Columbia River whose waters irrigated these hillsides and made Washington the apple epicenter of the world. Without the river, this would all be arid hardpan—perfect for a golf course, he said.

I had traveled to the other side of America to find my Scotsman. It seemed a reliable trope of golf odysseys that at some point, perhaps under the influence of weariness or whiskey, I would hear a bearded brogue whispering answers into my ear and, in frustratingly simple and absolute terms, telling me what made a golf course great. But my Scot wasn't wearing wool or a cap, and his beard was a tightly trimmed goatee. He was holding hands with an English beauty, both of them in aviator shades.

David McLay Kidd grew up the son of Jimmy Kidd, the longtime superintendent at Gleneagles in Scotland, and spent his summers with his grandparents around the links of Machrihanish. Great golf was in his blood, so it was no surprise that he had thrived as a course architect, especially as taste in American designs took on a more Scottish, linksy mood. He built the first course at Bandon Dunes, followed by designs like Mammoth Dunes in Wisconsin, Nanea in Hawaii, and here at Gamble Sands in Washington that cemented his reputation as someone who could bring the best of the British Isles to America. In David's view, "the best" could be boiled down to two other words: The Bounce.

Gamble Sands took its name from a pioneer whose family now farmed every hill and hollow within sight of the golf course. One hundred thirty-five years ago, a gold-hungry Dan Gamble hoofed it here all the way from Nova Scotia. He eventually swapped prospecting for fishing driftwood out of the river and milling it into apple crates. Sawmills, cattle, and orchards followed, and around 2012, David was hired by Gamble's ancestors, the Gebbers family, to help diversify their vast land holdings around Brewster. They had the apple, cherry, and beef markets covered; golf sounded like a chance to expand the family business, and a way to use some of the hills that didn't catch the right sunlight for crops. If their golfing venture failed, they figured, so be it—David would have at least laid the irrigation, and they could turn the fairways into farm. With low stakes and full creative freedom, David crafted the course he wanted to play, and I could tell Gamble Sands was close to his heart. Of all his designs, he explained, it was his dad's favorite.

The proximity of the driving range to the clubhouse, putting green, and first tee—all within fifty yards—was no accident: David designed a place where he wanted to hang out, a spot where you could grab a beer and watch the golfers or sit at a picnic table by the eighteenth green at sunset, eat steak skewers, and relive your round, as the five of us were happy to do. The hang at Gamble Sands was surpassed only by the course, on which David had blended drivable par 4s with reachable par 5s replete with speed slots and sneaky kickers. It was a golf fun park, and not just because David shaped it that way. It had everything to do with that elasticity underfoot.

"Golf in America, in literary terms, it's become a limerick, a simple formula," he explained while his wife, Tara, and my friends Gretchen and Amanda and I chowed on tenderloin that came from just over our shoulder. "Over here, you know where your ball is going straightaway. You know the result of a shot from the moment it's left your clubface. And that's crap. That's turning a round of golf into mere seconds. Golf should feel more like a novel, with chapters that unfold. You hit a shot, then have to watch and wonder and pay attention, and see how it turns out. The ground and the grasses we have here allow that to happen."

He was referring to the most indulgent choice he was empowered to make at Gamble Sands: wall-to-wall fescue, that firm, crispy grass of unmistakable crunch. It felt like Scotland to my feet, and in America, I knew of only two courses draped entirely in golf's original playing surface: Old Macdonald at Bandon and this one. Other courses used fescue in some fairways, but as it browned easily, few were bold enough to seed it in their greens. *Their loss*, I thought. Fescue made the magic happen. Fescue brought The Bounce.

"If the public would decide that playing conditions were more important than the color of the course, then we wouldn't have all this *Poa annua* grass,"

David continued. "*Poa annua* is the lazy fat kid on the couch—keep feeding it water and chemicals and it won't go anywhere. But starve them, and fescue is the marathoner that will win out. It doesn't need all the expensive inputs that we're pumping into our courses, but it's going to go brown. And until people can accept brown, they aren't going to get the best conditions. But we have them here."

David had asked us to trust those conditions earlier that day. We arrived at sixteen, a two-hundred-yard one-shotter where he pointed us thirty yards to the right of the flag. "See that hill?" he said. "That's your target."

"Over there? But I want to go at the pin," Gretchen replied. She was a scratch golfer and the best pound-for-pound player I knew (as I doubted whether she tipped a hundred on the scales, it wasn't a close contest). But David assured her he'd built up that kicker to allow a variety of shots to curl toward the green. I had played with a few designers, and it was always a thrill to peek behind the curtain and see which levers had been pulled.

We all followed his instructions, and it was like watching some unmissable catcher's mitt collect our shots, then push them toward the pin. David was right—not just about the friendly bounces but about the joy of watching a golf shot unfold. Instead of a split second of inevitability, we watched our balls meander and pause and restart themselves on their journey. The genius of sixteen was that the backstop allowed better players to go pin-hunting with high irons but gave shorter hitters who needed a 3 wood the same chance of holding the green, if they dared to aim far away from it. Because we had guided them thoughtfully, and because David had left them a path, our shots snuck up on the pin like lost ducklings who spotted their pond and bolted for home.

I couldn't help but watch the smile on David's face as our balls behaved as he'd predicted. *What a thrill that must be*, I thought, *to see an idea you dreamed years before come to life before your eyes.* I suggested as much to David as we approached our birdie putts, and reminded him that we were playing for five pounds (I couldn't play a Scot for dollars), and that he was welcome to keep feeding his opponent local knowledge.

"You know, the funny thing is," he said, "I loved reading your Scotland book. Loved it." I felt my cheeks warming—praise from a Scot for *A Course*

Called Scotland was as good as it got for me. "But the difference is, you couldn't see me enjoying it. I get to come out here and watch you enjoy what we created. How amazing is that?"

It was extraordinary, I told him, and I caught myself indulging the fantasy of every golf-head I knew: that someday we would tee off into one of our napkin sketches.

We shared a long dinner on the picnic benches that evening, then retired to our rooms with plans to meet up in an hour on the putting green just beyond our balconies. Gamble Sands—which is entirely public, by the way—had about fifty guest rooms that enveloped a two-acre putting green that was lit at night, with a firepit in the corner. In the distance, dark mountains stood like sentinels over the Columbia River, its waters reflecting slivers of a pink sunset.

I grabbed my putter and stepped out my sliding door and onto the green, where Gretchen was putting in bare feet and Amanda and Tara were laughing as their balls scaled Himalayan humps, then peeled away from light-hearted hole placements. Tara was a former Tour pro who had met David at an industry meetup, and her path to elite golf was one of the more impressive that I'd encountered. On her twenty-eighth birthday she was struck by one of those where-is-the-time-going epiphanies and decided that she wanted to be a professional athlete. After a few years of relentless practice, the formerly casual golfer was teeing it up on Tour in Europe. Gretchen's story was intimidating as well, at least to us lifers. She had first picked up a club just ten years ago, while dating a guy on the NYU golf team. A woman of rare intensity, she channeled her focus into golf, and in short time was a semifinalist in the US Women's Mid-Am, a winner of Oregon's Women's Mid-Am, and a qualifier for the US Women's Four-Ball (with Amanda, who could play stick, too). She had the state Am coming up in a few weeks, and when she wasn't busy playing slow golf, she had become a world speed-golf champion along the way. So, I wasn't surprised to see her blond hair leaning over six-footers in the dark, still grinding.

We had met in Scotland when she was working in Amsterdam and weekend-tripping over to the Highland links and had remained good friends. She'd been to my home in Philadelphia and played hide-and-seek with my daughters. The greatest miracle to come out of that Scotland book David mentioned was that every new friend who joined me for that adventure—folks from London, Canada, Arizona, Georgia, Chicago, Florida—all showed up in Philadelphia for the book launch, then came back to my house for an after-party. From a window upstairs, I watched them laugh together on my patio, this band of unlikely comrades—women and men, old and young—who continue to text and call and golf with one another to this day.

I watched and didn't just feel gratitude—though my gratitude for these friendships was profound—but an almost cosmic awareness of the good. It would lessen the moment to credit it all to golf, as great a connector as our game could be. It was a sense of joy and purpose and even relief to see proof that this thing where people had to all be together and get along—otherwise known as life—had its own path and way of working, at least when we stepped back and let it be, and took a moment to watch it.

David watched us from the edge of the putting green that evening, where he reclined in an Adirondack chair beside a blazing fire. I joined him, and he confessed that he didn't like losing five quid to me that afternoon. I told him the five-pound note was going on my wall, but he could get it back if he told me the ingredients of a truly great golf course.

It didn't take him long to answer. "Fun," he said. "Fun, and memorability. Golf isn't just a sport. You know that. It's a game of life and drama and narrative. So, a great golf course, it has to do much more than a basketball court or baseball field. It's something far more than just a place to play. If it's just about the execution of golf shots on the pitch, then that's not golf. Not to me."

I agreed by saying nothing. The only sound was popping embers, until he continued: "I know a course is great if I get to the fourteenth hole and don't want it to end. On some courses, most courses, you get to fourteen and you're kind of ready for it to be over. You've probably had enough. But when you're approaching the end and you don't want it to come, then you know you're somewhere special. You know that's a great golf course."

We sat there and watched our friends' shadows roam back and forth across the putting green. They were laughing like children and putting across a course of their own imagining, with no clear beginning and no discernable end.

COEUR D'ALENE, IDAHO

I asked nine people in Coeur d'Alene what Coeur d'Alene meant, hoping it had something to do with the island green we all traveled here to play, or maybe potatoes. This was Idaho, after all, and I expected to be able to lean down and pluck russets out of the rough.

In response to my query, I got nine shrugs and two people who turned to their phones for an answer: It translated to *heart of an awl*, a name given to the local tribe by French-Canadian fur traders. I asked them what sort of potato an awl was, and Google revealed it was a pointed tool for making holes in hide and leather. Heart of a hole puncher wasn't quite the romance I was looking for, but I trusted the floating green would be worth the visit.

The resort itself had a 1989 vibe with blocky white buildings and towers of condos beside a lake. It was a cart-only facility where our caddies would walk along, and I waited in my buggy for a playing partner, Brian, who arrived with rental sticks. Maybe thirty years old, his wife was here for a conference, so he'd spent the week taking the water taxi over from their condo to the golf course.

We paired up with two guys who'd pulled in on motorcycles. They both had handlebar mustaches; Ricky had a shaved head, and Joe sported a curly mullet that spilled out the back of his black leather cap. Dark jeans and wide belt buckles, sucking on Marlboros and tiny cigars; I took them for patched members of a biker gang who would cut us for a gimme. But as our round wore on and I learned one was from Idaho and the other Colorado and that they had met up here for the weekend, I surmised they might be on a date. There was a fine line between the machismo of biker blood brothers and biker boyfriends; either way, they were the sort of unexpected company I was hoping for.

As we rode along through Coeur d'Alene's claustrophobic routing—the course was jammed into a footprint that felt like golf in a clown car, with slivers of green stuck between the pines and the water—I couldn't get my eyes off Ricky's bag. It was one of those rotund leather barrels that, back in the '90s, had made us caddies scatter like roaches. Ricky's was adorned with a rulebook peeking out of a pocket, a ball retriever strapped to its side, an umbrella frayed like a dying bouquet, and one of those club-holder stakes that he would—whoops—jam straight into the green and lean his chipper against. Five woods were topped with giant novelty headcovers (a shark, a parrot, Yosemite Sam), and of course his iron heads were sheathed in plastic. (When iron covers showed up in the bag room at Rolling Green, we had a rule that you wiped the covers and considered yourself done.) And yet his Scotty Cameron putter sat amid all that padding with no cover at all. Cameron covers were collected like Fabergé; golfers queued up online for the latest offerings, and the fact that Ricky owned every pro shop accessory aside from the one we all actually used spun my mind into distraction. I spent the rest of the round trying to make sense of his setup, and what it must mean about the man himself. I hardly noticed the holes (they were tight but fun, with some leading you to the rocky ledges of the lake) until fourteen, where our eyes tightened on the trial ahead.

Considering how little land they'd been given to work with, I thought it made sense that the designers would float one of the greens out into the lake. There were other famous island greens out there, but this was the only one I'd seen without a land bridge. Here, you boarded a boat—a mahogany dinghy called *The Putter*—to chase your tee ball, and towlines tugged the green to a different distance every day. If you made par, the skipper gave you a certificate of achievement. Damn how golf could make grown men who had everything become willing to trade it all for a piece of paper.

Joe's tee ball caught a corner of the green. Ricky and Brian had to drop up beside the dock, while my 7 iron left a ball mark three feet from the hole, rolling out to a distance of about nine. Joe lagged his long one for a tap-in par, while my need for a pat on the back from the skipper saw me jamming my first putt past and lipping out the next. We stepped back over to the dock and sailed for shore, Ricky taking a picture of Joe's wide smile and his certificate, while I stewed in my seat in *The Putter*, hoping for an iceberg.

We shook hands on eighteen, and I bid my biker friends farewell. I dumped my sticks in the trunk and headed for an afternoon of redemption at nearby Circling Raven, a top-one-hundred-you-can-play designee, and aside from its connection to a casino with a parking lot packed with RVs (people camped out at casinos?), it was a quiet retreat of soft Idaho hills and herculean golf holes. It occupied a vast expanse of property that absolutely required a golf cart, and I shared one with a social media contact named Chris. He was nineteen and caddying over at Coeur d'Alene and had fiddled around with community college until a counselor asked him what his passions were. Golf topped the list, so he decided to enroll in the PGM program at Idaho (PGA Golf Management—boot camp for club pros), where he would be starting classes in the fall.

I congratulated him on finding his path. I'd worked with undergrads who would rather take a three-hour final than write a paragraph about what their passion was; rare was the young person who knew what they really cared about, who could locate the thing they felt compelled to pursue. Were the distractions of social media to blame? Was it the pursuit of grades over ideas and curiosity? I don't know, but I watched unsure eighteen-year-olds sign up for business majors because the easy answer to what they wanted in life was comfort. The great American dream, from my point of view, wasn't life, liberty, or happiness—it was salary. Maybe salary could win you that other stuff, but before I'd finished my tenure carrying golf bags for rich dudes, I understood that was rarely the case.

Chris had a good swing, and that he'd come out to join a stranger and pepper me with questions about golf proved this game was indeed a passion. He inquired about where I'd been and where I was going, about favorite rounds and most famous partners. Then he asked me if playing made me nervous.

"Like, this kind of golf?" I asked. "Just playing a round of golf? No, I don't get nervous."

"It makes me nervous," Chris said. "Just even a round with friends, I get really anxious. When I saw you pull in today, I almost shit myself."

"Seriously?"

"Yeah. I don't know what it is. Maybe I care too much, or I want to be better too much. I don't know."

I told him it probably had something to do with his decision to dedicate his life to this. That was pressure, and a lot to process. I explained that golf had made me tremble, too; it used to take three beers to get me to the first tee, which, when I had a seven a.m. start, made for some awkward breakfasts.

"So that changed?" he asked. "How does that change?"

"Time, I guess." I knew that wasn't the answer he was looking for, nor was it the whole truth. "It probably changed around the time I quit drinking," I added, regretting the sentence before I finished speaking it. Now he was going to swear off beer, and that wasn't going to do a thing for him. He looked confused, and rightly so.

"What I mean by that is, when a person like me quits drinking—it's like when anyone tries to figure out why they're miserable or have this habit that holds them back. Eating, shopping, sitting on their ass—whatever. You do a lot of soul-searching. You look at how you act and think, and try to figure out why. For me, I worried too much about things I had no business worrying about. And I cared too much about what everyone else thought of me. If I was ever going to be genuinely happy, I had to work on that. What other people thought of me was none of my business."

"Okay," he said. "That sounds . . . difficult."

"It's not an overnight thing," I said. "But I realized, if everyone else was worrying about what everyone thought of them, like I was, then they probably weren't thinking much about me anyway."

He said that made sense.

"It also doesn't hurt when you've been through some shit," I continued. "Not that you wish for that, but it helps your perspective. I can get nervous over a putt, no doubt. If you throw up before a round because you really care, I don't think that's a bad thing. But you'll probably get to the point where other things will scare you more than golf."

"Great," he said. I smiled. We got back to our match, and on sixteen I won our five-dollar closeout, which had been my standard game since playing with Jimmy Dunne. We said our goodbyes, and I drove over to the casino hotel next door.

Of all the northern Idaho Native American casino hotels I'd ever stayed in, the Coeur d'Alene casino hotel was the finest. My room was clean, but the walk to it through dark corridors crowded with smoke and white-haired gamblers on a sunny Sunday afternoon robbed my soul of hope. I stood in line at a burger stand behind a guy in a tank top with eyes bleary from the slots; he fished out just enough change to buy himself a coffee. I hoped the local tribe was getting every penny this place was taking, because reparations were the only way to feel good about this display of wealth redistribution.

Just as I reached the counter to order, I heard someone calling my name.

"Tom. Tom!" It was Chris, jogging through the casino lobby.

"I forgot about this," he said, handing me five dollars. I smiled and said thanks, and he walked his way back out to the parking lot. Chris, it was clear, was going to be fine.

ANACONDA, MONTANA

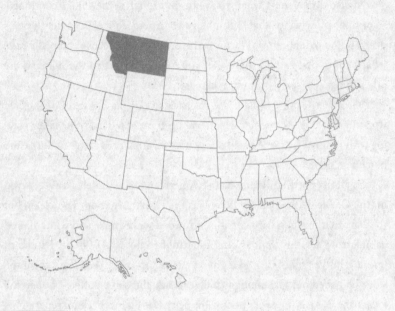

I was hoping Hertz meant it when they said unlimited miles. I played a driving game in my head in which five hours was a lot, four hours was progress,
and three hours left to my destination was practically there. Along the way,
I tried to snap a picture of every state welcome sign I passed, if I could do
so without spinning my car into a ditch. I'd collected a handful already,
but there was something about crossing into this state that had me sitting
up a little taller in my seat, pushing out my chest, reaching behind me to
stroke an invisible gun rack. MONTANA—BIG SKY COUNTRY, the sign said. I
didn't know why, but I felt like more of a man for being here. I didn't know
how the sky could be bigger in this state than it was in others, but I didn't
dare doubt it; Montana wasn't a place for soft-minded questions. It was all

bigger here—the sky, the mountains, my pecs, and, most of all, the drives.

With my cruise control set at ninety mph—the state let you fly on the highways, since the grocery store could be fifty miles away—it took an entire morning to make my way down to Old Works in Anaconda. The golden bear on its sign announced it as a Nicklaus course, which tended to be reliably good layouts with a somewhat manufactured feel. I wouldn't have come this far for a Nicklaus course if it hadn't been built here, atop a former mining operation.

The holes at Old Works were hemmed by tall walls of blond stone, some bearing the gashes and trails followed by mine carts, remains from a time when they pulled a thousand tons of ore from these hills every day. The bygone smelter at Old Works had enough capacity to treat half of that haul, but when a larger operation next door put it out of business, the land lay vacant for nearly a century before it was made a Superfund cleanup site in 1983— smelting agents had thoroughly polluted the area, and the Works had left behind mountains of black slag. Golf was proposed as a solution for repurposing the acres, and with so much fine slag to work with, it was no surprise that the bunkers at Old Works were plentiful, and entirely black.

Rusted mining buckets now dotted the property as decoration, with faux copper stones spilling out of one beside the putting green. I met my playing partner there, another friend I'd made two days before on Twitter; anyone who said they'd meet me in Anaconda, Montana, was most welcome, especially since I wouldn't have to juggle tee time promises to find him a spot. Ryan was a fit, firm-jawed lad in his twenties, tall with black hair. He had a friendly but formal air about him—he called me *Mr. Coyne*, which I nipped in the bud—which made sense when he told me he was in the air force. I asked if he flew planes, and he told me no, he was a missileer. I asked him what that meant.

"Well, the title we prefer is Nuclear Launch Officer," he explained.

"Wait. So, you turn the key?"

"I turn *a* key," he said plainly, as if telling me he collected stamps.

"So, hold on," I said, the questions lining up in my head as I realized I was golfing with a guy who, for his day job, awaited a call to destroy the planet. Had he seen *WarGames*? Matthew Broderick? He hadn't, which made me feel both old and anxious about the qualifications of our missileers.

Ryan explained he was meeting me on the way from his training base in California to where he was being stationed by the silos in Great Falls. He was married with two small children, and I asked if they'd gone ahead to Great Falls to move in already.

"No. They're here. My wife took them to McDonald's. Then they're going to find a park or chip at the practice green or something."

I liked this guy. I trusted him, too. Anyone who sent his family to McDonald's so he could golf with a stranger not only had his priorities in order but possessed the home front support that an officer in his position required. Still, I said, his job had to be stressful.

"They do a pretty thorough screening process to identify people who are right for it," Ryan said. He shared that he had gone to BYU and done a mission in Minnesota, and though our time together was brief, I decided the air force had chosen well. A levelheaded, non-substance-abusing Mormon seemed a good candidate—though if he started tossing clubs and spewing profanity, I was ready to freak out.

He didn't. He did explain how their system had so many redundancies that accidents were an impossibility.

"So—the big question," I ventured further. "Would you turn your key?"

He didn't need time to think about it. "If I have to turn that key, then things have gotten really, really bad. So yes, I would launch."

It was hard to appreciate all the rugged Montana beauty while visions of nuclear holocaust danced through my head. As I imagined these rock walls melting all around me, a cart approached, and out hopped our two other itinerary newcomers to whom I'd apparently given the wrong tee time.

Sean and Shoeless Gerry were both golf badasses, which seemed the only sort of golfer you should be in Montana. Considering that my other playing partner fired nukes, I thought they really needed to bring something to the table. They did—of Montana's 115 golf courses, Sean had played 113 of them, and Gerry had played all but one.

Neither could get on Crystal Lakes, a public turned uber-private by the millionaire who sped up the drive-thru by inventing the dispenser that pours a perfect medium soda with the push of one button. They weren't sure if the course was any good, but since only the owner and his relatives got to play it, it remained their golden goose. The property was said to include a full-size replica of Stonehenge, along with an air museum that housed a rare British bomber on which the Queen of England had the right of first refusal should the inventor ever decide to sell. Sean had heard that the course featured a greenside lake that had been filled to leave just two inches of water, so golf carts could roll across it like Jesus in Galilee.

Sean was young and stocky and dressed in branded gear from his website, Montana's Longest Drive, where he documented his cross-state golf quest as part of a master's thesis in communications. Blending academic pursuits with golf indulgence was a trade I knew well, and I applauded his turning his 8,700-mile drive into a blog that passed for graduate research. His buddy Gerry was not an academic; Gerry was a Gerry, in all the best ways. He loved golf, cold beer, his beard, and the Boston Bruins, and he wasn't much for shoes. Apparently, they stressed his Achilles, or his lack thereof.

A few years before, Gerry had been packing to head south and knock out five Montana courses on his list when the tendon popped. Rather than go to the doctor, he taped his foot into a stiff boot and played on. He ended up losing half his tendon, getting a staph infection from the surgery, and nearly dying in the process, but he'd gotten himself five courses closer to 115, all of which were noted on the walls of his basement golf bar that featured floor-to-ceiling golf flags and scorecards and pencils.

As we finished up on eighteen, Sean shared what had become my three least favorite words in golf: "Are you playing . . . ?" It was a question without an upside. Either I was, in which case the query was redundant, or I wasn't, which, at this point, I was powerless to change, and I'd leave the conversation dejected at my itinerary's shortcomings. Sean's suggestion, however, made me consider gutting the calendar—Heaven on Earth wasn't just his embellished description, it was the place's actual name. Nine holes of clifftop golf in the Montana wilderness, accessible only by a long, teeth-jarring drive or five days' floating down a river. It sounded like golf's *Apocalypse Now*, albeit with a happier destination, where you were met by an eccentric gatekeeper who handed you a stiff cocktail and the keys to the course.

I shook myself from visions of paddling my way through white rapids to play golf among the clouds; I didn't have time to do laundry, let alone take a five-day detour. I'd have to join Gerry and Sean's ranks as Montana golfers with a someday course still on my list.

As we played on into the afternoon, I relished Old Works for the quality of its holes—credit to Nicklaus's team, they'd laid out a fun one—and for the history we got to walk through. As we navigated heaps of slag and scraped quarry walls, I couldn't help but imagine the lunch-pail generations who had worked this ground (well, the ground under all this new grass). I also admired how something good had come of an environmental disaster. The smelting process shed nasty outputs—a lake in nearby Butte was a mile long and completely toxic. Its water was so metallic that you could literally skim copper from its surface. Yet here, they had done enough remediation to make it safe for golf, and unknowingly protected the course for decades to come.

Sean explained how tee time demand in Anaconda could be rather mild, but they were virtually guaranteed this course would last without having to hike greens fees to cover costs. The mining company was happy to stroke a check every few years to keep the place going, versus the billions they'd have to spend if they had to dig it up and clean the acres underneath. Now there was a new model for sustainable, public golf: golf courses as toxicity toppers.

I filled in a closing bogey on my card and headed for the clubhouse, where I met Ryan's wife and his boys by the putting green. Four and five years old, they were running in circles and swinging putters and waiting for Dad. His wife never found a park, so they'd been hanging around here, happy to be out of the car for a while. I shook their hands, and we walked out to the parking lot together.

In my trunk, I dug around for some of my Titleists and gave each of the boys a ball with TC on it and the number fifty—for all fifty states, I told them. They eyed the shiny plastic spheres like they were rare nuggets we'd just pulled out of those hills, turning them over in their hands. In return, Ryan reached into his bag and handed me a military challenge coin from the base where he'd trained. I'd seen these tokens of honor, but I'd certainly never been given one before. It was a thin piece of metal with the air force insignia on one side, and on the other, a rocket rising from a cloud of smoke. Maybe they gave them out to everyone, but I felt moved by the notion that there were people who were willing to do impossible things, and if you were like me, you took them largely for granted. And now I was linked to one of them—the proof was here in my hand—and suddenly, my being American felt less like a happy accident.

I thanked him with a speechless sort of gratitude, and then we said our goodbyes. As I headed to my car, I heard the boys still talking about the balls I'd given them, how new and clean they were, and I kind of wanted to cry.

Watching Ryan move his family across the country, meeting his boys— our lives as countrymen were distinct yet interwoven, and I felt like a better person just for having spent some time with a guy who said yes, so that I could ask why. I felt shortsighted for not having felt this connection before, especially since I already knew a man who had moved across the country under similar orders, in a convertible with my mother by his side.

SENECA, OREGON

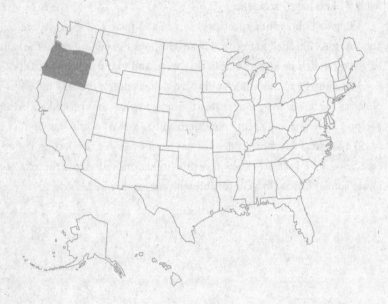

I made a U-turn at Anaconda and pointed myself west toward the lower corner of Washington. This time it wasn't Smokey the Bear but a cartoon bull with wide horns and a brass ring in his nose waving to me from the side of the road. The sign advertised a local testicle festival, with its smiling mascot imploring me to "Come have a ball!" I had committed to sampling as many regional dishes as the schedule allowed, but mercifully, today that was not an option—I was late for a tee time in Walla Walla.

The small city had been reborn thanks to the wine boom, with a downtown revitalized by new tasting boutiques. My hotel, once rundown, was now a bustling hub for Seattle couples looking for new vintages. It was no surprise, then, that the local course recommended to me was called Wine

Valley, with one of the better logos I'd seen: a golf flag terminating in a cork-screw. The course was spread over a wide alfalfa seed farm where a particular breed of tiny bees was required for pollination. In the fields all around us, blue boxes buzzed with little workers (I was told they didn't sting).

The irony of my playing a place called Wine Valley wasn't lost, but it was also part of its allure. Wine Valley was a name that could once have been ap-plied to my kitchen, so I appreciated this chance to try the golf variety. You could see almost all of it from the clubhouse, which gave me a false sense of confidence—I anticipated a benign trek across wide fairways, but once we were out in its hills of dense fescue, our balls were lost to the bees with alarming regularity. I backed up an opening birdie with a string of doubles that I was happy to blame on the six-hour drive, but as I progressed through the scorecard, the holes leaned and bent and twisted in a dizzying proces-sion. It was supposed to be tame farmland, but the builder had cleared off the alfalfa and found rumpled linksland underneath.

The greens were large and angry, and fronted by bunkers that felt as if they'd been clawed into the earth. Wine Valley was just ten years old, but felt like it had been here before the farm, so settled was it into its surroundings. Put Bill Coore or Gil Hanse's name on it and Walla Walla would be more than a destination for wine. I didn't know the name of its designer, but that would change in two days, when I found myself battling him for five bucks.

I met my life's first tumbleweeds as I ventured into eastern Oregon, where bundles of golden brush blew across roads where cell phone signals didn't dare to go. I was grateful to have a caddie at my next destination—my shoul-ders could use the break, and I was told I wouldn't have to tip him—but before we reached the first green, I was ready to fire Bruce.

He came off as bored and uninterested, and worst of all, lazy. He was silent as well, which only added to my frustration. His eyes were large and strange, and I don't think he cared if I was golfing or fishing or chasing butterflies—he was just out here for the walk, and the snacks. When I reached the green, my putter was fifty yards behind me as Bruce stood in the brush, chewing on his lunch.

His handler pulled on his leash—"Come on, Bruce, come on"—but Bruce had camped beside a thicket of tasty branches and dug in his hooves. I warned him that we had goat for dinner last night, that this caddie gig of his was a real cushy job for a quadruped like him, and not a forever one. His jaws just kept grinding. I grabbed my putter from the bag he was wearing and didn't bother asking for a read.

It was a place I'd lopped off the itinerary a dozen times before committing to the drive. Silvies Valley Ranch was near absolutely nothing, a two-day commitment at minimum, but their invite was so gracious, and their business model so curious—a working and entirely sustainable ranch, with a reversible golf course and goat caddies—that I had to make it fit. I trimmed my visits in Seattle—sorry, Aldarra, I'll catch you next time—and made room for what I feared might be a golf gimmick of a place but turned out to be two of the best days of my golfing life.

I spent the long, dusty haul from Walla Walla with John Day—if not in body, then in spirit. I had never heard of the nineteenth-century trapper and explorer before, but his name followed me through eastern Oregon. John Day the town, John Day the river. I would learn he had been robbed and stripped naked by natives along the Columbia River before losing his mind in the wilderness that now bore his name. I found myself conversing with JD as I drove, my brain softened by hours of bare and bony earth. He didn't know the way to Silvies Valley Ranch, either, and we both wondered if seeing my golf clubs strapped to a goat was worth wandering beyond the edge of the known world.

I exhaled as I passed through the ranch's gates with a sliver of gas left on the gauge, but it was all nearly gone before I saw any more markers of civilization—a house and another gate, with some cabins behind it. I wasn't going to miss the chance to play both directions of my first reversible routing, and since they played it in opposite directions every other day, Silvies required an overnight—not that I was in a hurry to get back in the car. I entered the first log building and found a reception desk in front of tall glass windows, where a young woman took my keys and handed me a walkie-talkie, since there was no cell or phone service on the ranch. She showed me what buttons to push in case of emergency and gave me a refillable water bottle—no plastic cups either—and the keys to a fat-tired golf cart that I could take to my room, and farther up to the golf course. She offered me some ranch-made pepperoni and told me dinner was just across the way at six p.m. It was already three o'clock, and I had two courses to play first. There was one dinner sitting per night, and dialing out for pizza was clearly not an option, so I told her I would hustle.

I raced my off-road cart up a dirt road to an open-air clubhouse, where I was given a less juiced-up ride, and played the empty clockwise routing in two hours. I'd never played at elevation and wasn't sure I would enjoy the inflated distances or feel like I was cheating, but after my first 310-yard drive, I got over it—not only was the air thin but the fairways were Scotland-firm. Silvies used as little water as they could get away with, implementing an eco-forward sprinkler system that measured precisely how much moisture had evaporated from the property and put back not an ounce more. From perched tee boxes, I rocketed drives through pine tree goalposts and dared myself to carry ponds and corners; I could see for miles from the course's crests, and without another human on the course, I felt that beautiful loneliness that only travelers understood as a gift.

I didn't understand how we were meant to play it in the opposite direction tomorrow, as it felt like a proper eighteen-holer without tricks or concessions to make it run both ways. I would find out soon enough, but in the meantime, I headed for some mountain ridges where I was told I could find some bonus golf that I would want to talk about at dinner.

McVeigh's Gauntlet was about as un-cart-friendly a stretch of golf holes as one might find in North America, so I left my driver and woods in my cart and threw my irons over my shoulder. Its holes had been built as a sort of experiment by its designer—can we really put golf holes there on that ridgeline?—and they found enough room for seven of them. Beside the first, a sign spelled out the "Lucky 7" challenge that, should you complete it, won you a T-shirt and Silvies immortality:

1. Complete scorecard and all 7 holes (par 23)
2. Take and use less than 7 clubs
3. Use or lose less than 7 balls

4. Drink less than 7 beers

5. Complete the course in less than 77 minutes

6. Have a score less than 27

7. If you birdie the "Par = 2 bonus hole" (which has a 7-inch cup), for the remainder of the round you get a bonus of: an extra ball you can lose, 1 mulligan, and a bonus of 7.7 inches to add to all lies

Four over par on a par 3 course seemed easy enough. I was ready for my T-shirt fitting until I hiked to the first tee and saw a small green dish perched on a mountain peak in the distance. I hit a ball somewhere near it, then hiked down and back up the ridge to find myself with a long look at birdie. The course was seven of the most wonderfully absurd par 3s I'd ever endeavored, with a short hilltop bonus hole that was a sixty-foot putt, with benches and a cooler of beer should the climbs have you sucking for air.

I had never had that much fun playing golf alone before, and came off the final hole giddy about the expanses I had just traversed, and with a winning scorecard. When I found they were out of prizes in the pro shop, I pretended not to mind. Rule #5 when you're being hosted by the resort: Don't complain about not getting a free T-shirt. The pro told me he'd see me at dinner, which was a surprise—one meal for everybody out here, I guessed—but I was glad for the company. There would be plenty of us, he said. The designer was on his way in as well.

The restaurant had walls of tan logs that stretched to a cathedral ceiling, and when I arrived, a dozen folks were sitting at a tree-slab bar, nibbling on jerky and sausage and goat cheese that all came from the livestock on the property. I couldn't pick the designer out of the crowd, nor could I tell the difference between employee and guest. Everyone spoke as if they knew one another, a quick and easy sort of community born of being together in the middle of nowhere, and they welcomed me right in to a plate of smoked homestead meats.

A man in jeans and flannel approached and introduced himself. "Dan Hixson," he said, shaking my hand, and I recognized his name from Wine Valley. The designer himself. Tall and thin with a bald scalp and round glasses, he looked more like a professor on sabbatical than a golf pro turned architect, but that's what he was. He had a laid-back Oregon vibe, and at maybe fifty years of age, he was humble and more interested in hearing about my trip than about how great I thought his golf course was.

The bartender told us to grab seats at the long table in front of the bar, and Dan and I took chairs next to each other. The chef walked out from the kitchen to tell us what was for dinner—there was no menu, but the courses sounded sumptuous as he listed that evening's selection of ranch-to-table offerings. I had somehow avoided beets until arriving at Silvies Valley, but now I found they were quite delicious when stuffed with goat cheese. All the veggies and herbs came from the fields outside. Even the bread here had a sustainable bent—it was all sourdough made from a family starter that was over a hundred years old.

Our waitress handed me a steak knife forged for Rambo—I was sure there was room for a flint and fishing line in the handle—and I felt like a true Oregonian as I used it to tear apart what the chef had called chevon. The woman next to me asked me what that was, but I just chewed it and shrugged. Whatever it was, it was tasty. Dan answered that it was goat, and she slid her plate toward mine. I enjoyed a double-goat dinner while Dan explained how he ended up building a golf course all the way out here.

The ranch had had a few former lives—one as a failed safari, another as a dude ranch for city slickers—before an Oregon veterinarian named Scott Campbell bought it with a vision for turning it into a high-end ecotourist destination, thus bringing outside dollars to an overlooked portion of his home state. He'd made millions by franchising pet hospitals, and enlisted Hixson to bring golfers to his new venture.

Dan had grown up the son of a golf pro, and both he and his brother were PGA members. He had a comfortable head pro job and an accomplished playing career, but ever since he was a kid sketching golf holes in his notebooks, Dan had dreamed of building courses. So, at age thirty-nine, he walked away from the family business, ready to do whatever it took to get work as a course builder. He didn't go to architecture school or study Scottish templates or know how to drive a bulldozer, but he started with short courses, bunker renovations, and practice areas as he learned the business. "I knew what a good golf hole was," he explained. "I don't really have a design philosophy, I don't think. I see what the land has to offer. I try to find a good hole that's already there, and then I see if I can find others to go around it."

It was an approach that worked, both philosophically and financially. While known-name architects were charging half a million for a new practice area, Dan could do it for a hundred thousand, and do it well. "Initially, working cheaper held me back. Places thought you had to spend a lot to get a good hole or short-game area. But once the economy tanked, my business took off. I've been busy ever since."

Celebrated designs at Wine Valley and Bandon Crossings (across the street from Bandon Dunes) put him on the map, and eventually won him the job at Silvies. Still, I couldn't help but wonder—every golf geek dreamed of building golf courses, but few of us dare try it without the learning and expertise. How did he learn to build a bunker? Install irrigation? Grow grass?

"Well, I learned to build bunkers by digging some holes. I learned to drive a bulldozer by getting on one. Irrigation, well, I called a friend to do that. And superintendents grow the grass," he said. Still, I insisted, it couldn't be that easy.

"It wasn't easy. But how'd you learn to write a book?" he asked.

I paused to think. "I don't remember. I just wanted to write one."

"There you go," he said.

We stepped outside onto the patio and melted s'mores for dessert. The meadow before us stretched for miles, and the grasses glowed red at sunset. Dan agreed that five dollars sounded like a good wager for tomorrow, but first we'd take a morning walk around the fourth course he'd built on the property, with some chevon to guide us.

Named after a War Chief of the Paiute Tribe who camped here while battling the US Cavalry in 1882, the Chief Egan course was a nine-holer of undulating par 3s with creeks to carry and goats to follow you around. I was joined on the Egan by Dan and a Portland couple who'd sat across from us at dinner last night. As we greeted our low-slung caddies, I felt badly that my breath still tasted like chevon.

According to the Silvies website, the idea for using goat caddies began when the goats started complaining about their limited career options, and the ranch felt inclined to offer them upward mobility and an opportunity to grow as employees. The subtext was that the ranch had the largest herd of meat goats in the world, and golf bags on goats would bring some eyes to the unconventional resort.

Seamus Golf, an Oregon company specializing in bespoke woolen golf goods and hammer-stamped ball markers, had become one of the new taste-makers in the game; these boutique companies were changing golfers' shopping habits, and it was rare to find a millennial player without one of their custom headcovers. They took up Silvies' challenge to craft caddie saddles to fit the goats and invented a double-sided leather satchel with a pocket for peanuts, which I quickly learned were the only way to ween Bruce off the brush and get my clubs over where I needed them. It was a publicity gag for sure, but it worked—it's how I'd learned about the course in the first place. Beside the pro shop, a small goat pen was labeled the caddie shack, and inside the shop you could buy stuffed versions of the caddies to bring home to your kids (I grabbed two of my buddy Bruce). It was easier to just carry my own wedges around the short course, but it was a welcome bit of whimsy to make a putt, then come over and scratch my caddie and feed him a handful of peanuts in their shells while he dropped turds in the fringe.

When we finished on nine, Bruce was busy munching wildflowers as I pulled my clubs off his back and headed for the big course with Dan. The opening hole I had played yesterday was still there, but I felt like I'd been duped by a magic trick as I turned around and found a new hole hiding behind me. I trusted Dan that I was hitting in the right direction, and by the second tee, I had somehow forgotten that I'd been here before.

Dan's thin frame belied his game; the dude hammered it, and worked his ball with intimidating precision. He got me three-down before I battled back to where I missed ten-footers on seventeen and eighteen for a win—nothing motivated my golf like trying to best the guy who built the place, but the fivers remained in both of our wallets.

Silvies wasn't a truly reversible routing in the mode of the Old Course at St. Andrews or Forest Dunes in Michigan—it had twenty-seven greens versus a true eighteen—but it seemed a useful variation for the Silvies property, as each direction took you to corners of the ranch you'd missed the day before. From either route, drivable par 4s and reachable 5s made for brazen match-play strategies, and the concept held to the Silvies ethos: use the land thoughtfully, and disturb as little of it as possible. Done well, a reversible course was a model for golf's future, requiring less maintenance, less water and chemicals, less cost overall—two courses, literally, for the price of one.

Dan was aware of these benefits and the legacy of two-way golf in Scotland, but his reasoning for implementing it here was born of fortuitous indecision. While touring the property, he had found a valley that was destined to be an all-world par 4; he just couldn't decide which direction made for a better hole. The idea struck him: What if they played it both ways? When his boss gave him the green light, Dan was suddenly building two courses instead of one. The fact that he made each feel distinct and new elevated Silvies to the top of a list I was keeping of places for the trip after this one, with a foursome of friends in tow. Two eighteen-holers plus the two short courses made it a three-day stop—maybe longer if you mixed in some saddle time—even though I'd budgeted only two.

Later that day, I traded in my walkie-talkie for my car keys at reception and headed down a long road away from a golf heaven nobody knew about and toward another one that everybody did.

BANDON, OREGON

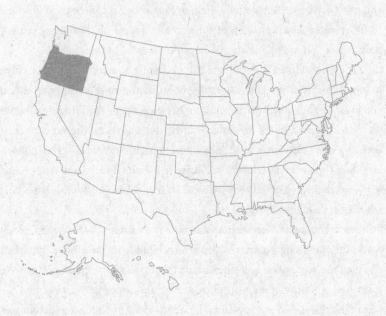

I had driven across Pennsylvania plenty of times; Ohio and Indiana, too. I guessed crossing Oregon couldn't be all that different—it looked only slightly bigger than my home state on the map. As I drove, I passed small communes in the brush, rusted buses and lawn chairs spread around dusty encampments. I saw more pot shops than gas stations and slowed down to eye a rally of one guy and his teenage son with a sign that said FUCK GUN CONTROL. It was a dozen different countries and landscapes—from pines to desert back to forest and rivers and into mountains, and then the sea—and eight hours later, I was somehow still within the borders of never-ending Oregon. But at least I had arrived somewhere really, really good.

Plenty has been said and written about Mike Keiser's wonderworld on the coast; on previous visits, I'd sung some of those praises myself, when I discovered how a greeting card magnate had transformed not only a giant chunk of Oregon coastline but also reinvented golf in the twenty-first century. Rather than cover costs by preselling memberships to wealthy friends, Keiser had kept Bandon public and gambled on greens fees, counting on golfers to drive five hours after a flight to Portland. And when they did come to this remote southern strip of Oregon cliffs—and oh, how they came— destination golf in America flipped upside down.

Golfers had been traveling for golf ever since someone figured out how to zip up a travel cover, but Bandon redrafted the rules by proving that if you build it, golfers will come. And not begrudgingly—the farther the better seemed to be part of the formula, as if the trek enhanced the experience. It certainly invested guests in the adventure. Plunk down four thousand dollars, then fly across the country and drive five hours down a one-lane coastal highway and you arrived well inclined to love what you found. Especially when it was so damn lovable.

Bandon spawned Keiser outposts in Wisconsin and Nova Scotia, along with other far-flung golf retreats in which he didn't have a hand. And this changed not just public golf's landscape in America but private golf as well. It severed golf development from real estate and timeshares and altered the way golfers budgeted their dollars. The standard for public and resort courses was raised across the board—trips to play a Pete Dye and stay in a Ramada didn't seem so sexy anymore. Millennials, the studies said, were more interested in accumulating experiences than they were stuff, and younger golfers seemed less inclined to drop fifty grand to play the same course every day when they could spend that money on excursions they'd talk about for years. Golf trips now had to be cool and audacious and, aside from the travel, create an expectation of easy fun.

Arriving at Bandon Dunes was a true hold-my-calls experience; the setting felt wonderfully severed from calendars and commitments (aside from tee times, of course), and its team excelled at forecasting your preferences: Your bag, which you probably shipped there, was already waiting on a caddie's shoulder. A shuttle would bus you from your foursome's cottage to the infinite driving range to a first tee, then to a handful of hangouts or a massage or back to your room, where four soft chairs and a stocked bar awaited you by a wide TV. Put your spikes on the shoe dryers by your bed and dream of doing today again tomorrow.

Bandon's most essential golf menu item was the menu itself—Keiser was often quoted as saying, "One course is a curiosity. Two courses is a destination." Over the past twenty years, Bandon's offerings had grown to four eighteen-hole courses (with a fifth ready to open), plus the greatest thirteen-hole course in the world (a small sample size, perhaps, but playing the par 3 course at BD was as close as I got to feeling drunk anymore) and a sprawling putting course replete with drink holders and lights for late-night putting duels.

With shoulder-to-shoulder courses by David McLay Kidd, Tom Doak, and Coore & Crenshaw, it wasn't all just convenient; it was dune golf of the highest order. With firm fescue fairways, the bounces at Bandon were Irish links in Oregon, and the connection was not entirely accidental. The area had been settled by George Bennett back in 1873, and he named it after his hometown in Ireland. He also imported gorse to remind him of his homeland, which today gives the courses a distinctly linksy flair, even if it remains their biggest threat. An intractable and invasive species, its oily leaves burn like kerosene—a gorse fire in 1936 turned the town of Bandon into a smoldering wasteland—and today its growth is strictly monitored by the Gorse Action Group of the local city government.

Five courses competing for one's affections, plus so many cozy hangouts, made Bandon Dunes a hot spot for rankings. Best course? Best meal? Best course logo? (They each had their own—Keiser was a wise merchandiser.) A visit would be incomplete without taking a stab at an ordering of preferences, so for me, my excitement over each offering rates thusly:

1. **BANDON DUNES:** Where it all started, a cliffside head-spinner of deep blue backdrops with a risk-reward sixteenth I see in my sleep.
2. **BANDON TRAILS:** Probably the best collection of holes on the property, it gets knocked for not being on the water, which isn't always a bad thing when it's really blowing.
3. **PACIFIC DUNES:** Another oceanside compilation of postcard holes,

I nudge it down the list for an awkward opener (I loathe kicking off with a layup), but it's stuffed with magical moments.

4. **BANDON PRESERVE:** The thirteen-hole short course; if it had twice as many holes, I might put it at the top. Any course with a hundred-yard hole where you can tee off with a putter (it plays like a ski slope) is a champ to me.

5. **OLD MACDONALD:** A tribute to Charles Blair Macdonald and chock-ablock with Oregonian versions of his template holes, it's a great match-play course, and a stroke-play shellacking. I love firm and fast and fescue, but at modern speeds versus Scottish pace, your ball does unmentionable things.

I gave the Preserve top billing for logo (a bloom of silvery phacelia, an endangered plant species that was now thriving around Bandon's 13-holer), and ranked Bandon Trails' rice bowls as best eats (others will swear by the pub's meat loaf, and it's good, but it's still meat loaf). But of all Bandon Dunes' accoutrements, the loopers were the true list-toppers for me. Maybe I'm a logistics geek or a nostalgic bag toter, but the caddie program at this walking-only property is the ingredient I found most impressive. It didn't hurt that I had Ken and Phil to show me its inner workings.

Hanging around the Bandon caddies can be a dangerous business. Three days in their easy company and you might find yourself reassessing your life's decisions, ready to shred your spreadsheets and come join their ranks. Sure, there were guys scraping from loop to loop, but the crowd I hung with seemed like they had life sorted.

Ken was a lanky gentleman with a gray beard who had retired from his day job to come loop at Bandon; he rode his bike to the course every day, earned his roll of cash, and squirreled it away for the month he spent golfing in Ireland every summer. We bonded over Ballybunion, and he gave me my most cherished swag—a Bandon pullover with LOOPER stitched on the shoulder. Caddie bonds never die. I felt even more like one of the gang when he took me into the Bandon caddie shack for a tour. And by shack, I mean command center.

It was the size of the clubhouse at my course back home, and like my home club, it had a large putting green out front where caddies could hone their strokes while they waited for a loop, unless they preferred to be inside. When Ken took me in for a tour, I could see it might be a tough choice: leather sofas faced a giant TV playing Golf Channel reruns, next to those massage chairs you always wanted to try in the airport but skipped for fear of cooties. Beside the lounge was a full canteen with trays of hot food sliding out a window, and past that, a locker room with a washer and dryer for keeping caddie jumpsuits a crisp white. Around the corner, the caddie masters managed their legion of 350 jocks from a bustling office, and every few minutes they announced over a loudspeaker: "Max and John Q on Trails in twenty minutes," alerting two reclining caddies to step outside and hop on the shuttle that would deliver them to the first tee.

It was caddie clockwork, and at its heart was a smartphone app allowing loopers to pick which days on the calendar they wanted to work; their tee times would pop up in their notifications. It all felt centuries away from leaning up against a wooden fence at Rolling Green, waiting for a hungover guy in a collared shirt to point at me. Caddie culture was in decline elsewhere, which threatened golf culture as a whole (the First Tee program sounded nice, but it was caddie yards that created lifetime players), yet Bandon Dunes was doing its part to help it thrive and push it forward.

As Ken and I headed for the exit, I was happy to bump into Phil. He'd just been dropped off by the shuttle after a twosome on Old Mac (the Bandon caddies' least favorite loop—so many deep bunkers, so much coaching to do) and we hugged hello. He was heading out for an afternoon round with some other caddies and invited me to join them. I had the afternoon free—that morning I'd gone around Pacific Dunes in a gale and had nearly become persona non grata in caddie HQ when I caught a breeze on nine and didn't see the looper ahead of us, tucked into a bend in the fairway. My *FORE!* was inaudible in the tempest, and I missed him by a yard, from what I could tell. They left behind the telltale marker of a group that has been hit into—my ball sat atop a tee in the fairway—and I lifted a hand in apology, which was met by shaking heads.

I was glad Phil had been on another course and that it wasn't his head I had nearly plunked. I told him I was in for golf and asked which course we would be playing. Trails? Dunes? The Preserve?

"Nah, we're going to go over to our place," he said. "You got a car? Follow me."

I had met Phil on my first visit to Bandon, when luck of the caddie-app draw put him on my bag. He had a thin, scruffy face with wild black hair tangled beneath a flimsy bucket hat. I'd have guessed his age to be near fifty, but he had a timeless dude quality about him; he probably looked this way ten years ago, and would look the same in ten more. His eyes had the tanned crow's feet that befit a lifetime caddie, and his gait and style revealed he was a surfer, loose as water. He lived in a converted garage on a nearby bluff, where he probably covered his rent in two loops, and could tell if the breaks were good from his bed every morning as the roar of the waves shook his walls.

Phil caddied, surfed, fished, golfed—repeat. And he golfed well, I was told; probably a few strokes better than scratch. Bandon's caddie ranks were full of former journeymen pros and Tour loopers, so I was curious about who we'd be playing with that afternoon, and where. I followed Phil's weathered white compact off the resort and pulled into a parking lot across the street, passing a sign for Bandon Crossings, another Dan Hixson design. It seemed I had accidently plotted myself a Hixson tour, and found the place where locals and Bandon caddies played their golf. Now in a T-shirt and torn jeans, Phil walked behind the counter and checked us in—this was clearly his daily spot—then went outside and strapped my bag next to his on a chitty-chitty-bang-bang golf cart. There was no way our group was walking, Phil explained. They did enough of that across the street.

As I inspected Phil's bag of aged Ping irons and a makeshift long putter where a shaft had been jammed into the butt of a standard mallet and secured with electrical tape, I overheard him talking to the two other caddies who were joining us, explaining my intrusion into their regular afternoon game.

"A writer?" the larger of the two said. "What's he write?"

"Golf," Phil said.

"Golf? A golf writer. Super," he said. His tone lacked sincerity.

Suddenly I was twelve again, hoping to win the approval of hard-knock veterans who'd earned their gruff sarcasm over so many summers. Phil paired me on his team against his buddies Ron and Brian, and as we drove to the first tee, he did everything he could to explain the match into which I was headed. It would have taken a very long ride for me to understand half of it.

It was clear there were no gimmes, and that strokes were not allotted by common math but rather by a first-tee negotiation based on Phil's actuarial tables of potential hole-by-hole outcomes. Ron didn't need a stroke on five; Brian couldn't take one on fourteen. Phil couldn't give Ron a stroke on two— he had no advantage on the drive. Phil haggled me out of having to give strokes because I had never putted the greens before, and of course nobody got shots on par 5s, nor could anyone press where they were getting a pop— otherwise, there was a press on every hole (I think), along with KPs (closest to the pin—why it's a K remains one of golf's great mysteries) and specials galore. I did understand the Russian Reversal, which meant your closest-to-the-pin prize flipped into your paying out double if you three-putted.

Solid play won me some acceptance, and by the back nine, our foursome settled into a competitive chumminess. Ron was thick but not fat, with a neckless fullback sort of build; I doubted whether he even noticed the golf bags on his shoulders when he was caddying. As we waited to tee off on the twelfth, he started recounting his morning loop for Phil and me, where apparently he'd nearly been killed by some asshole in the group behind.

"We were over in the hills on the right of nine, looking for my guy's ball, and this ball comes whizzing over my head. Swear to God I felt it zip past my ear. I walk out in the fairway and they're hitting into us and I'm like, *What the fuck? Are you kidding me?*"

Oh boy.

"What course were you on?" I asked.

"Pacific," he said.

Yup. "What was your tee time?"

Ron paused and looked me in the eyes for the first time that day. "Seven forty. Was that you? Were you the seven fifty group?"

I was taller than Ron, but there was no doubt he could roll me up into a ball and stuff me in his pocket. I considered a more careful response, but settled on, "Yeah. I'm really sorry about that."

"Are you serious?" he said. "That was you?"

Phil promptly burst into laughter, diffusing the tee box standoff. We were one-up and he needed his partner to finish with limbs intact.

"That's great," he said. "I can't believe you hit into Ronny. That's awesome."

"Yeah, really awesome," Ron said, walking over to his ball.

"Now you're really in his head," Phil whispered to me. And I guess maybe I was. Ron launched his next one into the pines—they were towering and abundant—and Phil added another birdie to our card. Birdies applied some sort of multiplier, and thanks to seven between Phil and me (I made everything, and Phil played with a magical nonchalance, going 'round in 72 strokes and 0 practice swings), we each left with thirty more bucks in our pockets.

As we loaded our bags into our cars, Ron and Brian both lamented how well I putted. "These greens are hard to read, man. New guys never putt like that," Ron said. The greens did have angry tilts to them, but for some reason, the lines that afternoon all looked like sidewalks to me. Maybe they were tough for a newcomer, but I wasn't going to tell them that Dan Hixson and I went way back.

I drove through a tunnel of tall northern pines, and as I watched for signs for the Oregon Coast Highway, it occurred to me that the only bad hole in Bandon was the final one. It meant the golf you'd spent a year anticipating was over, and all that remained was a long drive to a long flight. I'd felt the Bandon hangover before, but not on this trip. The anticipation wasn't over; it was just kicking in as I set a new destination and saw the good news on my phone: just two hundred more miles to Gearhart.

GEARHART, OREGON

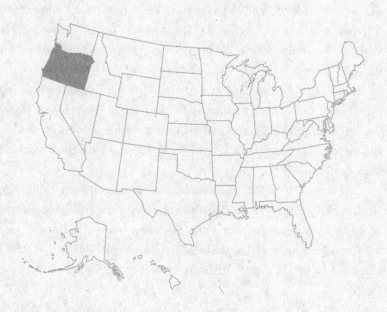

At home we called them hipsters, that bearded lot in flannel shirts and sec-
ondhand sweaters, trucker hats, and thick-rimmed glasses. But here in Oregon, I think they just called them people. And the people were everywhere
at my next course the following afternoon, after I'd left Bandon Dunes and
headed north toward Oregon's hippest farmhouse.

The McMenamin brothers' trippy empire of hotels, pubs, and music
venues spans Oregon and Washington, and from an outsider's perspective,
it seemed they'd captured the former's peace, love, and dope aesthetic and
turned it into a beer-flowing bonanza. They converted schools and rundown boarding houses—and old farms, in the case of the hotel I'd landed at
in Edgefield—into places at which you'd expect Jerry Garcia to be picking

notes in the lobby. The brothers—both in their sixties now, but still an untucked and bearded business team—had nailed a formula of wall-to-wall psychedelic art, microbrews, and gastropub kitchens, with the Grateful Dead ever-present on the speakers. Their locations had a dedicated following who traveled the state like Deadheads chasing the next show, getting stamps in their McMenamins passports to prove they'd had a pint in their fifty-plus locations, thus achieving rare status as "Cosmic Tripsters." My Grateful Dead phase was far in the rearview, so I was here in Edgefield for the golf.

I'd read that the Edgefield property held two par 3 layouts where you played amid the blackberry bushes and looked for the Garcia bronze to pay homage to Jerry. This blend of golf and counterculture sounded irresistible, and a good way to forget that it was Father's Day and I was three thousand miles from home.

Unfortunately, the McMenamins faithful had not forgotten the holiday, and had all decided to reward Dad with some homebrew among the gardens of the compound. In the early 1900s, the seventy-four-acre county "poor farm" was used to house Portland's indigent denizens. Today it was full of shops and bars and a pottery studio, with an open-air concert venue in the back.

I weaved through the Sunday crowd of half-drunk dads pushing strollers, carrying a handful of wedges and feeling terribly conspicuous in spikes and golf attire. I finally found the golf holes, where guys in sandals and women in flowy dresses giggled around the hills in eightsomes. The tee sheet was packed; if I could play tomorrow, a woman told me, she could get me the first slot. As my tomorrows were always five hours away, I told her I'd give it a go and see if they'd let a single play through. She wished me luck; these weren't golfers out here. I was the only one who'd bothered to bring my own clubs, so the wave-through was etiquette with which they would be unfamiliar.

I made the best of it, playing a few extra balls and enjoying the clever assortment of tiny greens tucked into pocket gardens. The second green was set back on a hillside where I interrupted a couple of twentysomethings who'd had their afternoon's share of IPA and sunshine. The girl scrambled to replace half of her sundress as they lay there smiling in the grass like some sort of French sculpture, tangled up in boozy bliss. *You don't see that at Shinnecock*, I thought to myself.

With the course well clogged, I surrendered after eight holes. I never saw that Jerry sculpture, but I had the scorecard and could cross Edgefield off my list. I hurried to check into my room within the stately main house, eager to catch the final group of the Open at Pebble Beach. I rolled my bags through the restaurant, then down a long concrete corridor with wide and heavy doors that recalled its days as a state institution and into a room painted with bright psychotropic murals and doilies and stained-glass chandeliers. I felt like I was here to get my palm read. The room was cozy enough, but it lacked one essential—no TV.

I can think of few moments in my life when I felt less cool than in that lobby full of tie-dye, asking a girl with dreadlocks where I could watch the US Open.

"The what?"

"The golf. On TV."

She informed me that they didn't have any TVs—this was a getaway from screens, and televisions would spoil the vibe. I understood her point, but Gary Woodland was making a run, and I was playing Pebble Beach for the first time in a few months. So, like a grumpy dad who'd been driving with the kids for too long, I checked out on the spot and headed for a McMenamins where I knew there'd be golf on in a room named Caddyshack.

I had found Gearhart by way of the greatest golf course in the world, and when I began dreaming up this search for its American counterpart, I had kept the Gearhart Links in my back pocket should the rest of the trip not provide a clear front-runner.

Dating to a three-hole layout in 1888, the Gearhart Links was the oldest golf west of the Mississippi, and had recently twinned with my beloved Carne in Ireland. Twinning with a course basically meant your members visited each other's courses every few years and maybe hung their sign in your pro shop. Given Gearhart's connection to Carne, its members had decided to invite me out the year before to talk about my Irish travels. What I found when I arrived was the rare American course that deserved the label *links* in its title. It was built on sandy earth with windblown features and showcased a treeless landscape of bounding fairways that I fell hard for.

It had been a regular childhood haunt of Tour champion Peter Jacobsen, and the course had been thriving since Timothy Boyle, CEO of Columbia Sportswear, took full ownership in 2011. Boyle owned a house nearby and wanted to see his local public track survive, so he oversaw a deforesting of the layout and restored its seaside style. Boyle also brought in pro Jason Bangild from Nanea in Hawaii, likely irking some of his fellow CEO members (Nanea was a small Fortune 500 fraternity) for stealing one of the best head pros in the business.

Not only did Gearhart's golf mimic the style of the British Isles but its setting as a community hub was that essentially Irish and Scottish ingredient that even our sandiest American links tended to lack. Beside the first tee sat a cedar-shingled McMenamins hotel with its comfy Sand Trap Pub, near a patio and firepit crowded with folks who'd come down from Portland for the day. At the turn, its new Sand Bar was more than a halfway house—it had a little putting green and a homey bar that was crowded even in wintertime, when locals would light fires and hang there with hot toddies in the snow.

With beach just beyond the mounds at the edge of the course, the Gearhart Links bustled with walkers and diners and drinkers, and some golfers, too, all milling about a shared space of tee box, bar, and hotel. And in that hotel, Jason had reserved for me the same room from my first visit. It was called Caddyshack, and it indeed held a television, along with a painting of a witch riding a golf club. There were carved gophers sticking out of my headboard, too, but that didn't distract me from catching the final three holes at Pebble. Good on ya, Gary Woodland.

Losing track of whom I was meant to play with, and where, had become a reliable snafu on this trek, leading to awkward pro shop negotiations regarding the six guys who'd shown up for the four spots they'd offered me. That wouldn't be a worry today; my buddy Jason, the head pro, would make room for whatever platoon of partners turned up—and good thing, because when

I turned the corner the next morning, Rob Ahlschwede was on the putting green, along with a gaggle of Northwest Hickory Players. I ran back to my car to slip the hickory putter he'd given me into the bag and headed down to say hello and thank them for this surprise reunion (surprise to me, at least—I couldn't remember if I'd invited them).

They knew Gearhart well, a hickory favorite for its fairways' low-ball hospitality. Rob's Santa-size beard and personality could be overshadowed only by the guy who happened to be standing next to him.

Penn. We hadn't met until he decided to spend ten days with me in Scotland, where we bonded over Highland golf, harrowing drives, and a meal of singular culinary perfection. We played Ireland together the next year, and Scotland again the year after. Golf brought people together, but it was golf travel that truly cemented the friendships in my world. It was clear after those long-ago days in Machrihanish that Penn was going to be a part of the rest of my life. Chasing golf courses helped ensure that was the case, and seeing him on the practice green at Gearhart sparked a flash of joys past, reminding me what I was doing out here.

He greeted me with a big hug and his Georgia drawl: "Tommy Coyne! Love you, man." *Love you, man* was his catchphrase for *hello*, *goodbye*, and *nice putt*, but I believe he meant it. We texted a few times a week, and he still told confused strangers about beating me on the final green at Tobermory. Pushing seventy now, he was relearning golf with a new knee, but remained dedicated to walking the course and carrying his own bag. He was Georgia red to the bone—Go Dawgs—but had also sent me pictures from a #MeToo march in which he donned a knitted pink hat. He'd come up to Gearhart after a visit to his daughter in Portland, to see if everything I'd told him about the place was true.

It was honest, intriguing, public links golf, with that breath of brackish air Bamberger talked about. Penn agreed it was special. While I loved that Gearhart had figured out a way to welcome daily fee golf while still cultivating a membership—how Scottish of them—I was pretty sure Penn's favorite feature was the Sand Trap, where he made fast friends with a crowd of locals. Within fifteen minutes they were buying him a dram and slapping him on the back.

"The name's Penn!" he called over the roar of happy hour. "With two Ns!"

A soupy-eyed gentleman put his arm around him. "Well, I'm Bob! With one O!"

Jason met us at the bar for dinner. He was a towering but soft-mannered guy who had brought an unbothered Hawaiian air with him to Oregon. In his hand was a brown paper bag.

"You didn't," I said.

"Oh yes, I did," he said, opening the bag to reveal a tall pile of clean clothes. "You said you needed laundry."

"I said I needed *access* to the laundry. I didn't expect you to wash these yourself."

"We're a full-service club here at Gearhart," he said, lifting a finger to order himself a beer. If there was ever a club where the pro drank with the members, this was it.

I dug through the bag. "Dude! You washed and folded my skivvies?"

"Yeah, let's not talk about that."

Penn tore himself away from his fan club to order his meal. He eyed the menu over his glasses, then asked the bartender, "What can you tell me about this barbecue chicken dish here?"

She eyed him with little enthusiasm. "It's a pizza," she said.

"Yeah," I said. "It's round. It comes on baked dough."

Penn dropped his head and smiled. "I didn't see that it was in the pizza section, asshole," he mumbled to me without malice, then told the waitress, "I'll have that."

I replayed the last month for Penn and Jason as the bar crowd thinned out. On the stool next to Jason were a pair of sneakers I had been staring at for the last two hours. I finally took a break from my stories and asked who had forgotten their shoes.

Jason looked over at them, unfazed. "Oh. Those are Joe's. Hey, Joe! Come get your shoes!"

A guy in golf spikes fell out of a booth at the other end of the room. "Hey, thanks, man. I need these."

Gearhart was no Bandon Dunes (at Bandon they would have wrapped Joe's shoes up and delivered them to his cottage), but if forced to choose between a getaway to either, I'd have no easy time of it. Bandon was the can't-miss trip, but Gearhart felt like the jaunt for budget-minded buddy trips, or a Bandon add-on for golfers in the know. An idyllic beach hotel overlooking a dozen fairways wasn't its only draw: The Highlands nine-holer up the road sustained the Scottish theme, aside from the gang of elk that the course's owner, Mayor Matty Brown, tried to keep off the greens by spraying wolf piss (it was worth a visit to Highlands Golf Club just to meet him, a forty-year-old PGA pro who looked about nineteen and had been elected mayor of Gearhart in a landslide). And after a few more minutes in the car, you could find yourself at lovely Astoria, where geologic sorcery turned their linksland into long, high-banked gullies; it was golf through a halfpipe park that had hosted the likes of Palmer, Watson, Couples, and Sneed. Its wild dunescape earned it the title "St. Andrews of the Pacific," though I didn't recall any hills like these in Fife.

I left Gearhart with clean laundry and a candidate for the Great American Golf Course. The Gearhart Links was a course of the people, by the people, and certainly for the people. It had melting-pot grit, with city-upon-a-hill quality. Add some apple pie at the turn and it ticked every Yankee cliché I could conjure. Whether it would hold the top spot in five months' time was too far a forecast, but it would surely rank high among golf destinations when my bags' wheels stopped spinning.

I navigated my way to the Portland airport, where I awaited a flight to the greatest tee time I had ever booked. And in this case, it was far more about the time than the tee.

FAIRBANKS, ALASKA

It didn't take long to find the bear. A stuffed grizzly was flashing his claws beside the baggage claim, and my hotel—the Bear Lodge—had two more in glass cases. When friends heard I was playing all fifty states, a regular question was, "Alaska?" And I assured them it was top of the list for two reasons: my first potential bear sighting, and my first golf beneath the midnight sun.

Fairbanks was as far north as I could find golf in America, and north was key for catching a full twenty-four hours of sunlight. It meant I might have to settle for posed bears in a lobby, as grizzlies were more abundant down south around Anchorage, but it was an easy compromise; I was here on the summer solstice to see a sun that didn't set.

At one a.m., I checked in to the Bear Lodge under dusky skies and slept hard. In the morning I headed out for a look around before golf at America's most northerly course, the elaborately named Fairbanks Golf Course. I expected the town to be a burg of swinging-door saloons set into rocky crags, muddy streets full of shaggy prospectors who paid for their whiskey with nuggets of gold. Instead, I found Starbucks, dollar stores, and two-lane highways beside apartment complexes and parking lots full of unpolished trucks. I zoomed past one spot that grabbed my eye and spun my car back around. It was a squat, whitish shack that may have been abandoned, but its hand-painted BARBER sign was a welcome discovery. I couldn't show up at home tomorrow looking like this.

I pushed open a torn screen door, stepped over empty bottles of antifreeze, and as my eyes adjusted to the darkness within, I made out a man standing over a chair, trapped in some sort of jungle. Dusty vines and fake plants choked the room, and when he looked over at me, the guy with clippers called out with a southern twang, "Come on in, stranger. Be right with you—grab a seat."

He was a tall Black gentleman with white hair and a bent frame, and was busy cleaning up the sideburns of a guy in a polo shirt. He wore a loose yellow button-down and his fingers looked shakier than I preferred in my barbers, but how many chances was I going to have to get my hair cut in Alaska? Plus, there was plenty to look at while I waited.

The barbershop seemed to function as some sort of outpost general store where pioneers could acquire anything their homesteads required. (There was a food market and hardware store across the street, so I wondered if any of this stuff ever sold.) From the pipes hung umbrellas and wide-collared shirts and fur coats draped in plastic, above a tabletop *Pac-Man* machine that I would have played if I had any change. There were piles of old VHS movies and racks of CDs, sunglasses hanging from a wire, and a semi-legible sign advertising fresh eggs and ice cream. In a glass case stood old dolls next to a neck massager, and by my feet was a watercooler jug full of pennies. On the chair next to me sat an old ammo box of unspecified contents, but at only $12.95, it seemed a good deal. The barber sent his current client off with a handshake—old pals, from what I could guess—then waved me up into his forest.

I took my seat in his cracked leather chair just as the phone rang. "One second," he said, picking it up from behind one of the plants.

I was going to be late for golf, but I was committed to this haircut, too curious about what might be looking back at me in the mirror when he was done. For ten minutes, I listened to him barter with a voice on the other end of the line. Someone, it seemed, wanted to buy this property, and while I typically preferred getting my hair cut in places that weren't going out of business, I felt powerless to leave. The cape he had already draped over me weighed heavy.

He hung up the phone, complaining how the son of a bitch wanted to rob him blind, and from there, our conversation came easy. Joe had been cutting hair up here for fifty years, and at eighty years old, he was looking to retire. He'd come from South Carolina, and his daughter was visiting next week from California. He hadn't seen her in thirty-seven years. "My daughters, they're still mad at me for not marrying their mother," he said. "What can you do? I was young. Wasn't the marrying type."

Just then, the mailman pushed open the door, and Joe kicked up a conversation with him as well. "Say, where's that good-looking lady who was delivering the mail last week? What's her name?"

"Beatrice?" the mail carrier said.

"Yeah, Beatrice. You tell her I was asking for her, all right?"

The man laughed and said he would, and Joe turned on his clippers.

"I hit on all those ladies," he told me. "They love it."

Our conversation turned to why I was here, and when he heard golf, he got pretty passionate about Tiger Woods.

"Now you tell me: Why did Tiger go and get married? Tell me, why?"

I said I didn't know.

"Come on, Tiger," he continued. "You know who you are. You love women. You want to play the field, then you go and do that."

While twenty minutes before I'd taken Joe for a half-mad haberdasher, I soon realized he was something of a Fairbanks tycoon. He owned four hundred acres of property down the road that he was turning into a subdivision, and asked me how many acres he would need for a nine-hole golf course.

"Fifty, maybe? Seventy-five?"

"That's all? Damn. I got plenty more than that, my friend. Plenty more."

He cut my hair using only clippers—"Hands don't do so well with the scissors anymore"—then flipped on some sort of vacuum-tube apparatus to suck the loose hair off my head.

"You want a shave?" he asked, and I paused. I had always wanted a straight-razor shave in a barber's chair, but I was late, and that tremble in his hands . . . I wondered how many types of hepatitis were out there, and if you could catch them all in one sitting.

"Absolutely," I said, curiosity winning over caution. A box on his shelf spit warm cream onto his hand that he spread across my cheeks; I left without a nick, and with a pretty fair haircut—everything the same as when I came in, just a half inch shorter.

As I pushed open the door on my way out, Joe called to me: "Hey, if you wanna go halves on that golf course, you let me know!" I told him I certainly would. *Now* that *would be my Great American Golf Course*, I thought, *me out there mowing the fairways, and Joe inside selling eggs and VHS copies of* Weekend at Bernie's. I filed it under future book ideas and headed for a tee time I'd already missed.

The gravel parking lot at the Fairbanks nine-holer was more crowded than I had hoped, and I found three chagrined guys hanging around a tailgate—my playing partners, I guessed. I'd met them all through emails asking if I was coming to Alaska; Scott had traveled from Anchorage with Kyle, and Gerry had flown up from Seattle, which made me feel a little worse about being late, but we had all day and all night to get our golf in. Literally.

The head pro squeezed us into a full tee sheet and asked his assistant pro to shepherd us around. It was a thoughtful gesture, though the instructions Chuck the assistant apparently heard were, "Go show them how awesome you are." He swaggered up to the first tee and introduced himself without smiling. "I'm supposed to play with you guys," he said, then teed his ball up, giving himself the honors. Kyle was documenting our round for his YouTube webisodes, so he asked Chuck if he minded being filmed.

"Nah. Doesn't bother me. I'm used to it."

I swallowed a laugh when I realized he was serious and watched as he banged one out into the fairway, holding his follow-through with muscles taut. I don't think we asked, but he told us he played on the Adams Tour for a while. I looked at the smiles on my partners' faces. Every one of us wanted to ask him what the Adams Tour was, but we refrained; we were getting big-timed by the assistant pro at the nine-hole Fairbanks Golf Course, and that was too awesome a thing to interrupt.

As a course guide, Chuck really let his boss down. His lone advice on a twisty, confusing course was, "Stay left on every hole." Okay. On number five, a hard-turning dogleg, I stayed left. Well left.

"Not left enough," he said. "That one's gone." Then he stepped up and aimed fifty yards farther left of where I had been pointing. He popped it over a pine none of us were looking at and said, "That's on the green." He putted out for birdie while the rest of us kicked around poisonous Alaskan foliage in search of our balls.

While Chuck may have given us no help that afternoon, he did give us something to talk about at dinner. Downtown Fairbanks was hopping: The streets were closed off for pedestrians, and locals wove their way from bar to bar. We'd wandered into a Thursday-night festival, and Kyle explained that energy levels in Alaska were off the charts during the summer as folks emerged from hibernation. Kyle worked in finance for the oil companies, and Scott sold pipes to them. Everything up here was oil dependent, they explained; every Alaskan received an annual oil dividend check, and the state's budget was tied to the price of crude. As I listened, I saw my and Joe's course coming to life before me. Greens fees be damned, we'd always have that oil money.

We had time for dessert before our eleven p.m. tee time, but were careful to budget an hour for procuring clearances to get on base. Chena Bend GC is on Fort Wainwright, home to the army's Arctic Warriors (and the perch from which they could see Russia, so I'd heard). Kyle said it was the best course in Alaska. As a military course, its budget wasn't linked to customers, and it was guaranteed to be in good shape. I recalled how my dad said you could always tell whether the commanding officer was a golfer by the condition of the base's course.

We were a bit early for peak conditions—they started in July and lasted all of two months—but it had been a mild spring, so Kyle expected the greens to have thawed by now. It was June 20. *Sorry, Joe*, I thought. *I'd never survive up here as a golfer.*

We waited in line at Fort Wainwright's welcome center behind a queue of girlfriends dressed in bits of pink and black, ready to start the weekend early. Officers ran our driver's licenses through some sort of database, then gave us passes to present to guards with big guns, who waved us through and into a village of low, quiet buildings with an empty golf clubhouse at its far end.

One woman remained to check us in for our tee time, then locked the door behind us as we yawned and headed for the first tee. My body wasn't quite sure what I was doing, but unblemished fairways framed by Alaskan pines were like smelling salts, and we hustled forth to join the mosquitoes, who clearly didn't give a damn that the sky said they shouldn't be out.

Joining us at Chena Bend was another Scott, from the nearby town of North Pole, which was south of here, which he admitted was confusing. He was a builder and a two handicap who loved to play this late; this was his busy season, but when you could tee off at midnight, you could get your golf in without losing hours on a jobsite. Between golf shots and reapplications of black-market Alaskan DEET (I think Scott mixed it in his bathtub), we kept checking the time. Finally, on the sixth hole, we paused to take a selfie of us golfing with phones that read midnight. At around one a.m., the sun dipped and slid along the treetops, then lifted itself into an orange sky as we finished the back nine.

I remember playing well—the card says 73—but the details are lost in a drowsy fog. There were dark trees and a river and glossy greens, and we got soaked by the early morning sprinklers. It all felt like a kids' sleepover party: we went into it on a sugar high, with laughter and loud voices and bold plans for the night, and walked out of it with sagging shoulders and sleepy eyes, wishing our moms were there to drive us home to our own beds.

The ride across base and back through town had an eerie, apocalyptic vibe. The sun was glowing, but the curtains were drawn tight, the stores all closed. I stopped at the Bear Lodge to rinse off the repellant—a fire hose would have helped—then headed to the airport, where I found Kyle passed out on a bench, waiting for his flight home. I boarded a four a.m. to Seattle, then connected for Philadelphia, and walked in my door at ten p.m. Eastern Time, not quite sure how I'd gotten from the Bear Lodge to here, and still smelling like bug spray.

The girls had waited up to hug their dad, and I gave them their stuffed goats from Silvies before Allyson reminded me where the bed was. I wanted to sleep, but my head and body were on opposite coasts, and I had just finally nodded off when my alarm buzzed. Allyson shook me out of bed and wished me luck. It was club championship weekend, and I was on the tee in thirty minutes.

BEACHWOOD, OHIO

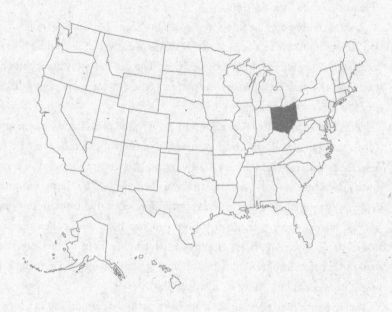

His name tag read BIG MONEY, and by the seventh hole, that was what we were losing. He'd been a caddie at Canterbury for twenty-three years, so I couldn't blame his reads. The place was a sneaky beast from the back tees, and Big Money elucidated the problem as our team went four-down.

"CPR. That's what we need." Up to this point, he had been all jokes and smiles, an African American looper with a gray beard and a golf shirt worn thin at the shoulders. I wasn't playing great, but mouth-to-mouth seemed excessive.

"CPR," he continued. "Caddie-Player Relationship. I'm getting a copyright on that, CPR. That is what we need to establish here. I'm the caddie, but I'm the psychiatrist, too. I read the putts, I get you a cocktail, whatever you need, but I keep you motivated and inspired. Once we get the CPR rolling, then we work on the PPR."

Points per reception? I wondered to myself.

"Player-Player Relationship. You got to get gelling with your partner, 'cause y'all are getting killed right now. Then when we have the CPR and the PPR working, it's time for CCR."

I was catching on. "Caddie-Caddie Relationship." I nodded.

"That's right. We're a team, too. I read a putt for the other caddie if he's raking; he reads for me if I'm forecaddying. The caddies working together, the caddies helping their players, the players getting on the same page—that's how this all's supposed to go."

Big Money had nailed the recipe for a great round of golf, and I was ready to run through a wall for him. But nowhere in the CPR step-by-step did it describe how to find Canterbury's fairways, and his inspiration was lost on a loose driver. Still, an ugly card couldn't ruin Canterbury. The Herbert Strong design was intimately shaped and expertly rumpled, a ride through uneven lies and history. Strong, an English-born pro, had been one of the originators of the PGA of America, helping to establish it in 1916 at the behest of department-store mogul Rodman Wanamaker, who thought an association of golf pros could help boost equipment sales.

Set in a suburb of Cleveland, Canterbury occupied a bright star in Cleveland's beleaguered sports constellation. Next to Oakland Hills, it was the only other club to host the US Open, PGA Championship, US Senior Open, US Am, and Senior PGA, and had crowned champions like Walter Hagen, Jack Nicklaus, Arnold Palmer, and Mark O'Meara as a twenty-two-year-old amateur. Its US Open in 1946 took a whopping 108 holes to crown a winner, when Lloyd Mangrum returned from winning two Purple Hearts in World War II to finally best Byron Nelson and Vic Ghezzi on a very long weekend (the US Open used to end with thirty-six holes on Saturday, and when all three remained tied after an eighteen-hole Sunday playoff, they had to go around one more time).

The '46 Open was the first time the tournament had been held since 1941, after golf took a detour during WWII. With rubber in high demand for military tires, golf balls were a rare commodity, and even though Roosevelt was pushing the game as a means of exercise, folks were hoarding their Spalding Dots. Golfers resorted to playing refurbished balls that had been repaired with a new compound called balata; it would become the go-to for back-spinners for the next fifty years (I'd spend many an allowance on sleeves of balatas, only to gash them useless by the fourth strike).

The courses had also been forced to adapt. As detailed by John Strege in *When War Played Through*, Augusta was turned into a cow pasture, providing beef to nearby Camp Gordon. Congressional became a covert training facility for special ops, and other layouts around the country sprouted victory gardens to help augment the food supply as commercial crops went off to the troops. The Red Cross shipped clubs and balls to POW camps, where German guards were happy for soldiers to be golfing on improvised layouts instead of plotting another escape.

Ben Hogan and Sam Snead had enlisted in the army and navy, respectively, while Byron Nelson, barred from service due to a blood-clotting disorder, toured the country putting on exhibitions to raise money for the war effort. Before shipping off, Hogan may or may not have won the US Open in 1942. Its official title was the Hale America National Open Golf Tournament, and though it was meant to be a wartime substitute, it sure sounded like a US Open: hosted by the USGA, featuring a field of elite professionals, and offering the winner a medal that was almost an exact replica of the US Open prize. The debate as to whether it counts as Hogan's fifth Open persists among historians. In the field that week was Lloyd Mangrum, who would win that next official US Open at Canterbury, and who would go on to say, "I don't suppose that any of the pro or amateur golfers who were combat soldiers, Marines, or sailors will soon be able to think of a three-putt as one of the really bad troubles in life."

I taught *The Canterbury Tales* every other semester, so I was keen to hear the backstory on a course from Ohio borrowing the name of an ancient English city and using its coat of arms as a logo. Turned out the club was named after Canterbury, Connecticut, the birthplace of city founder General Moses Cleaveland, who was alleged to have traded Cleveland's first NFL draft pick for a wagon. The logo was a must-buy in the pro shop; its medieval heraldry depicted a royal leopard above three black crows borrowed from the arms of everybody's favorite martyr, St. Thomas Becket, the erstwhile Archbishop of Canterbury.

At Canterbury I posted a score that was triple my handicap, but that was a better result than the heavy number I'd hung on the scoreboard a week prior in the club championship. I had decades' worth of club championship catastrophes to compare it to, and it ranked toward the top for both embarrassment and lack of fun. I expected my game to be sluggish with jet lag, but after keeping it close to par on a seven-thousand-yard test in Alaska, I figured I could sleep-walk my way into the championship bracket at my backdoor track. Instead, I walked my way into an afternoon nap after 92 whacks and a missed cut—my highest score ever at my course—alongside a caddie who was stumbling through his hangover. As I struggled to manage my own meltdown, I had to keep an eye on his, too; he was tilting leftward as he walked, and nearly tipped over trying to pick up a flag. I might have been upset if I had a number going, but instead I just tried to get us through our respective messes, both finally able to go home and sleep it all off.

My swing through western Pennsylvania and Ohio and Michigan and Illinois was a stark contrast to that morning, as pro loopers like Big Money became the stars of my midwestern travels. Caddie culture was thriving in the heart of America, thanks in large part to the Evans Scholars Foundation, named for its creator, elite Chicago amateur Chick Evans, who wrote a popular golf book in 1921. Fearing the royalties would jeopardize his amateur status (I harbor no such anxieties), he put the proceeds toward a fund that, today, awards hundreds of full college scholarships to caddies every year, including room and board at Evans Scholarship Houses.

The allure of a full ride kept caddie standards high through these middle states, and it also meant you were as likely to have a young woman on your bag as a young man. Two African American high school girls carried for me at two of the most esteemed clubs in Chicago (Chicago Golf Club and Onwentsia), which was, unfortunately, something I had never witnessed back east. It reminded me that carts were golf's nemesis, and that while junior programs were fine, the best way to build a lifetime golfer was to put a couple of dollars in a kid's pocket during summer break and let them learn.

Oakland Hills in Michigan boasted two Donald Ross designs (one of which went public during the Depression), and had hosted six US Opens, three PGAs, two US Amateurs, and a Ryder Cup—its walk of fame down to the first tee was a trail of famous bronze faces, but the best I met was Gavin's, a skinny fifteen-year-old whom my wife would have called adorable. He'd already done eighteen that morning but was happy to grab my bag and do another loop. Gavin had a bit of teenage swagger to him, and during one of our rain delays camped out at the halfway house, I asked him if he played.

"Of course I play," he said. "I had a hole-in-one last week."

"Did you?" I said, and asked for the play-by-play.

"I had a pretty good round going through hole fourteen. This was over at Pine Lake. I had one forty-five and hit a knock-down eight. The pin was front, and it kind of landed in the fringe over the bunker on the right side, and had some crazy draw spin on it. My buddy was like, 'It went in!' and I'm like, 'There's no way.' Sure enough, walked out to it a couple minutes later, ball's in the hole. First hole-in-one of my life. And best round of my life, even-par seventy-two."

I congratulated him and told him he was pretty young to be firing 72s and dunking 8 irons.

"I'm a swimmer, too," he said. "I've been swimming since I was seven, competitively. I swim distance freestyle, the two hundred and the five hundred. I do it every morning, and yeah, it's great exercise."

"You're a pretty impressive young man, Gavin." I smiled.

"Thanks. I'm a cancer survivor, too."

I stopped. "You're what?"

"I'm a cancer survivor. I was diagnosed with leukemia when I was ten," he said. "Three years later, I finished chemotherapy. So now it's been two years since the end of my treatment. I'm cancer-free, living a healthy lifestyle." Gavin's upbeat stoicism belied his age. He sounded like a wise man recounting a life void of regret or resentment.

"And here you are now," I said.

"Here I am. Caddying thirty-six a day at Oakland Hills."

Four days later, I would meet another caddie full of surprises in Chicago. North Shore was a level layout by the prestigious design firm of Colt, MacKenzie, and Alison, and had hosted the US Open in 1933, when Johnny

Goodman became the last amateur to ever lift the trophy. Today the club was a Catholic golfing haven (I was surprised to find that Chicago's private clubs remained organized along religious lines), and it seemed as if half the membership was there to welcome a fellow Notre Dame alum to their course, including my caddie, who had just graduated that spring. Jackson was looping his way through graduate school, and by the look of him, he was pursuing a master's in the bench press. He was a block of a dude, with a chiseled jaw and thick brown hair with a careful part. He had to roll up his sleeves to let his biceps breathe, and his shoulders were like side tables on which he rested two bag straps. I don't think he put down our bags once the entire round; I doubted whether he noticed they were even there.

I wondered aloud if he had played football at Notre Dame, and he explained that no, he had been a boxer. Notre Dame's boxing club had been around for ninety years and was one of the campus's more celebrated intramurals. Jackson had been its captain. *God bless your sparring partners*, I thought. I asked him what he was studying in graduate school, and when he said fine arts, I checked my ears and asked him to say that again.

"I'm doing a master of fine arts. I'm a painter," he said.

"Wait a second. I have a master of fine arts. You don't look like any MFA student I've ever seen."

He laughed and showed me some of his work on his phone. He specialized in pop art paintings, and his oil-on-canvas collages were good—outstanding, really. I looked forward to adding one to my art collection. Well, I looked forward to starting an art collection, with some work from my friend Jackson Wrede, the caddie-painter-pugilist.

En route to Chicago, I'd enjoyed more standout looper performances back in Pittsburgh. At Fox Chapel, where Brian Silva had restored its Raynor punch bowl and Biarritz and Redan features, I called my caddie Adam by the name Andy for sixteen holes, and like a true pro jock, he didn't correct me once. Over at Oakmont, I stepped back and placed my life in my caddie's hands. If there was ever a course for taking directions, Oakmont was it; we all knew it as America's sternest test, and when my caddie handed me a putter for my second shot on number one—I was 150 yards away—its reputation was validated.

As I watched my ball roll down a sloping fairway, through the green, and into a backside bunker, I felt my legs wobble with fear. *This place really is impossible.* But I left Oakmont convinced of a few things: One was that the Fox Chapel/Oakmont combo was in a dead heat with Merion/Pine Valley in the Philadelphia versus Pittsburgh debate. In all my travels, I had never felt more engrossed in a round of golf; every step, every shot, I was at full attention. You couldn't rest for a single breath, and even as we got pulled off the course twice for lightning, the focus never faltered. It was difficult, but it never played unfair. I'd visited a half-dozen Florida courses that I'd consider crueler, simply because tedious architecture filled them with water. Oakmont required you to play away from pins and from greens sometimes, but it was delicious medicine to take; every shot demanded strategy, every swing deliberate purpose. How a steel baron named Henry Fownes designed this place, and this place only, seemed one of golf's great riddles. Was his creation the Great American Golf Course? For slopes, speed, challenge, I'd played few better. For courses bisected by a turnpike, it had no rival. Oakmont had hosted more US Opens (nine) than any other course, but I couldn't help thinking that at least some of its stature came not from its golf course but from its pro shop.

Bob Ford had grown up in the town next to mine, and when I arrived at Waynesborough on a morning back in 2018, the property was already buzzing with the news: *Bob Ford's out here. Did you hear? Bob Ford's in the group ahead of us.* He was the only lifelong club pro I could recall whose name people actually knew, and he was back in town to be inducted into his high school hall of fame. He had already received the Bob Jones Award, the USGA's highest honor, and had recently retired from Oakmont, where he'd been the golfer in charge for thirty-seven years—and for sixteen of them he'd done double duty as the winter pro at Florida's Seminole (two of the most coveted jobs in the PGA world, held by the same person), where he was still head professional.

On a previous trip to Florida, I'd had the chance to ask him how he'd achieved such celebrity status when club pros so frequently came and went. Ever the humble statesman, he explained that he didn't consider himself a celebrity, and that any reputation he'd acquired was likely due to his playing career. He had teed it up in thirteen majors, plus eight more senior majors, and was the last head pro to make the cut in the US Open at his own course, when he did so in 1983 at Oakmont, finishing four strokes ahead of Jack Nicklaus. He came in twenty-sixth place that year but took home the biggest paycheck, since head pros used to run merchandise sales at the US Open (a scenario I find unfathomable, considering how shopping pavilions have overtaken major championships). A tall and soft-spoken man, Bob had gray hair cut tight as an admiral's, and he exuded the sort of class and confidence I associated with a high-ranking officer. His family tree of former assistant professionals now populated head jobs at all the best courses in America and carried forth his attitude of "It's nice to be important, but it's important to be nice."

Mr. Ford (if you've ever met him, you know why Bob doesn't feel right) helped make Oakmont's name a misnomer by way of a tree removal program that liberated its vistas and turned it into one of the meanest yet most visually stunning courses in the United States. Today its deforestation is used as a model for tree remediation projects elsewhere, but at the time it was highly controversial. As the story goes, Oakmont's trees had to be cleared at night so as not to alert the membership; the wood was chopped and removed under cover of darkness, with replacement sod laid before sunrise. When members came into the shop wondering where that tree on seven went, or if they had imagined a tree by the fourteenth tee, Mr. Ford explained it had been felled by thunder and lightning. (Far be it from Bob Ford to lie to his members: Thunder and Lightning were the names the Oakmont staff had given to their two chain saws.)

Mr. Ford had his own book's worth of stories—a favorite of mine was how Ben Hogan paid his bets at Seminole with a signed check, knowing its winner would never cash it—but two that he's reluctant to tell prove the kind of person he is: A member had told me that Mr. Ford was given an Oakmont membership upon his retirement, but he refused the gesture; he insisted on paying full fare and joining just as any other member would. And when he had the chance to break Arnold Palmer's course record at Mr. Palmer's own Latrobe Country Club, Mr. Ford finished his round in dramatic fashion.

"We call it the Palmer Cup matches, and we play it at Arnie's place. He goes out first, and I'm in the second group behind him," Mr. Ford explained as I took notes in the bag room at Seminole one afternoon. "I just got off to a ridiculous start. I hit a three wood on number three, which is a par five, and it went up into the trees, and we went looking for it. We never could find it, until we got down to the green and it was in the cup. It had obviously hit a tree and went in the hole for a two. I'd birdied the hole before, and birdied the hole after, so all of a sudden I'm five under early. I guess I got to nine under through fourteen, with two par fives coming up, both reachable. It so happened that that morning I had seen Arnold's scorecard in the clubhouse, with his course record on it, sixty. Well, if I make another birdie, I tie him, and if I birdie both of the par fives, I beat his record. We closed out our match on fourteen, and the guys in the group said, 'Come on, let's finish up, you're going to beat Arnold's record.' And I said, 'No, we're going to go have a beer. I'm done.'"

I suppose there are two kinds of people in the world: "Play On" people, and "Let's Go Have a Beer" people. I'd like to think I'd have called it Miller time, but with two reachable par 5s still to come?

Sorry, Mr. Palmer, but there's only one Bob Ford.

ROSCOMMON, MICHIGAN

It pained me to find Ann Arbor so enchanting, with its bevy of bookshops and cafes and theaters and brewpubs—it was a downtown quite unlike South Bend's, a place we rarely ventured to from our golden bubble up the street. I donned all my shamrocks for golf at a lovely Ann Arbor muni called Leslie Park, where across the sweeping hills of a former apple orchard I battled a "Michigan Man" for five bucks. I had him down three at the turn, then went out there and tied one for the Gipper, three-putting the last green for a halve. It stung all the way up to Forest Dunes, where I arrived at sunset and checked into my cottage. I caught a late dinner on a patio that overlooked a green hugged by water, then went to bed only to be awoken at three a.m. by pounding at the door.

It was Brendan, my hometown cohort and one-putting nemesis, standing in the rain with a ponytail that had grown an inch since I'd left Philadelphia. Brendan was handy with a camera, so I'd asked him to meet me at Forest Dunes to help film Doak's new reversible routing for YouTube. He had arrived eight hours late, and without a golf bag in sight. The airline believed his clubs might be in Detroit.

Planted deep in the woods of northern Michigan, Forest Dunes was one of the less convenient rendezvous points on my itinerary, but Brendan was curious about its two-courses-in-one routing, and I was eager to test my game against my short-legged rival, who, when he wasn't crowing about his record in our matches, sent weekly texts of encouragement that made home feel a little closer.

Brendan had waited five hours for a delayed flight to Grand Rapids, then drove four hours through dark forest roads in a downpour, slapping himself awake with a tub of coffee and a sack of gas station donuts as his lone provisions. But he was up early the next morning armed with a toothbrush and a drone—the rest of his luggage was set to arrive tomorrow—and headed to the Forest Dunes clubhouse, where he shopped like a doctor forced to golf at a convention. Shoes, clothes, hat, rental clubs, and glove; for a golfer who so carefully curated his bag and attire, Brendan was way off his beam, and I felt his agony. Losing our clubs was like surrendering an appendage. He pulled his rental driver from his borrowed bag, gave it a few swings, and said, "Man, this is like holding someone else's dick."

I doubt he would have played if Forest Dunes wasn't such a venerated destination. It had three courses in two—its original Tom Weiskopf layout, plus a recent design by Tom Doak called the Loop, which played in truly reversible Black and Red routings. (A short course by the geniuses behind Orlando's Winter Park was also set to open soon.) Carved into densely wooded land within the Huron National Forest, this secluded getaway had a wonderfully shady history. The land was originally owned by William Durant, founder of General Motors, who in the 1930s sold the acres to "The Detroit Partnership," aka the Detroit mob's notorious Purple Gang. They called it South Branch Ranch, and it became a five-star getaway for mobsters, replete with indoor horse-riding barns, an Olympic-size swimming pool, airplane hangars, a dance hall, a grand mansion, and a private runway. The house was a popular spot for getting whacked, and the road that's now the entrance to the resort was once guarded by a Gatling gun. The property was even searched when Jimmy Hoffa went missing, and was eventually seized for tax evasion. It remained unoccupied for decades, aside from the gunned-down gangsters whose ghosts made regular appearances around the Ranch.

The GM walked me into the woods off one of the holes on the Loop to see the pieces of a rusted-out Ford Roadster hidden in the brush, its rear panels dotted with bullet holes. I thought Brendan might be more excited to witness this remnant of gangster glory days, maybe fly his drone over this overgrown hideout, but I could tell he was still mourning his clubs. We decided to play the Loop as a friendly and save our match for when the van from the airport arrived. Hopefully.

I wanted to nitpick and find the course inferior to Hixson's two-way in Oregon. Dan had been such a gracious host and playing partner, while I had reservations about Tom Doak. "Socially remote" would be a politic way to sum up what I'd been told about his demeanor, but he was given a pass for being aloof because he was golf's wunderkind. I was less convinced, and preferred Bob Ford's "It's nice to be important, but it's important to be nice" perspective. But then I played the Loop, and I found myself reconfiguring my thoughts on Doak. Dammit, he *was* a genius. And plenty of savants had rubbed people the wrong way.

While Silvies Valley utilized twenty-seven greens in its two-course design, Doak restricted himself to using only eighteen, à la St. Andrews, which seemed a simple task if you wanted to build two boring courses, and an impossible puzzle if you were after something as good as the Loop. Each route felt distinct from the other, and Doak snuck bunkers in under tee boxes and banked hazards in such a way that they were invisible in one direction, then dead in your face when the course flipped around. It transcended smoke and mirrors; true artistry demanded that a gimmick not overtake the integrity of a piece, and art was what Doak achieved here at Forest Dunes. It didn't hurt my impressions that on the second hole of the Black routing, a 180-yard one-shotter, I scored a ½. Brendan wouldn't let me tally it as such, but my tee ball crushed the lip of the cup before striking the base of the pin and spitting back out. At least 50 percent of the ball had been below the surface, I told him, but he wasn't having any talk of a half ace. Neither was I; I was just trying to stock the battlefield for tomorrow.

Brendan's clubs arrived on the next day's flight from PHL to Gerald R. Ford International (an airport in Grand Rapids seemed about right for a three-year president), just in time for our final round at Weiskopf's original Forest Dunes course, and a match of no excuses. It was more familiar golfing fare: a parkland course of defined, doglegging fairways with ponds and tidy bunkering to negotiate, whereas the Loop had been wide swaths of short grass where most of the adventure was within fifty yards of the pins.

Our match was a silent four hours of grind. I had prepared myself for Brendan's gamesmanship—stroke-play mindset, ready to putt everything out—and while most of our matches involved a few giveaway holes either way, no balls were abandoned early at Forest Dunes. The margin never grew larger than a hole, and on the scorecard we were both playing close to par. We came to the par 5 eighteenth all square, and with two drives in the fairway, I expected Forest Dune's bye hole (a bonus nineteenth hole) to come into play for settling the match; it was a semi-island par 3 and would be a fitting finish for Brendan's journey.

Eighteen was guarded by a lake that hugged its left side and ran around the green's back edge, so I laid up judiciously, as Brendan looked poised to do the same. I watched him look at the pin, his ball, the pin, and then put away his 5 iron and reach for the hybrid. *Fine by me*, I thought. He was a course manager, and such audacity didn't suit his game. That bye hole might not matter after all.

Seconds after the ball left his clubface, Brendan was still posing in his follow-through when he announced, "I just broke your heart."

It landed safely on the green, twenty feet and pin high. I scrambled for par while he tapped in for birdie, and I reminded him that this was just another warm-up for Ohoopee.

"Can't wait," he said. "Do I need to say it again?"

"No, you don't." But he said it anyway.

"You can't beat me, Tom." He smiled. And I once again wondered if he was right.

I left my bitterness back in the woods and drove alone toward Michigan's watery western edge. My room at Arcadia Bluffs overlooked golden dunes set against the lake, and at sunset I listened to a bagpipe echoing across the fairways. The Bluffs Course was as scenic as any I'd yet visited, its contours irresistible as I tunneled my way around fescue-topped sand hills. It would have been one of America's best links-style courses if only the fairways weren't so lush; there was nothing less links than watching your drives bounce backward.

The ground was considerably firmer at nearby Crystal Downs, a MacKenzie-Maxwell collaboration set between Crystal Lake and Lake Michigan, a course beloved by so many yet played by so few that its took on a Sasquatch-ian quality in the imaginations of golf architecture disciples. As it was told to me, you had to own property in its small community of lakeside holiday homes to become a member, so the numbers remained intimate, with a waiting list that required you to sign up around age twelve to enjoy the place by your thirties. When word spread of Tom Doak's rare affection for its layout, Crystal Downs became the GCA crowd's most coveted badge, and I was fortunate to receive an email from a retired Philadelphia gentleman who claimed he had an old colleague who played there. He said he'd be happy to make a call about us playing Crystal Downs, if I didn't mind giving him some strokes. I thanked him and promised his scorecard would look like it had been dotted by a woodpecker.

At seventy-six years of age, Steve had driven seven hundred miles from eastern Pennsylvania to join me, picking off rounds at Arcadia and Forest Dunes along the way. He played 120 rounds a year, walking most of them, and was a steady straight-knocker who still played to a twelve. He had retired from a notable business career, and as he marched the fairways at a healthy pace, I thought of my dad. They had the same haircut—a little bit of white left behind the ears—and both still played whenever the sun shined, though I wondered if Dad's back was going to let him join me this year. Steve hoped so; he had signed up for a Scotland trip I was hosting that August (because golfing all of America just wasn't enough), and Dad was booked to join us as well. Steve had read about him in my other books and was looking forward to teeing it up with him in person. I was, too.

Steve had been playing for sixty-three years, after picking up the game as a teenage caddie. Golf had taken me hither and thither, but not as far as it had transported Steve. As we walked the fairways at Crystal Downs, he told me how he had run into LPGA legend Betsy King many years before and learned of her Golf Fore Africa campaign. He soon found himself with her in Africa, working with communities to provide water and schools and AIDS education. While there, he met a twenty-six-year-old refugee who had fled to Uganda as a child, eventually returning to Rwanda to find that his father had been killed in the genocide. His dream was to bring education to the children of his country, so Steve decided to help make that happen, starting his own organization called Arise Rwanda Ministries. They built preschools and dug wells and created a vocational academy where three hundred young people were currently enrolled.

Here was a man I had admired solely for his golf longevity, an acquaintance I had placed on a long list of wealthy white guys whose greatest achievement was belonging to clubs I couldn't get into. I had to start giving people more credit. I presumed they were shallow until proven otherwise, and those assumptions, it turned out, had made me the superficial one.

Steve added that he had given up on the game at one point. He had been playing too much and losing time with his wife and his kids. "And then I learned about you," he said, "and wow; I realized my wife and kids were lucky!"

Touché, my friend. I told him the kids had been with me last week on a quick side trip to Missouri—we had all traveled out to Big Cedar Lodge in the Ozarks. The place was Bandon Dunes for families, a mountaintop mega-resort built by Johnny Morris of Bass Pro Shops, who spared no expense in building his playground. There were courses by Gary Player and Jack Nicklaus and Tom Fazio and Coore-Crenshaw (the clear standout of the offerings, though Player's short course was a blast), and a new eighteen coming from Tiger Woods. But with all the golf came fishing and swimming and canyon trails and drive-thru wildlife and an arcade fortress where the girls would have been happy to spend the remainder of their childhoods.

With Branson just fifteen minutes away, we couldn't resist a trip to Dolly Parton's Stampede dinner theater, where we drank from plastic cowboy boots and ate chicken with our hands. We watched horse-riding gymnastics and hooted for cowboys draped in red, white, and blue. The crowd was a lot of grandparents with grandkids, and I saw some dads with fanny packs and high socks and wolf T-shirts. What I saw everywhere was an eagerness to hop up out of seats and chant *U-S-A*, and this heartland hootenanny felt very far from home. We all loved America, but I felt like the clever coastal guy who couldn't abide commercialized patriotism without a cynical smirk. But something occurred to me as I watched my kids laugh and smile and wave their flags: This was all good. Horse shows were good. The heartland was good. Eating chicken by the fistful—it was very good. While I sat on the side-lines waiting for everyone else's America to fit my own ideal and enlightened version of it, there was plenty to cheer for in the meantime, so I got up off my seat with my kids and rooted for the cowboy in the American flag bandana.

Steve was glad to hear I had gotten Allyson and the kids out on the road with me, and I told him they'd be in Scotland with us as well. As for the course we were currently playing, Doak was right: Crystal Downs was as good a Golden Age course as one could find, and given its small and thoughtful membership, little about the place had changed since its inception. The stretch of short par 4s from four through seven had me wondering if I'd played a more exciting string of holes anywhere; the 350-yard fifth was a front-runner for what might be the best tee shot in America. A hogback fairway that leaned right, then cambered upward to the left allowed you to lead off with any club in your bag and make a 2 as quick as a 6. The safe drive left a blind approach; the bold line brought bunkers and an unseen landing area into play, thus capturing that most seductive blend of playable and penal and making Crystal Downs exhibit A in the distance debate: thoughtful architecture trumps ball speed every time.

The short ninth felt a bit out of place given the offerings that preceded it, a pretty simple par 3 back up to the clubhouse, but I appreciated the legend behind its creation. The story goes that as they collaborated on Crystal

Downs, MacKenzie was well in his cups when he showed Perry Maxwell his sketch for the first half of the course. Maxwell studied the drawing and found his inebriated partner had designed a front nine of eight holes, so they squeezed in a wee par 3 that's still fun, if not as compelling as its counterparts.

Each tee conjured the same four-letter refrain—*pure*—and if it hadn't been so exclusive, I might have found the course to cap my search. The Great American Golf Course, I figured, should be a bit more accessible to Americans, and as good as Crystal Downs was, it still wasn't the coolest course I'd seen in Michigan, which was hardly in Michigan at all.

MACKINAC ISLAND, MICHIGAN

The dulcet tones of my GPS sang out the most affirming, hopeful words in the English language: *You have arrived.* They were daily proof of my sanity, announced through car speakers: Destination. Arrival. Itinerary upheld. The only problem was, I was supposed to be looking at a golf course. This looked more like Lake Huron to me.

As I approached the northern tip of Michigan's lower peninsula, I had been growing suspicious of my navigational app's ability to find me this first tee. The usual markers of an impending golf course—distant flags, service roads, receding homes and storefronts—were nowhere to be found. Instead, the street was getting busier, with T-shirt shops, motels, and seafood shacks.

When I reached the end of that street, my rental car pointed at a vast expanse of dark blue.

To my left, a long line of tourists in tank tops and sunglasses stood between ropes, waiting for something—and there it was, steaming toward us across the water. A ferry. I waved down a woman with a name tag who appeared to be directing traffic and called to her from my front seat.

"Wawa-what?" She could barely hear me as the ferry's engines roared into reverse.

"Wawashkamo! The golf course!" I called.

The mention of golf seemed an easy excuse for her to disengage. She shook her head and turned away, pointing a colleague my way. His name was Jerry.

"I'm looking for the golf course. My GPS stopped here."

Jerry smiled. "It's on the island. You need to take the ferry."

What a quaint wrinkle, I thought. I hadn't envisioned any ferry rides on this journey, but this would be some welcome time for reflection upon one of our Great Lakes. I had ferried my car all over Scotland, and these island hoppers had become my favorite conveyance.

"Where's the car line for the ferry?" I asked.

"It's not a car ferry. There are no cars on the island. You have to drive back to the lot and park."

What a shitty wrinkle, I thought. I had budgeted enough time for a quick nine holes around an obscure golf course that I knew nothing about, other than that it was at the top of Michigan and that nobody seemed to have heard of it. I'd come for a quick golf curiosity, and now I was about to board a shuttle bus from a parking lot to a ferry to a carless island where somewhere there existed a golf course with a name I couldn't pronounce.

I bought a ticket and waited in line. Funny—I was the only one carrying golf clubs. A crewman on the ferry spotted my bag and nodded as I boarded. "The course is just a five-minute walk up the road," he assured me. "I play it once a week. You'll love it."

With my concerns about finding the course sans automobile alleviated, I left the ferry dock and headed up a hill—the island had the shape of a turtle's back—and after five minutes of dodging bicycles and horse-drawn taxis, I arrived victorious at a pro shop, pleased with myself for having sailed unknown waters in search of a golf hole. I'd found some, but as I eyed the merchandise in the pro shop, nowhere did I find the name Wawashkamo.

"That's the *other* course on the island," the pro behind the counter told me. "Nine holes. You're going the right way. It's a few more miles up the road."

After a half-hour hike past cottages and stables and bike racks, through silent woods that opened into wide fields of tall grasses, I spied a white building hiding behind dark evergreens. I found a path between them, and then a small gathering of low buildings with worn roofs and white siding. I'd either found the golf club or had stumbled into the base camp of a covert island cult. A statue of a golfer in knickers assured me it was the former, and I opened the screen door beside him.

No racks of golf balls for sale, no computers behind a counter. But there was a short desk with a book of what might be tee times; as I looked for my name, sweat dripped from my nose and stained the page. Eventually a man with a mustache came through a doorway and introduced himself as Chuck Olson, the head pro. Then he told me they had been expecting me hours ago. Still sucking air from the hike, I informed him that I'd had no idea that there was a ferry involved, or that I would be walking here. He saw the red in my face and had mercy.

"Yeah. It's a little different up here," Chuck said. "Well, you made it. You've found the toughest golf course to find in America."

The head (and only) pro at Wawashkamo, Chuck told me the course remained unchanged from its 1896 routing, laid out by Carnoustie's Alex Smith, making it popular with hickory players. They adored its turn-of-the-century yardages, as well as the sandbox by the first tee, placed there for constructing dirt tees as golf's forefathers did. Hickories were for rent, but I opted for my own sticks. The distances on the scorecard tempted me to grab a sack of old clubs from the spartan locker room—just a few wooden doors with some nails on the wall in a dark room, with the same toilet Alex Smith may have used—but I couldn't stomach the idea of hauling fourteen clubs over on a boat, then leaving them beside the pro shop.

Chuck was dressed in jacket and tie. Apparently, I had shown up on the afternoon of the club's annual summer party—thus the concern about my late arrival. He was worried no one would be here to welcome me. "All the members will be over in the tent next door, so you should have the course to yourself," he explained. He gave me a hundred years' worth of course history in ten minutes and showed me around the clubhouse—which felt much more *house* than *club*. It had a small parlor with a piano and fireplace and a porch outside. Chuck explained that *Wawashkamo* came from a Chippewa phrase for *a crooked trail*. A local chief known as Eagle Eye was credited with giving the course its name, when he observed the wandering golfers and described them as those who "walk a crooked path." Had straighter hitters been playing Wawashkamo in its early days, I wondered what the course may have ended up being called.

"You have to enjoy the quiet here, because that's why you come," Chuck told me. "The islanders say that the island chooses you, or it kicks you off. Once you're here for a little while, out here isolated at night, you understand what they mean."

The island had clearly chosen Chuck. He had been the head pro at Wawashkamo for eight years, and lived in the cottage beside the pro shop. In winter, he returned to a home in Traverse City on the mainland. He had a bike—everybody on Mackinac did—which he used for grocery runs, but the challenges of island life only began with trying to figure out how you were going to fit all your provisions into a bike basket.

"Everything transportation-related on Mackinac has to be planned," Chuck said. "Let's say you need a new refrigerator. First, it has to come across on a cargo boat, and then be transported onto the dock, and then be lifted onto a flatbed trailer, and two horses will bring it up the hill. And then it has to be unloaded by two or three people. There aren't any forklifts to do that kind of stuff; there's one at the dock, but once you get the fridge to your house, you have to drag it in, and take out the other one yourself. So, everything that has to do with transportation—the horse is king here. And it has been for over a hundred years."

With over six hundred horses on the island serving as taxis and hauling freight, they outnumbered the island's five hundred or so year-round residents. Snowmobiles were permitted in the winter, when roads were impassable for bikes, but more essential on Mackinac than a bicycle or stirrups was a good towel.

"To live here, you have to know that if you're going out to a five-star restaurant for dinner and it rains, you get wet," Chuck explained. "People have towels and rain gear in their bags all the time. The weather is a big part of life out here, and you have to be able to handle that. And that brings a certain type of person who likes to live here. The people love the peace of the place, the quiet. I don't think there are too many places left on earth, or certainly in America, that are like Mackinac."

The same could be said for its golf course. After Alex Smith staked its holes, never once had a digger or dozer broken the soil, and they never would, thanks to the island's ban on engines. "Wawashkamo has been preserved, just like everything on the island. The bluff houses and all the Victorian homes—if someone from 1910 visited, they would find that the place hasn't changed very much," Chuck told me. "It just looks like something that's been lost in time, because, basically, it has."

As Chuck hurried off to the festivities, I headed for the first tee, which Chuck told me featured a remnant from the Battle of Mackinac Island in the War of 1812—a black cannon pointed toward the fairway below, marking the vantage point from which British soldiers awaited the American advance. While America would ultimately reclaim the island in the treaty that ended the war, Mackinac was a decisive British victory, aided by local Native American forces. Chuck had explained that the remains of American soldiers killed by Menominee warriors were still on the course, buried in the rough between the fifth and sixth fairways.

I found a marker pointing to an approximate burial site, as well as plenty of other plaques around the property. For a nine-hole course spread across just a handful of acres, Wawashkamo simmered with intrigue. Flat land had been made interesting by cross bunkering and, as the signs explained, chocolate drops and a circus ring. I had never heard of either on any golf architecture podcast, but I learned that chocolate drops were piles of rocks meant to serve as hazards—without equipment to move stones very far, they were left as mounds in the rough. The circus ring made an otherwise sleepy par 4 into a treasure; a simple ring of knee-high grass encircled a small green, harkening back to, as the plaque explained, a time when lifting one's ball off the ground presented golfers a unique challenge. I felt like I was playing within museum exhibits, information accompanying the displays. The course was dotted with storm shelters that looked like tiny New England churches, and Chuck's welcome took on new meaning—this wasn't the hardest golf course to find in America because of the ferry or the ban on motorized vehicles. I had golfed to and fro and had never played a place like this. And that, for me, was the hardest golf course to find of them all.

As I crossed Wawashkamo's fairways, I wasn't thinking about the soldiers who stood post here, who fought and died in this field, nor was I recalling the Native Americans who called it home for centuries and gave the place its name. Instead, I was trying to keep my drive out of the chocolate drops and get my ball over the circus ring with enough spin to settle close. But as I awaited my taxi back to the dock—they called a carriage for me; no sweating back down the road this time—I looked back at the cannon by the first tee and read the stories posted on the signs beside the members' bicycles, and wondered how I had arrived here. I knew the logistics of it—car, boat, walk; a crooked path indeed—but how was I really here, feet planted upon history I couldn't have fathomed when I plugged a course name into my GPS this morning? It was because I enjoyed rolling a ball into a hole in the ground. And as I boarded my carriage, I felt more keenly aware than ever that I loved this game not just because it transported us in geography, but because it tossed us around in time as well.

Twelve dollars later, I climbed down off my taxi with my clubs and headed for the line of returning day visitors, a long row of sunburns and ice cream. I'd been gone a few hours, but it felt like years. And then they called *All aboard*, and the ferry's engines roared to life.

NEW BUFFALO, MICHIGAN

I drove past it twice, then parked in an empty dirt lot with no golf holes in sight—just thick Michigan forest. I sat on a bench and dialed for help, and a man told me to walk fifty yards up to my left, and I'd see a few cars and a bus. I knew the place was a private retreat for the lucky few, but its tiny clubhouse set back in the woods made it feel like I'd arrived at somebody's weekend home—albeit somebody who happened to have a few holes in their yard. On a small patio, a dozen well-groomed guys drank beers from a cooler, presumably cans they'd brought with them on that party bus behind me.

I peeked my head inside the lone building and found a man sitting at a table in front of a laptop. No office or pro shop; just a bathroom and a closet off to the side with some hats and shirts for sale.

"You found us," he said, and welcomed me to Mike Keiser's Dunes Club.

Before Bandon Dunes, Keiser had first dipped his toe into course construction with this nine-holer set just across the street from Lake Michigan. Built on a secluded ninety acres, the place had a small membership comprising Keiser's friends, from what I'd been told, and had been designed by him and the late Dick Nugent. They wanted to build something of modest scale with an unfussy feel to it: pure golf of a dynamic nature. The Dunes Club felt like a club in the most youthful sense of the word, like a tree-fort hangout where buddies met up when they could get out of the house. A small, nonlocal membership meant it was never crowded, and now that the Chicago crew was finished, I was told I had the course to myself, and that a kid from down the street was waiting outside to carry my bag.

It was a good course for a guide, as the property was devoid of signage or tee markers, and my caddie helped point out the abundant tee options. The winner of the previous hole typically picked the next teeing ground, and the variances were wide. The par 3s had a stockpile of starting points to ponder—different yardages, myriad angles—so when we went back around for a second nine, it felt like a fresh slate of holes. They were immaculate without feeling phony, and the closest comparison I could conjure was Pine Valley, for the way it wound through the conifers and its variety of shots and rugged bunkers and standout par 3s. I left with a hat to prove that I had indeed found the Dunes Club, and as I pointed my car south toward Indiana, I felt myself already missing the Wolverine State. It had been a Pure Michigan few days.

"Sorry that you can't play the fifth hole," Mike said. He was the course superintendent, and had good reason for rerouting our group. "We don't want you hitting the president of Mexico's kid out there," he explained.

"We don't want that, either," I assured him.

"When the kids go off for their games at four o'clock, we might be able to get you through there. Five just runs too close to their cabins, and summer camps are in full swing, as you can see."

I'd toured much of the campus that afternoon by accident, lost amid Indiana's amber waves of grain. This wasn't a course that showed up on my navigation apps, though Culver Academies did, and as I drove loops through its parking lots in search of signs of a golf course, it looked as if I'd left Indiana and arrived at some sort of storybook fortress.

Its sprawling campus was covered with handsome citadels, bright red bricks shaped into battlements and barbicans, all of it set beside a shimmering lake where young men and women were pulling on sculls. I saw other kids riding horses in formation and a group of teenagers practicing archery beside the water. To drive an hour south from Notre Dame, where I'd enjoyed the Coore-Crenshaw course that morning, and to emerge from the wheat fields into what looked like a small Harvard was like stepping through an enchanted wardrobe. A teacher pointed me down the road to the golf course, and that's where I met Mike Vessely.

Mike maintained and managed the nine-hole course at Culver, a prep school of plural institutions—they operated the Culver Military Academy, which dated to 1894, along with the Culver Girls Academy and the Culver Summer Schools and Camps. I felt dim for never having heard of the place (I was there on the recommendation of golf-writing friend Jay Rigdon, who lived beside the course with his girlfriend, a Culver instructor), and Mike assured me my ignorance was forgivable. Few people knew there was a nine-hole course here, he explained, and not just any course but a Langford & Moreau masterpiece untouched by time.

I'd left William Langford and Theodore Moreau out of my architect's glossary. They were two designers overshadowed by other Golden Age counterparts, but Andy Johnson called them "the sultans of the steam shovel," a team of great maximalists who sculpted some of the Midwest's most audacious layouts. The Great Depression left them with a thin portfolio, but architecture pundits swooned over their builds. Mike explained that when one such guru, Ran Morrissett of Golf Club Atlas, visited a few years ago, he told the Culver folks they had no idea the treasure they held in these forgotten nine holes. The alums themselves were unaware, but when word got out about Ran's take, the money came in for a restoration in 2013 by Bobby Weed. Weed was careful to ensure that his team merely peeled back the years to reveal what Langford & Moreau had created, giving the golf world a rare time capsule.

The nine holes had originally been slated as the first leg of a twenty-seven-hole complex that was meant to include a resort hotel beside the lake, but the Depression squashed those plans, and what remained had been left to the Culver campers as a place to knock it around. It had been "a Rembrandt in the attic," as Mike said, and I wondered if the teenagers out there today in their all-whites understood what they were playing. The campers came from over thirty different countries to this summer sanctuary, including the kids of high-profile dignitaries who sent their children for its celebrated leadership training (how European grandees knew about this place in Indiana was mystifying). The prep school cost more than most colleges, and its alums included senators, governors, and Olympians. Roger Penske spent his summer here, and George Steinbrenner was an academy grad. So was the movie critic Gene Siskel, though I had a hard time envisioning him marching in formation around the lake.

Jay walked down from his house to join me for two loops, and from the course's first tee, perched above a sweeping valley, to the vaulted green on the par 3 second to the subterranean swales guarding the short third, my eyes were wide open. I'd lived in flat Indiana for six years and had never walked land like this. The course was downright rowdy, with head-high bunkers and fairways bent around tilted hillsides. Nowhere in its geometry could I find one sleepy angle, and I wondered if this might be the merriest nine-holer in America.

It was a tough call, considering the holes I'd played yesterday in New Buffalo, and the nine-holer waiting for me up in Chicago. Downers Grove was the remaining half of America's first full-size golf course, and as I set off for Illinois, I wondered if it could stand out on a menu of Chicago heavyweights. With eight US Open courses plus two publics to play in five days' time, I was leaving Indiana's empty roads and open fairways and driving directly into a golf rush hour.

EVANSTON, ILLINOIS

"This hole is called Murray," Joel explained as we walked the fourth fairway at Canal Shores, just north of downtown Chicago. "My brother Billy used to run the snack shack up by the green. He started here mowing grass, and somehow promoted himself to the snack shack, which was funny because he's not *really* a morning person. He would show up at noon, not as early as most golfers might actually like a snack."

Some people looked sloppy in an untucked shirt; others made you wonder why your shirt wasn't untucked, too. Joel Murray was among the latter, his blue golf shirt hanging over his shorts. It was from William Murray Golf, the clothing line created by him and his brothers, and was dotted with a bicycle pattern. It recalled their days riding bikes here to play, or to caddie over at Indian Hill, where the six Murray brothers grew up carrying golf bags—and where his brother, Brian, collected experiences that would inspire him to write the film *Caddyshack*.

"This is back in the long hair, Fu Manchu mustache days," Joel said. "Bill liked to get up when the sun was warm. He'd come heat up some hot dogs when most of the golfers would already be done for the day. But there was a certain clientele that wore Dingo boots and cowboy hats that used to hang out with him and laugh. Who knows what went on there? I do. But I'm not going to say right now."

Canal Shores had been part of Joel's golfing life from the start. He'd followed his brothers into the entertainment business as an actor and comedian, but first followed them to the local course. "My relationship with Canal Shores has changed many times over the years," he explained. "When we started out, it was illicit. I was sneaking on and playing without being asked or wanted. Then I learned I could find balls in the canal and negotiate with the pro to play the course, and as I got older, I actually paid to play the course. And now we run a charity tournament here for first responders, and it's been great for us but has also helped enlighten people to the existence of this place. And the course—it has gotten so much better than when I was a kid. Then, it was hard dirt with patches of grass, and now it's really a proper course all of a sudden."

To call Canal Shores a community golf course would be underselling its role, and its routing; the four-thousand-yard par 60 layout rubbed shoulders with fire stations, the Chicago L, and the local hospital. Joel noted that before the trees grew up, slices from the original first tee ended up in the emergency room rotunda across the street. The holes wandered through backyards and across busy streets as you dodged taxis en route to the next tee, following Chicago's North Shore Channel connecting Lake Michigan to the Chicago River.

The metropolitan courses I had played were parks with gray buildings for a backdrop, but Canal Shores fit snugly between the city's walls. It was the sort of place that didn't survive in urban America anymore, no matter how much cities needed places like them. When I arrived with Joel, who was home from LA visiting family, fifty kids occupied the first two holes for a summer golf camp; out on the course, we played through dozens of young people taking their first swings.

Had Canal Shores been left to the hands of local government, it would have met the same fate as so many muni courses, sold off to fill budget gaps because the land was too valuable, the course too expensive to maintain, or the conditions too poor to drum up revenue. They had dodged that eventuality by incorporating Canal Shores as a nonprofit, relying on fundraising to keep the tees open and suggesting a new path for struggling community courses. They made decent money from tailgaters who parked on the holes during Northwestern University football games, but the budget required Canal Shores to lean on its neighbors to care for the course.

A local golfer named Jason Way had recently taken the course's conditioning on his back, rallying the Chicago golf crowd to come out and clear sticks, dig bunkers, and chop overgrowth. Volunteers were relied on to make the course not just playable but intriguing: They'd built replicas of the principal's nose bunkers from St. Andrews, installed a shrunken version of Oakmont's church pews, and dug a wee burn that recalled Carnoustie, just at one-tenth the scale. While a stranger's shovel would never be allowed to touch a municipally owned course, here was a chance for those who wanted good golf next door to get involved, to roll up their sleeves and make it happen.

Joel showed me no mercy on his childhood track; he fearlessly navigated fairways that were only slightly wider than the L tracks above us, closing me out on fourteen. As we put my five bucks toward pizza in the American Legion post that occupied the upstairs of the clubhouse, I was grateful I'd come to Canal Shores on my last morning in Chicago. I'd been in town for five days playing through golf's past, and it seemed fitting to end with some hope for its future.

Golf history ran deep in Chicago: The first ball ever holed in the West happened just north of Chicago proper in Lake Forest, thanks to none other than C. B. Macdonald. In 1892 he built a tomato-can seven-holer in the gardens of Senator Charles B. Farwell for British friends who were coming to Chicago for the 1893 World's Fair. Macdonald designed the short routing reluctantly, objecting to the flower beds and trees that felt nothing like Scottish golf. He struck out for more interesting terrain at Belmont, where the Chicago Golf Club was born and the first eighteen-hole layout in the United States was completed in 1893. They must have been an impatient bunch, because in 1894, Macdonald found new land that reminded him of Scotland, and the operation moved to Wheaton, where it still exists today. As Macdonald was a slicer, he routed his course counterclockwise around the club's polo field to keep his misses from drifting out of bounds.

The golfers who remained in Lake Forest would become the Onwentsia Club—its name meant "meeting place" in the Iroquois language, and the earliest pictures of its annual Pow Wow tournament showed members sitting down for dinner beside local Native Americans. The Scottish saltire waves above the Onwentsia clubhouse, and for good reason—its current course was designed by three Scots: golf writer and US Amateur champ H. J. Whigham and noted pros Robert and James Foulis Jr.

The five Foulis brothers were born in St. Andrews, where their father was the foreman in Old Tom Morris's club-making shop (the Foulis family home on South Street still exists and can be rented; my family spent an idyllic two weeks there in 2015). They all got to know Macdonald during his St. Andrews period, and Macdonald recruited young James, who would later win the second US Open championship, to come to the States and be the head pro at Chicago Golf, making him the first golf pro in western America.

James's brothers followed him across the Atlantic, and Robert Foulis not only designed Onwenstia but became its first pro. The Foulises designed and consulted on courses throughout the Midwest; the Morrisses may be golf's most written-about family, but the Foulises led American golf's Scottish invasion and helped pull golf westward from its coastal roots. They also inherited some of their father's workshop ingenuity; golf writer Jim Healey later discovered and credited them with the invention of the American Eagle ball, and the mashie-niblick (7 iron). Dave Foulis, noticing how golf holes deepened as caddies dug sand out of them for building tees, created golf's first cup liner. Not far behind was the first modern golf pin. Dubbed the Foulis Flag, it stood perfectly straight in the newly protected cups.

The rivalry between their clubs, the gold-and-blue puritans of Onwenstia versus the red-and-white scotch-drinking ruffians of Chicago Golf, was American golf's first great club rivalry. An article by H. C. Chatfield-Taylor, Onwentsia's first president, detailed how he grew his team by recruiting Americans to this new game; he flouted Lake Forest's temperance laws to his advantage: "When they came in, hot and tired, I lured them to the dining-room, where decanters of Scotch whiskey were placed enticingly before their innocent eyes. Alas! they fell to a man. Whether it was owing to the game or the whiskey, I would not venture a guess."

Taylor went on to lament their losses to the Chicago GC golfers, who practiced golf on the sabbath and also used their bar to their benefit, serving scotch before the matches, "thinking to entice their Puritan brethren from the straight and narrow path, and thus encompass their ruin." The rivalry grew so intense that it divided families, a golfing Hatfields versus McCoys. "When Onwenstia won the series [in 1896] . . . it was not safe for a Lake Forester to venture in the wilds of Wheaton unarmed." In time the matches simmered down into a friendly exhibition, and the two clubs' memberships began to overlap. On Onwentsia's wall of winners, Chicago Golf's C. B. Macdonald and his wife are listed as former husband-wife club champs.

With eight Open venues to visit—the most of any American city—Chicago was a busy shuffle up and down Lake Michigan. At Medinah, I was somehow paired with the voice of the Chicago Blackhawks and hockey Hall of Famer Pat Foley, who proved that cold cans of beer stood no chance against a hockey announcer in the off-season. We hurt our backs trying to imitate Sergio's 1999 hop, and we would have re-created Tiger's 261-yard cut 2 iron on the seventh had either of us been carrying a 2 iron. We didn't talk very much about the Miracle at Medinah, where Team Europe rallied on the final day of the 2012 Ryder Cup to overcome a four-point deficit and steal the champagne bottles away from the American side. I noticed that while Medinah's domed Arabian clubhouse (founded by Shriners, it was the site's most striking feature) held plenty of history about its PGA and US Open championships, far less wall space was dedicated to its Ryder Cup. It occurred to me that hosting the biggest event in international golf was a tricky gig: It was only worth the effort if your side won. Otherwise, all the memorabilia ended up in the basement.

For months, I had wondered how I was going to win access to all the Chicago privates on my list. And then a guy who knew a guy emailed a guy, and I was introduced to Sully, a Chicago golf keymaster. Sully had friends in every suburb of the city, and had planned my week's itinerary to the minute. The only key I didn't need him to turn was Chicago Golf Club, which, aside from Cypress, was my white whale. With barely more than a hundred members, sheer odds made it an unachievable get, but I found myself there with an ND alum, his son, and a former golf pro who now sold flagpoles—not the pins but the big ones out front.

With just a handful of other players on the property, playing Chicago Golf was a sacred experience befitting the oldest eighteen-hole course in America. On the course, the strategic demands of a Macdonald offering were all there, along with slick and squared-off greens. Though it was a relatively flat plot, Macdonald was able to use his templates to pump drama into the drives and the approaches. It had hosted a Walker Cup and three US Opens, including one won by my friend Johnny McDermott, but unlike the other Chicago venues where trophies were displayed in elaborate halls of fame, Chicago's vibe was understated in an almost somnolent way. Confident restraint was Chicago's calling card, even in its simple, white-walled grillroom with a vaulted ceiling above modest wood tables. The room had been built on a bet—the loser, Addison Stillwell, had been tasked with "building the Club a proper drinking room," and had delivered; his name still hung above the fireplace. It felt more like a genteel space for a contemplative cocktail than a party spot, and I'd heard it described as a one-drink hang; get your beer and get going.

The bar and clubhouse operations were overseen by a Filipino family who had been at Chicago GC for nearly a century. "Grandpa" Isidro Aspuria came to CGC around 1934 and lived to the age of one hundred. He had credited his longevity to brand loyalty—"I smoke Camels; never switch brands"—and, as my host explained, purchased a statue of himself that was erected in his hometown in the northern Philippines so that everyone there would know him. Grandpa and his descendants tended bar, cooked in the kitchen, waited tables, and did administrative work in the office, and still do. Most important, Grandpa had helped my host learn to roll the bones in the members' dice game. "I teach you to roll," Grandpa told him after witnessing another loss. "You no good."

The following morning, I joined Sully at Chicago Golf's rival club, where I got to witness the miracle that was his backswing: The clubhead barely reached his waist before he whipped it back through. He had a thick Irish build and looked younger than his sixty-four years, so I couldn't figure out why he refused a proper lash, but he assured me it was a result-driven approach. He was a good putter but a better negotiator. As he leaned over a four-footer in our match at Onwentsia, he murmured in the direction of our opponents, "All those millions spent on curing the common cold. And they haven't spent a penny on curing lockjaw."

Sully introduced me to friends at Skokie that afternoon, a course where Gene Sarazen had won the Open in 1922. My host, Peter, had a Purple Heart and a Bronze Star from Vietnam, and a proud Boston accent. He wore a Red Sox cap and jokingly described himself as both the token Catholic and token democrat at Skokie (the other member in our foursome was quick to note he was Jewish, lest their club be judged by yesteryear's biases). My favorite feature on its Bendelow-then-Ross course was a row of bells posted between the driving range and the eighteenth fairway. If you snapped a drive left onto the range, rather than hit another, you rang the "bell of shame," which told practicing golfers to wait and watch you hunt for your ball in a sea of thousands. It seemed a brilliant, if not humbling, alternative to the worst feature in golf: internal out of bounds.

Skokie might not have had a lot of papists in its pro shop, but it did allow women, which for Chicago was moderately progressive. The city was home to roughly a quarter of the remaining American golf clubs that still excluded women (Butler National, Black Sheep, Bob O'Link, and Old Elm), yet when I arrived at Midlothian Country Club the next morning, my playing partners proved Chicago golf wasn't just for the boys. I joined new friends Sandy and Sue for eighteen holes where Walter Hagen had won the Open in 1914, and with female caddies to guide us, I was the only dude in the group. (It was a welcome break from the I'll-just-piss-here crowd.)

Sue had just turned sixty but possessed the energy of a teenager. I struggled to keep up with her pace in the heat, and between shots she hustled over to speak with friends in passing groups or find hats for our caddies to save them from sunburns. (As a fellow ginger, I assured her I was fully lathered.) As we walked, I asked her where she got all her energy, and if I could have some.

"If you're not going forward, you're going to stop, Tom," she replied. I told her I hoped so. I'd been moving forward for some time now and could do with a little stop. But Sue shook her head. "Keep going. And enjoy every minute."

Sue was a true believer in this philosophy, I could tell; she had won an astounding twenty-five club championships at Midlothian, capturing the first one while she was pregnant.

I decided to heed her advice and keep moving forward, toward Olympia Fields that afternoon, where I found a club that befit the city of broad shoulders. The complex was vast, and had once been even bigger—they had to sell off two of their four courses during WWII—but its enormous clubhouse and iconic clock tower loomed large as ever. During my tour, I was shown a high-arched Tudor ballroom where professional prizefights used to take place. I imagined a smoky room of bowler hats and cigars, wide men chewing Chicago beef and cheering on bouts that were surely fixed by Tommy gun gangsters—this was Chicago, after all.

Olympia's US Opens had been won by Johnny Farrell in 1928 and Jim Furyk in 2003; Nicklaus had won the Western on its North Course, and James Foulis had done a stint as golf professional in the club's early days. But to me, Olympia's best history was found in its locker room. It was the size of a convention hall, but its layout forged a kind of intimacy. Creaky metal lockers were divided up into alleys. Every locker room had rows, but at Olympia Fields, they were wide, with card tables and televisions in between, and at the end of each row a sign noted that alley's team insignia and name: Alley Cats, Swingers, Tin Pan Alley, Gasoline Alley, Sin Alley. The alleys played challenge matches against one another for locker room bragging rights. They were clubs within the club, though I was told the alley rivalries had died down over the years—the decline of four hours of golf followed by five hours of cards and cocktails had diminished locker room bonds, and changing-room culture in general had diminished across America. The rooms were getting more lavish, yet we seemed to have less time to hang around in them. For most of us, they were a spot to change your shoes and check your phone and find that you were needed elsewhere. Gone were most of the old loiterers who spent their retirements reading the racing forms in that chair no one else sat in or arguing over gin hands in the corner. We had called them "the homeless" when we were caddies—they never left, but somewhere along the way, someone had pointed them home. Or maybe we were all just getting worse at doing very little.

There was no locker room to inspect at Downers Grove the next afternoon, where nine holes held the remains of Macdonald's first American eighteen-hole golf course, before Chicago GC moved out to Wheaton. Five of its holes were said to be originals from Macdonald's day, and aside from a bizarre fifth hole that was added later—I would have been better off tossing my ball into the marsh and heading for the sixth—the muni course was muni-ficent. Hefty hills made proper exercise out of a nine-hole walk, and when I showed up there to play before my flight back home, a dozen thirty-somethings were hanging around the pro shop. I'd discovered impressive golf and history in Chicago, if not the Great American Golf Course, but at Downers Grove, a public venue operated by the parks system, I may have stumbled across the Great American Golf *Club*, in the last place I'd expected to find it.

The NewClub (no space) was a golf society with all the trappings of a traditional club—logo, bag tags, handicap services, a full slate of tournaments, and a growing membership. The only thing they were missing was a course, and while that seemed like an essential omission, golf's first clubs in Scotland operated in similar fashion. The Honourable Company of Edinburgh Golfers, those writers of golf's first rules, bounced around before settling at Muirfield. The Burgess and Bruntsfield players did the same. Golf societies existed as separate entities from golf courses, and in recent years organizations like the NewClub, the Outpost Club, the Friars Club, and Sugarloaf Social Club were following that Scottish model; not one home but many (less formal associations, like the Royal & Ancient Company of Dishonourable

Golfers, were coalescing on Internet message boards as well). As country-club memberships declined, America's new itinerant golf societies could be viewed with fear or hope by the private-club world. There were large groups out there who would pay to play a private course. They just wanted to play lots of other places, too.

NewClub founder Matt Considine took the name from The New Golf Club at St. Andrews, one of five distinct golf clubs attached to the St. Andrews courses. He'd visited their clubhouse beside the eighteenth on the Old Course and was inspired by its ethos, where bankers, policemen, and schoolteachers were all equal members. He decided to transport that model to Chicago, where so many of his millennial counterparts were hard-core golfers without a home, rejecting the elitist trappings of the game. Social media and chat rooms made brick-and-mortar clubhouses less necessary for these next-generation patrons; all they wanted was a tee box. And by organizing tournaments and meetups at Chicago's public offerings, plus trips to visitor-friendly venues around the Midwest, the NewClub offered them that at an affordable rate, along with camaraderie, trophies, and bragging rights battles.

When I heard that Matt played off a +1, I challenged him on the first tee for those bragging rights, suggesting a match of five-dollar stakes. My bravado sparked a buzz among the dozen NewClubbers in attendance, all eager to witness this unexpected showdown between their pin-firing leader and an upstart interloper. Matt seemed surprised by my wager and asked if I would require any strokes. I was the senior of the group, so I gave him a sideways glance and answered like a cocksure cowboy: "I don't take strokes, Matt. I just give them."

I was the darkest of horses against this lanky former college player. He whipped his clubhead at speeds that struck me as inappropriate, and squaring off at his regular loop didn't bolster my odds. But after two holes I found myself one-up, and as his fellow members followed our match, I felt myself fighting for every Gen X dad out there who might not know how to Snapchat but knew a thing or two about getting up and down. I rained buckets to halve Matt with birdies on the third and fourth, then gave away a hole on the abominable fifth. The math regressed to its likely mean, but I was pleased that Matt at least had to birdie the final hole to finish me off. We shook hands and traded stories on the Downers Grove patio, which had become the NewClub's grillroom for the day. I soon left for the airport, but not before becoming a NewClub member myself. And unlike my other memberships, I could take this one anywhere. And I did.

ST. MICHAEL, MINNESOTA

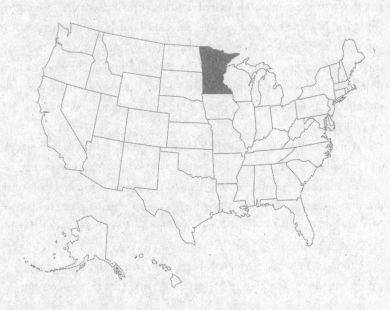

Poetry readings were typically nod-and-smile affairs where your mind drifted off to your dinner plans and your gaze drifted off to your shoes. But there was no shaking eye contact with Ranger Paul, who had gotten word of my day job when we teed off at Fox Hollow, then met me at the turn with a stack of pages retrieved from his car.

He'd been boss of the tee sheet at Fox Hollow for ten years, but not until today had he finally found the audience for which he'd been waiting. His cheeks were covered with white stubble, and in a faded Titleist cap, he read one of his "little ditties about the game of golf" from a collection I could see he had titled *Golf Scapes*.

"This one's called 'Short Putt,'" he said, and while the two teenagers working the snack shack covered their faces and giggled in the background, Paul read on, infusing enthusiasm into each syllable as he rhymed the tragic tale of a glorious approach spoiled by a jittery lip-out, leaving him nothing but "a story, of unfulfilled glory." I applauded his poem and patted him on the back—and when I reached for my camera to take his picture, Paul took it as a sign to read six more. He shared stanzas called "Ball Marks," "Wounded Paper and Broken Tees," and my favorite, "Golf Courses and Women," which confessed how "We seek to conquer them; but they / Actually enjoy this challenge, as / They know they will always win." This spotlight had been a long time coming, and while it seemed ironic that the course ranger was now putting our group well out of position, the cause of golf poetry demanded we wait and listen.

When Paul finished reading his pages, he handed them to me to keep, and I thanked him for my first encounter with on-course poetry; it had reminded me of one of my greatest golf days. The previous winter, I had snuck down to Florida to play alongside America's most popular poet (so claimed the *New York Times*). He didn't share any of his work while we played, though I wished he had.

I admired Billy Collins not only because we were both golfing academics, a rarity among the teaching and researching ranks (not many of my university colleagues have had to cancel class for a Mid-Am qualifier), but because I had cherished his writing for years. His poems had complexity masked as simplicity; they read like handshakes with a wise friend, and his lines were made of the most essential ingredients: wonder and joy. So, when presented with a chance to play golf with Mr. Collins, I was as nervous as an apprentice on his way to meet the mage. People traveled from around the country to hear him read, but our day was about a match of dear stakes between a golf drifter and one of his heroes.

Rather than meet at the golf course, Billy suggested we catch up at his home first, and while I would never say no to an opportunity to see where an icon lived and wrote, it put me on unsteady footing. I arrived early, of course, so I drove through the neighborhoods of Winter Park, Florida, until it seemed a suitable time to pull into the driveway. I circled his block three times. The Porsche and BMW had me wondering if I'd arrived at the right place (no poets I knew drove Porsches; few poets I knew actually drove), but within a minute Billy was on the front porch, making sure the cat didn't escape as he opened the door for me.

Billy and I had met via email months before, sharing our mutual appreciation for Old Tom's far-flung Askernish in Scotland. Our exchange further revealed that we both loved the Winter Park nine, so it became inevitable that we would one day peg it there together. I just didn't expect to get to poke around his office first.

Among the papers scattered around his wide desk—I was pleased to find it appropriately disorganized, like I'd caught a master at work amid piled books and manuscript pages and inky journals—Billy showed me a faded sepia photograph, no bigger than a driver's license, of a young boy holding a hickory golf club that reached his chin, with a big smile and a small cap. BILLY COLLINS was typed on the reverse side.

Billy had grown up in New York City and learned the game from his father. His dad had died in 1994 at the age of ninety-three, but Billy confided that, "If he were somehow alive today, he would be prouder of me for the courses I've played than for any of my achievements in poetry." A bold assessment, given that Billy had won just about every award a poet can win. He had been both a state and national Poet Laureate, and was asked to read a poem to a joint session of Congress on the first anniversary of 9/11. But he had also just returned from Augusta National, where he'd stayed in the cabin beside the tenth tee and visited various club offices to read poems for the staff, like one of the old bards reciting odes for his supper—so what he said about his dad made sense to me.

We headed to the Winter Park nine, where I sensed that they knew Billy was a somebody but that it didn't really matter, and that he preferred it that way. One of the many beautiful things about the Winter Park muni, aside from its genius Keith Rhebb–Riley Johns routing (through the streets of a quaint downtown, making it an archetype for neighborhood golf), is that the place lacks any and all airs—a good spot to tee it up with a literary lion who lacked them as well.

We decided we would play nine holes for a poem; the loser would have to write one for the winner on the spot. I had played for dinners and hundred-dollar stakes before, but never had I made such a bold wager on the golf course, especially when having to give my opponent seven shots. A napkin poem from Billy Collins would be the crown of my collections, both literary and golf, but the prospect of losing and having to invent lines for a poetry superstar was pure terror. I quickly went two holes down and tried to remember how many syllables were in a haiku.

Billy played with a soft slice that he attributed to his golfing DNA; lessons be damned, it had been with him since his father taught him the game. One of the things that fascinated him about golf, he said, was how our swings had a certain genetic footprint that we had to accept and overcome. His gentle slider kept him well in play at Winter Park, but he generously missed a couple of short ones so that we kissed sisters in the end. An impromptu Collins poem would have been nice, but the prize was golfing with a man I so looked up to—and he was treating me like a friend. In fact, he *was* a friend, sharing dirty jokes and telling me why he still loved golf as much today as ever.

"Golf is the union of the social and the solitary," he explained. It seamlessly blended time with friends, conversations, cocktails—group time—with moments when it was just you, your mind, your ball. As writers, we both required the solitary and felt most comfortable in that setting, but we needed that other part, too, to keep us sane. No wonder we played this game that gave us both. We weren't the weird ones, the writers and academics who needed golf. The weird ones, I realized, were those who somehow got by without it.

As big a part as golf had played in Billy's life, he had published only one poem about the game, and like all his work, it reminded me of something essential that I had overlooked. Golf had given me a lot of things, but better than most of them, on many a sleepless night, it had given me rest.

Night Golf
I remember the night I discovered,
lying in bed in the dark,
that a few imagined holes of golf
worked much better than a thousand sheep,

that the local links,
not the cloudy pasture with its easy fence,
was the greener path to sleep.
How soothing to stroll the shadowy fairways,
to skirt the moon-blanched bunkers
and hear the night owl in the woods.
Who cared about the score
when the club swung with the ease of air
and I glided from shot to shot
over the mown and rolling ground,
alone and drowsy with my weightless bag?
Eighteen small cups punched into the
bristling grass,
eighteen flags limp on their sticks
in the silent, windless dark,
but in the bedroom with its luminous clock
and propped-open windows,
I got only as far as the seventh hole
before I drifted easily away—
the difficult seventh, "The Tester" they called it,
where, just as on the earlier holes,
I tapped in, dreamily, for birdie.

—Billy Collins

I was playing some dream golf of my own at Fox Hollow, where I turned at three under and wondered if I should ask Ranger Paul to immortalize my front nine in verse. Fox Hollow was a forty-dollar public tucked into the banks of the Crow River, packed with brow-raising tee shots on the best conditions I'd found in a sub-fifty-dollar layout. Minnesota's cupboard of quality public options was crowded, and its private clubs contributed to a tally I called the Minnesota Miracle: four hundred courses thriving in a state with a blink-and-you'll-miss-it golf season. I received twice as many invitations from Minnesota golfers as I did from those of any other state, a phenomenon born of two factors: Minnesota Nice was a real thing, and when the sun did finally shine in the Land O'Lakes, its inhabitants attacked warm days like bears after a winter's nap.

A golf-writing friend of mine, Eric Hart, had generously built me a two-week itinerary from one edge of the state to the other. I was sorry to have to curtail his home-state pride into a four-day visit, but my schedule was unyielding. We packed two or three courses into a day and discovered that this place of parkas and hockey was one of America's great golfing venues, you betcha. Oh yah.

At Fox Hollow with Eric, his wife, and their sixteen-year-old son, Dylan, I followed a self-patented formula of topping a –3 front with a +4 back; it was a recipe I'd tweaked through the years, playing smart, measured golf before studying my scorecard and abandoning all reason in pursuit of 62. It was a number I'd never sniffed, yet my mind remained convinced it was just around the corner, if only I tried a little harder. One might have blamed Ranger Paul's intrusion as a turning point in the round, but it wasn't. If there was any blame to cast at Fox Hollow, it was for the group behind us that fired a magic bullet through our cart.

It served us right for riding, but with two more walking rounds on the calendar that day, we had opted for the free carts the pro offered. We pulled up to a dandy par 3 that played down to a green hugged by marsh and river. As much as I championed accessible golf, the private club world offered some luxuries I missed, and one of them was not getting stuck behind two foursomes of dudes on a bachelor party, three of whom had never played golf before. Another one was safety. We waited behind a lineup of carts, scooching our wheels up as far as we could, out of the firing line from a tee box to our right. We didn't scooch far enough. As we sat waiting in our carts, we heard a succession of *zip, crack, boom, Fore?* in that precise order.

I wasn't hit by a ball—that unlucky honor went to Dylan, in the cart ahead of mine—but I was struck by a sharp piece of black plastic. Dylan and I looked at each other, silent and confused about what had just happened. I turned around to see a guy on the tee behind us mumble *Sorry*; he had a wood in his hands, yet I knew the laws of physics prohibited a 3 wood from making a ball move at such an obtuse angle, and at such velocity.

The offending golfer zipped off in his cart without another word (another public golf shortcoming: douchey nonsense from unaccountable strangers) as we tried to re-create the events. The zip in my ear was the ball from the tee behind us, but it had somehow split the two golf bags strapped to our cart, brushed Eric's wife's leg, and then turned toward Dylan's cart, where it shattered a plastic joint on his stand bag, kicking shrapnel back into my face, then careening left to strike Dylan in the shoulder before bounding forth through their cart and onto the tee, where the dudes looked up from their beers to ask where the hell that ball came from.

As I pieced together the ball's trajectory, I discovered a new appreciation for the Warren Commission and their single-bullet theory. We were lucky to survive the incident with only a few scratches, though Dylan's bag was less fortunate. He lifted it off the cart to find its leg dangling and broken, and my heart went out to him; he'd worked hard to save up for a Sun Mountain bag and had high school tryouts in a couple of weeks. I knew what it meant for a sixteen-year-old to show up for a tournament with a cool bag, so I reached out to the folks who had been following my travels on social media, and within a day, a half dozen had offered to send him a replacement. For every golfer who broke your bag and drove away, there were a thousand to remind you that people are good.

CHASKA, MINNESOTA

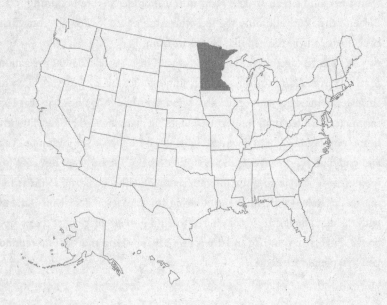

The Twin Cities offered three US Open venues for inspection. Minikahda and Interlachen felt like the quiet classics, while Hazeltine was a muscle car idling at the starting line, ready to host another major tomorrow. Minikahda was a charming Golden Age track where Chick Evans won the 1916 US Open as an amateur. Its name came from the native Dakota words for "by the water," and so it was, with a white-pillared clubhouse overlooking the largest lake in Minneapolis. It shared designer DNA with nearby Interlachen— Scotsman Willie Watson laid out the first holes at both—but Donald Ross overhauled Watson's Interlachen holes in 1919, adding angry false fronts protecting perched greens and an eighteenth that was downright devious. Set high above a pitched fairway beside the Tudor clubhouse, you had about three yards to make your approach stick on a tilted Slip 'N Slide. Interlachen would go on to host the 1930 US Open, where Bobby Jones took the medal en route to his Grand Slam, and a plaque on its ninth commemorated his clank heard 'round the world. Distracted by spectators running across the fairway, Jones topped his second shot on the par 5, skipping it across a pond where lily pads carried it across the water and tossed it onto dry land.

Eric and I arrived at Interlachen on the Sunday after Member-Guest. The caddies were whipped from back-to-back double-loop days; their pockets were already full of cash, so we were lucky to find two willing to go around again. Keith and Mark warned us that this was technically their day off, and that they might still be feeling the effects of their Saturday night. I didn't care; I'd carried some of my best loops pie-eyed, and I just needed someone to help me over the false fronts. My guy, Keith, was ex–Special Forces, and we laughed a lot that afternoon—until a former caddie buddy of mine, Mike, who'd relocated from Philly to Minneapolis, joined us to walk the back nine.

Keith busted my friend's chops at one point, to which Mike casually replied, "Shut the fuck up." Now, in Philadelphia parlance, "Shut the fuck up" translates to "Oh, go on, you silly fool." But in Minnesota, it translated to "Shut the fuck up." Keith sat up straight in the seat of our cart (our caddies had opted to become chauffeurs at the turn) and said, "What did you say to me?" The jovial looper was suddenly a Green Beret. I hit the gas and sped off, explaining that Mike meant nothing by it, that it was a Philadelphia thing. He was quiet for a moment, then laughed. "I get it. I served with guys from Philly. Ball-busters. I like that." The moment passed, and Keith tried to coach me through eighteen, but I couldn't help sending one long and capping a solid scorecard with a 6.

We retired to the clubhouse, where I could see that Interlachen was clearly a hang-around family club, with a bustling campus of kids bounding down the steps in bathing suits. Hazeltine National, on the other hand, felt more like a dormant coliseum waiting for a bout. I arrived the next morning to find a sprawling property with plenty of room for tents and merchandise pavilions, with an earth-toned clubhouse of wood and stacked slate. It was a national club (like Augusta—when you see "National" in the name, it means the club caters to a membership from beyond its own ZIP code), so it lacked the intimacy of Interlachen and Minikahda. It lacked their age as well—Hazeltine opened in 1962, built for the express purpose of hosting big events, and that it had. The Robert Trent Jones layout hosted a controversial US Open in 1970 after half the field didn't break 80 on day one. Tony Jacklin eventually won it, and after the course was softened a bit, the Open came back in 1991, when Payne Stewart pulled off a playoff win. In 1977, Nancy Lopez took second at Hazeltine in her first US Open as a professional, but the only tournament anyone was talking about by the time I arrived was the 2016 Ryder Cup. If Medinah downplayed its losing experience, the opposite was going on at here, where it seemed the champagne was still flowing.

Hazeltine was the only US Open venue on my itinerary where I didn't have to worry about the number of gift posters remaining in my trunk. Chandler, the head pro, was an old friend from Philadelphia—he'd been an assistant at Merion—and had hand-drawn the poster for me that winter, painstakingly sketching each club logo and lettering the names and scores of every Open winner. He already had a copy of the artwork in his office, though you might hardly notice it in a room where the widest side was wallpapered with floor-to-ceiling photographs of the first tee at Hazeltine's Ryder Cup. His course went ahead and crushed me, but I hardly noticed the hurt. I was too busy listening to Chandler tell me stories of American victory, when captain Davis Love III had given Hazeltine's head pro rare access to the team.

Love was Chandler's golfing idol; he'd gotten into the golf business because of him, and carried himself with the same quiet class as his hero. When Davis was announced as the 2016 captain, Chandler had hoped he'd have a chance to bring something to the team, so he'd spent the long Minnesota winter rewatching every recent Ryder Cup and taking careful notes. When Davis came out for a scouting round the year before the Cup, Chandler joined him, and when they reached the long par 5 third hole, Davis mentioned that there was no way they'd be using the back tee in the matches. Chandler saw his chance.

"Why wouldn't you play it back?" he asked.

Davis explained that they needed to make more birdies. They hadn't made enough birdies at Gleneagles in 2014 and lost. Chandler took his shot and disagreed.

"We lost at Gleneagles because we got crushed on the par fives," he said. "We were plus four on the par fives in alternate shot. The Europeans were minus eight."

Davis stopped. He was listening.

"McGinley put the blocks at five hundred yards. He knew they had the better long-iron players. Our team has eight of the twelve best wedge players in the world. So making the par fives into three-shot holes is going to be to our advantage."

That was precisely what they did. From that suggestion on, it was very much a team effort for Chandler and Davis. Eager for more insight, Chandler asked Davis why he thought America lost at Medinah. The captain said they couldn't close five tight matches that went to the eighteenth hole. Chandler offered his take: In those five matches, any one of which could have given America the Cup if they had taken a single point, no American player won the seventeenth or eighteenth hole. The Sunday pins had been pushed to the edges, and the more aggressive Americans kept taking the bait.

"If you're leading on Sunday," Chandler replied, "just put the pins in the middle. Take bogey out of it." They did, and Justin Rose notably lamented on Sunday after losing the Cup at Hazeltine, "I thought the setup was incredibly weak. I thought it was very much a pro-am feel in terms of the pin placements. They were all in the middle of the green. I didn't quite understand that, to be honest with you."

It was music to Chandler's ears. The PGA's own analytics team would back up the math Chandler had done in his basement, but he had earned himself a spot in the team room that week, where he had a role in deciding who would be let inside it.

The team room had formerly been a hangout for players and wives and coaches and celebrities. Chandler was playing with Tom Lehman a few months before the Cup was set to start, and he asked him why Michael Jordan was allowed in the room. Lehman said it was meant to be a social place where the guys could relax and blow off steam; they wanted it to feel comfortable, so players were free to invite whomever they chose. Chandler said that sounded fine if America had been winning the Ryder Cup, but they hadn't. Lehman heeded his advice and took the idea to Davis, and that year at Hazeltine, the team room was players only. MJ would have to hang in a hospitality tent.

An awkward legacy of that decision manifested in 2020, when Chandler was in Florida playing at Grove XXIII, a high-end private club owned by his Air-ness. Jordan happened to catch Chandler's group on the back nine and joined up, then sat with them in the bar afterward. Conversation turned to the Ryder Cup at Hazeltine, and Chandler's friend told Jordan that the guy who got him barred from the team room was sitting next to him. Jordan raised an eyebrow, and Chandler grinned.

"Michael, let me ask you: Would you have wanted wives and celebrities in the locker room at halftime during game seven?"

"Fuck no," Jordan said without hesitation. He nodded and said he understood. "You did the right thing," Jordan said. And Chandler quietly sighed in relief.

I used the drive out to Spring Hill that afternoon as a chance to remind myself that I knew how to play golf, ignoring the Hazeltine scorecard in the passenger's seat that suggested otherwise. Interlachen and Hazeltine grabbed the Minneapolis spotlight, but Spring Hill was likely the most coveted Twin Cities tee time. A mutual friend of Eric's and mine had arranged for us to play with a member who'd won a gold medal—and not just any gold medal, but the most meaningful gold medal in American Olympic history.

Rob McClanahan was a Minnesota hockey legend who had played for the Rangers, Whalers, and Sabres, but was best known as a member of the 1980 Miracle on Ice team. I usually operated under the assumption that hockey players were good golfers; I'd seen it proven back home, and it was proven again by McClanahan, who played off a three handicap and still had the build of a guy you wouldn't want following you for a puck in the corner. He'd scored five goals in the '80 Olympics, including the gold-medal winner against Finland. But perhaps most impressive, Rob was a normal guy who was happy to share stories about coach Herb Brooks and the 1980 team.

The Tom Fazio course was a chef's kiss of brave shots spread across terrain that moved like a potato chip, but we had our eyes and ears pointed at Rob, who indulged my request for another Brooks anecdote. He told us about the coach's parting words before the gold-medal game, after the US team had just beaten the Russians in perhaps the most emotional game in hockey history. A letdown seemed inevitable, and their coach knew it.

"Herbie walked into the locker room before the game, and he's pacing back and forth. Now, Herbie used to speak for five, ten minutes. He always had a speech ready; he knew how to motivate his players. So he's pacing back and forth, not saying anything, then he looks at us and says, 'If you lose this game, you'll take it to your fucking grave.' He turns around and walks to the door, then stops and looks back at us again and says, 'Your fucking grave.' Then he walked out. That was it," Rob said. "There was absolutely no way we were gonna lose that game."

I felt the goose pimples as I looked down at my ball in the fairway, an acre of shoulder-height marsh between me and the green, and I thought to myself, *If I dump this ball into the shit, I will take it to my fucking grave.* Then I did. And I believe that I will.

When I reached the drop zone, Rob tossed me another ball—it was a Titleist 80, with USA printed on the side. I putted out with it before slipping it into my bag for safekeeping, and in the grillroom afterward, he pulled the gold medal from Lake Placid out of his locker and let us each put it on and snap selfies.

Our introduction to Rob had been made via a local golf-head named Guy who distilled his own vodka and was a celebrity on the golf message boards. He invited us out to his curiously named club—White Bear Yacht Club—the next morning, where I walked two laps around the docks before being told the course was across the street. They didn't have polar bears in Minnesota, though there were a few cement ones on the White Bear course, placed as driving markers for its blind tee shots. It was a course to embrace or to balk at, the quirkiest Donald Ross I'd encountered, where you aimed at bears and played from tee boxes perched on the edge of a busy road—listen for the cars to pass, then swing, quick. For me, it struck the ideal blend of eccentricity, quality, and adventure; its hills were heart-stoppers, and its layout had all the twists of a great novel. It actually had ended up in a short story by F. Scott Fitzgerald, under the name Sherry Island Golf Club, after Fitzgerald and his wife, Zelda, had spent a summer living in a room there. Or most of a summer—their drunken antics eventually got them booted from the property. *Too bad for Fitzgerald*, I thought, because I flat-out adored White Bear. Per usual, the company influenced that impression.

It was hard to guess Guy's age. He had a kid in college, but dressed like one himself—golf-cool, with a flat-brimmed hat that belied his years. As we played, we talked about the metrics one might use in identifying the Great American Golf Course. I wondered if I might be standing on it, even though I'd hoped the title holder would be a public, to embody our democratic republic. As I covered more of our country, my list of characteristics for a representative American course was expanding: it should feel bold and idealistic with an individualistic bent, showcasing blended shades of the experimental and the innovative. It needed to be welcoming—America had been so to me thus far—yet it should be imperfect as well, though not without an abundance of hope. It would have a little revolutionary spirit with an ounce of wholesomeness, an upstart that should operate by an ambitious but simple credo. Plus, it should inspire and aspire while fostering both agreement and discord and tolerating both. And it should have a damn good hot dog at the turn.

It was a lot to ask for in one course. White Bear fit some of the bill, but not all of it. As for what made a course great, if not quintessentially American, Guy had some ideas to share.

"To me, a great golf course is one where you get to eighteen and want to walk back to one," he said. "This course is like that. Because of the lack of flat lies, every round is different. You might play thirty-six holes, and play the first eighteen and love the course, and the next eighteen just have your brains scrambled. But what really makes golf great is you and me. It's the friendships, the people you play with. I really don't care where we play. It could be a goat track, but if I'm with the three best dudes, I'm going to have a great time."

I thanked Guy for ranking me as a best dude. It was as high a status as I'd achieved in golf, and it reminded me that my Great American Golf Course was going to have more to do with the Americans with whom I played it than its red, white, and blue bona fides.

I had walked with teachers and drummers and actors and firemen and bankers, with students and grandfathers and moms and soldiers. I left Philadelphia with a simmering skepticism about my countrymen; we didn't agree, we didn't listen, and, worse, we didn't seem to care. We had retreated into our own righteousness, living in universes of disparate ideas, and I of course felt there was no hope unless everyone moved over here into mine. But when I tuned out the ranting hordes, I found that while we might be failing as Americans the plural—we weren't *E pluribus unum* but rather *E pluribus pluribus*—American the singular was still best-dude stuff. He or she was generous and hopeful, in search of fair work and happiness, and inclined to agree more than disagree when we found those rare face-to-face minutes. Such dialogues were going extinct in a screen-to-screen world, but not on the golf course, where I was reminded daily that our pastimes were now more essential than ever. There were still places where nobody was a snowflake or a moron; they were usually playing grounds of universal accord, where we all had something in common: a pursuit of victory or teamwork—or, in our case, par.

THE SANDHILLS, NEBRASKA

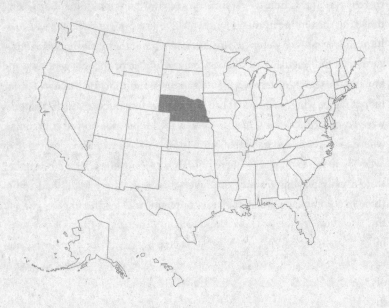

Explorers had eschewed the place for its useless mounds of beige—couldn't grow much, couldn't build much—but I was here for that sand in August. I had landed at the heart of one of the world's largest desert ecosystems craving the crunch of fine granules underfoot. They were crap for growing corn or soybeans, but when it came to holding golf holes, there were no better handlers than the dunes.

I had spent chunks of my life shaking Irish and Scottish sand out of my shoes; little did I know that every golf hole over there could have fit neatly into the dunescape in front of me, that the purest golf property on the planet wasn't in the British Isles or in California or Australia but in the heart of my own country, in the last state my imagination would connect to golf. I considered myself a connoisseur of golf in the dunes, yet I'd been deaf to the call of earth's mightiest sandhills. Now, America's greatest golf miracle rushed past my open windows as I licked the grit from my teeth and waved hello to the sandhills of Nebraska.

How the largest grass-stabilized dune system in the world landed in the Cornhusker State is uncertain—it may have been born of sediment spilling off the Rocky Mountains, or by sand blown from dried-up riverbeds. Its ancestry mattered little to me; I took the surroundings as proof that our game was rooted in phenomena. In the divine, even. Golf's greatest playing grounds were not shaped by software or backhoes but by an ancient and inscrutable confluence of wind, water, and sand. I eyed the hearty grasses waving atop soft slopes in every direction and felt myself cradled in evidence of golf as not a game but the great reminder to get outside and wonder.

"That's a golf course, right there," I found myself saying to the windshield. "And another one. And another one." Every few minutes I spied a new stretch of rippled landscape—so many designers had struggled to re-create this elsewhere, yet here it was, untouched and unending. I imagined myself hiking it in heavy boots, hammering stakes into the sand for a green site or a tee box. But dreams of my personal paradise were interrupted by reminders of the toil it took to get here—too remote, too unpopulated; golf could never thrive here. And if it could, it would take a bolder soul than me to roll those dice. Thankfully, there are plenty of such souls out there, and one was named Dick Youngscap. He had not just created a Nebraska golf course but shifted a paradigm.

When the architects of the early twentieth century went looking for exciting new ground, they were drawn to seaside tracts on Long Island and Monterey, or to the pine barrens of New Jersey and North Carolina—all near population centers or railroad stops, and all accessible for a newly mobilized set of American fun seekers. Some builders wandered farther afield, but none dreamed as Youngscap did in the 1990s, and by doing so he transformed course development and helped usher in the new Golden Age of golf design.

I didn't understand any of this until I played his course. I was just here to see if the holes were worth the drive and the letter I had written to Mr.

Youngscap, in which I pleaded my way onto a yonder golf course called, appropriately enough, Sand Hills.

As I sat at the bar in the lodge after my first loop around Sand Hills, awaiting the meal I had been instructed to order—*You have to get the bone-in ribeye*, friends told me—I made small talk with the bartender, a kind woman in glasses with blond hair puffed to a height that recalled the schoolteachers of my youth. When I discovered that she was indeed a teacher who worked here during the summers, it made sense, and not just because of her demeanor—for a place like this to function in Mullen, Nebraska, it would take all the schoolteachers and college kids home on break. The job applicant pool must have been small, but the people who took those jobs were proud of Mullen's acclaimed course and dedicated to the place's success. When she heard I was from Philadelphia, she told me that she had once been to Pittsburgh. And from where I was sitting, here on some faraway planet called the Sandhills, Pittsburgh might as well have been right outside our windows back home.

The bar grew crowded with the arrival of a buddy trip of twelve golfers from Chicago. Somebody's father was one of the club's founding members, whom Mr. Youngscap had tapped to help fund the construction, and so this crew made the trip out here every year, to golf dawn to dusk, gorge themselves on Nebraska beef and California wine, and then crash in the simple but clean cottages behind the lodge. There was no Hilton or downtown nightlife around the corner from Sand Hills, so a trip here was a true compound experience.

We're used to these sorts of getaways today—trips to Cabot, to Streamsong, to Sand Valley are now staples on golf calendars, where you eat, drink, golf, and repeat in the most inconvenient destinations. Bandon Dunes deserves credit for popularizing remote golf in America, but there is no Bandon without Sand Hills. This was the epicenter of the destination-golf movement, as its success emboldened Mike Keiser to take a shot on Bandon, and soon developers were seeking great land first and clientele second. We now live in a golf world where architects get to elevate their artistry on the best plots of land in the country, regardless of location. And those geographic handcuffs were first unlocked at Sand Hills, a golf oasis unlike anything I'd seen in America. Playing it felt like sailing a vast sea of grassy swells, where both your ball and your mind rolled with the tides.

Just that afternoon I'd met one of the men at the center of this new day in golf design—Gil Hanse was building a course not too far from Sand Hills, and had come over to play with some of his crew. Gil and I lived five minutes from each other back in Philadelphia, but we had to come all the way to Nebraska to finally meet in person.

Gil was taller than I expected, and if I hadn't recognized him from TV, I would have struggled to peg him as the designer of the Olympic course in Rio or the architect charged with restoring an inordinate amount of American classics, from Sleepy Hollow to Brookline to Baltusrol to Oakland Hills to Winged Foot to Southern Hills to Olympic to Fishers Island to Merion. He just looked like a dude, with relaxed posture and dancing bears on his belt.

As he walked from his truck toward the clubhouse, I stopped him and introduced myself. He was gracious and said some nice things about my books (it's a kind thing to say to an author, but congenital insecurity leads us to assume you haven't actually read them, though I think Gil had), and we talked about the Eagles for a bit; whenever they played near one of his job sites, he said, he was in the stands in green.

I followed him inside to poke around. There were plenty of architects with egos of legend, but Hanse spoke in thoughtful and humble tones, somehow managing to give the impression that he was as pleased to meet me as I was him. As we don't rank anywhere near each other on the golf notability scale, I quickly identified that quality in Gil that I searched for like Diogenes with his lamp—simple class.

We both scooped up some Sand Hills souvenirs in the pro shop. He would be giving his to friends and employees, while mine would be peacocked around for the next decade as proof that I was golf anointed. After we'd gathered our spoils, Gil told me to follow him, and we went searching for a map.

Down a stairway we found a creased drawing on the wall. It looked like a framed spiderweb to me, but its black-and-white dots and lines actually sketched out 136 different golf holes that Bill Coore and Ben Crenshaw—two more heroes in golf's new chapter—had identified on the property. Creating

Sand Hills, for them, was not a matter of building golf holes as much as it was a matter of eliminating the unnecessary ones. Blessed with natural green sites and ready-made fairways funneled through the dunes, they moved precious little earth during construction, and the course was completed for the absurdly low sum of $1.2 million. Some courses spent more shaping a driving range.

Gil was quiet as his eyes studied the map with the reverence of an art buff in a museum. He took out his phone and snapped a picture of it, and I was again impressed by the modesty of such an accomplished designer who had come here not just to play but perhaps to learn as well. A less noble mind might have resented Coore and Crenshaw as competitors, but it looked to me like Gil was paying homage to his peers.

As Gil was leaving to get back to his worksite, he posed for a picture with me in the parking lot, and I asked him about his own answer to the question that had set me on the road for the last four months.

He paused, and in that silence I admonished myself for asking Gil Hanse such a broad, high school newspaper question. Why not just ask him the meaning of life, as he's trying to get into his car to leave? But he answered as cool and clear as the pro he was.

"I think a sense of place. I think that's a really important thing, and I think that a golf course needs to tie in naturally with its surroundings. With how diverse the topography in our country is, there are so many great examples of golf courses that just fit where they are," he said. "The best examples of golf architecture take advantage of the natural advantages that are already there. And that gives them that identity that I think is really critical to any good architecture. I understand when we talk about strategy and interest and character, and any great golf course is going to have all that. But I think it's really about that sense of place that makes a golf course feel like it belongs."

In that brief moment, Gil had not only aced his golf architecture exam but he had done more work to soothe my psyche than the therapist back home who kept wanting to talk about my trials as a grade-school ginger. *Place. Belonging.* They were words we often applied to our own search for happiness, but to extend them to golf, and to think that when a golf course possessed them, it impacted our own happiness—I was knocked off my

"Every great golf course has a bell."
—Anonymous, Sleepy Hollow, New York

A soggy start at Newport

This damn close at the Loop (Forest Dunes, Michigan)

Nationally grateful

Pick your course

Caddie whispering wisdom at Silvies

A driving range unlike any other
(Big Cedar Lodge, Missouri)

How David McLay
Kidd cleared the gorse
at Bandon Dunes

Lax border security
(Aroostook Valley,
Maine/Canada)

How foursomes were made
before smartphones (Marion
Golf Course, Massachusetts)

The other one (Arkansas)

Not Shinnecock

Chasing the midnight sun (Alaska)

The citizens of *A Course Called America*

Pulling into the literal island green at Coeur d'Alene (Idaho)

Rez Golf is the best golf (the Navajo Nation)

All those rounds in Scotland, and it was in Vegas the whole time . . .

Rake your bunkers. And your greens. (Missouri)

A yardage buffet at Ballyneal (Colorado)

Spot the six sports
(Southern Hills, Oklahoma)

Real saints fight
with 5 irons

Dad pushes, Mom plays
(Schoolhouse Nine, Virginia)

The taxi home from
Wawashkamo (Michigan)

Yujin
the Wonderdog

Targets at White Bear Yacht
Club, of course (Minnesota)

Torrey Pines
(California)

Fishers Island
(New York)

Tobacco Road
(North Carolina)

horse. The mystery of why sometimes a nine-hole muni felt perfect while an elite rankings topper sometimes felt incomplete finally made sense. It didn't have to be in Scotland or Ireland or Nebraska or Monterey—it just had to be the right course for wherever it was. Because when it was, it was place and belonging and comfort; it was home. And damned if I hadn't roamed the golfing world searching for precisely that.

That evening, the ribeye was as good as had been foretold, and as I sat at the bar with upturned wineglasses dangling overhead, a few of the Chicago group recognized me, and one of the more well-served of the party insisted he had read my book about golf in America.

"No, you haven't," his more sober friend told him, pulling him back by the shoulder. "You read his Ireland book."

"No!" he insisted, leaning in closer over my empty plate. "I read about you playing America. I swear to God I read that book."

"He hasn't written it yet!" his friend explained. I confirmed that was indeed the case, but the gentleman insisted that he had read about my American travels, waving his glass of red wine for emphasis.

He was confusing some social media posts for a book, I surmised, but I silently wished he was telling the truth. So many more miles and states and courses ahead—I looked at the Nebraska twilight past the windows and dreamed of the moment I could say *America, complete*. Such a moment felt like myth, but as I reminded myself every morning, all I had was the day in front of me, and there would be a time not too long from now when I would miss all of this, a day when I could tell the guy at the bar at Sand Hills that no, he hadn't read my book about playing all fifty states over the course of eight glorious, enlightening, maddening months in America—

But you are now.

SPRINGFIELD, PENNSYLVANIA

"Here comes your old man," the guys in the pro shop would call down to me from the window. "Bud and a dog."

Other caddies had members who requested their services, and while my dad never made an explicit appeal to have me on his bag, he would always ask the pro if I was here today, and I always was. None of the other caddies at Rolling Green minded the nepotism; Dad's was a heavy leather sack and he paid the standard rate, while most caddies were holding out for reckless tippers. Dad's routine was to tell whoever was minding the shop that he'd be on the tee in a minute, but first, a late lunch at the halfway house. Or, as he always put it, "I'm gonna go grab a Bud and a dog."

While he did so, I'd hustle down from the bag rail to the basement, hoist

Dad's bag off the rack, and head for the first tee. I preferred the storytelling hours waiting around the bag room to the actual caddying, but Dad was an easy loop—driver, 4 wood, 9 iron, putter, in that order. It was amazing how many times he turned that combination into par. He was a short, straight hitter who didn't require reads or raking, as his ball rarely veered into bunkers. As we all settled into our steady loops over the course of our caddie careers, I found I would rather wait around to see if Dad was coming over from the office than play roulette with a guest's bag or get stuck with one of the assholes. I learned early that the disparity between an asshole and a hero had nothing to do with skill or demeanor—the difference was about ten bucks.

I know Dad was pleased that I took to caddying, and that the caddies took to me, a member's kid. He'd spent his childhood in upstate Pennsylvania, where his father had run an orphanage during the Depression, and a summer caddying job was a similar lesson in humility and empathy. Some of my co-workers were living very raw lives—while I was saving for Air Jordans, their tips went to booze or a fix or a bed for the night, and not getting a loop meant begging trolley fare off those of us who did. Dad appreciated that his country-club kid was learning that the world was not, in fact, a country club, and carrying bags taught me plenty more than how the greens tilted. Carrying *his* bag taught me who my dad was—and years later, how much of that was in me.

We weren't club-tossers, but we both played a little angry, two golfers who hated giving away a hole. He did bend a 5 iron around a tree once, then handed it back to me as if I was supposed to slip a V-shaped rod back into his bag and carry on. I'd carried his bag in club tournament triumphs, and listened to him replay every shot for my mom that evening. Like me, his mood was dictated by his ball striking. Good golf cast a clear light on the world; bad golf made everything a little cloudier.

I'd watched him make three aces—all on the same hole at Rolling Green, with the same club—and launch bunker shots into backyards, never quite mastering the sand in his fifty years of golf. But when I think of my dad and Rolling Green, I always come back to one afternoon before any shots were struck at all.

I was waiting in the pro shop for him to return with his Bud and a dog. When he did, he pointed through the window to three kids heading toward the first tee and asked who they were and why they had just jumped ahead of us. The pro explained that they had come over from the US Junior at Aronimink and were playing at the request of a Rolling Green member named Stanley. Stanley fancied himself as something of a golf mover and shaker, floating around the club with an air of tiresome self-importance.

"Is Stan playing with them?" Dad asked, the ire in his voice suggesting he already knew the answer. The pro told him he wasn't. I could tell that no one was a fan of this break from protocol; you didn't just show up with unaccompanied strangers and tell the pro to let them go play.

"So, are they his guests or not?"

The pro shook his head. "Mr. Coyne, I can only ask the members to follow the rules. It's your club."

That was all Dad needed to hear. He turned for the door and pushed it open, and I watched through the window as he marched over to the carts where Stanley was laughing with another member. I could hear his voice through the glass: "Excuse me, Stan. I'd like to have a word with you."

He pulled Stanley aside into a corner, but not out of view. Dad's face was stern; he looked like he did that time I sprayed Mom with the garden hose through the kitchen window. Dad jabbed a finger to emphasize his points, and we watched as Stan's face went white, his lips frozen. My dad turned around and walked toward the tee, and Stan headed for the pro shop door.

The pro and I hurried away from the window. Within seconds, in walked Stanley. "I'm going to go put my spikes on," he said with a little flutter in his voice. "I'll have three guests with me today." He stepped briskly across the shop and into the locker room.

The pro turned to me and said, "Your dad is the fucking man."

Many years later, Mom and Dad moved to a seniors' apartment complex, too far from Rolling Green to use it anymore. His friends at the club were mostly gone anyway, deceased or relocated to Florida, so after forty years, they moved on.

We all have that course that has stuck with us like a first crush or a childhood home; it's our golf imagination's stock footage, and every other course has been a remix—sometimes a better one, but more often not. For me, and for Dad I'm sure, that was always Rolling Green. It's where I took my first swipe at a golf ball and followed a trail of holes six days a week—even when we weren't playing it, some part of our mind was. Before I chose a single course to visit on my tour of America, I wrote *Rolling Green* atop what would become a long list.

Dad hadn't been back since the move—nor had I—and word was they had redone the clubhouse, chopped down half the trees, and were restoring some of the holes. That all sounded like good news, but what the place was becoming didn't really matter. For us, it could only ever be what it had been. It existed for me in a sort of radiant stasis in some immutable part of my memory, where it's always sunny and I'm forever fifteen years old. Put the words *golf* and *course* together and I see Rolling Green. Probably always will, no matter how far I wander or how many courses I play.

The only way I would ever play it again was with Dad, but when I was last at home, he had called to tell me he wasn't coming to golf with us in Scotland. He had woken up one morning the week before unable to stand. The doctors suspected sciatica, then confirmed he had a few degenerated disks. At eighty-five, he was too old for any back procedures, so he hoped physical therapy would help, and accepted that he was stuck pushing a walker.

He learned to use Instagram so that he could follow my travels, and I called Mom often to get his status—he'd of course tell me he was fine, but she could offer an honest assessment. He wasn't doing great. His spirits were low, and a guy who had lived without complaints now had plenty of them.

I know I'm luckier than most to have so many golf memories with my father. We'd played across the Irish county where his grandparents were born, and had crossed the Swilcan Bridge together. I knew he'd start acting his age at some point, but it had seemed a distant, abstract notion, not something we'd ever actually witness. The wobble in his legs was hard to watch; worse was the look in his eyes as he reached for something to steady himself. I'd seen my dad worried, but this was my first time seeing him afraid. It wasn't a fear that he would fall or break his arm, though I'm sure that was a concern. It was a fear of not knowing who he was like this, unsteady and unable. I stopped expecting to golf with Dad again and bargained with unknown forces to trade his golf for the return of his bad jokes and his battles of wit with my six-year-old, for his email forwards and his easy confidence that I didn't know how much I relied upon until I found it missing.

JUNO BEACH, FLORIDA

I had spent months entrenched in Florida golf while writing my second book, *Paper Tiger*, so I'd long dismissed its courses as a song I'd heard a thousand times—flat Bermuda grass, golf carts, alligators. Golfing in February was never terrible, but it was never very special, either. That opinion shifted when I finally visited Jupiter and Hobe Sound, where the Atlantic Coastal Ridge forged an undulating golf canvas along Florida's eastern shore. A geologist friend—everybody needs one—explained how the prehistoric ripple was formed by mineral deposits dating to when the edge of the East Coast was seabed: The sediments created sand hills and limestone crests that could be found as far north as the Pine Barrens in New Jersey, meaning Pine Valley was a geological cousin to Seminole. It seemed poetic; a lot of the same people belonged to both clubs. I was eager to become one of them, but couldn't find the applications on their websites. I couldn't find their websites, for that matter.

I did, however, find Seminole at the end of a residential street in Juno Beach, where the road ended at a left turn before the beach, pointing me at a Spanish-style manor, pink walls with the bronze bust of a Native American out front. Seminole had been home to Fords and Kennedys and Chryslers and Vanderbilts when they wintered in Palm Beach. It was a favorite retreat for Ben Hogan, where he spent a month every year in preparation for the Masters, and where he palled around with Seminole's pro, Claude Harmon. Harmon had won the green jacket as a club pro in 1948, and like Seminole's current pro, Bob Ford, who had done double duty at Seminole and Oakmont, Harmon had kept a decent summer gig up at Winged Foot as well.

Seminole's Donald Ross layout had recently been updated by Coore & Crenshaw in preparation for the 2021 Walker Cup, and it was most renowned for its confounding green complexes, where a ball was never safe until you marked it. I gave kudos to Ross for finding such a beguiling routing on a square plot of land. The Atlantic Ridge helped, as Seminole offered climbs you'd never expect along a beach in Florida. While it had no peer in this panhandle state, raters debated whether its lofty ranking was inflated by mystique, or if its routing would hold up against the likes of Merion and Shinnecock if placed in the Northeast. I was the wrong person to ask, because I never subtracted mystique from the course equation—and at Seminole, the mystique was so thick I could taste it on my tongue. It tasted like SPF 50.

From the moment my foot hit crushed gravel and a valet whisked my car off to elsewhere, I felt intimidated in all the best ways. Sure, I'd railed against golf elitism, but as Uncle Walt once said: "Do I contradict myself? / Very well then I contradict myself, / (I am large, I contain multitudes.)" Golf was a big game, and there was enough room for at least a few places behind the gates. How else were we going to get goosebumps when they opened before us?

Things got more serious when my phone buzzed in the locker room and I made the mistake of removing it from my pocket to look. It was my host telling me he was running late, which earned me a reprimand from the locker room attendant. I apologized, and resisted blaming my host for setting me up. If there was any golf room where I didn't want to be asked to leave, this was it. Seminole's locker room felt like a lair for Victorian redcoats and their big-game-hunting friends. Around its perimeter, wooden doors were set into the walls, reminiscent of the sunken lockers I'd once witnessed at the R&A. In the middle of the room, tea tables were elegantly set amid glass cases displaying club artifacts. On the high walls, the names of Walker Cuppers and elite amateurs were painted on gold-lettered lists of club trophy winners, and above them hung the stuffed heads of water buffalos, antelope, and elk. It was a perfect blend of class and machismo that made me feel like I was sitting in Teddy Roosevelt's parlor.

The course was a comprehensive exam in angles and careful strategies, demonstrated most effectively on Hogan's favorite, the short par 4 sixth, where the diagonal green required not just a savvy approach but a bold drive to save you from an unsavory second shot—brave the bunkers or be left with a hopeless hundred yards. The whole place felt like an exhibit in the distance debate, proving again that thoughtful design could cut the legs out from under bombers.

After our round, I shopped stupidly—of course I knew nine people who needed a hat—then headed a few miles south to a course that may have shared some of that Atlantic Ridge with Seminole, but that was as far as their similarities stretched.

When my summer-fall itinerary left no room for the Sunshine State, I was unfazed by the prospect of lopping it off my map. I'd spent so many winter weeks there that skipping Florida seemed an easy omission to write my way around, but my conscience prodded me into planning a pre-Newport tour during my spring break from school. I didn't expect the courses I chose to be impacted by the influx of March revelers, but this one apparently was; I had to wait for a foursome to come off eighteen before a parking spot opened. The tee sheet was jammed at the very public Palm Beach Par 3, where Raymond Floyd had designed eighteen one-shotters that wound along the beach, over ponds, and around a bustling restaurant—and judging by the golfing

multitudes on a Monday afternoon, Palm Beach had nailed a winning recipe. I arrived as a bus of senior citizens was unloading at the bag drop, so I
hustled inside to check in ahead of them. I asked where I could change my
shoes—my Seminole locker room faux pas was still fresh—and was given a
tired glance from the guy at the counter, who said there was a bathroom in
the restaurant. I told him I'd go back out to my car, and there in the parking
lot, I found the old friend with whom I was playing.

I hadn't seen Johnny since my *Paper Tiger* days. He'd nearly made it
through Q-school on three different occasions, then hung around the mini-
tours before his back gave out and he pivoted to the business world, where
he was currently killing it as a cannabis speculator. Marijuana had gotten so
respectable of late. Guys who used to have a cousin who could score a baggie
of trashy pot were now hemp fund managers with shareholders to please.
Johnny drove a Mercedes, and his slick curls and designer shades shouted
investment banker.

The Palm Beach Par 3 is the poster child for community golf: fun shots,
sunny scenery, smooth greens. Palm Beach just needed three more of them
to accommodate the demand. The slower pace allowed Johnny and me to
catch up on many years of in between, and by the back nine, he had me
sold on CBD as a cure for cancer, Parkinson's, and three-putts. He plied me
with products I was reluctant to sample (I'd forfeited my rights to chemical
mood adjustment), but he assured me the stuff wouldn't get me high. Or
not *that* high. I was less convinced as the round progressed; the stuff he'd
been rubbing on his lips and gums had widened his eyes and inspired talk of
metaphysics and the true nature of the universe. We went from debating the
merits of a claw putting grip to discussing how life beyond our solar system
could be accessed via an expanded consciousness.

"The stuff I could tell you would blow your mind," he said with a knowing grin. "People have no idea." And maybe Johnny did know. Maybe he had
tapped into a font of cosmic well-being; he sure was happy, and far be it from
me to judge anyone for that. Mindfulness and meditation were very of the
moment, and I, too, had dabbled—it didn't help me commune with extrater-
restrials, but it did make me a more peaceful golfer, and thus a better one, so
my friend was surely onto something.

That night, I hopped on a late flight from Fort Lauderdale, an airport I would recommend to anyone looking for a place to spend the shittiest three hours of his or her life, and headed for Jacksonville to meet up with my friends from No Laying Up. On this next leg, my spring break circuit around Florida would shift from a tour of reclusive treasures like Seminole and McArthur (a quiet Nick Price enclave where I hit balls on the range next to Bill Parcells, and didn't even tell him the Giants suck) to Florida's bevy of quality everyman courses. The NLU boys played their golf at Jacksonville Beach, a muni around the corner from their Killhouse headquarters (named for Tiger Woods' Navy SEALs "kill house" training regimen). The course had been renovated the previous year by noted architect Harrison Minchew, and was a steal at forty dollars for a Florida muni in private-club shape. The guys were known for their elaborate golf gambling machinations—games were loaded with specials and side bets and presses stacked like pancakes—but the common thread in all of them was my losing money to Tron. I did win his blessing when I named the rest of the courses I was visiting that week; I'd already played plenty of Florida's edges, so I was eager to head for unexplored territory in its red center. When I told him one name in particular, he pumped his fist in approval.

PALATKA, FLORIDA

I arrived before dawn, but the first box was already busy with pushcarts and practice swings. The pro said he could find room for a single if I waited on the putting green, which I did until I was called to the tee, where a man with a bushy red mustache and jeans was arguing with the starter.

"I told you I got to be done by eleven," he complained in a surprising accent; I'd never heard a deep Florida drawl before. Come to think of it, I'd never met anyone in Florida who was actually *from* Florida.

"I know, Randy, you told me. You on graveyard again?" the starter asked.

"All week. And I got to be in bed by eleven or my night is screwed."

Randy was sharing a cart with his buddy Jim, and I imagined being paired with an unknown single had stirred some protest. I assured him I wouldn't hold them up, even though I was walking. When I hit a deep one off the first tee, he said, "Looks like I'll be holding you up, looking for my balls in the woods!" But Randy was a Palatka hustler; you wouldn't see his swing in any magazines, but it squeezed out four birdies as he banged his chips through the Ross false fronts, his ball skipping forward and snuggling up to the pins. The Palatka Golf Club's holes worked their way around and through a cavernous rift, and its Frisbee-size greens added another good thousand yards of difficulty to its 5,800. I had been warned by a friend that Florida was full of dubious Donald Ross layouts—if his train so much as passed through town on the way to Palm Beach, a course would claim him— but this one felt like the genuine article, and along with Bacon Park up in Savannah, they had to be the two best values for a Ross devotee, both getting you on the tee for around thirty dollars.

By the back nine, Randy and I had become old pals. He told me Palatka had once been a busy railroad junction and a retreat for Northerners who visited its fancy hotels. A fire destroyed most of the town in 1884, after which Palatka lost out to Jacksonville as the area's industry and shipping hub. It still had a paper mill on the St. Johns River, and a Sheetrock factory where Randy worked. "The people here are hardworking, good country people," he said. "You can be in the big city in an hour, but it's better here. Jim lives in Orlando now but he's here today. The place pulls you back."

I could see why. This north-central strip of Florida was ripe with southern charm, and as I cruised down to Ocala after our early round, I passed horse farms and ranches and a lot of pawn shops, too—a world far away from the condo-golf developments I'd once called home down in Naples.

Ocala's main square was dotted with whimsical horse sculptures painted by local artisans, and the businesses here had actual age, so unlike the P.F. Chang's Florida I was accustomed to on the Gulf Coast. At a busy barbecue stand on the edge of town, I finally met Florida Man. He was in line behind me, keys dangling on a chain that hung from beltless jean shorts. His shirt must have been at the cleaners, I thought, and his deep tan had an unbathed sheen. His tattoos were of a two-for-one quality, and in his fist he clenched dollar bills and a pack of menthols. He had a patchy blond mustache below bright green eyes that I could feel staring at the back of my head, but I didn't dare turn around again. That evening, I met Florida Woman outside my motel, where she was mumbling to herself in the parking lot in a ripped white T-shirt, one hand clutching a plastic bag and the other a bottle of iced tea. She paced in circles and bobbed her head back and forth.

It was all a reminder of the puzzle that was this planet at our southeastern tip, a state of both last and first resort. You were here because you'd either won at life or life had kicked your ass. For every country club, a rehab; for every gated community, a block of halfway houses where some folks got better, but most ended up clutching plastic bags in dark parking lots. It had Mickey Mouse and Sea World, too, along with "The Horse Capital of the World" in Ocala, where the most elite thoroughbreds came to stud, but opioids had ignited a treatment boom backed by both capable practitioners and junkie-chasing profiteers. No wonder its state motto was In God We Trust; it was a place only He could explain.

My phone found four courses with Ocala in their name, and I visited three of them to find the two where I had tee times—Ocala National and Ocala Golf Club. The former was a perfectly acceptable Rees Jones course packed with northern snowbirds, but Ocala GC was the twenty-dollar gem I was looking for. Its holes ran up and down a hillside, a tidy locals' hideout where I got paired with a ten-year-old named Tyson, who was playing hooky to golf with his dad. I felt badly for intruding on their father-son morning. The dad kept reminding Tyson to hurry up and pick up his ball; he seemed too worried about spoiling my pace, and I assured him that I was in no rush, and Tyson should take as many swings as he needed.

On the seventh green, Tyson stood over his ball, digging in his pocket for his lucky ball mark.

"Come on, Tyson, let's go," his dad told him.

"I can't find my marker," he said, sounding distraught. For a moment, I remembered being ten and so carefully arranging my bag the night before golf with my dad. I couldn't shoot par, but I could lay out all my golf accessories and plan for it like a pro, and my chosen marker seemed more essential than my 7 iron. I reached into my pocket and pulled out the heavy Seminole marker I had bought a few days before and handed it to him. I felt like Mean Joe Greene tossing him a towel.

"Here. Keep this one. You heard of that place?"

Tyson stared at it in his palm like it was made of gold. "Seminole," he said. "Yeah. Florida State. But we're Gator fans."

"Well, yeah, that's okay. It's a different Seminole," I said.

Tyson thanked me and marked his ball, and went on and missed his putt for five.

I first met Scott on the Isle of Skye, after he emailed to ask if he could join me on my Scottish adventure. We'd been close ever since, and his running the best golf resort in Florida made it an easy friendship to maintain. He was also the only director of golf I knew of whose checks were signed by a fertilizer mining conglomerate.

Who would have guessed that most of Florida's middle was a phosphate field? I wouldn't have, but I learned that in 2007, the Mosaic Company went looking for a way to responsibly repurpose their churned acres—and it occurred to them that the sand hills they'd created looked like a pretty special spot for golf. They were right. They'd accidentally turned the heart of Florida into sublime linksland, and with new courses by Gil Hanse, Tom Doak, and Coore & Crenshaw, Streamsong was a gluttonous golf getaway, forty-five minutes removed from any signs of civilization. But unlike yonder Bandon Dunes, it offered the ease of weekend trips for golfers from the Northeast—fly to Orlando, drive ninety minutes, then peg it—and was thriving from a steady stream of New Yorkers escaping the cold.

After three calf-burning loops through the sands of Streamsong's modern links masterpieces, I recharged in the luxury of its lodge before heading for the epicenter of American golf. Streamsong, Pinehurst, Bandon, Long Island, Monterey—mere outposts and also-rans in the race to be America's golf capital. There could be only one true champion, where a trademark promise of *Free Golf for Life!* sounded like a miracle popped from a genie's bottle.

THE VILLAGES, FLORIDA

Fifty golf courses. Thirty-two square miles. One hundred twenty thousand members with seventy thousand homes, and, according to the *New York Post*, a ten-to-one female-to-male ratio with an appetite for golf cart quickies. Simply put: a sprawling golf heaven. The only downside, it seemed, was that its residents were inching up on real heaven, with an average age of sixty-eight. But as members passed, there were plenty of relocators ready to take their place; according to census data, this golf hub was actually America's fastest growing city, though when I visited it felt more like a sprawling village than a metropolis. Which was precisely what they were after.

While wintering in Florida had once been a ritual reserved for wealthy northern families, it was now a commonplace migration, and I was eager to visit one of the places that had made it so, selling every American their slice of the Florida dream. *Retirement community* didn't capture the Villages at all. It felt more like a religious commune where everybody worshipped at the altar of happy-hour specials, an elderly Eden where all the automobiles had been replaced by golf carts and the residents were aging backward. As I toured its town squares—there were several, with live music seven nights a week, and more bars than Bourbon Street—I watched as grandparents danced and clapped out of rhythm and hopped from one watering hole to the next. At dinner, a loud table of ladies celebrating a seventy-fifth birthday had ordered a tray of kamikaze shots and sent one my way. I politely declined, and was pretty sure one of them was eying me like a late-night snack. It wasn't even five o'clock. Suddenly, it struck me: This was no retirement community; this was Nanna and Pop-Pop on spring break. This was our parents acting like our children. It was heartwarming and awful at the same time.

My hosts were in their late sixties and dedicated members of the Villages' Parrot Heads, America's largest club chapter of Jimmy Buffett lovers. "Party with a Purpose" was their motto, and they used their trimonthly cocktail parties to raise money for local causes. Their golf cart was decorated with Buffett beach scenes, but their wheels were humbled by the pimped-out rides that crowded the town squares, some transformed into mini Rolls Royces and shrunken Humvees or retrofitted to look like antique Ford pickups. I spotted a Yankee mobile with pin-striped leather seats and was pleased to see an Eagles cart decaled in green and white. The retirees' surplus of time had sparked a cart arms race, it seemed, and there was a cart shop nearby to help you keep up with the Joneses. The Villages, I could tell, was a one-stop shop for its citizens—there were churches for every creed, a Target, a Walmart, and supermarkets aplenty. With its own hospital and myriad doctors' offices around the complex, you never had to traverse its borders. My hosts admitted it might all feel a bit odd to an outsider. "But once you drink the Villages Kool-Aid," the wife explained, "the place is pretty much perfection." There was some vodka in that Kool-Aid, from what I could tell, but the Villagers seemed happy to chug it.

The community began as a mail-order business in the 1960s, when Michigander Harold Schwartz started selling plots of paradise sight unseen.

It was born as a glorified mobile-home park, a few of which remained today, as the Villages catered to retirement at any budget. Whether you were in the market for a mansion or a double-wide or something in between, there was a neighborhood for you. We took a golf-cart tour of the community, and my friends were sure to bring along an extra tank of gas—the place was too vast for electric carts to stay powered, and when they went to visit their friends on the other side of the Villages, it took them forty-five minutes and a fill-up.

"Why don't you just drive your car?" I asked, and they laughed.

"You don't drive here. They don't give out DUIs for golf carts. It happens, but not very often," the husband explained.

"Unless you hit something," his wife said.

"Right. Unless you hit something. People get their carts juiced up to thirty-five miles an hour, which is against the rules. They can have real wrecks."

I imagined a grandmother inviting some dodgy mechanic over to turbocharge her cart engine under cover of darkness. There were some scofflaws here in paradise, and apparently some libidos, too. My hosts—whose names I'm not using because the Villages fiercely protects their image as a late-life utopia—said the stories about the STDs were probably exaggerated, but it depended on who you asked.

The *New York Post* did an exposé in 2009, which described a dramatic spike in gonorrhea, syphilis, and chlamydia among the retirees and quoted a local doctor as claiming she'd treated more herpes cases at the Villages than she did when she worked in Miami. The story described a vibrant market for one-night stands, and for bootleg Viagra, where outnumbered bachelors had their pick of the flock.

"You should see how some of these women get done up," my lady host told me. "The big hair, the tight dresses. My God, you can cut the perfume in these places with a knife. They've got the bodies, but the faces, eh. The helmets are a little rough."

She added that one doctor told her the numbers in the newspaper were overblown, but another she knew admitted that she had written plenty of prescriptions for STDs.

"People come down here and turn back into kids. It's great. We weren't sure we were going to like it, but I tell you, once you get into it, you're always doing something—golfing, going places, having happy hour every day. It's Friday all the time. What's not to love?"

The *Free Golf for Life!* tag was a bit of a Villages bait and switch; you were welcome to play any of their thirty-two executive (par 3) courses for free in your own golf cart, but the twelve eighteen-hole "country club" courses came with a fee. They had designs by Arnold Palmer and Nancy Lopez and some other names I'd never heard before, but notions of architecture took a back seat to golf's real purpose here: fill the days with diversion, and crack beers in the sunshine.

I chose the Nancy Lopez course from the menu—I suspected I wasn't going to find another one this year—and it played like a reassuring hug. I hit from the last of six tee options—it was a solid 4 iron to carry the front boxes—and discovered a course where you couldn't lose your ball if you painted it green. These tracks were designed for ease and pace, with fringe-height rough and yawning green mouths. And damned if I didn't like it. Tiger's dad made him play from the forward tees so that he would learn what it felt like to go low, and to expect it. There was nothing wrong with a little ego boost, and Nancy's layout had me believing I was a better golfer than I was. I'd fallen for worse deceptions on the golf course.

We watched from our carts as my friend's husband putted from a hundred yards out and left his ball pin-high. "He putts from everywhere. You can do that here. He'll putt on a par three. Doesn't care."

She was the longer driver of the two, and while I was succumbing to the comforts of Villages life, the idea of Allyson outdriving me while I putted from the middle of the fairway dampened any visions of a future here for us. Allyson wasn't a planned-community sort of person anyway, even if the monthly list of activities was fifty pages thick. We weren't big joiners, and she'd get bored fast, especially if I kicked the bucket first. She'd be too busy mourning my ashes for any bar-swinging, bed-hopping shenanigans. Of that I was sure. Pretty sure. Plus, the promise of a lifetime's worth of golf was less appealing when you were about to play that much in a year.

I thanked my friends for the peek into a golf world unto itself, then headed back to my university for a final month of classes before hitting the road full-time. My students laughed when they heard I spent spring break at the Villages, and I smiled a Cheshire grin; little did they know what gramps and grammy were up to. Cancún had nothing on late night in the square.

NEKOOSA, WISCONSIN

The sky was flashing white at midnight. Cars were pulled over on the side of the highway, but I still had a long haul up into the wilds of Wisconsin. My wipers struggled to move all the rain, so I clutched the steering wheel and pushed my face toward the windshield. As I rolled through the Dells at twenty miles per hour, I considered stopping for the night in Wisconsin's fun-land of waterslides and river rides, but I had a room waiting somewhere up in the woods, with a list of directions on the seat next to me. I dared not look over at them as the thunder shook the windows.

A few passes up and down a wet forest road, and I finally found the blue mailbox and turned down a muddy driveway. Deep in the pines, I spotted a cabin. I turned off the car and sat in the front seat, not entirely convinced

I'd found my destination. I stepped out into the rain, wary of approaching badgers or bearded men, and peered in through the dark windows. No clues, until I saw a lockbox on the door and breathed relief. I let myself in and got under the covers in a bed upstairs and dreamed of the days before everybody knew about Sand Valley. I used to be able to get a warm room in its cottages, but they were sold out for the season now, and off-site accommodations were the only other option.

In the light of day, I found I'd actually scored some pretty swanky digs, with a half dozen beds and a renovated kitchen; too bad I was spending only five hours here. I left at sunrise for a tee time down the road with my buddy Jeff, who had come from Texas to join me for a tour of America's new golf wonderland.

Centuries of glacial shift had shaped what was formerly a sandy lakebed into dunes, wetlands, lakes, and forests—a geomorphologist's dream spread over golf-able sandy soil. Over the last twenty years, developers like Mike Keiser and Herbert Kohler Jr. had caught on to what Wisconsin had to offer and, despite its tight weather window, helped make the Badger State as good a golf destination as America had to offer. The quadrangle formed by Sand Valley, Lawsonia, Whistling Straits, and Erin Hills presented an ideal week's trip, where cheese curds and brandy old fashioneds were always on the menu. As I sat at the bar at Sand Valley eating a lunch of the former soaked in Buffalo sauce, I watched a bartender mash cherries into a dozen short glasses. And then another dozen. And another.

Sand Valley's original course, by Coore & Crenshaw, won all the awards when it opened in 2017, and rightly so—it showcased the beauty of its brush-and-dune setting with dual fairways, sandy rifts, and big, wavy greens. David McLay Kidd's Mammoth Dunes joined it the following year, winning those same new-course awards and making Sand Valley a two-round must—three, actually, as its seventeen-hole short course, the Sandbox, was a maze of wild humps and template-inspired greens. We got out there with our wedges and partied. In the Sand Valley playlist, the Coore & Crenshaw course was fine opera—a thoughtful, heart-melting classic—but Mammoth Dunes was what the kids were listening to, a hooky chart-topper you couldn't stop humming. Its fairways were preposterously large, and its banks and speed slots a pinball-like experience. As with Gamble Sands, Kidd mixed in drivable par 4s and positioned bounces to the players' benefit. The boomerang green on the sixth was as much fun as I've ever had two-putting, watching my ball take its own magical U-turn, and for shared fun among a foursome of varying abilities, Mammoth Dunes had few peers in American golf. Hackers and ball-strikers walked off wearing the same smile, making it buddy-trip perfection.

Our Wisconsin tour rolled on to Lawsonia, where the Woodlands course was a fine warm-up for its Links by Langford & Moreau, the 1920s masters of the steam shovel. Their creation had all the muscles of a built-up layout, yet its contours felt effortlessly natural as they pushed us through swales and across ridges toward hoisted greens that hid their engineering. In one case, the evidence was literally buried; the hill on which the seventh green sat had been built by entombing a sand-filled boxcar. Its treeless landscape was a chance to take a wide view and ponder the artistry of America's great design era, and recall how those architects could make subtle strokes play so boldly. Best of all, you could walk the Links at twilight for forty dollars. This wasn't a resort course; it was a locals' hang, with Bud Light specials and a fish fry advertised on the chalkboard out front. A downpour nearly washed away news of the specials, but between storms we savored every hole at the Links, then packed up for the next leg of our 'Scansin tour. And then I found Jeff standing sheepishly by the trunk of his rental. His keys were locked inside. We weren't going anywhere.

We spent a soggy hour prying and prodding the front window, aiming for a clear shot at the lock button. We cheered as we wedged the jamb wide enough to snake a stick downward toward the lock button, but victory was short-lived—the car had to be turned on for the button to work. Storms had knocked out the power in the clubhouse, where a hundred wet golfers were waiting in the dark for the all-clear horn. The beer taps were running, but the one toilet was clogged, and the smell of it all kept me out in the rain with Jeff, waiting for a mechanic to come find us in the woods.

He eventually did, and lucky for us, he was a former larcenist who was able to unlock the door with a slim jim in four seconds flat. Our hopes were again dashed when the trunk release wouldn't work without power, so our friend was forced to take apart every piece of Jeff's back seat—seats, cushions, and metal plates—stripping the car down to pieces. Golfers heading home stopped to stare, probably wondering what we were trafficking into northern Wisconsin. A guy asked if we'd called Triple-A or border patrol, but before we could answer, our hero finally cleared enough daylight to squeeze his torso into the trunk and pull the release. The lid sprang open, and Jeff showered him with cash like he'd been dancing for us on a pole.

The ordeal was far behind us by the time our caravan reached Kohler, where our rooms in the American Club befit golfers who arrived by private jet, and we supped on tenderloin after washing the rental-car grease from our fingernails. I'd been told that Kohler used the hotels at its four-course resort, home to the eminent Whistling Straits, as a showcase for its most luxurious bath fittings, and my shower of myriad nozzles did not disappoint. With my every crevice blasted clean, I left early for our tee time on the Irish course, only to be admonished by the starter for being late. I told him I was right on time; it was 6:57 and we were off at 7:00 a.m. He warned me to be ten minutes early next time, and I walked to the tee thinking that the Irish course needed a lesson in Irish time, where five minutes late was ten minutes early.

The Kohler courses occupied a rugged stretch of cliffside dunes overlooking Lake Michigan, and the Irish course indeed possessed moments that felt lifted from Baltray or Enniscrone. The herd of sheep that stampeded across the fourth green and through my line was a nice homage to the old sod, and as I spooned a bowl of stew in its snug clubhouse pub, the tricolour waving out front, a very Irish feeling came over me. That was precisely Mr. Kohler's intention—in the late 1990s he had asked Pete Dye to build him Ballybunion beside Lake Michigan, and after our stew, we headed out into the breezes to see how close he had come.

Likening any course to the granddaddy of Irish links is an unfair comparison, but in the spirit of unfairness, Whistling Straits, home to multiple men's and women's majors, was no Ballybunion. It was certainly tougher than Bally-B, with about 975 more bunkers—it held roughly a thousand in total, most placed as décor on hillsides that were out of play. Maybe they'd been set there to cast a natural vibe, but for me they did the opposite, distracting from the scenery by reminding me how much designing had been done. Even if the place had handprints on it, it was a colossal course of rare quality, and a giddy experience for both its blue vistas and the shots it asked you to execute. Some part of me is still launching Titleists into Lake Michigan on the par 3 seventeenth, where 220 yards into the wind to a sliver of green above lapping waves required more fortitude than I possessed.

It was clear by the third hole that Whistling Straits' name was not inspired by its pace of play. As we waited on another tee box, our caddie, Evan, told us he had a second job as a day-trader. He had no stock tips to share, but he possessed a droll bedside manner when it came to describing the fate of our golf balls. I wiped one deep right on the sixteenth, and he told me I had found lion country.

"How is that lion country?" I asked.

"Because if you find it over there, you're fucking lyin'."

On eighteen, he delivered the tragic news that the only bunker we actually wanted to find that afternoon was no longer there. They had filled in the Dustin Johnson bunker, where DJ had famously grounded his club in what was, or wasn't, a sand trap, denying him a spot in a playoff for the PGA Championship.

"Too many people were stopping and taking pictures in the bunker. It was backing up the course, so they got rid of it," Evan explained. My mood was lifted by a closing par—pars were dear that day—and though it wasn't Ballybunion, Whistling Straits had been a grand golfing spectacle of audacious offerings, with guest room showerheads mightier than any I'd found in Ireland. (Considering Ireland still had electric showers where you had to flip a switch for a dribble of hot water, that category wasn't even close.)

We bumped into Ireland again in Erin, a small town settled by Irish immigrants who named their burg after the word for their homeland, Éire. Its golf course, Erin Hills, had been open only since 2006, yet it had already hosted a US Am and the US Open, and was on the schedule for a Mid-Am and Women's Open as well—quite a coup for a rural community of 3,700. But Erin Hills' success wasn't a straight-line story. Much like Ireland itself, its history detoured into tragedy and heartbreak.

I had read the painstaking research compiled by Josh Sens for Golf.com, which recounted the story of Steve Trattner and his dream of building a golf course. For a Milwaukee software programmer like Trattner, who lacked the capital or connections, it seemed like just another golf geek's fantasy, but he ultimately quit his job and went searching for a site where he could somehow convince somebody to break ground. He found that land in Erin, where the hills were begging for golf holes, and enlisted the help of another dreamer named Bob Lang, a wealthy Wisconsinite who'd made millions in the calendar business. Lang wasn't a golfer, but he quickly became enamored with the Erin Hills project; he busted the construction budget, fixated on making it a US Open–caliber venue, and spent much of his fortune to do so.

The duo spent ten years bringing it to life, but when it was finally announced that the US Open was indeed coming to Erin Hills, making it the youngest course to ever receive such an honor, neither of them was there to celebrate it. Trattner was serving a thirty-five-year sentence for reckless homicide after he had killed his wife during an argument in their kitchen (he claimed self-defense, and continues to seek a new trial). Lang was out as well; he had poured everything into Erin Hills, borrowing heavily and sparing no expense, until the debt was too great. He was forced to sell at a loss to a Milwaukee money manager just a few months before the US Open announcement.

Lang was mentioned in some of the coverage around the 2017 US Open, but thanks to the dark details, Trattner's story was largely unacknowledged. History as a whole took a back seat that week to the controversy surrounding the scoring, and a relative unknown named Brooks Koepka who brought the course to its knees. The week had started with Kevin Na sharing a video of the thigh-high fescue beside the Erin Hills' fairways, claiming the course was unplayable, but the narrative flipped when in benign conditions Justin Thomas shot the lowest-ever round to par in a US Open (–9), and Koepka won with a record-tying sixteen under. Since someone had once decreed that the US Open wasn't allowed to yield great scores to great players on great courses, Erin Hills got bashed in the media. I didn't put much stock in the backlash; people liked to pick on the new kid, and blasting Erin Hills was a hot take. Plus, second-guessing the USGA was most golfers' favorite couch pastime. Had Koepka won his fourth major there instead of his first, we would all have celebrated Erin Hills as a course built to identify a true champion. After playing its landscape and hoofing eight miles across its hillocks, it was clear to me that the Erin Hills story had been miswritten, because this course kicked all the asses.

The clouds from its past had all cleared out by the time I visited; the tilted meadows of tall, golden grasses were dotted with a farmhouse lodge and stone cottages, and a barn for the caddies where guests could hang as well, playing pool and Ping-Pong and shuffleboard late into the night. In the pro shop, I met Mr. Wisconsin Golf himself, Rich Tock, who'd been a PGA pro for forty-plus years and recently had been inducted into the Wisconsin Golf Hall of Fame. He'd taken up the game when he was tending bar as a twelve-year-old at a course in Illinois, and today served as an ambassador at Erin Hills, ensuring new visitors like myself enjoyed the visit. It was great to have Rich with me, but I could have walked the place alone with one club and just as easily fallen for its charms.

In the British Isles, they talked of machair and loam and gorse when they described their linksland; in Wisconsin, the word was *moraine*, which referred to the sediment that slid off glaciers, the silt and sand deposits that shaped the mounds and valleys. A trio of designers—Michael Hurdzan, Dana Fry, and Ron Whitten from *Golf Digest*—had been unconventional picks to mold the moraine at Erin Hills, considering Tom Doak had already laid out a routing for previous owners of the property, but a bold choice begot bold results, and a course full of fascinating decisions. *Full* seemed the right word—the property was titanic, and as it was a walking-only facility, I wished I had eaten my Wheaties. I was pleased to find its fairways coated in crispy fescue, allowing our shots to scurry over hills and up to its raised greens, or to roll back down from them. It was challenging, sure, but it didn't break your spirit, and I smelled Oakmont in the air. That was the last place where my eyes had seen punishment ahead but my mind said, *You got this*, whether it was telling the truth or not. The walk left me legless, but I didn't want to leave Erin Hills. I would have had to crawl a second loop, but if the daylight had allowed, I would have been out there on my hands and knees.

I had yet to discover what California had to offer, but in a States-wide competition, Wisconsin seemed the lead dog when it came to accessible, extraordinary golf. I could think of one other place that might have something to say about that assumption, and I was ashamed it had taken me so many years to get there. I had two weeks until I'd finally tee it up at Pinehurst, but first, somebody needed a haircut.

PHILADELPHIA, PENNSYLVANIA

Before leaving home again to explore golf in the South, I had blocked off a week to reacquaint myself with my hometown courses, lest I overlook them like some local who only went to the museums when guests were in town. There were few golf sections with more history, and probably none with better architectural chops. Philadelphia had its own coterie of designers—George Thomas, Tillinghast, Crump, Hugh Wilson, Flynn, Oakmont's Fownes, and, later, Dick Wilson formed the Philadelphia School—but I was keen to get back to see Cobbs Creek first.

A friend of mine had been the pro at Cobbs twenty years before, and when I asked him what that experience had been like, he told me of a morning when he arrived at the shop at sunrise, and the Philadelphia police were waiting for him. They asked him to come take a ride with them out onto the course, and when they reached the creek beside the fifth green, they asked him if he knew the woman whose body was lying in the water.

"Are you serious?" was all he could muster. He wasn't sure what happened after the scene was processed; sadly, murder in this corner of the city hardly made the news. He tried his best to get on with his day and do his job, which at Cobbs Creek wasn't your typical PGA gig.

The goals were simpler, if not more taxing: Get the golf moving, make sure most of the golfers had paid (bisected by a busy street, it was Sneak-On National), keep the homeless off the course, and try to keep the neighborhood kids' motorbikes off the greens. A caddie friend of mine had been mugged on one of its tees during a high school match, but carried on and won without his wallet. The course had been a patchy pasture for decades, with barren tee boxes, flooded greens, and impenetrable forest masking the richness of its holes. Tough times had come to Cobbs Creek, or Slobs Creek as we referred to it in my youth, but it had once been a beacon on America's golf landscape, with exceptional design pedigree.

Well-researched historians are quick to dissent when Hugh Wilson gets all the credit for Merion and Cobbs Creek—C. B. Macdonald and William Flynn and George Crump and A. W. Tillinghast all played their part—but in broadest strokes, Hugh Wilson was a Princeton grad and top Philadelphia amateur who laid out Merion's celebrated East and West Courses before being tasked with giving Philadelphia a public golf venue.

His course at Cobbs Creek opened in 1916 to wide acclaim, and it remains one of the most important sites in the history of African American golf. While other courses around the country were still whites-only, Cobbs never held such restrictions, and players like Howard Wheeler and Charlie Sifford sharpened their craft there, alongside heavyweight champ Joe Louis, who joined Sifford whenever he was in Philadelphia. It hosted the National Negro Open three times, as well as a PGA Tour event in the 1950s that saw Arnold Palmer and his contemporaries playing alongside Black players, a rarity on Tour at the time. Philly golf writer Mike Cirba once unearthed an even more notable piece of Cobbs history: The land had once been a stop on the Underground Railroad, where the Quaker abolitionists who owned the property operated a tunnel to what is now the fifth green. Escaped slaves could work their way north through the creek, losing their scent in the water and throwing off the bounty hunters' dogs.

When I arrived at Cobbs, I could see that change was afoot: I was met by a member of the newly formed Cobbs Creek Foundation, which had successfully lobbied the city council with VOTE YES golf balls, securing the property for a rent of one dollar. As he showed me slides and sketches of the group's plans, it seemed we weren't going to be able to call it Slobs Creek for much longer. A cadre of area golfers had raised a hefty chunk of capital to help return the course to its former glory and establish it not just as a place to play but as a community hub. I flipped through drawings of a practice facility that would house a First Tee program for kids, as well as an education center for after-school academic support. They already had plans drawn by Gil Hanse's design partner Jim Wagner, and were now getting ready to return Cobbs to its original layout, before the US Army had commandeered a chunk of holes for a Cold War antiaircraft battery. They were preparing to add a new nine-hole course as well, with holes that could be blended into a composite routing with the old course, thus producing a layout long enough to host the PGA Tour. Philadelphia remained the largest market without a regular Tour stop, and the Foundation was eager to see that change.

As I played my way through the front nine, however, it was a dream that felt a long way off. The fairways were mostly dust and crabgrass, and the greens had turned to browns, their surfaces cracked like sunbaked desert. There were lost basketballs stuck in the creek, and on the fifth tee, a man was washing his socks in the water cooler. This was Cobbs at its Cobbs-iest; they were on a maintenance hiatus as they prepped to dig the place up, but it brought back warm memories of sneaking on with caddie friends who looped upon much grassier fields up the road.

I wished the best for Cobbs as I made the short drive to one of those playing fields. Philadelphia Country Club was the sixth club to join the USGA, just missing out on the notoriety of being a member of the founding five. Its William Flynn layout had hosted Byron Nelson's only US Open win in 1939, and remained a Philly blueblood stronghold. I ranked it in a similar class as other prestigious clubs where the status attached to membership perhaps inflated the reputation of the course. It was a solid layout with one standout par 4—its hard-bending seventeenth—but my heart was over at the other PCC, Philadelphia Cricket Club, and I headed there early the next morning.

Philly Cricket traced its roots to 1854, making it the oldest country club in the United States. It started as a clique of University of Pennsylvania grads who bounced around Philadelphia playing cricket matches against all comers. In 1883, they settled in the Chestnut Hill area of Philadelphia and added golf to their rotation. That original course, the St. Martins, hosted the 1907 and 1910 US Opens (it's since been reduced to a nine-holer that includes six of the original Open holes, and is one of the great short walks in golf). George Thomas and A. W. Tillinghast were both members, and Tillinghast was responsible for its championship course, the Wissahickon, which was situated on a separate golf campus in nearby Flourtown. Tillinghast so loved the course that his ashes were spread in the creek beside its eighteenth hole, not far from where, on one sunny afternoon, the greatest snowman in golf history was made.

I detailed Garth's struggles as a new golfer in my Scotland book, so rather than rehash all the non-golfing objects his ball struck on that trip, I'll just say my friend's introduction to the game was hard-earned. It was his first season at Philly Cricket, and maybe his third year since first picking up a golf club, when he decided to sign up for the club championship. He was trying to get to know more of his fellow members, but by the second hole, he had met plenty more than he was planning to.

Garth had gotten off to a fair start, double-bogeying the first hole for a net par. They played the gross and net championship on the same weekend at Cricket, so the Wissahickon first tee and putting green were buzzing with members, which is where Garth deposited his approach shot on the second, cracking it off the roof of the cart barn, where it kicked further right into the bushes beneath the patio.

It should be noted that Philly Cricket possesses the most plus-handicaps in the section; its membership roll is fertile with elite amateurs, which Garth knew as he nodded to most of them and walked past the barn, through the cart parking area, past the pro shop, and over to where his ball was lodged in the shrubs behind the first tee.

"I didn't really know the proper rules at this point, so I grabbed the ball and started walking back to play my provisional," Garth told me. "I assumed it was out of bounds, but the director of golf, Jim Smith, nicest guy ever, comes over to tell me it's still in play and that I have to play it as it lies. I'd picked it up, so I took the penalty, no big deal. I just wanted to hit it and get out of there. I punched it out across the path, and now I'm next to the practice green. About forty guys were watching at this point, wondering what I'm going to do, because the clubhouse is directly between me and where I need to go. I told myself, *I just need to take a wedge and hit it really, really hard to get it over the clubhouse and onto the second green.* Yeah—that wasn't the best idea."

He choked the grip and swung with muscles that should not be engaged during a round of golf, exhuming a hoagie-size divot that went soaring across the golf carts, but not before nudging his ball forward. It trickled down a path and hopped into a flower bed. Jim approached with the good news—"Hey, you get free relief from the flower bed"—and Garth decided to lighten his grip a little this time, knocking one clean over the cart barn and back into play. The members erupted into applause, and Garth waved and tipped his cap.

He was now lying six in the fairway, and the battle was on to finish the hole without having to take his handicap maximum score of 9. He wedged one close from 110 yards, and good for Garth, he made the putt. When he turned in his scorecard at the end of the day, Jim came running out of the pro shop to catch him as he walked toward the parking lot, head hanging low.

"Garth! You made an eight on that hole!" he exclaimed. Garth confirmed it was true. "That has got to be the greatest eight I've ever seen," Jim told him, and they shared a laugh and a high-five. Garth said it helped him see what golf was about—here was a pretty well-known golf pro who wanted to make a newcomer feel better. He did, and it showed Garth there was a place for him in golf, and a place at Philly Cricket, too.

Merion was situated on the other side of Philadelphia, closer to Cobbs. It had been so long since I'd played it that short-term memory had me leaning toward Philly Cricket's Wissahickon as Philadelphia's champ (its eighteenth won me over every time, requiring a deep drive to the crest of a fairway, then a long iron dropped down into a backdrop of white clubhouse set behind a diagonal creek; making four there brought applause from the lunch crowd behind the green), but it didn't take long for the Merion tingles to return. The portrait of Ben Hogan's 1 iron at the top of the locker room stairs was enough to remind why this was my hometown's best day of golf.

Soon I would be playing the hole where Bobby Jones completed golf's only Grand Slam, Merion's number eleven. An altered iron tablet marked the spot. Legend had it that the plaque had arrived with Robert *Trent* Jones, the golf architect, inscribed as the Grand Slam winner; you could see where a raised strip with "Robert *Tyre* Jones" had been welded to cover the error. It wasn't the only plaque snafu at Merion: A plate marking Ben Hogan's legendary 1 iron into eighteen had been installed with the wrong date on it. They had the round correct, but somebody assumed a Sunday finish, forgetting that the US Open used to finish with thirty-six holes on Saturday. Surprisingly, the error went undetected for ten years.

Merion had been closed for over a year while Gil Hanse replaced every blade of grass on the property and installed eighteen SubAir systems in the greens. I'd heard the project cost around $30 million, with an assessment to the members of $0 million. *Must be nice to have access to that kind of cash*, I thought—my club wanted a new bar, and we got assessed for every cent of it. Considering that Merion was a member-plus-three-guest-fees machine from sunup to dusk, I shouldn't have been surprised that its reserves were so robust.

Our group was three guests plus Michael, a member I'd known long before he played at Merion. Michael and I had grown up playing junior golf against each other—Rolling Green and Llanerch were about two miles apart, and we had been pretty evenly matched as kids. Michael wasn't the first man on the Llanerch team, or his high school team, or even his college team where he played with Brendan, but his name started popping up in the newspaper after college; he made a deep run at the 2003 US Am, defeating top-seeded J. B. Holmes along the way, and was winning the Philly Am and taking home our player of the year award regularly. He was a medalist in

US Mid-Am qualifying, where he made it to the quarterfinals, played in the Concession Cup against Great Britain and Ireland, and won a few Crump Cups as well (Pine Valley's annual invitational for the world's best amateurs, and the few days when they open the gates and allow spectators to come have a look).

Michael's accomplishments, plus his gracious manner, had earned him entry into clubs like Merion and Pine Valley (where one of his scorecards hung by the bar—his 62 was the lowest ever round from the members' tees), and eventually an invitation to join that place at the end of Magnolia Lane, where if I had to guess, he was a candidate to be a playing marker in the Masters. We used to top tee shots together as twelve-year-olds, but somewhere in the golfing woods, two roads diverged, and I took the one more traveled by.

It was fun to watch Michael bend drives around Merion's corners. He was a tall masher with a handicap of +4 whose golf ball made a different sound than ours; more like a mortar launch versus the clicks from our clubfaces. There was a league of pseudo-amateurs out there who played golf full-time, bouncing from invitational to invitational, with family money or no-show jobs to support them, but Michael was one of a few top nonprofessionals who was a genuine amateur with a full-time job (he ran his own money management firm) and kids to chase at home. We caught up on the places golf had taken us since the days of scrambling for sixes in our junior matches, and I couldn't help but ask how Augusta had happened. All he would say was that he had no idea he was being considered for membership until a friend called and told him to hang out at home; a very special letter was arriving that afternoon.

I would have pitched a tent beside the mailbox, but Michael had promised his kids a weekend at Hershey Park, and off they went. He was a good dad, too. I don't know how he didn't lose his kids among the rides that weekend, knowing what was waiting in his mailbox. And to get home and finally open that envelope; I was sure his first stop had been his dad's house. His father had retired from the electric company and, like my own, was a dedicated golfer who started his boys early. For the kid you used to take to the driving range to hand you his invitation to join Augusta National—there had to have been some tears.

After our morning round, we had lunch on Merion's famed patio (it sat directly beside the first tee, making Merion's opening shot one of golf's most terrifying), where Michael stopped by Buddy Marucci's table to say hello. I told Michael I was heading south to meet up with his old college teammate Brendan, and explained the stakes of our match. He laughed and said he'd just gotten back from Ohoopee himself, and it well exceeded the hype. He wished me luck; nobody wanted to see Brendan in a scrunchie.

Later that year, Michael spotted Brendan at a team reunion, and he crossed the room to grab him.

"Your hair is short!" he said. "You lost the match!"

Brendan smiled. "You'll have to wait to read about it."

VIDALIA, GEORGIA

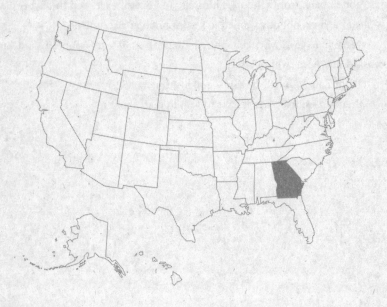

Our match in Georgia had begun years before, in 2012 at a golf sanctuary laid upon yonder Pennsylvania farmland, when I spotted a guy in psychedelic-print golf pants at a golf outing for a league of less ordinary gentlemen.

My introduction to the league was an October invitation to its two-day end-of-season event. A friend had told me about a group of sober guys who were playing golf together in Philadelphia and asked if I was interested in joining. I hadn't touched my clubs since quitting drinking, but I was curious how anyone like me went to a golf course without stuffing four beers in his bag, so I gave it a go, spraying golf balls into the margins of exquisite golf holes. After golf, we had a steak dinner and played poker and hit the putting green at two a.m., gambling with whatever chips were left in our pockets. We slept in rooms in the clubhouse, then pegged it again early the next morning. It was the sort of dream golf weekend I had erased from my board of possibilities, and here I was, walking around in it.

I knew my companions had all taken the same boozy ass-kicking as I had, yet they were smiling and laughing, two practices I was just beginning to relearn. I wanted in, and was relieved to find I'd already passed the primary entrance requirement: be a drunk who doesn't drink. The guy in the crazy pants qualified as well; Brendan had been in the league for fifteen years, and when he introduced himself that evening, he admitted he'd been surprised to find me here, and then not surprised at all.

That afternoon, he told me, he'd overheard his playing partners talking about the Irish golf book I'd written, the one with an empty pint of Guinness on the cover.

"I heard about that book," he said to them. "I saw that guy on TV. I have no interest in reading some asshole's drunk-alogue around Ireland."

They looked at Brendan like he was missing something, then pointed to me across the fairway.

"Who's that?" Brendan asked.

"That's the guy. He wrote the book," they said.

"But he's a drunk. What is he doing here?"

They smiled, and Brendan let it register. "Shit," he said. "He *is* a drunk. That's awesome."

I was in.

The league had started twenty years before, with eight sober guys getting together for regular golf at Philly's public tracks. In the decades since, it had grown to become an association of seventy-two golfers, split into thirty-six teams for better-ball matches. We played five matches over the course of the summer (league rules required one member of each team have a home club for hosting), and the playoffs stretched on through the fall.

The league was well organized, with a website, a logo, apparel, and a trophy; we also had awards dinners and side trips to Bandon and the Homestead. We had all joined to meet like-minded golfers and to reacclimatize ourselves to the game sans cocktails, but we stuck with it for the courses we got to play. There were members from every notable club in the Philadelphia section, which included some of the top-ranked courses in the world, and I was constantly struck by the lives this gang of sots had built from their ashes. Walking into that first dinner and seeing proof in every seat that being an alcoholic was my strength and not my shame—it told me I could do anything, because so many of them had. Former crack-smokers and guys with gin bottles hidden under the bed were now CEOs and business owners, real estate developers and hedge fund managers, and writers, too.

We kept one another from getting too impressed with ourselves. Plenty of guys credited the league and the friendships they'd made there with saving their lives, and Brendan made it clear he wouldn't be alive today without golf. It was there for him when he needed it most, when he was struggling to get clean and needed to fill his time with a habit that wasn't going to kill him. He poured himself into his practice, turning the thing that kept a lot of us stuck in a booze-soaked cycle—our golf club—into his recovery retreat.

We were the same age, but Brendan had decades on me in terms of time since his last drink. While the rest of us had been funneling beers off apartment balconies, he was the miracle case who'd somehow kicked the sauce in college. He'd grown up as a kid who hit balls every day after school, rain or shine. He covered his copy of Jack Nicklaus's *Golf My Way* with brown paper and wrote *SCIENCE* on the cover so he could sit in the back of the classroom and study what he was going to practice that afternoon. But golf soon took a back seat to other interests, and the first time he shot par at age sixteen, he didn't remember much of it.

He'd head out for high school practice with a one-liter bottle of Coke and Jack in his bag, and whenever the coach joined his foursome, Brendan would aim for the trees or dump a shot into a deep bunker so he could squat down and take a few stealthy swigs. In college, his coach took him under his wing, lending him the team van at night so he could find a recovery meeting when they were traveling and keeping him away from the team parties in the hotel rooms next door. By the time he graduated, Brendan was three years sober, and today he owns a network of recovery clinics. He still practices nearly every afternoon, grinding on the range like a proper addict.

There's a quick connection among drunks who've dangled their toes out over the abyss. It's a lifeboat sort of bond that Brendan and I share, where we don't have to explain ourselves and can laugh about the portfolios of stupid shit we've survived, and that's exactly what we did on our way out to Ohoopee. I'd picked Brendan up the night before at the Savannah airport, and that morning we made the ninety-minute drive through flat fields of bronze earth, finally finding a small sign in the woods with an onion on it— Ohoopee's logo—that told us we were nearly there. It was a golf hideaway in the literal sense, tucked away on forgotten acres, with a clubhouse that might have been a farmer's barn if the lines weren't so sharp and modern. We went inside for lunch and found two places set for us at the bar. We eyed the wall of bottles in front of us and joked that we'd come here about twenty years too late. Our fee that day was all-inclusive: food, beer, and cocktails could be ushered out to us on a whim, and here we were spending a few hundred bucks on club sodas with lime.

We discussed our morning on Ohoopee's Whiskey Loop, an alternative par 69 routing made up of Gil Hanse's four bonus holes. Beside the tee boxes, a cubby held a bottle of bourbon with plastic shot glasses, and our caddie tried to convince us that a dram would unlock all the birdies, a story Brendan and I were used to.

"It's funny; guys talk about playing better when they're loaded, or needing their swing oil," Brendan said as our lunches arrived. "But I'm playing the best golf of my life right now, college or any other time."

"You're two-down," I reminded him.

"Not right now, not today, but in general. I've never hit it better. You'll see. There's a lot of golf left."

I conceded that there was.

"The caddie was funny, though, with the whiskey shots," Brendan said. "Like, yeah, I'll take one of those. Then you can call the cops and an ambulance."

I laughed and studied the scorecard. Instead of admiring my two-hole lead, all I could think about was how I wasn't three-up. Brendan was losing, but as usual, his head was in a better place.

"There's probably a lot of guys who get shit-canned out here and don't remember how awesome it is," he continued. "I remember this one time when I was out with the team in college, and we were practicing on this beautiful golf course, and the sun was setting, this awesome red sunset. The rest of the guys were talking about where they were going to party that night, and I said, 'Guys, look at that sunset. It's beautiful.' They all literally stopped and looked at me, and were like, *What are you talking about?* They didn't get it. They couldn't appreciate that we play a sport out in the middle of nature, in the most beautiful places on earth. I look around, and I think, *Man, I get to play golf today.* And I'm relaxed."

As we headed back to the first tee, I thought of the ball marker that I knew was in his pocket, the one that read, "The more relaxed you are, the better you are at everything." During our morning eighteen, Brendan had uncharacteristically surrendered a few holes by getting stuck in Ohoopee's everywhere sand. Short holes could get angry quickly; reach for the driver and leave yourself a fifty-yard bunker shot, a trend I couldn't rely on him to continue. As we walked down the first, I was sure of three things: I was lucky to be winning. Brendan was relaxed. And I wasn't.

I wasn't shit-canned, but I was missing out on the magnificence of Ohoopee for sure. I didn't see a fun-packed golf oasis in the Georgia brush. All I could see was a scorecard, where I was powerless to reverse the numbers' trajectory. Two-up slid to one-up to even. Once Brendan had established himself as the tee-chooser on this course of optional starting points, he pressed his advantage, pegging it to where the par 4s became reachable, forcing me to match his straight driving. He was finding greens while I was climbing into bunkers, and by the sixteenth hole, it was Brendan's card that read +2.

It was fun during the first eighteen to update our wives via text with the score of our match. The messages, however, were considerably less amusing in the afternoon, and as I heard my phone buzzing in my bag with another update from Brendan, and then another, I felt something I hadn't experienced on a golf course since getting cut from my college team: rage. I was veins-popping pissed. I didn't want to look at Brendan, or hear from my caddie. I thought I'd matured to where golf could only make me depressed, not angry. My eyes were leaking fire as I watched my ball hop past the pin on sixteen, then grab. I picked my birdie out of the hole, and Brendan said, "Lots of golf left," to which I did not reply.

It was clear I'd taken this friendly contest too far. I hadn't said a word to Brendan since lunch, and I wasn't sure why I'd let myself slip into a competitive black hole. The monthslong buildup added to the unpleasantness, or maybe it was that Allyson was getting regular updates on my failure. But if I broke it down, I got angry when I got fearful, and this vitriol was born of the fear that Brendan was right—I couldn't beat him, and I wasn't going to get the bragging rights to which I felt entitled. I'd been golfing my ass off from one ocean to the other, and if I wasn't going to win today, I never was. I think I was also a little afraid about the course Brendan might choose to play if I lost. My reserve of friends and favors was thoroughly depleted.

Brendan's drive found the right junk on seventeen; at Ohoopee you were either in the fairway—they were big enough—or you were wiggling through branches and dodging thorns in the dusty wilds. He punched out, but the advantage was all mine from the center of the short grass. It wasn't much longer than the wedge I had just jammed on the last, and a part of my mind was already composing the next text for Allyson—*All square, headed to the last.*

As we watched my ball squirt right at an entirely unnatural angle, I realized I wasn't angry anymore. All the air emptied out of me, and I was a golfing void. I think Brendan was disappointed, too—to end it all with a shank wasn't fun for either of us. I found my ball beside a tree stump, took two chops to blast it through the branches, and shook Brendan's hand on the green.

"Where did that shot come from?" he asked. I told him I didn't know, though I suspected it came from deep within my fractured psyche.

Before the match, we'd poked around the pro shop and identified an Ohoopee Match Club belt as the champion's prize, and Brendan now held it proudly for my camera, both of us forever knowing the answer to the question stitched onto it: WHO WON THE MATCH?

The drive back to the airport was quiet. I'd managed to suck all the fun out of a round with a best buddy, and didn't even have a belt to show for it. I'm sure Brendan didn't want to bring it up, but it needed to be discussed.

"So. Where are we going?" I asked.

"I think you know," Brendan said. And I did. I just didn't know how the hell Cypress Point was going to happen.

I dropped Brendan curbside in Savannah and started working my way north. I needed some time to recalibrate; I'd been building my golf up to the match, and now that it was done, I had to refocus on what this journey was about. I had a few days in the Carolinas ahead of me, and that was good timing. A cradle was precisely what my ego required.

PINEHURST, NORTH CAROLINA

It was a blank spot on my résumé, a blot on my golfing escutcheon. I had been to the Pinehurst resort before, but had never struck a shot on what many called the cradle of American golf. Who went to Pinehurst and didn't play? I did once, and I wasn't going to repeat such a malfeasance.

It was 2014, and I was working on a *Sports Illustrated* story about spreading the golf love around. Having played my share of dream golf, I wanted to make some happen for other players, so I asked readers to tell me their fantasy foursome, and I'd pick a winner and make it happen at Pinehurst, the site of that year's US Open.

I expected a lot of Tiger and Phil and Arnie requests, and got them. Some voyeurs wanted to get Obama and Trump on the course together, while others requested Fred Couples, Tom Watson, Ernie Els, Bill Murray, and Tony Romo (who my Philly sensibilities shuffled to the bottom of the pile). And then I read a submission from a veteran who wanted to play with the three men who saved his life, and what I'd expected to be a light story about golf with celebrities, replete with pats on the back and posed photos, was suddenly a round of golf that really mattered.

Lieutenant Aaron Ojard had brought his golf clubs to Kandahar in 2009. He built a tee with a piece of carpet and a wooden pallet and hit balls into a net, or sometimes out into the minefields. He joked that they had the Taliban shag balls among the mines, but he had a friend at home sending him a steady supply.

Aaron worked in the Bethesda Naval Medical Center for two years before going to Afghanistan and joining the Role 3 Multinational Medical Unit. During his deployment in 2009, it was the busiest trauma center in the world. It wasn't like *M*A*S*H* from television; they weren't working in tents but in a building with real beds, beeping monitors, and some of the best surgeons and specialists in the world, fixing friend and foe with precision and efficiency. It might even have felt like a hospital back home, if it weren't for Rocket Man.

He roamed the hills above the base and launched on them three, four times a week. Some other bases would fire back when under attack, but not them—it was a waste of time. They knew he wasn't there. Rocket Man set up hours in advance with a bottle of ice for a trigger. When the ice melted and the contacts connected through the water—*whooosh*—launch, and the alarms came over the base, a recording of a woman with a British accent declaring, "Rocket, *attack*. Rocket, *attack*."

As we sat in the dining room at the Carolina Hotel in Pinehurst, I watched as Aaron's eyes scanned the room, quick and restless. I pulled our waitress aside, and though they'd given us the best table in the house, I asked for one away from where workers were fixing something in the basement, their drills buzzing up through our table.

She looked a little unsure—we had just ordered—but when I told her, "I'm dining with guys who were in Afghanistan, and the vibrations . . ." I didn't need to finish before we were seated across the room. Aaron later explained that he could feel it coming on through his feet—*Birds incoming*. The vibrations had put him right back in the suck, waiting for helicopters full of our wounded, or theirs.

For his playing partners on Pinehurst #2, Aaron had chosen James, Jim, and Marc.

James had sent shag balls and a turf mat to Aaron while he'd been overseas, and they now worked together in the NICU in Bethesda. James enabled Aaron's golf addiction, the two of them sneaking away for nine holes whenever Aaron needed to talk. James was the guy who got Aaron's worst stories, and he told me that, while Aaron claimed he had been ordered to Afghanistan, he had actually volunteered to go.

Unlike the rest of our Pinehurst contingent, Jim Estes was a straight-up stick. He'd played in four US Opens and a PGA Championship, and spent a year on the Tour in 1998. He was now a prominent instructor who found most of his students at Walter Reed, where he worked to get wounded vets out of the hospital and onto the course. He spent a month swinging on his left leg to understand how to instruct leg amputees; he'd learned to teach a one-armed swing as well. Jim had helped get Aaron back to the golf course, and Aaron told me he had saved more lives than he would ever know.

As for Marc—when Aaron first walked into the trauma unit in Kandahar, he turned a corner and froze. In front of him a young soldier was screaming. Soaked in red from head to toe, he had one limb left, and his testicles were splayed on the table. Aaron couldn't move, and that was the moment he met Major Marc Dauphin, surgeon and commander of Role 3, who told him in very clear terms—not barking orders, and not cheerleading—the things he needed to do. *This is your job. You're the ICU nurse. This is what you need to do to save a life.* Aaron did his job. They saved a life, and many more. Role 3 didn't lose a single American soldier during Marc and Aaron's deployment.

Aaron was six-foot-five with eighteen-inch arms and a shaved scalp that won him the nickname Shrek around the base, and he towered over Marc, the French-Canadian surgeon. Still, Aaron said he would have walked across any battlefield on earth to serve in Dauphin's MASH unit; he credited Marc with keeping him alive in Afghanistan. When the bodies came through the door, Marc was ice, and he had showed Aaron how to survive the daily routine of pain and death. Marc was part comedian, part Aaron's boss, part Aaron's therapist, and was now retired from the Canadian Army, making art and writing novels in Quebec.

Marc was the guy who understood how it could still sneak up on Aaron: rocket, *attack*. Aaron had been knocked down hard in one of them, leading to a neck fusion and ten follow-up surgeries. He'd made it home upright and able to walk, but the dust was still on his boots when the nightmares started, his pager calling him back to the trauma beds and the bloody scramble. Sleeping stopped. Going places stopped. He finally reached out for help and started practicing the only real fix for PTS (he's adamant about dropping the D, to also drop the stigma of its being a disorder): talking. Talking about his thoughts and visions loosened their grip, and it was on the golf course where he found that the words came easiest.

It was his first stepping-stone, luring him out of the house for a few minutes of practice. Soon he was away from home for five hours, feeling natural with a club in his hands. Eventually he got back to work at the hospital in Maryland, but not without his sticks. On the night shift he'd roam the hallways carrying a 5 iron, because the feeling settled him. The world felt familiar with a golf grip in his fingers.

He explained that he still struggled in the grocery store—the look and smell of raw meat was a trigger—but overall he was doing well and playing often, his back problems confined mostly to a golf swing that had more slide than turn. He had a therapy dog now, an Akita named Yujin that I couldn't help hugging, even though I wasn't supposed to touch a working dog. The round with Marc and James and Jim had provided a lot of laughs (and some tears), and Webb Simpson even showed up to say hello and thank Aaron for his service. Little did any of us know that the best thing to come out of that weekend wasn't a story or a reunion of friends but thousands of lives changed for the better.

On our first evening at Pinehurst, we had all met for dinner in the Ryder Cup Lounge, and Aaron invited an Army Ranger buddy from the area to join us. His name was Josh, and they got to talking about how they needed to play more golf together, and how cool it would be if there was some way they could play competitive golf with other vets.

I'd watched plenty of good pub ideas evaporate into the evening banter, but these guys weren't the type for idle promises. Aaron and Josh pursued the project like the soldiers they were, quickly securing nonprofit status for their association, along with a slate of eager sponsors. It took them less than a year to host their first veteran's national championship back at Pinehurst, and in the five years since that conversation in the lounge, the Veteran Golfers Association had hosted two thousand tournaments for over seven thousand vets and their families, with regional playoffs and a national championship where the winner won the VGA red jacket and an exemption into the PGA Tour's Military Tribute at The Greenbrier. Some eighty thousand rounds of golf had been shared by veterans thanks to the VGA.

I had asked Aaron to meet me somewhere along my America journey. A reunion at Pinehurst seemed the obvious spot, where this time I would be playing instead of observing and scribbling notes for a story. He and Yujin were waiting beside the practice green when I arrived, and as we walked Pinehurst #2 again, Aaron shared the VGA stat he was most proud of.

"We've had exponential growth. Three hundred fifty members the first year, and now over seven thousand. But the number that matters the most is that, out of our seven thousand vets, not a single one has committed suicide. Not a single *one*." His voice cracked as he described it. "I have guys come up to me with tears in their eyes at our events. They say, 'Thank you. If I didn't have this, I would have killed myself.' And I know exactly what they're saying. Getting golf back, getting that competitive drive back and having something else to focus on, that's everything. That's the whole point. We want to get guys to pick up a golf club instead of a bottle or a Glock."

After a parade of bogies along #2—the crested greens weren't as perilous as its pine straw outskirts—we had lunch with Yujin and Aaron's new girlfriend on the patio, and Josh came over in a VGA golf cart and took us into town to visit their headquarters. And there it was, on a green awning in the heart of the village of Pinehurst: Veteran Golfers Association. It was the American equivalent of a storefront on The Links road in St. Andrews, and inside the walls were crowded with photographs of their members and tournaments, as well as a pro shop stocked with VGA gear. A long oak bar ran the length of the room, with a few beer taps ready to welcome any veterans who might be passing through. In the back of the room was the Wall of Honor, where VGA members had stuck hundreds of their military patches. Every branch was represented, with Airborne and Ranger and Special Forces labels pinned to the wall.

The VGA's growth and prosperity were hard stories to believe, yet in golf, you seemed to hear such good news all the time. I too often sold it short as a game that brought rich people together to make them richer; maybe it did that, but it also excelled at connecting large-hearted people as well. Golf made good happen, and over the next twenty-four hours, it would happen again. Twice.

It started with a text of last resort that morning to a friend whom I'd promised I wouldn't be bothering again. He had already been generous in arranging some of my most unfeasible tee times, but every other wagon to which I'd hitched my Cypress star had landed in a ditch. This was my last and only shot, and I paused before hitting send; if this text was met with no reply, I would have burned my best golfing bridge. But I put my trust in golf's goodness and sent off a request for a twosome at Cypress Point.

By the time I was back in my room after visiting the VGA with Aaron, a message was waiting on my phone. The member would be happy to host us, it said—and I could bring a third friend if I wanted to round out the four-some. It felt like a diamond bulging in my pocket, an open spot that I should protect and share only after the most careful deliberations.

Brendan was an automatic invite. He had earned his spot. Dad's back was in no shape to walk Monterey, or else he would have solved my lucky dilemma. Aaron was a contender, but the fact that I was already hosting him at Pinehurst was a blow to his candidacy. It was the best golf proposition I would ever get to make, and I was confident a front-runner would identify him or herself during my travels. Maybe he or she already had.

Pinehurst got its start when James Walker Tufts bought up six thousand acres of North Carolina sandhills in the 1890s and turned it into a health retreat for middle-income folks. Frederick Law Olmsted, who had designed New York City's Central Park, was enlisted to lay out the village, and it eventually grew into a golf colony when Tufts spotted guests knocking white balls around a cow pasture. In 1900, Donald Ross came to Pinehurst, and by 1919 he'd built the resort's first four courses (a rudimentary eighteen-holer was already there when he arrived, which he overhauled). The total course count would grow to ten, including a short course by Gil Hanse called the Cradle that had become one of the tougher tee times at the resort, even though eightsomes were allowed. Music played from hidden speakers, and Aaron and I went around it with wedges tucked into canvas sacks, pausing by the wood-paneled drink cart to sit and soak in the glory of the Cradle's 789 magnificent yards.

Hanse, Fazio, and Nicklaus added eighteen-hole designs to Pinehurst's roster, but the place belonged to Ross, in legend and otherwise. He had a home overlooking his pièce de résistance, Pinehurst #2, that he named the Dornoch Cottage after his hometown, and where he lived until his passing in 1948 (the resort now owns the cottage, and guests are occasionally invited to spend a night there).

I feared it was blasphemy to prefer Hanse's new #4 over Ross's #2—the latter was the Open venue and Pinehurst's biggest draw, and the former bore the sin of replacing a Ross original—but I simply had more fun on Hanse's varied layout, which benefited from a more undulating piece of the resort. And my next foursome agreed.

Over the course of my tour of America's two-star accommodations, I had mastered a traveling maneuver in which I could unpack my toiletries, lay out the next day's clothes, and order a delivery pizza within the first ninety seconds of entering a hotel room. I could pack it all up and be out the door in about sixty. But at Pinehurst, I was indulged by three nights in the same bed, dropping anchor at the Holly Inn (Ross's Cottage must have been booked), with a bevy of tee times to share on #2 and #4. Aaron could join me for only some of them, so I put out the word on social media, and by random scroll of the finger picked a dude named Jeff to come play both courses, and to bring a buddy.

I had been meeting up with golf strangers from one coast to the other, and I'd yet to get stuck with an undeniable asshole (there was that one guy, but I'll get to him). The people of golf kept showing me their best side—*our* best side, rather. I knew that golf grossly skewed the sample when it came to judging my country's welfare and unity, but wherever my wheels stopped, I didn't find any of the complainers I watched on TV. I didn't see the barkers of incivility that filled our Twitter feeds, where outlier jackasses got far too much screen time. I didn't hear the acrimony I'd come to accept as our destiny. Most people couldn't be bothered, it seemed; they were too busy getting on with their lives.

That wasn't to say we were saints, but we were entirely tolerable, and I was now collecting hope by the mile, and not just for my country but for golf as well. The game was getting younger and smarter and more creative—you just had to get out there and look. If country clubs were being culled, maybe that's what needed to happen. It wasn't cause for worry for this golfer, because there was a flock of inspired and informed players ready to carry it, and as my two hundred new golfing friends had shown me, the kids were alright.

Jeff and his friend Anthony weren't quite kids—both my age, with young families—but they were more proof that golf's invisible hand moved in benevolent ways. After I'd selected Jeff at random for a Pinehurst rendezvous, he sent me a picture of him and Anthony from three months prior. It wasn't another shot of two buddies beside a flagstick but a picture from the hospital, where Jeff was dressed in a gown with his arm around Anthony, who had just given his friend a kidney.

Jeff had long suffered from deteriorating kidney function, and when it got to the point where he needed a new one, he turned to his twelve golf pals, a regular traveling troop they called the Minors. Anthony was quick to step to the plate. Jeff was grateful for the chance to thank his friend with an overnight at Pinehurst, and I was grateful for the chance to witness friendship of the most genuine order. Meeting an organ donor makes one wonder—who would I ask? Who would ask me? And would I say yes? If Brendan wasn't a match, I'd be stuck hunting for a kidney on Facebook, unless I got in with the Minors. Jeff gave me one of their headcovers and said I was now an honorary member, so I had options.

We played #2 and #4 back-to-back on a sweltering September day, and Jeff soldiered forth with a smile, stopping often to hydrate and catch his breath. Walking thirty-six holes through an oven wasn't his post-op prescription, and his afternoon face seemed paler than his morning one, but after a shower, he arrived refreshed at dinner, where we all agreed that the only knock on Pinehurst was pace of play. My visit had convinced me that this was indeed the home of American golf, but I wasn't the only one to come to that conclusion—with so many eager visitors, the starters cranked out foursomes on #2 and #4, where our rounds had each failed to break five hours.

I wouldn't have been inclined to mind if I hadn't been spoiled by so much rapid golf that week, at places like Coore & Crenshaw's Dormie Club, where its new model for membership—join the Dormie Network and get access to six top-tier courses spread around the country—seemed a trend that was going to change the club scene. Or at Pine Needles, where I'd gone to golf camp as a kid, and still found its Donald Ross track a quiet gem with a sweet-tea-on-the-porch vibe. But the course that ruined me for most any other was just a few miles up the road, through the woods to a place that went ahead and wedged itself into my world's top five. Someday, when my kids are older, if they ask me where I was that year and what I was doing, I'll have this book to give them, but I'll have a simpler two-word answer as to the road for which I was searching.

I'd been refining my metrics for greatness in a golf course: architectural attribution had become more important as I studied designers and their choices, and as Gil Hanse had described, a seamless blend of golf and setting mattered, too. A great course presented a cerebral experience, requiring calculation and strategy and forcing a player to make choices according to their own mettle. It should challenge good players, and at least entertain the strugglers. Sheer enjoyment remained a vital component, but a truly great course, to me, required something more abstract. It had to inspire. And not just inspire you as a golfer but as a human being; it should make you ponder your gifts, wonder at the earth, and prize your moment. It should leave you a more mindful person than when you arrived, and reward you with awe, the kind you used to summon so easily as a child.

It was a pretty high bar. I might have been inclined to lower it, but Mike Strantz's Tobacco Road proved it could all linger in one plot.

I was reluctant to briefly leave the embrace of the Holly Inn, where I didn't have to use rewards points for a lobby waffle every morning, but I was excited to pack an overnight bag for Tobacco Road, where I was offered an evening in the cabin beside the fourteenth green, where Strantz had lived and worked as he plotted the golf course. They were simple accommodations—a few clean bedrooms and a kitchen—but the outdoor space was five-star. I flipped on the spotlights and chipped and putted until eleven o'clock, a dark pond beside me, and high on the hill above, a tee box where I would be tested tomorrow. I was alone in the shadows and the quiet, and it was perfect.

Mike Strantz grew up in Ohio, and after studying fine art and then landscape architecture at Michigan State, he joined Tom Fazio at Inverness, as Fazio prepared it for the 1979 US Open. Strantz had a bushy mustache and a dark mullet, a cowboy type who enjoyed riding horses and sketching landscapes. He worked alongside Fazio until 1987, then struck out on his own. He partnered with PGA Tour player Forrest Fezler to create a firm called Maverick Design, and at places like Caledonia and True Blue, Strantz put the name into practice, building courses with a fearless aesthetic and ridding the landscape of every last boring note.

At Tobacco Road, he had been given a former tobacco farm turned sand mine and full license to shape its jagged landscape. Even today, his background as a fine artist was evident; some of the holes felt surrealist in quality, while others were impressionist masterworks. He was the rare architect who designed his golf courses to look dramatic from every direction, walking the holes backward to make sure each ditch and mound was thoughtfully placed. He literally painted the dirt; writer friend Jay Revell sent me video of Strantz wandering around with a spray can, hand-lining every fairway and bunker and green. If a team member moved one of his lines by three inches, he noticed and would paint it again. Like any art, his work had both its devotees and its detractors; he was named one of the top ten architects of all time by *Golfweek*, yet some derided his uncommon courses for their difficult and inscrutable holes. To me, that was the last piece of that puzzle of what made a course truly great: somebody had to hate it. I had played only a few of his designs, and tragically, he left us only nine. In 2005, he died of cancer at the age of fifty, shortly after completing his final build at Monterey Peninsula Country Club.

My round at Tobacco Road took me back to my first time on a links course in Ireland; not because of the design but because playing a links felt like an altogether different sport. And Tobacco Road, with its blind shots and sand craters and preposterous greens and hulking mounds, felt like golf as I'd never before considered it. All the ingredients were the same—fairway, green, flag—but they'd been arranged with such imagination that other courses look like thin broth. It was golf through the funhouse, which I knew wasn't for everybody. But it was damn sure for me.

As I drove back to Pinehurst, I wondered if I'd finally found the Great American Golf Course in the North Carolina woods, or if the routing that best represented this country should appeal to a broader palate or have more accessible rates. In-season fees peaked at $180 at Tobacco Road—which was the best $180 a golfer could spend, but that didn't mean it fit every budget. The course that would tick every last box was out there, I was sure. There were plenty of roads left to discover, and one to get back to as soon as I could.

BETHESDA, MARYLAND

I was in a hotel in DC when my phone rang around midnight. I was relieved it wasn't Allyson, but that relief passed when I realized it was Paddy.

"Dude, hey. Where does LJ live?" he said. It sounded like he was in a car, with his head hanging out the window.

He was referring to one of my buddies (Little Jon) with whom we'd played Congressional that afternoon, ticking off another US Open spot where the courses were good but the palatial clubhouse was the draw. It felt more like a resort than a golf club, with bedrooms upstairs and multiple pools and a bowling alley, plus sundry restaurants and ballrooms. When I left the lads after dinner, I had a feeling Paddy wasn't making it back to Philadelphia that evening—the Barenaked Ladies were playing a wedding on the upstairs patio, and he looked too comfortable in his seat by the pool, guarding a small army of Bud Light cans.

"Don't tell me you're driving," I said.

"No, I'm in a taxi. I'm crashing at LJ's. He gave me his address, but I can't find it."

I sent him LJ's number and went back to sleep. It had been a long thirty-six in the sun with my friend from Ireland-then-Philadelphia; Paddy had shepherded me around the Irish counties when his wife's job landed him in Kinsale, then moved back to our shared Delaware County, and later traveled to meet me in Scotland as well. While he was one of my most loyal pals whom I treasured for his fearless authenticity, he was also that friend that you had to pre-introduce with a disclaimer: Paddy is going to make you laugh or maybe cringe, depending on your taste in off-color jokes, and I am in no way responsible for anything that comes out of his mouth.

I couldn't set out on another cross-country journey without him, so we identified DC as a convenient spot for Paddy to join the story. The day started early at Columbia Country Club, where in the 1921 US Open Chick Evans had bested a young Bobby Jones for low amateur. Columbia could have fit within one-fifth of the Congressional property, a tight layout packed within a neighborhood. Columbia traditionally welcomed the president as a member (Trump had his own course in the area, so no need to invite him to join), though accommodating a president's golf was no simple matter. It ruined the place for the members; the Secret Service took up most of the carts, the tee sheet had to be blocked off, and the roads that circled Columbia's snug routing had to be closed. Legend had it that in the 1990s, when Clinton's secretary called Columbia's president to schedule a round, he offered the commander in chief eighteen Mondays to choose from; when none fit the president's schedule, the secretary demanded they be more flexible. "We're talking about the president of the United States," Clinton's assistant protested, to which Columbia's president replied, "Well, you're talking to the president of Columbia Country Club."

Obama, I had been told, was sensitive to the disruptions his visits caused, and chose to play most of his DC golf at Andrews Air Force Base, hardly using his Columbia membership at all. As a senator, Nixon had once shown up looking to head straight out and play before a vote on the Hill; Columbia's matchmaker told him, "Mr. Nixon, you might be in charge up at the Capitol, but when you're here, I'm in charge." He told Nixon to take a seat on the waiting bench, and he did.

The matchmaker was Columbia's most brilliant innovation; he stood guard at a podium by the first tee, and if you wanted to play, you gave him your name and waited to be called. He arranged all the teams and foursomes, then handed you your scorecard with your match's strokes already dotted. He didn't always use your handicap index; he allotted strokes based on how he knew members would match up against one another, or he'd send out one side already up two holes if he felt they were the underdog. No one ever dared to argue with his math, and the result was close contests immune to sandbagging, a welcome throwback to the days before all our foursomes were prearranged, where you might actually meet somebody new on your golf course.

During our round, I met a Columbia caddie named Billy who had been looping there for an astounding sixty-five years—he started as a ball-shagger on the range at age twelve, and was still going around at seventy-seven as a forecaddie (he eschewed rangefinders, calling them "caddies in a can"). He kept coming back because Columbia treated their caddies well, he said. Like part of the family. He told me about another caddie, also named Billy, who had caddied there for just as long. This Billy took the bus to Columbia every day for forty years, until members decided to reward him for his loyalty and chipped in to buy him a car. The day after handing him the keys, they spotted him stepping off the bus again and asked him what had happened to his new ride. "I sold it," he told them. Apparently, they'd forgotten to ask Billy if he had a driver's license.

Paddy was in joke-telling form by the third hole—it didn't take him long to warm up to strangers—and shared a tale with our foursome about a pub toasting contest in Kinsale. As we were playing with Columbia's longtime head pro, whom we'd known for all of thirty minutes, I braced for the punch line—it involved Sunday mass, an angry wife, and an orgasm. Paddy delivered it shamelessly, and I couldn't bring myself to look up and see if the pro was laughing. I was, anyway. By the eighteenth hole, Paddy's candor had won the group over, and the pro told us we were welcome back anytime. You didn't have to laugh at his jokes to love Paddy, but it helped.

I was in Virginia when he texted the next day; he'd made it home safe and sound after a night in LJ's guest room. It had been only a few hours, but DC felt weeks away from where I found myself in Sperryville, surrounded by wavy green hills dotted with cattle and golf holes set beside a schoolhouse.

I was joined at the Schoolhouse Nine by its owner, Cliff, and its architect, Mike McCartin, a Doak protégé who at Cliff's request had turned some of his family's fallow pastures into a sporty routing for local denizens. Cliff explained that there was little future for small farms in the area, so they'd had to find new ways to make money off their land. He had already converted an abandoned schoolhouse into a pub and arcade when he decided a golf course next door would bring in some clientele. It seemed to be working; there were a dozen groups out there when I visited. We played behind a dad who was pushing a double-wide stroller while Mom whacked away in sandals.

I was excited to see that McCartin had injected some intrigue into the greens and bunkers around an otherwise flat parcel. He kicked off his shoes and played me barefoot, and after a quick loop, I put his five bucks in my wallet—cash won from a designer on his own course remained my favorite currency. Mike was a talented young architect dedicated to the cause of public golf, and had started up the National Links Trust with a mission of "promoting and protecting affordability, accessibility and engaging golf course architecture at municipal golf courses throughout the United States of America." Next, he had his eyes set on DC's East Potomac course, which I had played just that morning. It was an unpolished jewel that I agreed could use some of his vision; DC's busiest muni was a hundred years old, and the wear certainly showed, but the backdrops were hypnotic. Its holes played along the Potomac, and the Washington Monument seemed to follow us around the property. I'd aimed drives at interesting markers before, but that white obelisk topped them all.

The Links Trust also had their eye on refurbishing DC's Langston Golf Course, where the round I'd played two days prior had felt like more of a privilege than an opportunity. Its holes were on the Register of National Historic Places, and teaching pro Roy Savoy sat down with me to explain why.

The municipal course was named after the country's first African American elected official, John Mercer Langston. "Blacks had been given this place back in 1935," Roy explained. "It was a place they could say, 'This is our own, this is our place to come and play this great game of golf.'" He was in his seventies and had been running junior programs for Langston players since the 1980s, but long before his tenure, the Royal Golf Club (America's oldest Black golf society) and the Wake-Robin Golf Club (America's first female African American golf club) had been teeing it up at Langston and battling city hall to see that the course was properly maintained (its original greens lacked grass) and expanded to eighteen holes (it was, plus a fifty-slot driving range). In its heyday, Langston's Capital City Open had been considered the top African American tournament in golf and attracted the likes of Calvin Peete, Lee Elder, Jim Thorpe, Chuck Thorpe, and Bobby Stroble; its Wake-Robin Club produced Ethel Funches, an amateur who won over one hundred regional and national titles from the 1950s through the '70s. Her name was hard to find in the annals of golf history, unless you had someone like Roy Savoy at a place like Langston Golf Course to remind you that golf history was broader and richer than the version we'd been telling. I was grateful I did.

En route to DC, I'd made a pit stop in Wilmington, Delaware, to cross the First State off my list. While the Small Wonder had a big list of quality golf offerings, there was only one course I wanted to see again. Bidermann was my sleeper pick for the Mid-Atlantic's finest, and it was easily the best golf course nobody had ever heard of. As my Philadelphia golf writing friend Joe Logan once noted, for forty years, the place had a membership of one.

Devereux Emmet had designed the course's original nine holes for Henry Francis du Pont, who would blast opera from one of the windows of his 190-bedroom estate and play the holes alone. In 1963, Henry's cousin convinced him to expand the course and open it up to select family and friends, so William Flynn disciple Dick Wilson was brought in to build a proper eighteen-holer that, for me, was unequaled as a farmland golf experience. It was golf through a Wyeth painting, into hills of tall golden grass where each green and fairway was ensconced in pastoral bliss.

Wilson was a celebrated but irascible designer of the 1950s and '60s, with Cog Hill and Florida's Pine Tree among his credits. Booze got the best of him, and he passed away on the day the new Bidermann course opened—not with doors swung open wide, but more like a window cracked. The membership remained miniscule and predominantly du Ponts, and on a busy day the course saw maybe a dozen golfers. I was surprised to see it even show up on my GPS; the pro told me they only recently posted a street number by the road (no Bidermann sign, of course), after a member had needed an ambulance the year before and things had gotten a little complicated. It had a tiny pro shop and a spartan locker room with a few chairs that hadn't been reupholstered since Pierre Samuel du Pont de Nemours landed from France. He'd traveled to America in 1799 on the French ship *Aigle* (or *Eagle*), which was commemorated by a carved eagle above the Bidermann lockers, in a room that confirmed the inverse-locker-room theory: the less fancy the locker room, the more exceptional the golf course. (Gulph Mills, outside Philadelphia, existed as the pinnacle of this theory, where an extraordinary routing was accompanied by a room of pegs on a wall.)

It was a short trip down to Maryland to investigate the next US Open venue on my map. I wished I could have spent a week in Baltimore Country Club's redbrick clubhouse, nibbling their chunky crab cakes at every meal. The 1899 national championship had been held on the original BCC course, but like Philly Cricket Club—which had also moved its golf to wider pastures—the first hole was all that remained at that in-town campus, where racquet sports now reigned. And also like Philly Cricket, A. W. Tillinghast designed its flagship course as BCC expanded to its Five Farms property, where the hills were merciless and the back-to-front greens sloped like the deck of a sinking ship.

Baltimore had hosted a bevy of notable contests, but the one cup deliberately missing from its trophy case was the PGA Championship's Wanamaker—Walter Hagen had won the trophy four years in a row before Leo Diegel knocked him off in 1928 at Baltimore, but when it came time to pass the prize, Hagen claimed he'd left it in a Chicago taxicab after an evening of carousing and hadn't seen it since. They had no trophy to give Diegel at Baltimore, and so a replica was made for the next year's winner. The original Wanamaker would eventually be found in a warehouse that stored

Walter Hagen golf clubs—quite suspiciously so—though winners today still receive the replica, as the original is held by the PGA for safekeeping.

With Baltimore behind me, I was ready to move west and sink into the deep pillows at the Greenbrier in West Virginia, but my schedule conflicted with their PGA Tour event, so I wouldn't get to visit Dick Wilson's imaginary golf course. In 1955, Eisenhower called for a Cold War bunker to be built that could house all of Congress during a nuclear attack. They decided to build a massive covert facility beneath the Greenbrier resort, but needed a cover story for a construction project of such scale. Dick Wilson agreed to lend his name to a golf course they weren't actually building, though he did use leftover dirt from the project when the Greenbrier's Meadows course was constructed in 1962. A 1992 story in the *Washington Post* outed the Greenbrier's secret basement, and today guests can take an eerie tour of the emergency halls of Congress.

The only other West Virginia destination on my list was the Oakhurst Links; it claimed to be America's first golf course (you still played it with hickories), but as it remained closed from the damages of the 2016 floods, I picked the closest West Virginia golf holes to my route, a public course near Harper's Ferry on the state's eastern panhandle. I kept weaving between Maryland, Virginia, and West Virginia to find it, and when I did, the girl working the bar in a trailer turned clubhouse was surprised to see a golfer she didn't recognize.

I was simultaneously offended by the golf and pleased to find a specimen that fully exposed me to the plight of the public player. I would find only one track that was shaggier in my travels, a course called Pine Valley in Arkansas that I played for irony's sake, where the owners had sort of given up on the place as a golf course and seemed to be making more money on the Frisbee crowd: "The blue trash cans are where you tee off if you're playing golf. The white posts are for the disc golfers," I was told. Pine Valley II at least had good bones, so my West Virginia find grabbed that bottom spot on the list, as it incorporated nearly every element of awful golf: internal out of bounds, house-lined holes, fairways seeded with a careful blend of clover and dandelion, greens overtaken by anthills and goose feathers, tee boxes with grass grown higher than any tee in my bag, and cups with thick grass beards that reduced their size to roughly that of a bottle cap. If this was what public golfers in West Virginia were facing, I thought, they'd all better go looking for their Frisbees.

At least I played fast. The golf came to a hurried conclusion, and I rushed to get back on the road. That evening's drive was a haul. My tee time jigsaw had me heading south again, so I beelined it back toward Georgia and two places that were both somehow the home of Bobby Jones.

ATLANTA, GEORGIA

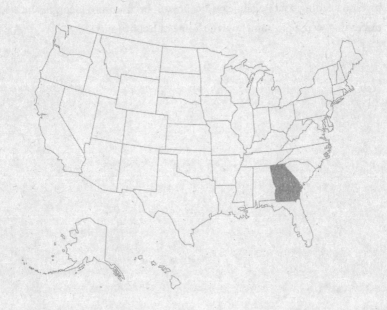

Playing the two clubs back-to-back felt like reading the same history book twice, but what a book it was. They seemed to be competing for chapters of the Bobby Jones story, and while Atlanta Athletic Club boasted a more abundant spread of memorabilia, East Lake had a few museum pieces as well.

Atlanta Athletic was the undisputed home club of American golf's original superstar. Aside from Old Tom Morris, Bobby Jones was perhaps the game's most influential and beloved practitioner. Born in 1902, Jones grew up at Atlanta Athletic Club, but in 1967 AAC left its downtown site and settled in Johns Creek, where they had enough room for two Robert Trent Jones courses. The course they left behind—where Jones had actually played—was now called East Lake, and it had floundered for decades after

AAC relocated. Throughout the 1970s and '80s its surrounding neighborhood suffered a plague of gun violence that earned it the nickname "Little Vietnam." The course was on the auction block when local philanthropist Tom Cousins emerged with an idea for purpose-driven golf, using East Lake as an anchor for raising corporate dollars that could revitalize the community as a whole. They added mixed-income housing and a charter school that now saw 100 percent of its students go to college, with the only all-Black golf team to ever win the Georgia state championship. Violent crime had dropped by 96 percent and the new YMCA was thriving, as was the new community nine-holer with practice areas for local youth.

The big course made its way back, too; today East Lake hosts the PGA Tour Championship and an annual collegiate showcase. Driven by the success of East Lake, Cousins later partnered with Warren Buffett to create Purpose Built Communities, an organization aimed at ending poverty through community revitalization. They have re-created the East Lake story in thirteen cities across America, with plans for several more.

The contemporary Atlanta Athletic Club welcomed you with a statue of Bobby Jones by the entrance, and their Jones history cases were more crowded than East Lake's, though East Lake still owned his old locker and the pocket watch he carried, with its four-leaf-clover charm. (He was born on St. Patrick's Day, and East Lake now uses the clover as its alternative logo.) East Lake was also one of two places where you could see the original US Amateur trophy, or its closest approximation. Bobby Jones had brought the Havemeyer Trophy back to his home club after winning it at Merion in 1924, and while it was on display there, it was destroyed in a clubhouse fire; a less ornate version was then created for future winners. In the 1990s, two replicas of the original were produced: one for the USGA's New Jersey headquarters, and one for East Lake. I found it in a case in the lobby, a stunning silver tower of baroque beauty.

Along with all the Jones history, East Lake could claim rights to the story of Alexa Stirling, a female golf prodigy who used to dominate Bobby Jones when they were kids at the former AAC (in fairness to Jones, she was four years older). It was said that her talents pushed Jones to dedicate himself to the game in the hopes of matching her, after he watched her win her first of three consecutive Women's US Amateurs at age eighteen.

Later in life, Jones would seek a more intimate Atlanta golf setting. His AAC had grown crowded with families and tennis players and kids swimming in the lake, and he envisioned a nearby spot for a handful of dedicated golfers. Along with his friend Dick Garlington, he tasked Robert Trent Jones with building them a hometown course that Jones requested be "as near like Augusta National as possible, and better, if possible." While the resulting Peachtree Golf Club was only marginally easier to access than Augusta, I was lucky to meet another friend of a friend who was willing to show me its hills and flawless fairways. If I didn't have a pocketful of Peachtree ball markers, I might have forgotten I wasn't reliving that singular day when the golfing deities escorted me down Magnolia Lane. (That story is in my Scotland book, obviously.)

Jones kept to the Augusta formula by selecting a former nursery for Peachtree, where the hills held the purest greens I'd found in America. Its firm fairways looked like they'd been vacuumed instead of mowed, and as my FootJoys floated across a layout of undulating variety, I was easily convinced I was playing Georgia's second-finest golf course. Peachtree's antebellum clubhouse was one of the few great buildings to survive the burning of Atlanta, when General Sherman used it as a temporary headquarters during his scorched-earth campaign through the South. A Civil War cannon out front stood as a reminder of the troops who had been quartered there.

The actual Bobby Jones Golf Course in Atlanta didn't have any such history on display; its pro shop was still in a trailer, as the course had just reopened a few months ago, but it had been Atlanta's first public course when it opened in 1932. Bobby Jones himself hit the ceremonial tee ball, and his grandson hit the first shot this time around, when the Bobby Jones Golf Course Foundation cut the ribbon on a $23 million renovation that literally reimagined the course in every direction.

I met Marty Elgison around the third hole to tell him that what he and Bob Cupp created had given hope to every struggling muni out there. Marty had been the Jones family's lawyer for years, protecting the golfer's legacy and licensing his name to select brands. That a golf course with Jones's name on it was in such disrepair felt like a dereliction of duty, so he committed to bringing his client's namesake course back to life. Working through city government to secure permissions and raising the capital had been a yearslong mission, especially given the course's tight city footprint. They had promised learning facilities for area kids, but there wasn't room to meet all the city's recreational needs and still build eighteen holes. Accomplished architect Bob Cupp saw that they could fit eighteen bad holes or nine great ones, so, borrowing from St. Andrews, he imagined the new layout as a reversible nine.

Cupp passed away before the project could be finished, but his son completed the vision, which extended beyond a course that played both ways. They wanted a course that truly appealed to all abilities, so you could play each hole on its Magnolia or Azalea routings (they alternated by the day) from any one of eight numbered starting points. The Longleaf Tee System was a new initiative from the American Society of Golf Course Architects Foundation and the US Kids Golf Foundation that removed gender from tee choices in favor of driving distance. It was like trying on shoes—you went to the practice tee and hit a few drives, and posts on the range told you the appropriate tee for maximum enjoyment. My pride was salvaged when I qualified for tee number eight, and from the back of the boxes, the course was all you could ask for in either direction. I visited on one of the days you could play it each way, approaching its huge double greens from opposite sides. For a newborn, the routing was packed with character and thoughtful shots, and if you liked fast and firm, Bobby Jones was your spot. The new sod was so hard that we were given rubber mallets for banging our tees into the turf. I wasn't sure what the course's namesake would have thought about golf with a hammer, but the ground would soften with time, and Marty Elgison's municipal miracle would have surely made his late client proud.

Five o'clock in the evening seemed a late starting time, but the friend I'd made on Twitter assured me it left plenty of daylight for the weekly game at his favorite Atlanta muni. I met a small group of guys in T-shirts outside the one-room clubhouse at Candler Park; they were sitting on lawn chairs and drinking canned beer from their own coolers as they waited for the regulars to show. I introduced myself and threw twenty bucks into the pot—I think we were playing skins, but I wasn't sure. I'd played a lot of golf, but I'd never walked to the tee with three balls in my pocket and one club in my hand.

Candler Park was said to be the first course in Atlanta to allow women golfers, built by Coca-Cola's founding family for one of their daughters who took to the game. Atlanta was a Coke town; its headquarters loomed large on the skyline, yet there was no Coca-Cola being consumed that evening as our eightsome rolled down the first fairway with beer coolers slung over seven shoulders. Candler Park was a beloved Atlanta public for its rock-bottom rates and bold terrain, and the one-club golfers had made their money match a Tuesday tradition. They even had their own shirts and logo, where instead of the traditional two clubs crossed in an X there was only one. One-club brought out a mix of young Atlanta golfers: a chef, a gelato shop owner, a teacher, and a CPA. I asked if anyone had a pencil—the things you forget when you golf without a golf bag—and a dude named Fish ran back to his car to grab one. When he returned in a soaked T-shirt, I apologized for sending him on such a sweaty errand.

"All good. Needed more whiskey," he said, jingling his Big Gulp in my direction.

The course was a tight, short track where you could leave your driver in the trunk. One of the guys had gotten the idea to leave his bag altogether and see how well he could score with just one stick. Pretty well was the up-shot, and Tuesday night one-club had been happening ever since. It made for more interesting gambling—the talent gaps shrank when you had to putt and drive with an 8 iron—and it left your shoulder free for a cooler. As cans were crushed with stunning rapidity, the true genesis of one-club revealed itself: swapping thirteen clubs in favor of thirteen beers.

None of those twenty dollars came back my way at round's end, and that was fine. Our eight-pack played fast—you picked up after par—and the one-clubbers had welcomed me as one of their own. I was sure they'd left me a better golfer, too. I was an unremarkable iron player, but two hours of 7 iron from all distances and predicaments was a boost of confidence. Being forced to consider drive placement versus drive distance was a mindset I'd abandoned when persimmon disappeared, and relearning how to lay up might treat me well as I headed north for an autumn sampling of American golf ancestry.

WORCESTER, MASSACHUSETTS

Tim landed in the booth at the restaurant, trying to catch his breath. We had met that afternoon at Worcester Country Club, a course of bad logo and brilliant Donald Ross golf holes where Willie Macfarlane had won the US Open in 1925. Legend had it that President Taft had taken a mulligan on his ceremonial opening shot at Worcester, though I was having a hard time finding a course in New England where Taft *hadn't* lost a ball or gotten stuck in a bunker. Tim was a Worcester (Woos-tah) member I'd met online. He'd offered to host me and my two Irish amigos at his club, and was quickly finding that he'd volunteered for more than he'd bargained. Keeping track of two Irishmen loose in America required both patience and resolve.

Cormac had reached out months before to tell me that he and Jack were coming over to join me for some of my northeastern weeks from Ardglass in County Down. I was thrilled for the company; since my Ireland book, Cormac and Jack had become dear friends, and I returned to Ardglass often to visit them. They were in their sixties and looked like a misfit pair: Cormac of wide frame, shiny scalp, and tan complexion, and Jack, the paler, skinnier, hairier partner. They both looked unnatural in shorts, their legs not having seen the sun since their last trip to the States, and they had custom golf shirts for their American tour—Ardglass logos with American flags emblazoned on the breast. While a rainy New England autumn had sapped my energy, meeting up with Jack and Cormac restored the vim and vigor. They were here for the craic, two lads from the village on holiday in America, and I knew it was best to let them find their way. If my years among the Irish had taught me anything, it was that they could always sort something out.

Tim was less convinced. We sat at our table waiting for Jack and Cormac to find us, and after twenty minutes, he went outside to look for their car. He'd given them the address for their GPS, and the restaurant was less than ten minutes from the course. After half an hour, Cormac finally called to say he was parked in a neighborhood full of homes.

"We're here at fifty Franklin Street, and it's somebody's house!" Cormac told Tim. Apparently, Tim had made a joke earlier that the restaurant was just over the second green, where Cormac had deposited one of his approach shots—"You can find your ball when we get there." Instead of plugging the restaurant's address into his phone, Cormac took Tim at his word and headed for the homes behind the second green. Not finding a restaurant, he kept driving, in the absolute wrong direction. By the time he typed 50 Franklin Street into his phone, he found one in an altogether different town.

Tim got them headed toward the restaurant, and eventually flagged down their minivan out in the street. Jack came inside and laughed about how much of Massachusetts they had accidentally seen, and a relieved Tim came in to join us. We were starving, and halfway through our appetizers, I realized something was missing: "So where the hell is Cormac?" I asked.

"He's not here?" Tim said.

"I think he's still parking the car," Jack replied, plucking steak from another skewer.

"Shit. I thought I missed him and he was in the bathroom. I'll find him." Tim was off again. He was in his twenties; plenty of energy, Jack and I decided, so we stayed put and polished off the rest of the plates. I wasn't worried. My itinerary forced me to let Jack and Cormac forage for themselves that week, and when it came to golf and accommodations, two guys who'd landed in America without a tee time or hotel reservation were doing just fine without me. They'd connected with Tim via an email I forwarded, and without my knowing, the three had become fast friends. Tim had taken them out on the town the previous evening, then pointed them toward a hotel down the street. It felt sort of funny to pawn my guests off on a stranger, but there were no strangers in Jack and Cormac's world.

When Tim returned once again without Cormac, he was properly worried, and I was beginning to wonder how my friend could have gotten lost between the sidewalk and the restaurant doorway. Twenty minutes later, Cormac strode through the entrance, all smiles, not a bother. He'd been sitting in the bar next door, waiting for us to show our faces. "It was a young sorta place, really loud music," he said. "I began to think I might be in the wrong place. Sure enough, I was!"

Entrees arrived, and we spent the evening laughing about how many different 50 Franklin Streets one might explore during a tour of America. Cormac was eager to learn about my travels and asked how long it was going to take me to write this book. (It's an author's least favorite question; I'd rather you ask me my weight.) A few hours among Irish friends had reignited the ball-busting, so I told Cormac, "Not as long as it took you to find this fucking restaurant!"

I had saved New England for the fall; friends said the northern fairways could be soft until July, and I'd never been on a leaf-peeping trip, so October seemed a bright and perfect window. I forgot that fall and spring lasted all of three days anymore, so at places like Brae Burn and Brookline, we raced gray monsoons of wintery spit. I got clear days at Eastward Ho! and Old Sandwich, two indulgent days of Massachusetts's best old and new courses, but I fell most deeply for Essex, a Donald Ross charmer where he had actually worked as the head pro, and the third course I'd visited with a Ross house on or near the course. These top-corner states were packed with golf history and heavyweight clubs, and stopping in New London, Connecticut, on my way up to boat out to Fishers Island and visit Seth Raynor's keynote course was a golf dream hard to believe, even as I wiped the salt spray from my eyes.

With a smile frozen to my face, I bounced across the waves beside three new friends I'd met on Instagram. We passed the fairways of Connecticut's Shennecossett (which felt like a course I'd played back in my teens) and hung a left at forbidden Plum Island, where the government researched animal diseases—unless you were partial to certain conspiracy theories. We docked at Fishers Island and soon found ourselves ascending its fourth hole, Punchbowl, where the oceanside fairway cresting at a ridge before falling to a concave green backed by miles of blue might very well be the best golf hole in America. But as impressive as Fishers was, the Hay Harbor nine-holer down the road hit me in my sentimental spot. It was a linksy walk with its own opportunities for seaside heroics, and best of all, it was a complete surprise.

I didn't know Hay Harbor existed until our host pulled up next to it; he was a real-life du Pont, and much of the island was populated by American industry's founding families. I jokingly asked him if he'd been to any family reunions lately, and he said he actually had. Every New Year's Day, hundreds of descendants of Pierre du Pont convened in Wilmington, Delaware, not far from where their fortunes had begun in a gunpowder mill. They all wore ribbons that listed their lineages back to Pierre. It was yet another surprise, and it set the tone for the miles ahead. Like a pilgrim landing at nearby Plymouth, the world ahead of me was teeming with revelations.

Who knew Vermont held masterpieces like Dorset Field Club and Ekwanok, the latter a Walter Travis design where Lincoln's eldest son, Robert Todd, was formerly club president. Both courses were enveloped by Green Mountain drama, but Ekwanok, a name taken from the Native American word for nearby Equinox Mountain, was white-picket-fence Vermont bliss. With serene slopes uninterrupted by trees and an idyllic white clubhouse, it felt like golf with Norman Rockwell, and appropriately so—one of the club's forefathers, Bartlett Arkell, had used his Beech-Nut fortune to collect art, and he gifted rare works to his two golf clubs: Ekwanok and Augusta National. Ekwanok received Norman Rockwell's caddie painting *On the Tee*, a reproduction of which still hangs in the Ekwanok clubhouse (the club eventually sold the original for millions, my host informed me). His latter club did fine by Arkell as well: he personally financed 40 percent of the cost of the Augusta National clubhouse and funded the winner's purse for the first nine Masters tournaments.

Located on the edge of the postcard village of Manchester, Ekwanok had me forecasting a Vermont retirement. Allyson had long dreamt of the New England farmhouse life, spending her days jarring vegetables she didn't know how to grow, or jar, or convince me to eat. But if I could hike Ekwanok's fairways every day, I'd fork whatever homegrowns she put in front of me.

More surprises awaited across the border in the Granite State of New Hampshire, where I was stunned by how much I managed to spend on my room at the Omni Mount Washington. Its Donald Ross course, updated by Ross restorationist Brian Silva, was good, if not a touch plain. Its backdrops provided the majority of the excitement, which included the Presidential Range (Washington, Eisenhower, Adams, and Jefferson each had a hill)— plus its white castle of a hotel, where somewhere behind one of its windows, a tired hotel room at leaf-season rates awaited me.

Maine shocked me next, with its girth and sense of humor. The other New England states were quickly traversed, but the voyage to Maine's end felt like an interminable expedition. Along the way, flashing road signs reminded drivers to "USE YOUR BLINKERS, PUMPKIN SPICE DRINKERS" and "PEEP THE LEAVES NOT YOUR PHONE." Belgrade Lakes was a jagged mountaintop eighteen built by the heirs of the Dexter Shoe fortune, and as scenic a public course as I'd found. I spent another afternoon at Maine's Northeast Harbor Golf Club, which was called "Philadelphia on the Rocks" for all the Philly folks who spent their summers here. It dated back to 1895, and I would have expected it to treat this Philadelphian better, but it was the toughest five thousand yards I'd ever traversed, as a golfer and as a walker. If you loved short par 4s, this was the course for you; they were all short, but with greens set into cradles of granite, the ricochets were unforgiving. Still, through my struggles I could see it was another remote treasure, and I played with a transplanted Scot who suggested we play our match for a book; loser buys the winner his favorite read. He hadn't read any of mine, but after beating me four-up, maybe he has now.

I was searching Maine's shores for a lobster shack but kept bumping into what were called lobster "pounds" instead. A local finally disclosed that they were restaurants named for the way lobsters were stored in large enclosures—like dog pounds, I guessed. I felt lucky to get the insight. Mainers were hospitable, if a bit guarded. They had a New England edge that was hard to penetrate; kind but wary of outsiders, and protective of their northern utopia. A grad school friend had moved up here after school, and when we met up at a lobster pound, he explained: "Your neighbor might not speak to you for ten years, but he'll help pull your car out of a ditch."

Maine lobster tasted like Philadelphia lobster; the price was the tasty part. With a full belly, I headed for the Canadian border, where I hoped I might find at least a few square feet of an American gem. At Aroostook Valley CC, situated at Maine's northern tip, I would have my first chance to drive my ball out of the country (the second would come later, at Black Jack's Crossing in Texas, where I would Sharpie *VAYA CON DIOS!* onto my Titleist before launching it across the Rio Grande). I'd heard that the cross-border club had been built in a scheme to circumvent Prohibition—the pro was cagey about giving too much credence to the legends, but there was no other explanation for a 1929 venue of this particular layout. The story went that golfers looking for a drink built a club with a US address—its modest American pro shop that was the size of a garden shed—but with a Canadian clubhouse twenty feet away, where whiskey could flow freely.

The international border was marked with a post by the parking lot, and like an idiot tourist, I straddled the line, then hopped back and forth between Canada and the United States, thumbing my nose at the border patrol, wherever they might have been. The holes were over in Canada; you could snaphook a ball back into America, but I kept mine safely on the maple-leaf side. It was a dandy of a hilltop layout with long views of gold and orange foliage, but as I was playing at an American club on a course in Canada, I had to disqualify it from my search and head for courses with less confusing addresses.

I cruised south along Maine's eastern coast, which held pockets of short-course genius at places like Kebo Valley, where a 68 was my best round of the entire journey (I was pleased to birdie the seventeenth, where President Taft once carded a 27, after seventeen shots in one bunker), and Cape Arundel in Kennebunkport. A clubhouse sign paid homage to George H. W. Bush, who had learned to play golf there under the tutelage of his father, Prescott Bush, former president of the USGA. (Prescott's father-in-law, George Herbert Walker, was also a USGA president, and lent his name to the Walker Cup.) The course was as pleasant a walk as I'd taken with golf clubs; from its cozy clubhouse to its gently fashioned Walter Travis holes, Cape Arundel felt like a big golf hug. No wonder it was the place where the forty-first and forty-second presidents became friends, after Jim Nantz arranged a round with Clinton and Bush where the two were spotted walking off the fifth green arm in arm.

Maine may have offered peaceful golf and hours of reflection behind the wheel, but it was Massachusetts's density of great courses that revealed the region's golfing heart. As I toured its volume of offerings, I stopped by another former presidential golf hangout in Hyannis Port, just around the corner from where the street was crowded with Kennedy Compound snoopers. John F. Kennedy had played much of his golf at the Hyannisport Club, and even if you couldn't get out to play it, the place was worth a drive for the parking lot view. The course was a low-lying eighteen that spilled downward from the clubhouse toward harbor and marsh, and in the distance, white flecks of an on-course residence were visible through the trees. It had been one of JFK's summer White Houses, a sufficiently secure location on the water's edge with only one road leading out to it. You can still see the boulders that the Army Corps of Engineers placed in the waters surrounding it, blocking off a perimeter from approaching ships. When I went around the front nine at Hyannisport without making a birdie, the head pro with whom I was playing told me my name was now Jimmy.

"Who's Jimmy?" I asked.

"Jimmy's the guy who didn't make a birdie on the front. And if he doesn't make a birdie on the back, Jimmy buys the drinks."

I cast off my Jimmy tag by eighteen and headed for the Open venues around Boston that were the pillars of my New England calendar. Brookline (The Country Club) owned the well-chronicled Francis Ouimet story, a David-and-Goliath tale in which young Ouimet beat British superstars Harry Vardon and Teddy Ray in the 1913 US Open, a victory that essentially

saved American golf. It had been considered a British game until this underdog American victory grabbed headlines and ignited a golf boom among
Ouimet's countrymen.

The Country Club's original membership featured a faction of Bosto-
nians who came over from the Myopia Hunt Club, which had US Open legends of the nightmare variety. Before heading for the first tee, the pro gave
us the scope of Myopia's punitive past: It had hosted four early US Opens and
still held the record for the highest winning score (331, by Willie Anderson
in 1901) and highest single-round score (157, by J. D. Tucker in the 1898
Open). In the 1901 championship, not a single player broke 80 in any round.
It was the bluest of blue-blood establishments, founded by a baseball team
of spectacle-wearing Harvard grads who called themselves the Myopia Club.
They built a compound for baseball, hunting, and polo, and eventually golf,
where Herbert Leeds, also a former Harvard baseballer, crafted what had
to be, yard for yard, America's least forgiving gauntlet, with greens tilted on
their sides and fairways canted to kick balls toward sandy bottoms. Caddies
used to keep a rope by the bunker on ten for President Taft; he found it often,
and liberating his 330 pounds from the sand required a cable tied around his
waist and pulled by a team of loopers.

That previous winter, as I compiled my list of aspirational golf clubs,
I'd wondered where I might most feel like an outsider. Myopia took the
prize in mere minutes as I drove through its fox-chasing grounds and past
its stables and kennels, parking between Land Rovers where moms dressed
in equestrian casual were dropping off children in riding gear. A chorus of
dogs yelped regally in the distance. Add the quaint yellow clubhouse dating
to 1772 and I felt as if I'd stepped out of a horse-and-carriage time machine.
It was no surprise that John Updike had been a member here; his golf tales
seemed born of a patrician milieu with which I was unfamiliar, but I felt
fortunate for the chance to pierce its curtain for a few hours. As for its layout,
if you had years to study its angles and brandished a bull's-eye iron game,
Myopia might be your perfect golf course. I had neither, so I set my sights on
nine Cape Cod holes that just might be mine.

· · ·

A Rob I'd never met before had emailed to offer me a room in Marion, across the water from the Cape. As I pulled down the road into his property, I was glad I had taken this stranger up on his offer. I'd gotten pretty good at judging whether an invitational email was offering a cot in a kid's room or if I might have my own suite or wing, and it was clear Rob's quarters were the latter. He was a member at Kittansett, a course at the tip of a peninsula protruding into Buzzards Bay, and his home was just down the street from the club, where we would be playing in two days. There were three buildings on his waterside property; one where his mother stayed, another where he and his family lived—the kids were off at college, so I had their whole side of the house to myself—and a cottage beside a dock, which they used only in the summer, or when Irish guys came knocking.

I expected to be meeting a new face when I pulled into Rob's gravel driveway, but to my surprise, through the cottage door came Cormac, arms spread wide, with Jack right behind him.

"Mr. Coyne! In the flesh!" he said. "We are having the time of our lives in America!"

I'd forgotten that I'd also forwarded Rob's email to Cormac when he inquired about my itinerary, and after a few back-and-forths I didn't know about, Rob had insisted the lads stay with him. The next morning, before I went out on a tour of Cape Cod shorties, I couldn't help but laugh seeing Cormac sipping his coffee by the water of his adopted estate, and Jack reading the paper in his cottage by a long window through which shined a million-dollar view. New England was full of surprises, but to see that the lads had America all figured out wasn't one of them.

"I take it you guys are doing okay?" I asked on my way out.

"We're doing amazingly," Cormac replied. "We've been playing at Kittansett and living here like a couple of kings."

"We go into town for the newspaper and sandwiches," Jack added. "It's been lovely. Just lovely."

I was relieved they were enjoying themselves while I bounced hither and thither, as there were only a few tee times where I could accommodate two extra guests—and it was great to have the company at Rob's. I was usually a pretty poor houseguest, arriving late and leaving early, with little time for

thanks or cordial conversation. I knew the lads would have the gracious-
ness department covered, and when Rob poked his head into the cottage, the
three of them greeted one another like former schoolmates. Rob had a whole
day planned for Jack and Cormac—a little time on the boat, a little lunch—
and I could only smile as I headed off for the first of my three tee times.

In the days before Bandon tilted the debate, the answer to the question of whether the United States possessed any true links or true dune golf
courses was an easy no, with one curious exception: a nine-holer at the tip of
Cape Cod called Highland Links. I was desperate to finally see it, and when
another virtual friend heard I was heading up to Truro, he suggested we
make a day of Cape Cod's short courses. We started early at Blue Rock and
quickly circled its eighteen merry par 3s, playing through the same group of
women twice as we went. (A woman in a visor and a hand-quilted sweatshirt
embroidered with a jubilant GOLF! generously waved us through, before
her foursome accidentally skipped six holes and landed back in front of us.)
We finished quickly and stopped in Chequessett for chowdah and nine more
holes of sporty public golf at its unfussy Yacht and Country Club.

We drove slowly up a long, skinny road at the top of a beachhead, and as
we pulled into a parking lot, we passed groups with cameras and rain gear;
they didn't look like golfers, and to my left I saw the lighthouse they must
have come to see instead. It was Cape Cod's first; none other than Henry
David Thoreau had retreated to these Truro highlands, living on a farm
where golf's most inconspicuous pro shop now stood. We entered the square
colonial building covered in bleached shingles, where we paid our greens
fees and were told we had the links to ourselves, and this self-proclaimed
links adjudicator set out to see if a links was what we really had.

It certainly had a links wind. Unprotected atop an oceanside bluff, we
were wobbling over our tee shots on the first. Highland Links had a sandy
base and hearty beach grasses—it even had gorse, or a brushy North American approximation thereof, thorny shrubs that were as eager to steal your
ball as any plants of the British Isles. Its landscape was uninterrupted by
trees, and rightly so—links lacked trees, as the sand was too fragile for their
roots—and though the bordering fescue had been chopped low, it was there.
Its nine holes held wild undulations, where we parachuted drives down into

sandy basins and teed off rugged perches. The only thing missing from its résumé was the brown; a modern irrigation system had spoiled the fairways by turning them a lush green. My host recalled former days when it played like a dustbowl, and how I wished I was watching my drives scamper along crunchy, dehydrated earth.

Regardless of its watering regimen, I could have kept going around its links holes (and that's what they were) for weeks, cheeks turned red from the wind and plagued by a runny nose that felt fundamental to a seaside golf experience. The lighthouse framed its closing shots, but it wasn't the most interesting installment on the Highland's horizon. On the hill overlooking the course's valley holes, I spotted two bizarrely juxtaposed structures: a spaceship sort of thing beside what looked like Rapunzel's tower. After I'd consulted the research of nature writer Robert Finch, the first was revealed to be a Cold War leftover from America's missile-detection system, a huge geodesic radar dome—it sort of looked like a golf ball—originally designed to give us twenty extra minutes to brace for incoming nukes. It now tracked commercial flights for the FAA.

The fairy-tale structure next to it was the Jenny Lind Tower, seventy feet of granite block that had once been part of the Fitchburg Railroad Depot in Boston, some hundred miles away. Lind was a European opera star who performed in Boston sometime during the 1850s on a barnstorming tour promoted by her biggest admirer, P. T. Barnum. When her show sold out, the "Swedish Nightingale" did an impromptu encore for fans who couldn't get inside the concert hall, singing from a window atop the tower. When it was later slated for demolition, a local businessman decided to save the tower, and for some reason transported it here to Truro, block by block. It was inaccessible nowadays, ensconced in brush and bramble, and it seemed like a lot of work to give golfers something to look at and scratch their heads, which was its primary function today.

The next morning, Cormac, Jack, Rob, and I caravanned to another nine-holer around the corner from our harborside digs. Marion Golf Club was a beloved if not somewhat forgotten public where the lobster-shack pro shop was locked and a sign on the door asked us to slip sixteen bucks into the mail slot. Beside a shaggy first tee, we found two of those old ball carousels, rusted relics from a time when you used to show up, drop your ball in the slot, and wait for it to reach the bottom, indicating your turn to play. A few decades ago, you could find them at modest public tracks, and while haughtier golfers would reject them as a trinket of the golfing masses, as I watched my ball spin around like a kid on a carnival slide, it occurred to me that these metal loops represented the best of American golf: no preferential tee times; a reward for rising early; a golf meritocracy based purely on passion; golf with new people; showing up solo and getting a game; golf arranged by chance versus text thread; and golf of the most accessible, democratic sort— Got a ball? Spin it and go play—and after figuring out how to make four sixteen-dollar greens fees out of four twenty-dollar bills, we did.

Wee Marion was one of George Thomas's earliest designs, and it was a golf-geek indulgence to play a course that predated his life as *the* George Thomas, of LACC, Riviera, and Bel-Air fame. The place had great bones beneath overgrown fairways that bent at strange angles and played through and over crumbling stone walls. Even in a downpour, it was all laughs as we navigated its quirks and enjoyed what a young Thomas could do without members to please or a reputation to uphold. We went around quickly in the rain, and as the sun came out, we ate sandwiches that Jack had brought from the deli where they now knew him by name. "I've been pinching myself every morning," Cormac told me. "This feels like someone else's life."

Pulling into Kittansett at the absolute end of the Marion road, with its holes laid across a peninsula that stretched into the bay, was another pinch-yourself experience. The other waterside courses I'd played around the Cape were perched above the waves, but Kittansett was low-lying golf along the beach; if you missed right on its par 3 third hole, it was literal beach you were playing from.

I was predisposed to love the place when recent research by Wayne Morrison and Thomas Paul revealed that William Flynn drew the plans (at 2,260 pages, their Flynn tome wasn't one you kept on the back of the toilet). Having grown up on a landlocked Flynn classic, I couldn't wait to see what he'd conjured by the bay. Crowning a Flynn as the Great American Golf Course might have been nepotism, but its blend of artful links holes and tree-lined tests presented everything one could ask for in a golf course. Each Flynn on my trip deserved careful consideration—unlike his Golden Age peers, he never traveled to Europe to study its links, so his layouts are considered by some to be the first truly American designs. At Kittansett, he'd made magic with minimal undulation and a tight plot of land, and was a master of finding and utilizing angles without leaving heavy fingerprints upon the acreage. If good artists borrow and great artists steal, maybe the best artists hide, leaving the glory to their compositions. The only problem with this canvas, I thought, was that its colors were in danger of washing away.

With golf's fortunes so closely tied to weather and its shifting patterns, you would expect its voice to be a leader in addressing climate change, at least in the sporting world. Though its constituents were frontline witnesses to the impact, the game's governing bodies were largely mum on the matter. Depending on region, golfers had seen their seasons squeezed by inordinate amounts of rain (the Mid-Atlantic's soggy 2018 was a golf washout), or their club's water budgets crushed by drought, or their playing conditions spoiled by a cycle of extreme wet and extreme heat that left superintendents battling rot and struggling to salvage grasses unsuited to nature's new curveballs. As Trump's own course in Ireland slipped into the sea, his company lobbied the Irish government for a protective seawall, specifically citing climate change as a cause of the coastal erosion. From his pulpit, our American president was at best equivocal about shifting weather; as American golfers, we can't afford to be: A head-in-the-sand approach to climate change is a threat to our game. We can call it vague science or political agenda, but when it starts coming for our golf courses, maybe we can all finally agree that this shit is getting real.

That was certainly the case at Kittansett, where they'd recently been forced to look on their coastal circumstances with clear eyes. They'd been proactive in seeking scientific counsel about the water levels in Buzzards Bay, and the news wasn't good. The communities around the bay were losing twenty acres of land every year to taller tides, and with warming water temperatures fueling more severe storms, Kittansett faced a future of steady flooding. The water was indeed rising at an ominous pace, and the verdict was that within eighty years, this top-100 layout was unlikely to exist.

The membership was discussing the possibility of building dikes or seawalls to protect the course, but as I'd found in Scotland, where links holes were washing away every year, walls could make matters worse by funneling accumulated force onto neighboring coastlines. The only solution seemed to be finding a way to raise the entire golf course by six feet in the next fifty years, a project of cost-prohibitive scope and engineering. I was grateful for the chance to see Kittansett now, and empathized with the members who wished their grandkids would get to enjoy it as well. There was nothing quite so wonderful as golf by the water, and it broke a golfer's heart to know that the dunes where the game was born were turning into temporary quarters.

A sign out on the course reminded those at Kittansett that the waters were coming, because they'd been here before—it marked the water's height after hurricanes, and the flood lines were well over our heads. It must have been one of those storms that deposited a large gray stone beside one of the tee boxes (I don't think Flynn had the machinery or interest to put it there), and as I walked past it with Cormac trailing behind, I couldn't help myself.

"Cormac, check it out!" I called, pointing to the stone. "Plymouth Rock!"

Rob was ahead of me. He turned around and grinned, shaking his head. "Oh man. That's not nice," he said.

I choked down the giggles and kept walking. When we got to our tee, I finally looked back. There was Cormac, filling his phone with snapshots of an anonymous Massachusetts boulder. He leaned over for a selfie, and I had to turn around again, my face in full blush.

"Now I feel kind of bad," I said to Rob.

"You should!" He laughed. "Poor Cormac. Are you going to tell him?"

"Why spoil it," I said. "It's a rock. Near Plymouth. That counts."

That evening, we had more chowdah for dinner in the clubhouse, and I said my goodbyes to Jack and Cormac. I would see them in a few months over in Ardglass, and that realization struck me: I no longer saw high school buddies who lived ten minutes away, yet I spent days with faraway friends every year, thanks to this silly endeavor of dropping a ball into a cup. Aside from my family, golf bonds were the best I had, and on my way home, I was about to make one more.

AMSTERDAM, NEW YORK

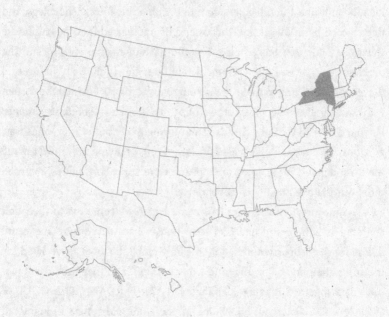

After three weeks crisscrossing New England, I had one unwrinkled shirt left for a round I contemplated skipping. It would have saved me a few hours to drive straight for Philadelphia, but I'd promised a man named Mike that I would come see his muni in New York. He had been one of the first to email with an invitation to his course, and while its location wasn't convenient to any particular golf route, he said his dad would be joining us, and they were going to have a dinner for me afterward. I was flattered that they were making a fuss, so I told Allyson I had one more course to see and drove toward the town of Amsterdam.

I sat in the car in the parking lot for ten minutes, pretending to be engrossed in my phone, trying to avoid the anxious-looking man pacing around the lot. I assumed it was my host, but I needed to catch my breath before talking about my favorite course or best meal or how I'd gotten my wife to agree to the trip; the questions were consistent and welcome, just not when I was road-weary and almost home.

I finally stepped out and found that it was indeed Mike waiting for me. He was built like a bulldog: a wide frame with a thick neck, short legs, and tight brown hair. We said our hellos and he apologized that the clubhouse was closed due to a busted pipe; I would have to change my shoes in the parking lot. That was fine with me, I told him, and I followed him around the clubhouse, trying to shake the lag out of my steps. As I turned the corner, I saw some golf course, plus a crowd of people in suits and holding cameras. I stepped over to the side, confused and trying to get out of everyone's way, and looked for where Mike had gone. He was busy moving the crowd toward me. I thought I'd interrupted an appearance of some sort, but as it turned out, I was the one making an appearance.

The mayor of Amsterdam had come out to welcome me to their golf course. His father, who had also been mayor, had played here and cared deeply for the property, and he told me how much the town appreciated my including their course on my tour. I met his staff, and they took some pictures of us together by a huge sign that read AMSTERDAM GOLF COURSE WELCOMES TOM COYNE! Some of the club's old-timers brought out black-and-white photos to show me, including one of Gene Sarazen hitting the opening tee shot. I was happy to get one airborne off the first as a small crowd clapped and wished me well, and Mike and his dad, Joe, escorted me down the fairway.

Joe was in his sixties with thick white hair, and by the fifth hole, I had renamed him Fairway Joe—his swing was homemade, but he shot bullets that didn't leave his target by a yard. Mike was more of a free-swinger who packed all his ounces into vigorous cuts. Together, they made a dangerous muni twosome, golfers who looked like easy money until you saw how they got around their home track with confounding precision.

Joe worked for the cable company doing home installations, and Mike had been a fireman for most of his life. Joe's grandfather had also played these holes, making Mike a fourth-generation patron of the Amsterdam muni. Their pride in their course was clear, and for good reason—the holes were interesting, the terrain was adventurous, and the conditions were tight. The course had been built as a WPA project back in the 1930s, and was designed by Robert Trent Jones Sr. "The greens used to be like putting on Norv Turner's face," Mike explained, "but they've got them rolling this year." I told Mike this was my first time visiting the area and praised the impressive burg of old Victorian houses set above a river that I had passed. He told me that looks could be deceiving. The small mansions I'd seen were once owned by carpet moguls who ran the factories along the river. "Those houses are chopped up into apartments now," he said. "The economy here isn't what it used to be. We've seen some pretty tough days, after all the industry left."

Amsterdam had been a thriving mill town and the carpet manufacturing capital of the East Coast, but the main business these days was beds, Mike explained. People lived here and worked in Albany.

Mike had been born and raised in Amsterdam, and was sneaking up on his pension from the fire department. He had a three-year-old son and was committed to raising him here, same as his father and grandfather. "The town's ready for a comeback. It's home, and this is our golf course. I've had a good life here; my son will have a good life here."

On the back nine, I spotted a garter snake curled up beside a walking path, and I called Mike over to have a look. When he saw what I was pointing at, he shot into the air, the terror rippling from his ankles to his cheeks. "Fuck you!" he shouted. "I hate snakes!" He sprinted away as I pretended to pick it up. Three holes later, he pulled me aside and apologized for the F-you, and I laughed. I told him that where I was from, it was a term of endearment. The same went for him, he said. I'd just met Mike, but he was that golf partner I most appreciated—a guy around whom you had to be nothing but yourself.

At the end of our round, Mike's wife, Kelly, was waiting for us with pizza and wings from his favorite restaurant, and we ate on the patio with his little boy, Harvey. Joe went inside the shuttered clubhouse to bring out more pictures from Amsterdam's early days and showed me snapshots of men in fine hats and long coats lining the fairways, erstwhile industrialists who watched as a Scottish band led Sarazen down the first fairway. I met Kelly's parents and hung around a lot longer than I'd expected to. I stayed not because I wanted to be a good guest but because I felt so entirely comfortable on the muni. Mike was authentic and generous, as was his family, and I felt like I'd been invited into a team of the genuine and good. Though it had been just one afternoon in Amsterdam, it was like I'd spent years of my life there.

I made it home late that evening, and the next day I texted Mike to thank him for a brilliant day. He wrote back and said it was a pleasure and that I should come back soon. Then I asked if he was available to join me at Cypress.

I expected him to fire off a quick reply, but it took a moment before he wrote: *Like the hip-hop group?*

That was Cypress Hill, I wrote back. I meant Cypress Point, the golf course. The reply came more quickly this time.

Dude. I will transfer to a fire department in California if I have to.

Followed by:

I WILL MOVE HEAVEN AND EARTH!

I had trusted that the final player for our Cypress foursome would identify him or herself somewhere along the road. And heaven and earth proved the road had gotten it right.

SOUTH PITTSBURG, TENNESSEE

Its lore had reached a level where it risked spoiling the recipe. Unexpected attention had brought impossible expectations, plus the pressure of a national ranking; one had to wonder if its success would threaten its soul, or if the abundance of coverage had ruined its reputation as an off-the-map golf heretic. It was the same predicament for any secret turned into Internet buzz: What if the magic faded, or the coolness turned common? It all crossed my mind as I headed south again, returning to Sweetens Cove for my second visit in two years—and then I saw Birdie, the resident wonderdog, and all those notions vanished in the Tennessee sunshine. The fun was still here, and until they plowed the place under, it always would be.

The enthusiasm had started shortly after Sweetens's 2014 opening, with high praise from Andy Johnson of the Fried Egg. By the time it reached the *New York Times* in a story by Dylan Dethier, a full torrent of GCA frenzy crashed upon it, as writers like myself hurried to investigate rumors of a golf messiah born by a backwoods intersection of Georgia, Alabama, and Tennessee. It landed on a top-100 list in *Golfweek*, and doing so as a nine-holer was rare acclaim. It was hard to imagine that its creators, architect Rob Collins and builder Tad King, had any idea that their formerly flat rectangle in South Pittsburg would spark a small golf revolution. Or maybe they did. As was usually the case, it took dire times to finally crack the mold.

The market crash of 2008 had sunk bloated golf projects around the world, but Rob Collins saw the shake-up as a chance to rethink the golf course construction model. He was six-foot-six with a bit of Mike Strantz maverick in him, an art history major with a singular vision and an appetite for risk. Rather than building big, costly, often repetitive golf experiences, Rob saw that the moment was ripe for a new approach: Build small. Build fearless. Build different. He and King created Sweetens Cove for the absurdly low sum of $1 million and packed it with wide fairways and wild bunkers and greens of uncommon scale and imagination. They built banks everywhere, turning the plain property into a jamboree where you dared to aim away from pins or putt in the wrong direction, looping your ball off backstops to cozy it by the cup. Double greens and multiple tees made it a nine-holer you could play for a full weekend, and plenty of golfers did. The design and course ethos encouraged improvisational golf—as long as you weren't hitting into anybody, guests were free to invent holes as they crossed the property backward or sideways, whichever route fit their fancy. Folks traveled from around the world to play holes they'd never seen before, like its fourth, a par 3 with a half-acre green that played anywhere from ninety to over two hundred yards.

Sweetens didn't sell tee times; rather, they sold day passes, knowing their clientele favored a dawn-to-dusk experience. There was no clubhouse to speak of—just a small green shed for buying a pass or grabbing a souvenir. There wasn't food service or a beer cart, but there was a porta-potty for a locker room. Guests didn't mind the lack of accoutrements; if anything, they seemed to desire it. The Sweetens simplicity forged an unfussiness that was essential to the experience, one that golfers seemed to be hungry for. As other golf clubs added gyms and swimming pools and day care to attract members, here was a place that proved we were happy to order Domino's for lunch if the golf made us smile.

Since my last visit, Sweetens had done some cosmetic maintenance, adding a bare-bones pavilion with picnic tables and a Himalayas-style putting green inspired by the version in St. Andrews. Peyton Manning and Andy Roddick had recently bought stakes in the course, and the rumors were that the property's barn would be remodeled into a microdistillery and tasting room for a Sweetens Cove–branded whiskey. As Rob told me, "If we can't make money with Peyton Manning, golf, and whiskey in Tennessee, then we don't deserve to be in business." They were considering adding a few bunkhouses, but Rob was well aware of the minimalism that made Sweetens special, and there would be no post-round spa treatments in South Pittsburg.

Is it really that good? I'd been asked that question often, as word of Sweetens seeped into the golfing mainstream (much to the chagrin of the non-mainstream golfers who flocked there), and I could confidently tell anyone that he or she had never played a place like it. Rob had had no one to please but himself when he designed it, and it played that way, with holes fashioned from a dream that no golf committee would understand. As to whether it could match the mountain of hype thrust upon it, I wasn't quite sure. Nor did I quite care.

Joining our group at Sweetens was one of Rob's original local investors. He told me that as much as he loved his golf course, he found it strange that so many people showed up here looking for the meaning of life, and left proclaiming they'd found it. It was just a golf course, after all, and he wondered how many folks fawned over it because that's what the cool follows on Instagram were doing. He had a point, but I had to admit that there was something in its acres that made its golf feel better than the golf we knew, and that hadn't happened by accident. Sweetens might have felt entirely new, but Rob had borrowed templates from Scotland and inspiration from MacKenzie in crafting his holes. It might have all felt like experimentation, but it was really a collection of golf's best bits amplified and then made entirely accessible.

I didn't know if it was a golf course perfected, as many claimed, but without a doubt it was a golf course perfectly timed. I couldn't think of a course that better fit its moment: as more golfers sought adventure and entertainment and novelty and affordability and simplicity, Sweetens hit all the sweet spots. It was an outlet for walkers and soul-seekers and architecture wonks, and its spirit spoke to the modern golfer who prioritized fun over tradition. Whether Sweetens had helped create that demographic or was benefitting from becoming its promised land, the result was something rare, and rare was what we course chasers wanted most of all. The only problem with a Sweetens trip, I found, was that when visitors fell under its spell and didn't leave the property, they missed out on the other nine-holer up the road.

Back in the 1920s, my grandfather had been recruited from Scranton to play football at Sewanee. Now a revered institution of high academic standing, it had once been a gridiron powerhouse, and its "Iron Men of 1899" team was among the best in college football history—they went 12–0, with an astounding eleven shutouts over schools like Georgia, Tennessee, Texas, and LSU. My grandfather could have been a part of that tradition, but he made the mistake of asking the coach what classes he would be taking at Sewanee. "Oh, you want to go to school, too?" was the coach's reply, and Pop took his talents to Penn.

Otherwise known as The University of the South, Sewanee's nine-hole campus course popped up in the magazine ratings, too, thanks to a 2013 restoration by Gil Hanse that cleared its mountaintop vistas. The drama at Sweetens was in the ground you were walking, while at Sewanee it was out there on the horizon past greens that bled into deep blue backdrops.

After making the short drive up I-24, I found a small but elegant clubhouse on the edge of campus, where I happened to get paired with a high school Spanish teacher whose family had sold Rob and Tad the land for Sweetens Cove. *Small Tennessee world*, I thought, and asked if he wished they still had a piece of it, now that Sweetens had become such a golfing mecca. He said he was happy with his membership and was glad they had done so well by the property.

The third in our group, an assistant pro named John, was unlike any pro I'd met on my travels, and I'd teed it up with dozens. Most assistants started working in golf after college and burned out pretty quickly, sliding over into the business world when they got tired of washing carts, but John's kids had been in high school when he decided to make golf his job. His wife had passed away a few years earlier, and he and his kids had needed a new start, and new scenery. They packed up and left the city, moving down to where John's memories were good—his alma mater—with no idea what he might do for a living. When he got a job at the campus course, he decided to give golf a shot. An above-average player, he had dedicated himself to his practice and passed the PAT (Player Ability Test), and was now taking classes to become a Class A PGA pro. He loved their life down here, he told me. His kids were in a good private high school, and he wasn't working in an office anymore.

We were both Yankees by birth, and I told him one souvenir I would be bringing home from the South was *y'all*—not all the people but the contraction. Philadelphia's version of the second-person plural was *yous*, but *y'all* was charming, and unlike *yous*, you could say it and sound like you had passed the third grade. John informed me of an even more authentically southern variation: *You'uns*. It was reserved for the most rural among us, he explained, so I should be sparing in my use of it. He pointed to the driving range, where two men in jeans and NASCAR T-shirts had hair pouring out the backs of their mesh baseball caps. They whiffed away with rented drivers, shaking their heads and pausing for a smoke. "That's *you'uns*," John said.

There weren't a lot of *you'uns* at Seth Raynor's nearby Lookout Mountain, which was another must-add to any Sweetens itinerary. It was a private club, but a call to its magnanimous pro might score you a tee time with a member eager to show off Raynor's only mountaintop course. They had a lot of pride in their rocky treasure, where every putt broke to one corner of the mountain; I never figured out which, but I swear balls rolled uphill at Lookout Mountain, a course of good golf holes and acrophobic views. I played it with two guys named Trey—I was definitely still in the South—and one of the Treys explained that they were doing their best to keep a Raynor classic going, as a once robust roster of vacationing members had either left or passed away.

From the 1930s through the '60s, the mountain had been a popular summer retreat for Coca-Cola executives looking for a fresh-air escape from Atlanta's pollution. In 1932, Tennessee businessman Garnet Carter developed the mountain as a resort, opening the hiking trails and gardens of Rock City for visitors (it would become famous from a farm-painting campaign where barn roofs from Texas to Michigan were plastered with the imperative SEE ROCK CITY). He had already built a mountaintop neighborhood called Fairyland wherein, if you plugged Lookout Mountain Golf Club into your GPS, you could enjoy getting lost. The drive up the mountain veered back and forth between Tennessee and Georgia, until I found streets with names like Peter Pan, Cinderella, and Tinker Bell. I pulled into what my phone said was the golf course but in fact turned out to be its sister Fairyland Club; I understood this only after I went inside with golf clubs and spikes and found myself standing in the doorway of a day care like some creepy golf prowler. I was politely told the course was two more miles up the hill.

My GPS would have been right fifty years ago; the Fairyland Club looked like a castle surrounded by explosive rock formations, through which Garnet Carter had routed the world's first miniature golf course in 1926. According to a chapter in *The American Amusement Park*, shrunken putting courses already existed, but Carter was the first to add pipes and hollow logs and playful obstructions; he franchised it as Tom Thumb Golf, and within three years, twenty-five thousand Tom Thumb courses had popped up across America.

As I rolled across the South, my imaginary retirement tour had circled plenty of candidate addresses; summers in Vermont were a quaint pipe dream, but we'd need a winter spot as well, and as Allyson had rejected any planned Florida communities, I kept an eye out for towns with gaslit lanterns and wraparound porches, her two retirement prerequisites. They were all over Charleston, where I identified a rotation of courses to keep me busy in my twilight years. The Country Club of Charleston claimed roots dating back to 1786—ancient even by Scottish standards—citing documents that described a "golf club" existing in the city at the time. Savannah Golf Club had similar documentation citing its origins in 1794 (its layout held old Civil War embankments you could find if, like me, you steered clear of the fairways), but these early starts didn't last; they were precursors to clubs that came into their current form around 1900.

Country Club of Charleston was a Raynor design where the templates were tougher to spot on its low-country topography, but the course was an easy walk, and the clubhouse was a happening scene of socialites clinking glasses by the pool. Raynor had also built Charleston's Yeamans Hall, which was simultaneously one of the most and least exclusive clubs in the South. It was a hidden classic at the end of a wooded road, and before passing its gatehouse, I crossed the tracks where New York trains used to stop by the club entrance, letting out the Rockefellers, Kelloggs, and Morgans who spent time here during the winter. It was a layover on the American royalty tour that ultimately ended at their Florida estates.

During their weeks at Yeamans, America's superfamilies would dine and drink together each evening and golf and stroll the grounds in the afternoons. Raynor laid out the golf, but Frederick Law Olmsted of Pinehurst and Central Park designed the rest of the nine hundred acres that had once been a working plantation owned by one Lord Yeamans. The property was populated by dozens of homes, which descendants of those original New York families, known as the "proprietors," still visited today. They didn't stay long, which made for a genius scheme of getting on the golf course: I played as the guest of a member of the Yeamans summer association. They were ordinary Charleston golfers who got access to the course during the summer when the proprietors weren't around. For a reasonable fee, they could get out on a course that had been restored by Tom Doak and Jim Urbina to its full Raynor glory, with conditions as pure as Raynor's Fishers Island, where they most certainly weren't allowing seasonal members. The summer golfers couldn't go into the clubhouse but they had their own little bar inside the pro shop, and were plenty happy for their slice of dynasty golf.

My host at Yeamans was a guy I wished I'd met thirty years before, though his occupation likely hadn't existed at the time. Rich ran a thriving college golf consulting business, where parents paid him to get their fourteen-year-olds on Stanford golf's radar, making sure they were playing the right junior tournaments, getting the right grades, and making the right scores. He offered tutoring and coaching services and traveled the country scouting for talent and clients at the top junior events. His primary task, however, was expectation management: UCLA and Duke were taking just a few players that year, but Fairfield and Toledo needed golfers, too. He'd been a summer golfer at Yeamans for a few years and described to me one of the club's best traditions. Since the property sat across the river from a top-secret naval weapons station (where some of the 9/11 terrorists had been held after detainees were moved out of Guantanamo), golf didn't begin until the base played the national anthem promptly at eight a.m. each morning. The members stood at attention on the range, and the first group of the day waited ready on the tee; when the anthem's final note was played, the day's opening ball was struck.

Should I be unable to snag a Yeamans summer membership, the Charleston Muni had good golf to offer—and thanks to its Friends of the Muni campaign, it was only getting better. Pledges and donations had raised $2.4 million to recondition the city's busiest golf course, where I was paired with a young guy named Mike and another named Tyler, who hopped into our group on the first tee. Tyler was a local and a Muni fixture; he had a patchy beard and played in a faded T-shirt, but he hit it like a sleepwalking stick who didn't notice he was shooting 68, so bored was he of making birdies. He explained that he'd golfed all over the South and hadn't found another place where players were more passionate about their course. "We've got seniors out here, junior programs, a Monday skins game, a Saturday scramble," he told me as we passed a few dozen old men sitting on lawn chairs outside a cement-block clubhouse. "This is these people's home," Tyler said, and with holes that played down to the river's edge, with trees draped in Spanish moss, I could understand why.

I had nearly scratched my visit to the Muni in favor of an extra loop at Yeamans, but the road got it right again. I asked Mike what he did for a living, and he said he worked as a drug and alcohol counselor. I didn't mention the fact that I used to work *with* a drug and alcohol counselor, but Tyler looked over at him and said, "No shit. I just got ninety days sober."

I laughed, which Tyler didn't seem to appreciate, but I told him why I found the coincidence funny—it wasn't really coincidence at all. I told him

how I'd been bumping into people like us all over the country; we were everywhere, even though we'd once believed we were the lone inhabitants of
our shitty little worlds. At the end of our round, I gave him my number and
told him to reach out if he started feeling squirrelly. He thanked me and told
me he would, and we both headed for our cars. I knew he was unlikely to
call—I had dozens of numbers from guys who'd said the same thing to me
when I was counting days, and I'd never dialed any of them—but just having numbers in your phone was sometimes enough to remind you that you
could make it to tomorrow.

I drove west for hours and crossed the Alabama state line well after dark.
I woke up early the next morning, ready to lose golf balls at a Robert Trent
Jones course called The Judge. It was an anchor on the RTJ Trail of courses
that stretched across 'Bama, and a plaque by its first tee read PREPARE TO
BE JUDGED. It was an absurd opening golf shot, from a vaulted tee down
to a sliver of fairway enveloped by bass-rich waters, and though I found dry
ground, I quickly decided I wasn't in the mood to be judged. Hard for hard's
sake was not only boring but idle architecture. Any novice with a pencil
could draw an impossible golf hole, so I checked it off the list and moved on
to Mississippi, where I didn't find a place I'd like to retire, but I did discover a
prime three-day golf getaway in the last place I would have expected to find
buddy-trip perfection.

WEST POINT, MISSISSIPPI

My northern imagination expected Mississippi to be stuck in pre-electricity poverty, with dusty roads of hungry children hanging off broken porches and Confederate flags waving from mud-splattered pickups. When I arrived, I noticed that it wasn't exactly Manhattan, but it wasn't a whole lot different from the other rural states I'd visited, where I passed a lot of silos and churches and Dollar Generals (their signs coated the South in yellow and black), and where the mailboxes were very far apart, unless I was approaching a town with a college, a prison, or a military base. I was nearing a large one now as I rolled into Old Waverly, just down the road from Mississippi State University in Starkville.

Old Waverly had been built in West Point by its native son George

Bryan, who had wanted to bring a world-class golf destination to Mississippi. The course opened in 1988, and after the addition of a Gil Hanse design called Mossy Oak across the street in 2016, Bryan had done precisely that. Old Waverly had a membership of Mississippi gentry, but it offered stay-and-play rates for visitors—and extremely reasonable ones at that. It was a refined southern dreamboat dripping with Mississippi charm, while Mossy Oak was its less delicate sibling, with rugged holes stretched across a treeless and tilted pasture. Both were five-star experiences, but Mossy Oak won me over for its bare-naked beauty, its quirks, and its five steps from green to tee. Old Waverly was Mr. Bryan's baby, but as he joined me to play Mossy Oak (he played both left- and right-handed, depending on which side was working better that day), it was clear he was warming to the variety of shots Hanse had given him. He wore cool sunglasses and his white hair was just a little longer than I expected from a Mississippi boss man, but he was definitely Mr. Bryan, not George, and not just because y'all called everybody "Mister" in Mississippi.

After graduating from Mississippi State, Mr. Bryan went to work for his family's meat business; a fountain by Old Waverly's clubhouse incorporated a few of the cauldrons in which they used to boil hogs to remove their hair (they were dead prior to boiling, Mr. Bryan assured me). It was the golf club that hogs built, because when Sara Lee bought Bryan Meats, he became CEO of Sara Lee Foods, where he did well enough to become a course developer and a benefactor to his alma mater. (He was named alumnus of the year in 2000.) After golf, he drove me around the school's campus, where I noticed that the athletics building had his last name on it.

The Little Dooey was closed on Sundays after football season, but Mr. Bryan made a call, and somehow we soon had a table at the Starkville barbecue institution. Mr. Bryan said the full rack plus pork platter was probably more than I wanted, and after I finished every last nugget of mahogany-slathered meat, I believed he was right, especially when the conversation turned to the six thousand hogs his plant had processed every day. Mr. Bryan described the rigors of pulling ribs, and how the long-knifed artisans on the line had to know the latest price of ribs versus bacon when they decided where to cut.

"Best hog is the Berkshire," Mr. Bryan told me. "You ever have a chance to try Berkshire meat, you do it."

I confessed my big-city ignorance. I thought there was one kind of pork: cooked.

"When you say hog, you're talking about pigs, right?" I asked.

"Yeah. But a pig is your friend," Mr. Bryan said, "and a hog is for dinner."

As we ate, we talked about the US Women's Open that Old Waverly had hosted in 1999; it was as big a sporting event as Mississippi had ever held, and I could tell he was proud to have brought the golfing world's eyes to his hometown. He had Scottish roots and had named his course after the novel by Sir Walter Scott. The club had its own Scottish room called Cameron's, named after his mother's Highland family, where a mural-size painting of the Swilcan Bridge was a touch of the old sod in Mississippi (it had been the official painting of the 2000 Open Championship, and the only other version was hanging in the Old Course Hotel in St. Andrews).

Mr. Bryan talked about working with Gil Hanse, whom he said he appreciated as a man who got his hands dirty. One evening, he'd found Gil driving a bulldozer, tearing the hell out of the seventeenth at Mossy Oak. He called to Gil to ask him what he was doing.

"Building a bunker!" Gil replied. "I'm calling it Grant's Tomb!"

Mr. Bryan knew he was kidding, but Gil had unknowingly given his bunker a fitting title: Mississippi State had just built a beautiful new building for Grant's presidential library. I was surprised to hear of such a memorial for a Union general landing in the South, since Grant had made his military reputation in a decisive victory at Vicksburg, Mississippi, a July Fourth surrender that its residents weren't quick to forget; it took them eighty-one years to start celebrating Independence Day again. But Mr. Bryan explained that Grant had spent a lot of time in Mississippi during the war and was good to the state during Reconstruction. He spoke about the general as if he'd passed away last summer. History did feel more immediate down here—and when Mr. Bryan dropped me off back at Old Waverly, I got another lesson in how the past tended to hang around these parts.

I was staying in the lodge at Old Waverly—Mossy Oak had fairway cottages as well, making West Point a golf–barbecue–SEC football winner of a trip—but rather than drop me off at the clubhouse, Mr. Bryan said he would just park in his driveway. His front door was pointed at the parking lot, and he laughed that he'd built a home here when his wife said she wanted to be closer to the club, but now she was wondering if they'd planted themselves a little *too* close. Mr. Bryan wasn't moving again, he said, especially after the time they'd spent securing this particular piece of property.

When mechanized farming flushed jobs out of the South in the 1930s and '40s, former agrarian families had headed north for industrial work, many of them abandoning their plots in Mississippi and Alabama. Records listed some fifty families as the owners of the empty acres across from Old Waverly, and in order to purchase them, lawyers had to track them down and get at least 30 percent to agree to sell. It was a tedious process but not an uncommon one in the South, Mr. Bryan explained, where large tracts of land could be owned by unknowing proprietors. Once you put in the work of finding enough owners willing to sell, then the property was put up for bid at the courthouse. After three years of paperwork, Mr. Bryan and his wife finally had their plot across from their golf club, and until I had one myself, I awaited the day when somebody called to tell me about the land I owned in Mississippi.

Mr. Bryan sent me off with a bag of pork rinds from Little Dooey's—"Pure protein," he said—and I broke it open the next morning as I drove for Arkansas and Oklahoma and Kansas. I was a few hours into the drive when my phone rang. It was an old friend whom I was meeting in Kansas; he'd been kind enough to invite me for a weekend of Perry Maxwell perfection.

"We're all set for Prairie Dunes," he said. "Bill's actually going to be in town. He'd like to join us, if that's okay."

I think I said that was fine, sure, okay by me. I don't really recall the rest of the conversation. You wouldn't have, either.

HUTCHINSON, KANSAS

At some point between moving a couch with Bill Murray to accommodate a massage table and helping him break into the safe in his room, a moment of awareness came to me: if it never bequeathed me another birdie or par or even fairway hit, golf owed me nothing.

I'd received emails from a dozen Prairie Dunes advocates who said my American trip would be pointless if I skipped it. It wasn't that I didn't want to visit Perry Maxwell's Kansas dreamland, but no matter how I tried, it remained a round peg of a destination that just wouldn't fit.

Born in Kentucky in 1879, Perry Maxwell was of a Scottish bloodline, and his travels to the homeland had shaped an architectural proclivity for large, wavy greens ("Maxwell Rolls," people called them). He was a master of locating intrigue within existing topography—of the land on which he'd been commissioned to build Prairie Dunes, he said, "There are one hundred eighteen holes here, and all I have to do is eliminate one hundred of them." He'd done work at Pine Valley and Augusta but was best known as the wizard of golf in the Plains states, and though he finished only nine holes at Prairie Dunes, it would become his most celebrated work. With plow and shovel and horses and mules, he uncovered Scotland in the middle of America. His son, Press, would complete the second nine twenty years later (they didn't play back and front; rather, the father/son holes were interwoven through the eighteen-hole course). Scotland, shovels, mules, minimalism—Prairie Dunes was speaking to my old golfing soul, and might very well be the course I was searching for. I just had to figure a way to get there.

As I divvied up my map of America into trapezoidal chunks, Hutchinson taunted me, that one flag I couldn't squeeze within the lines. It was too far south for my northern swing through Nebraska and the Dakotas, and too high for my Texas and Oklahoma leg. I'd promised some members I would be there, but as months passed and courses accumulated, Prairie Dunes was looking like a calendar casualty. Then I played with Joel Murray in Chicago, and his impressions of his brother Brian's throaty rasp reminded me that I owed Brian a call. Now living in Kansas City and averse to email, Brian wasn't the easiest cohort to keep in touch with, but after Joel gave me his number, he turned out to be a handy texter. I shot him a note to say hello, and then recalled that he had joined Prairie Dunes back when his wife was at Kansas State. If it meant I got to catch up with an old friend, I thought, I might just have to erase other visits and make room for some Maxwell with Brian Doyle-Murray (he'd added the Doyle fifty years ago when he started in showbiz, to avoid confusion with Broadway's Brian Murray).

My kids probably knew him from his voice work on *SpongeBob SquarePants*, but for the rest of us, Brian would forever be Lou the caddie master in *Caddyshack*, a film he wrote based on his and his brothers' experiences caddying outside Chicago. His TV and film credits were plentiful—from *Saturday Night Live* to *Groundhog Day* to *National Lampoon's Christmas Vacation*, his face or voice probably popped up on your TV weekly. A film you were less likely to know him from was *A Gentleman's Game*, the movie based on my first book, which is how we met back in 2000. He'd played a hard-luck caddie who drove an El Camino, and as Joel recalled it, "Yeah, Brian made tens of . . . tens of dollars on that movie." My job during filming had basically been to hang out with Brian while he was shooting in Philadelphia, so we played golf together and stayed too late at the bar beside the set. It was great to reconnect, especially when he said we should make a weekend out of Prairie Dunes and stay in one of the cottages. The plan hadn't been for his other brother Bill to join us, but I got the impression that Bill had an appreciation for spontaneity.

I later learned that Bill had been on the road following his son Luke's basketball games (he was an assistant coach at Louisville) and had an open weekend to come visit his brother in the heartland. As Brian had explained, it happened to coincide with our Prairie Dunes weekend, so I suddenly had a golf weekend with Bill and Brian Doyle-Murray on my calendar. It was a hard appointment to believe. Apologies to the member who got bumped when Bill joined our foursome, but I had one out clause when it came to golf commitments, and it was Bill Murray.

I pulled into Prairie Dunes in the dark, and Brian came out to direct me into the bar where, wouldn't you know it, there was Bill Murray, eating peanuts and watching ESPN. We said hello—he called me the new guy and asked what I wanted to drink—then we walked over to the restaurant and sat down for dinner. Brian told me he was enjoying life in Kansas City; the golf was good, and it was equidistant from his acting jobs in New York and LA. As for his brother, he was a nice guy who liked to talk sports. I kept forgetting I was sitting with Bill Murray, which was probably the best thing about sitting with Bill Murray. I hardly noticed that all the other tables were staring at us; I figured they must all love golf books about Ireland and Scotland, and hoped I wasn't making the guys too uncomfortable.

Later that night, the three of us sat around the TV in our cottage, and Bill flipped back and forth between *Saturday Night Live* and a rerun of *The Ed Sullivan Show*. I was watching *SNL* with two guys who'd put it on the map. *Surreal* was an adjective I avoided, but sitting there as Bill sang along with the crooner on *Ed Sullivan*, I understood the word in an intimate way; it felt like you were watching your body walk around in someone else's life. I hoped I recognized it as my own before the weekend was over.

The next morning, Brian and I were up early. When I came out of my room ready for golf, I found Bill practicing putts in sweatpants and socks in the living room. "Try this," he said, handing me his putter and placing a ball atop a yardstick. "Try to keep it from falling off."

I worked on it while we waited for Bill to get dressed. He couldn't find the pants he'd bought in the pro shop yesterday, nor could he get the safe in his room to open. I worked on the safe while Brian went looking for the pants in the car.

At breakfast we met the fourth in our group, the daughter of a Prairie Dunes member who had extended me an invitation before I enlisted the Murrays to join in. I wasn't sure how Bill and Brian were going to react to being paired with an eleven-year-old, but she played to a 10, and they warmly welcomed little blond Addison to our group. The only shame was that she was probably too young to know with whom she was playing, though her dad, who was happy to carry her bag that day, certainly did.

Brian and I teamed up against Addison and Bill. The two of them gave me and Brian a sound beating, though I can claim distraction and copious picture snapping as an excuse. It was a cold Kansas morning, and Brian found it tough to loosen up his swing. Both he and Bill, who was playing in a woolly beret, had the same classic, long, looping move—two caddie swings, for sure—and Addison was a fairway finder who wasn't afraid to blame her father for wrong numbers and bad reads. Like any golfing eleven-year-old, she wandered and enjoyed herself with no particular hurry, walking to the back tees with me and Bill before finding her own. Still, we were freezing, and the golf soon became a race to get back inside for the Kansas State game. On the back nine, Bill exhibited his celebrity superpowers by admonishing Addison at full throat: "Let's go! You're not playing with some tourist here. Get your head in the game! Walk to your tee and get ready to go!" Then he turned on her dad: "That goes for the caddie, too. Move it! Let's go! Show up, keep up, shut up, that's all a caddie needs to know." He kicked his feet around in the tee box in disgust. "I'm here to play golf. Let's go!"

And instead of making a little girl cry or turn her dad red with rage, everybody just laughed. It was magic.

"You're the luckiest guy in the world," I told him as we walked down the fairway. "You can say anything to anybody, right to their face, and even if it's true, they won't be offended."

He shrugged. "It can be useful."

It was useful again when Bill left a short par putt dead in the mouth. Addison smiled at him and said, "Nice lag."

Touché. Bill stood up straight and tilted his glance in her direction. "You busting me?" he asked. "You sure you want to do this? I'm a professional. I can make you cry. And I will."

On the closing holes, I wished I could have played better for Brian, but I was spending a lot of time in Prairie Dunes's legendary gunch; it guarded most every fairway and played like some sort of super-herb engineered by mad botanists. Brian said they control-burned it once a year, and after my fourth lost ball, I wanted to start my own burn of what had to be the thickest, least negotiable boundaries in golf. That Bill was kind enough to hunt for every one of my buried drives only made me feel worse; I was ready to drop another and get on with it, but Bill took his golf seriously and didn't give up on a ball. We were used to watching his larky play at Pebble Beach, but the truth was, Bill Murray was a grinder.

After our round, we joined the purple-clad Kansas State boosters in the bar and cheered on the Wildcats. We filled our plates at the chicken wing buffet, and Bill talked our waitress, Patty, into tasting the death sauce—*Here, try some, it's delicious.* It was good to be sitting next to the Murray brothers; the bartenders came by every three minutes, and we had four waitresses checking on our table—well, three, after Patty found herself slumped over the bar with her tongue stuck in a glass of water. The manager came by to ask if we needed anything, anything at all, and Bill mentioned that he was tight and would love a massage. She paused—he'd thrown her a curveball—and I think she contemplated walking around the table to start working on his shoulders. I had found myself in a can-do universe, so I wasn't surprised when the manager said no problem and told us she would go make some calls.

There was no spa at Prairie Dunes, and Wichita was an hour away. But when the manager returned, she said a masseuse would be at our cottage at four o'clock. Bill thanked her, and turned to me. "You want a massage?"

What a weird and wonderful weekend, I thought, before answering, "You're damn right I do."

Brian went to his room for a nap while Bill and I moved the furniture around to accommodate a massage table in front of the flatscreen. Of course we needed to watch the game while we got our massages—we weren't savages. The doorbell rang, and I helped our masseuse bring her table into the room. For someone who'd been called on a Saturday afternoon to come massage strangers, she was in great spirits. Bill let me have the table first—he had some calls to make—and as she worked the cold out of my back and legs, I couldn't help but ask her if, when she woke up that morning, she thought she'd be giving Bill Murray a massage in a cottage in Hutchinson, Kansas, that afternoon.

"No, I did not," she said, and laughed. "I was actually in Wichita at a brewery with my husband when they called. But I said, 'Hey, when's the next time I'm going to get to meet Bill Murray?'"

We still couldn't get the cash out of Bill's safe, so it was funny to watch him mooch twenties off his big brother to pay for his massage. The masseuse asked Bill if he wouldn't mind taking a picture with her, and Bill posed for a dozen campy photos as I snapped away with her phone. We handed her our money and she said it had been an honor, which in all my massages were words I'd never heard a masseuse speak. As I helped her carry her gear out to her car, she seemed pretty giddy about the whole thing.

"I'm glad I got pictures, because my friends would not believe this," she said. I told her I knew what she meant, and that I had plenty of pictures of my own. After spending a few hours with him, I admired Bill as a person and not just a star, because Bill Murray appreciated being Bill Murray. He didn't walk around cracking jokes like some sort of tableside entertainment, but he understood that he could make your day, and seemed to enjoy doing so.

There were only three of us in the grill that night, but we huddled around a small table in front of a football game on TV and ate bowls of chicken soup, still chasing the chill out of our bones. The conversation was quiet; we were tired and hungry. We were three guys eating soup around a television, and that didn't feel surreal at all.

• • •

I was in the Wichita airport when Brian texted the next morning to tell me they'd finally found Bill's golf pants in the trunk of his car. Black pants, black trunk—they'd been right under our nose. We got the safe open, too, when our waiter came back to the cottage and popped in the master code, and out poured bundles of Euros, a bankroll befitting an international money launderer. (Bill had just been in Italy with a guy whose credit cards weren't working, he explained, so he'd loaded up on cash.)

As I waited for my flight home, I wrote a note of thanks to Brian for being such a generous host. I told him I'd catch up with him in Kansas City soon, because I had a golf course I wanted to show him over on the Kansas side of his Missouri city (Kansas City, Missouri, was named for the Kansas River that ran along its west flank; Kansas City, Kansas, came later, co-opting the name in 1872 as a way to participate in the success of its thriving eastern neighbor). I was coming to the end of my travels, and after so much searching I was relieved that I finally had an answer to whether I'd found the Great American Golf Course. Other states had made their bid, but no better layout befitted this country in character, courage, and creativity than the one I'd found that summer—a course that was set, quite literally, in some guy's backyard.

KANSAS CITY, KANSAS

I wanted to make sure to get to the Dakotas during the warm months, so I'd planned an August loop from Missouri to Iowa and up to South and North Dakota before dipping into Wyoming and Colorado and wrapping up in Kansas. St. Louis started things off on a triumphant note. Macdonald and Raynor had worked together at St. Louis Country Club, where they designed my pick for US Open course I'd most like to call home. Oakmont and Shinnecock were the obvious Open front-runners, but they were too grand a meal for everyday consumption. St. Louis was a polo club (its driving range was the polo field, where regular matches still took place) where James Foulis, of that itinerant clan of golfing Scots, had built the first nine holes in 1896 before Mac-Raynor came to pump their templates into the landscape.

That I walked it during a flare-up of gout (a gift from my dad) and still enjoyed every step of its dense routing of peaks and hollows, plus anachronistic twists like back-to-back par 3s in its first three holes, was proof of its charm. I was a sucker for good logos, too, and SLCC's horseshoes split by a riding crop that recalled its equestrian origins was shopping-spree stuff.

I expected little out of Iowa but a long, flat drive through miles of green waiting to be shucked, but Waveland in Des Moines grabbed me by the shoulders and shook loose all my preconceptions. The name of this oldest muni west of the Mississippi hit the mark—the land moved like a typhoon, and for twenty-six dollars, lapped the competition in the race for America's best-value public. As I was in Iowa, the conversation with my local playing partners naturally turned to politics. Its kickoff caucus was still six months away, but they had all already met, or had been invited to meet, each presidential candidate, and they described to me a wily Iowa electorate of conservative values mixed with a penchant for rocking the boat. One member of our group worked in state government and said the rural Republican counties were being crushed by the trade war with China—the price of soybeans was issue number one for a lot of Iowans—and it would be interesting to watch as red voters tried to reconcile their principles with their pocketbooks.

Later, I felt a mild tinge of panic as I traveled north through the soybean fields, overtaken by an irrational awareness that if I should have a heart attack or stroke out here, with no cell signal and no civilization to save me, the crows would just pick my corpse clean. I was relieved to finally see other cars in the parking lot at Rice Lake; the pro told me I had chosen wisely, because there were only four golf courses within eighty square miles, and this was easily the best of the bunch. Its land moved like a pancake, but the greens were gorgeous patches nursed by the rich Iowa soil.

From the north edge of Iowa, I took a left turn toward South Dakota and Sioux Falls, where Prairie Green was one of three city courses where you could play unlimited golf for an annual fee of less than $1,000. By bizarre coincidence, I found myself playing it with three Eagles fans; Iowans were pro-sports free agents, and this group had all adopted the new team of former North Dakota State star Carson Wentz. One of the guys' actual name was Cat, short for Catlyn (his mom named him after a Dr. Catlyn from an

'80s soap opera she watched while pregnant), and Cat said his Eagles loyalty predated Wentz. For his honeymoon, he had taken his new bride to Philadelphia for a game.

"Wow, you *are* a real fan," I said, and I had to ask if they were still married.

"No, we are not," he replied. "Game was awesome, though."

Farther north, Sutton Bay was a first-class retreat with a course set high on the Missouri River, but as it sat in the lonesome middle of South Dakota, directly across from the five thousand square miles of the Cheyenne River Reservation, I had to wonder who was retreating here. I teamed up with the course's designer and winner of seventy pro international tournaments, Aussie Graham Marsh. He told me that the remote success of Sand Hills in Nebraska had stoked their ambition to make Sutton Bay happen, even after the first course broke into pieces—the original holes had been routed on low ground along the river, but after a few years, the shale beds cracked and destroyed the irrigation system. We played Graham's second take, a grand bluff-top routing that overlooked the water and the outlines of the first course. Graham—or Swampy, a friendly take on his last name—had nailed his do-over of strategic lines and absurd vistas. On one hill, he stopped and told me to look out across the river. "You can see more than a million acres from right here," he said. On none of them did I see any signs of our species. The new Sutton Bay course was bringing in golfers, but it already did big business as a hunting resort, where every season they imported twenty-five thousand pheasants for gun-toting guests. At forty dollars per bagged bird, it was a tasty revenue stream.

The road moved relentlessly north to Hawktree in North Dakota, where I got to sample some of architect Jim Engh's extravagance. He was known as a designer with a histrionic flare who sculpted holes that almost felt storybook in nature, using landforms to give them an audacious quality. The following week, I would visit his Fossil Trace course in Colorado, where we played against canyon walls and through golden rock stacks where prehistoric plants were pressed into the stone. At Hawktree, we navigated funneled fairways and black-sand bunkers in our rented golf motorbikes—you cruised around with your bag perched between your legs, and while I typically carried my sticks, I couldn't resist *Easy Rider* meets the golf course. The quixotic holes veered from inspiring to unfair, depending on your mood, and our moods were high as we popped wheelies on the way to the next tee.

Bully Pulpit, over on the western side of North Dakota, was the longest I'd ever waited on a golf course to play three holes. It was jammed with pseudo-golfing tourists who had all come to make 8s on the same holes, fourteen through sixteen, where you fired from the top of Badlands buttes, parachuting your drives onto green strips below. The camera clicking backed up the whole course, but it was a canyon ride worth the wait.

The next afternoon, I dipped my toe into Wyoming at Devils Tower near the South Dakota border, where its namesake hid from you on most of the mountainside holes. The course had started as a few holes built as an amenity for workers at the local sawmill. The mill's owner, Jim Neiman, wasn't a golfer, but he thought a golf course might lure more full-time residents and potential employees. It was now a proper eighteen-hole members' club with a lavish log cabin clubhouse that Neiman built specifically to house the 1901 bar-back he'd purchased from the Cowboy Back Bar in Belle Fourche, South Dakota. The huge mirrors and hand-carved cherrywood fixtures were gently moved up the mountain, and whether you played golf or not, it was another site worth seeing when visiting Devils Tower the rock, which I finally saw after driving back down the road from Devils Tower the golf course.

I veered back into South Dakota for more sightseeing, where I pulled over to take a picture and cross Mount Rushmore off my list. I was surprised to find the road to Mount Rushmore so crowded with arcades and tchotchke shops and two-star family motels; my imagination had placed it on a distant mountaintop accessible only by a dusty frontier path of donkeys and stagecoaches. Turns out, you have to drive through a neon western wonderland to get there, then climb another road and wait in a car line. I could see the presidents' faces right there in front of me, and I wondered why everyone else was clamoring to get closer; it wasn't like you got to scratch Lincoln's nose. I got my picture and turned my car around, a full day's drive to Colorado ahead of me.

I followed state roads down through South Dakota and Nebraska and Wyoming, where I learned a lesson about believing in the next gas station.

Perhaps the scenery distracted me—it was a curious ride, from scrubby dessert to red stone towers reaching out of the dirt. Millions of years seemed to pass my windows as I drove through rock cuts that exposed varying layers and shades of sand. You could stop every fifty yards to take a picture, or you could just zone out and motor, which is what I mostly did until the light on the dash started flashing.

I'd refueled back in South Dakota at a gas station that doubled as a gift shop; the farther I ventured, the more roles the American gas station assumed. This one was a restaurant, a souvenir store, and a flag shop, where I overheard a couple in leather motorcycle chaps ordering burgers and cheeseballs from the grill. I wondered if maybe this gas station was known for its cheeseballs, and if I should order some. Instead, I perused the flag section, where I found fifty ways to say *No, you cannot have my gun*. As I left, I didn't give a passing thought for the next gas station I would see, an ambivalence I now regretted as the light on the dash gave up and the needle pointed at my lap.

I was coasting as much as possible through Nebraska, hoping each new silo on my horizon might come with a fuel pump—the farmers had to refuel somewhere—until I rolled up to a squat building with two antique pumps outside. They were rusty and had those rolling-number dials on them, but damned if they didn't work, and I exhaled for the first time in an hour. Inside, a friendly woman took a break from working on a transmission to take a rubbing of my card with one of those credit card cheese grater things and pointed me to the bathroom, where I had to keep flushing lest she hear the uninterrupted torrent of my stream.

When I arrived in Denver the next day, I expected to find some Rolling Green in William Flynn's Cherry Hills, but as he was a designer who didn't work from a playbook, the similarities were hard to spot. Cherry Hills was curiously flat for a course in Colorado with Hills in its name, though I soon learned that Denver was largely situated in a mountain valley, albeit a very high one. The club had hosted three US Opens, and its 1960 tournament had been won by Arnold Palmer after he famously drove its first green in the final round, besting Ben Hogan and then Buckeye amateur Jack Nicklaus. Its closing stretch was an angry march, and while the place was pure quality, I preferred what Tom Doak had done over at Denver's CommonGround, an aptly titled public facility that was pretty much the perfect city golf course. If Winter Park in Florida was the great community nine-holer, Common-Ground was its eighteen-hole cousin, where for fifty dollars residents could play an impeccable and subtly cerebral layout. The fairways were generous to newcomers, but Doak angled his greens to require thoughtful tactics from low handicappers as well. With a busy teaching program and a caddie academy where Denver kids could prep for looping jobs at places like Cherry Hills, CommonGround was doing everything right when it came to the sort of golf courses we needed everywhere, and needed now.

I saw more Doak at Colorado's Ballyneal, a contrast of courses that highlighted his architectural chops. It was the opposite of a city muni, an unruly inland links with handsome lodges surrounding a lit putting green. Completed in 2006, Ballyneal was walking-only golf through rugged sand and fescue, and had recently added a short course called the Mulligan that was no wedge-and-putter stroll but proper second-shot practice that tested most of your irons. Ballyneal had a mini-Bandon feel to it, aside from its being private, which may have been what sank the place on its first go-round. With an original initiation fee of $50,000, a location convenient to very little, and a recession on the horizon, it attracted only one hundred members before it fell into a benevolent bankruptcy in 2012. The original owner's brother-in-law was able to buy it out of foreclosure, wiping clean the club's debt and eventually hitting the right price points for a course that members probably saw twice a year.

When I visited, the place was packed with golfing couples and four-man getaways, and I appreciated some of Ballyneal's customs more than others. I loved that the loser of the match had to carry the winner's bag from the eighteenth green to the clubhouse. It was a steep climb, but I wasn't too gracious a guest to stop my host from double-bagging it up the hill. I also admired its milkshake menu, which we did our best to work our way through; while Mormons might dodge booze, my host proved that there was nothing in their book about milkshakes. I was less enthralled, however, to find that Ballyneal was another course with DIY teeing grounds—pick your spot and go. It was a cute novelty the first time, but I struggled to embrace full tee box autonomy. If I was going to grind for four hours, I wanted to post a score, and without set tees and a course rating, I couldn't.

From Ballyneal I moved north for a reservation at Nebraska's Prairie Club, a place I hoped to return to with golfing buddies someday, if I could remember how to find it. Philadelphia to Valentine, Nebraska, was a very indirect flight, but with three golf courses and a cozy five-star lodge, it had earned a spot on the pilgrimage list. The Tom Lehman Dunes Course was another nod to the wonders of Nebraska's sandy basins, but I preferred my new pal Graham Marsh's Pines Course; the Dunes was a par-hard, bogie-easy course, whereas Swampy had swollen his fairways for a par-easy, birdie-hard experience.

I didn't have time for the Prairie Club's short course by Gil Hanse and Geoff Shackelford, and that was fine; I would have just sulked my way around it, forlorn over Gil asking a different golf writer to the dance. Three courses plus the Old Wagon putting course would be plenty to get my friends on a plane out here, and I felt like I needed to, if for no other reason than to see how they would have handled the appetizers.

There were any number of starters on the Prairie Club menu that might have satisfied my quest for regional flavors—the barbed-wire bites and the prairie rattlers were calling to me—but how many times was I going to have the chance to sample deep-fried bull testicles? When I read that the sandhill oysters were locally sourced, I couldn't resist; I was so tired of frozen bull balls from China. I was eating alone at the bar, and that the bartender was a college-age brunette gave me pause about my selection. I felt like a pervert for asking if she'd ever tried the testicles (she had, and wasn't a big fan), and once I did, I was committed to ordering them. I had to prove I was in the market for gonads, lest she think I got my jollies from quizzing young women about them.

When they appeared from the kitchen, they looked like slices of fried eggplant. Bartender Michelle looked away as I dipped my testicle chip into cocktail sauce (of course) and tried to chew through its rubbery casing. Honestly, as someone who had spent much of his life respecting the fragility of testicles and trying to protect their delicate constitution, I expected them to be more tender, but these had a jerky-like consistency, my jaws grinding until I could finally wash them down. I didn't taste much aside from fried coating and cocktail sauce, and after slice number two, I placed my napkin atop the basket of sandhill oysters and accepted defeat. I would soon discover that eating balls in public was not as awkward as nearly getting your own handed to you by two women on the first tee.

The next morning, the Prairie Club starter told me I could have the 8:20 tee time on the Pines to myself, but I would be stuck behind two foursomes, so if I wanted to hang back and join an 8:30 twosome, I was welcome to. It was an easy call; I almost always preferred company, and the starter said the twosome were two newlyweds, which was fine by me. I looked forward to meeting the guy who had talked his bride into a golf honeymoon—or was it the other way around?—and headed for the tee.

Up pulled a cart with my playing partners, but sitting in it were two women in their fifties named Amy and Darlene. *Good on ya, Nebraska*, I thought to myself; we really had moved into the twenty-first century across America. I was eager to show off my progressive East Coast bona fides, chumming it up with my lesbian buddies and telling them about my gay friends back home. As they stepped out of their cart, I said, "Congratulations!"

"For what?" one of them asked.

"For your wedding. This is a great place for a honeymoon."

They stopped and looked at each other, confused. Then they looked at me, and Darlene said, "You know, not every woman who golfs is a lesbian."

As my golf bag was not big enough to fit my entire head, I stumbled for a reply: "I, the starter, newlyweds, said I'm paired with . . ."

They laughed. Apparently, the young married couple had swapped their time and was playing behind us. These two were longtime friends from Charlotte now living in opposite corners of the country, and they got together for a reunion golf trip every year.

Despite my awkward greeting, we were pals by the third hole. Darlene and Amy hit their balls often, but they played like jackrabbits, and I had to suggest they take some more time, as we kept bumping into the group ahead. As I watched the men in front of us linger over their shots and loiter on the greens, never once considering the possibility of waving women through, it occurred to me that boardroom bias transferred to the golf course. These ladies were playing too fast, possibly overcompensating for women being branded as slow players. It was frustrating to watch that entitlement up ahead, vestiges of your grandfather's credo that the course belonged to men before noon, and I wanted to apologize on behalf of my gender for making Amy and Darlene feel like they had to play faster than men to not be considered slow.

Amy gave me a hug and apologized at the round's end: "I haven't played that poorly in three days. I don't know what happened out there." I assured her that I brought that out in most people, and that I thought she went around well, because she had. Any time you're standing over a ball waiting for a green to clear, you're doing something right.

Back in Kansas City, close to where my heartland loop had begun, I would have been remiss to skip a place called Heart of America. It would have been poetic if HOA identified itself as the Great American Golf Gourse, but like CommonGround, it was a model for the community golf complexes of tomorrow. Kansas City's own Tom Watson had been generous in helping bring the learning center to life, where a full-length nine was joined by a par 3 course and a three-hole beginners' loop, plus golf camps and junior programs spread across impressive practice facilities. It did a golfing heart good, I thought, to see such investment and innovation when it came to attracting new players, and Heart of America was an ideal gateway: make some contact on the range, move over to the three-holer, graduate to the par 3s and the full nine, and then you were ready for a place like nearby Swope Memorial, a thirty-dollar Tillinghast muni of billowing holes that I considered a very close second to Waveland for public golf perfection. When you made a birdie at Swope, spectators literally roared for you; the lions at the Kansas City Zoo were pacing just down the hill.

I'd circled Kansas City on my map as a potential spot for squeezing in some sand greens golf, so that afternoon I headed for Harrisonville Golf Club. Kansas was better known for sand greens—they still crowned a Kansas high school sand greens champion—but you could find a few over in

Missouri as well, low-maintenance layouts like Harrisonville. These courses used to be easy to find across the middle of America, but numbers had declined as more plains golfers got raised on grass. There was nobody at Harrisonville to take my greens fee when I approached; it had a few garages, a picnic shed, and a mailbox with scorecards in it. I waved down a gray-haired guy in a tank top who was riding a mower, but he wouldn't take my money. He said the course was maintained by volunteers. Only about fifty paid $200 a year to play here, and he said I was free to give it a go. He asked if it was my first time playing sand greens—my Shinnecock hat and Oakmont shirt must have outed me as a visitor—and gave me a quick tutorial on how to navigate the greens—er, sands.

Per his instructions, once your ball reached the circular sand putting surface, you grabbed the rope attached to the flagstick and used it like a measuring tape to note how far your ball was from the hole. Then you swung the rope around and placed your ball on the smooth putting lane according to the distance you'd marked with the rope. The paths were hard troughs of packed sand that they oiled every few weeks to keep the granules firm, and they ran at about a 27 on the Stimpmeter (thankfully, the greens were all flat as nickels). I'd read that fry grease was best for oiling sand greens, but my friend didn't want to reveal the source of their sauce; he said it was donated but all natural, so as to not upset the neighboring farmers.

There was very little here, I noticed, that would upset any environmentalist; sand greens courses originated in rural areas as a way to maintain courses on a shoestring and now seemed a fix to golf agronomy's reliance on expensive inputs. The place was a sustainable golf dream. Harrisonville didn't just lack an irrigation system; it lacked any running water at all. Forget chemicals and fertilizers—with fairways mowed to rough height, I enjoyed clipping shots off beds of clover, then trying to hit the hardest putts of all: dead-ass straight. I wouldn't give up grass for sand greens, but as a way to make golf possible on a budget of nil, it was a smart system that, to my surprise, felt like real-deal golf.

Two loops around Harrisonville and I was ready for dinner. I'd actually been ready for this meal for months, as KC barbecue was the regional fare I was most anticipating, and that morning at Swope, a local stick named

Christian had left me clear instructions on how to do it right. I found a Jack Stack restaurant and read off his prescribed order of cheesy corn, hickory pit beans, and burnt ends to the lady at the register. It was a combo that proved everything I had once considered to be barbecue was just soft meat slathered in supermarket sauce. I don't know which end they came from, or why they were burnt, but the burnt ends were tangy nuggets of caramelized beef that I wished were served in popcorn tubs. They were a Kansas City specialty, and before I finished licking my fingers, I knew I'd be back for more soon. I was already mulling a return to KC next year; I belonged to a golf club here, after all. Considering it had over a thousand members, I was surprised that so few Kansas City folks had heard of it.

I needed a street address to find Brough (pronounced *Bruff*) Creek National. It wasn't a course that popped up on the nav system, and as I drove through a dark canopy of trees leading me toward the Missouri River, my phone told me I was close, but the hills were dense with brush and branches; it seemed I was running out of space for a golf course until I reached the end of the road, where to my right was a clearing that looked about the size of a soccer field, its open space interrupted by towering walnut trees and leaning golf flags.

I pulled into a gravel driveway beside somebody's home and parked up against a long garage. Out in the field, a guy in muddy jeans was running from flag to flag, using a range finder to laser distances and scratching the results down on a notepad. His name was Ben Hotaling, and once he spotted me, he came over to welcome me to the golf course I'd been reading about for months. It was a place born of No Laying Up's message-board banter, after Ben posted a question about what it would take to build a backyard course. The idea captured an eager audience of would-be architects and wishful course owners, and through the benevolence and might of the online golf community, donations and equipment started flowing his way. Their theoretical golf club soon had a course design, a logo, a name, and a location—Ben's buddy Zach Brough was happy to lend his yard. Brough Creek merchandise became the stuff to wear for golfers in the know, and followers were encouraged to sign up for a club membership that cost you only your email address

(I am indeed a proud BCN member). So, with thousands of us design voyeurs watching on Twitter, Ben got to work and started to burn.

Clearing the acres was a herculean effort shared by Ben and four friends, who built tall burn piles before they could start sodding tees and carving out greens. They learned as they went, overcoming inexperience with passion and man hours, and after a year of round-the-clock blisters and beer, their creation was ready for golf. I was humbled to play its seven holes for the first time with Ben, though it was like being in the delivery room for the birth of someone else's kid; I felt I hadn't earned my place. But Ben was itching to play, having just lasered the distances for the first time that morning. They were penciled beside hole names on a piece of cardstock that now holds a spot of honor among my scorecards:

Brough Start	52
Road	117
Ann	81
Biarritz Punchbowl Pandemonium	88
Beer Break	92
Cottonwood Redan	62
Icarito	109

My barbecue sponsor Christian had pitched in on the construction—it was an all-hands endeavor—so he joined us for BCN's virgin round. At the ceremonial opening tee shot, a jostling throng of two people watched Ben rip a thick pelt of sod and dump his ball into the creek below. It was fitting for a hole called Brough Start, and after putting his every minute and muscle into making this moment real, we thought he probably deserved a breakfast ball.

The first hole was a nosedive that any course would plant on their homepage; we teed off a rocky outcropping through a tunnel of trees to a double green five stories below. It was one of the more dramatic sites Ben had found on Zach's property, but when they cleared his back hill and found a steep ridge hiding in the trees, Ben was gifted with another postcard hole where you fired between two framing tree trunks to a blind green backed by a rocky slope. Even the simpler holes weren't so simple; there were creeks to carry and canted greens with redan and punchbowl features, a horseshoe green split by a lion's mouth bunker, and a hole with a backstop so severe that you wanted to do tricks on it with your skateboard. They had recently unrolled sod on the greens, so the seams came into play, but it turned out that my stroke was made for sod seams, as I made 2 on the first, fourth, and sixth holes. I signed for a +2 score of 23 that would be, for at least the next hour, my life's only course record.

I'd played with designers before who were intimately aware of every detail of the property, but going around BCN with Ben was a different experience. He spoke of the course's features in an almost paternal way. Every bald patch and lush spot were his to fix or take pride in. It was that strange bond we all had with our own lawns, as we stared at a freshly mown yard and considered calling the newspaper to come document our accomplishment. But in Ben's case, his backyard was actually an achievement worth celebrating. In social media circles, the course was known as Some Guy's Backyard, and while it had just opened that morning, Ben was ready to make it some guy's career. He wanted to bring the BCN model to communities elsewhere, creating architecturally interesting, accessible golf parks across America. He'd proven he could build for peanuts, and his passion and confidence were so persuasive that I couldn't help but wonder if I was hanging out with Johnny Appleseed as he walked his first orchard.

As I drove from BCN to the airport, I had a hard time believing the truth about what I'd just discovered. So many miles and more first tees than I could recall, so many hours spent in conversation with the heroes of golf architecture, and the Great American Golf Course was seven holes built by a twenty-seven-year-old and his buddies. I reconciled reason with my emotions and knew it in my gut: Brough Creek National represented the best of both golf and America, at least in this wanderer's imagination.

It owned all the creativity and fun and drama that I required of a great course, plus the soulful and inspiring elements for which I was searching. It was indeed perspective-altering; you left the place and thought differently about golf, its playing grounds, and the people who walked them. It forced you to stop and wonder, and while others might cite conditioning and shot values in their course assessments, "stop and wonder" was all I was searching for. The place was a homegrown revolution. In a *Golfer's Journal* article by Job Fickett, Ben had been quoted as preaching an everyman's upheaval: "I'd argue that GCA is fucked! Totally wrong direction. The only new courses being built are on perfect land at destination sites by architects everyone already knows. . . . Why do I have to go to Oregon or Wisconsin or Scotland or New Zealand to see the places where the 'purest form of the game' is played? No. We need to see more construction on shitty sites. We need to start pushing the envelope in places no one expects it."

I wasn't sure I agreed with all of that, but I admired its guts and upstart perspective. Ben's denial of the status quo and his rejection of a perceived golf tyranny was apple-pie, tea-in-the-harbor stuff. It was our best ideals shaped into grass and dirt: Free. Independent. Brave. Bold. Self-made. Communal. United. Diverse. Ambitious. It was far from perfect, but it was born of an individual's belief that he could seek it. It was the height of golf liberty, and the fact that anybody with the desire to see them could come and play BCN's holes, that belonging required nothing but that you believed in the place—to me, that was golf's version of the great American invitation.

Maybe that invitation had been harder to discern in recent years. I wondered if we were no longer pushing the greatest assets our country ever offered: hope and safe harbor. Without them, I feared that America was quite ordinary. My dad's America was exceptional, but there seemed nothing exceptional about another country that traded in the easy currency of fear.

I'd embarked on this journey to prove that wasn't the case, that even if we didn't live up to our ideals, at least we still agreed on what they were. In every state of our union, I'd spent time in my father's America. I'd met resilience and fearlessness and true generosity of spirit, and on plenty of occasions I'd been its beneficiary. So many open hands had pulled me in and brought me along to places I'd never dreamed of going; places like Zach Brough's backyard, where some guys proved what was possible when, rather than bemoaning the state of things, you stuck a shovel in the ground and made something better. There was nothing ordinary about America or Americans, at least not the versions I had visited. But as I drove into another evening, so far from home and this country's well-beaten paths, I couldn't help but mourn the fact that Dad's America, once a light that reached all the world's corners, had required such a journey to find it.

I arrived back in Philadelphia in time to send the girls off on their first day of school. I wasn't teaching that fall—I still had dozens of states to explore, and would be on the road until Christmas. Maybe some spot in California or Texas would show me I was wrong about Ben's course, but I doubted it.

I might have found my Great American Golf Course, but I recalled what a friend had told me in Minnesota about the best course being the one you play with the best people. I had plenty of them left to meet, and one partner in particular for whom I still had hope.

AUSTIN, TEXAS

Robert handed me a pill bottle and said it would save my fingertips. I wasn't sure about sharing a prescription with a man I'd known only through email, but when I opened it, I found tees jammed inside, a genius golf hack to prevent sticking your hand into a pouch of sharp ends. He gave me a glove holder as well, and though he wouldn't be playing with me that morning at Lions Municipal, I told Robert that he had made my day—literally.

The sun was just rising over the stone lions guarding the gray clubhouse. Everyone in Austin referred to the Lions Golf Course as Muny, and it was sweater-and-vest weather at Muny that morning, with a brisk Texas breeze. These weren't ideal conditions for pictures and a ceremony—Councilwoman Alison Alter tried to keep her hair out of her face as the cameras rolled and the wind drowned out her reading of the mayor's proclamation, which seemed fitting. If she'd been shouting the words into my ears, I still wouldn't have quite understood what she was saying:

"Whereas renowned author Tom Coyne immerses himself in the people, food, music, culture, and history of each city he visits," the councilwoman announced, reading from a sheet of painted parchment, "and Whereas Golfer Tom Coyne is visiting Lions Municipal Golf Course in Austin, Texas, highlighting the advantages of maintaining a green space in the midst of urban Austin and drawing attention to a community's fight to protect a beloved golf course; Now, Therefore, I, Steve Adler, Mayor of the City of Austin, Texas, do hereby proclaim November fifteenth, 2019, as Tom Coyne Day."

I'd often told Allyson about the rules and rituals of Tom Coyne Day—I celebrated it often at home—namely leaving me alone to watch golf and allowing dishes to be scattered around the house with impunity. It was not a holiday she believed in, but now I had documentation drawn in calligraphy and signed by a mayor as proof. She could blame Robert if she disagreed.

I'd been introduced to him ten years ago when he emailed me about my Ireland book and extended an open invitation to come play Austin; I had no idea he had so many tricks up his sleeve, or city council connections. He was in his seventies with a gentle manner, and he stood in the background as the ceremony unfolded. He never claimed credit for the proclamation, but it had his generous fingerprints all over it.

I had resisted the urge to interrupt the councilwoman as she spoke, switching out some of the flattery for more modest descriptions of my accomplishments: *Whereas a golfing charlatan hatched a scheme to play golf indefinitely, and who has extended his boondoggle all the way to Austin, Texas,* might have been more accurate accolades. I stood there stupefied by the surprise and said thank you a lot.

The warmth of my welcomes had increased as the trip rolled on and word spread about my travels, but Tom Coyne Day was an almost intimidating amount of hospitality. Truth was, the writing life was rather lonely and insecure. It beat digging ditches, but it wasn't so much a party of pages as it was a daily scuffle with self-doubt. An atta-boy like this meant more than Robert understood, and if I was the tearful type, I'd have shed a few at Muny.

I'd read about the Save Muny campaign at Lions, and such community effort put the club atop my Texas must-visits. The history here was rich: It became the first desegregated course south of the Mason-Dixon line when, in 1950, two Black players wandered on and started playing. This was still a Jim Crow Texas—no Black golfers allowed. Employees at Muny called the mayor's office to ask what they should do about the trespassers, and after consulting with the city council, he replied with three groundbreaking words: "Let them play."

Both Ben Crenshaw and Tom Kite had grown up playing Muny, and Tillinghast had touched up the course during his consulting period for the PGA. Harvey Penick's brother Tom had been its longtime head pro, and Harvey himself had spent plenty of time on its fairways, once partnering with Ben Hogan for a legendary match in 1950, when Hogan looked out at the current sixteenth, now called Hogan's Hole, and asked, "Where's the fairway?" Muny's 141 acres were lent through a benevolent lease from the University of Texas, but as a state school with 141 prime Austin acres in its portfolio, the university was under pressure to find a permanent, profit-turning use for the land. They wanted Muny to have it, but the course would have to pay market value, so now the Save Muny initiative was raising funds and awareness to buy the place for good and preserve a city treasure.

It was certainly a city course worth saving, I thought, and not just for the backstory. The holes had architectural flair and were a soulful walk on a chilly morning, and they had a course greeter of rare pedigree: Ben Crenshaw himself met us on the front nine and talked about his childhood course (best Tom Coyne Day ever!). He told us he'd played his way around these holes more than a thousand times, and that Muny's closing would be an irrevocable loss, not just to Austin but to the legacy of the game. He'd lent his full influence to the Save Muny effort and was happy to see so many politicians, players, and regular Joes supporting the cause. He wished me well on my journey, and I thanked him for all he had done for golf, here and everywhere. I could have talked with him for hours about the courses he and Bill Coore had given us, but I was trying to fit Texas into one week, and that was proving to be a Texas-size endeavor.

• • •

I'd kicked off this last extended trek in New Orleans, where I played the Audubon Park course, America's only eighteen accessible by streetcar, with the two entrepreneurs behind Blue Oak BBQ. They gave me a pig headcover (which suited the declining state of my game), and were both passionate about their New Orleans municipal, where Joseph Bartholomew had gotten his start as a caddie in the 1890s. He would go on to study with Seth Raynor and design courses around Louisiana, most of which he wasn't allowed to play as an African American. The course was a dandy par 62 circled by walkers and bike trails, so public you'd forget you even paid. I wished I had time to sample the pulled pork back at Blue Oak, but I had to hustle off to Tulsa and points north.

On my way to Oklahoma, I played a quiet nine on the campus course at LSU Shreveport—walking nine holes alone was still the best way I knew to catch my breath—before a seven-hour haul up to Southern Hills. The following day, I pulled through the grass around lunchtime, eager to see how this host to seven major championships had been preparing for its next one. Gil Hanse had recently restored the greens' sloped edges so that marginal shots would wander off as Perry Maxwell had intended (I wondered if I'd visited a course with a major on its calendar where Gil hadn't been asked to push some dirt). The PGA Championship wasn't coming until 2030, but Southern Hills was playing firm enough to host it tomorrow; my ball meandered the wavy greens as if searching for letters on a Ouija board. That evening, I found sympathy for my scorecard among the members of the Perry Maxwell Society. They'd invited me to their monthly meeting at a Tulsa Mexican restaurant, and it was more fun than it sounds. They were a surprisingly young bunch; some were there for Maxwell talk, others for bottomless chips. The big topic of the night was getting better logo hats for their members, a subject on which I could actually lend some insight. I finished my taco platter and scooted before things got too wild—I had an early flight to Houston where tomorrow I had tee times at a classic and a comer.

• • •

I would have walked off the course if not for our appointment. So much for that Texas heat I was counting on—my hands were frozen clamps in which I couldn't feel my grips. We raced around Champions Golf Club in the sleet and arrived back inside for the reason I'd made the trip—a sit-down with Mr. Jackie Burke Jr. His assistant showed us into his office, where one of golf's greatest living legends got up from his seat and insisted on standing to shake our hands. He pointed us over to some leather chairs surrounded by photographs of him with Frank Sinatra, Bing Crosby, and Mickey Rooney. There was so much memorabilia that I couldn't have told you colors of the walls. At ninety-six, Mr. Burke was the oldest surviving Masters champion, and his accomplishments in golf (a playing Ryder Cup captain, sixteen-time Tour winner, PGA champion, and World Golf Hall of Fame member) were too numerous to cover in our conversation. Instead, we talked about how he had founded Champions with Jimmy Demaret as a way to introduce his rural Texas neighbors to golf. It was an effort, he explained, that was present in every detail. The clubhouse's main dining room, for example, had a gabled ceiling, and Mr. Burke said that was no accident—people in this part of Texas met one another in church; it was where they socialized and felt comfortable, so he wanted the club to give them a similar feeling. As a host to a Ryder Cup, a US Open, and a long roster of Tour events, Mr. Burke's Champions Club had overachieved when it came to bringing golf to his community.

He got up and walked over to his desk, returning with three fragile leather journals. On each page he had scribbled a swing thought or a brief notion; they were the collection of his life's wisdom, as sacred as scripture: *Play from the inside of the ball, and inside of yourself; You are always going to be your best instructor; Bad players think in terms of results, good players think of execution; You can't get lost on a straight road; Change brings hope!* Ever the instructor, he stood to show us that the golf swing was as simple as a slap: "If you want to smack somebody in the ass, you're going to square up your hand at impact!" he said, clapping his two hands together. He added that his Judo training in the Marines had taught him balance, and how the golf swing had to come from your hips. "It's the same as when you're delivering a punch," he said. "All the power comes from your legs and the middle of your body."

His stamina for conversation was impressive, and it was tough to leave the comfort of the chairs in his office as his insights washed over us, but I had a tee time that afternoon outside Houston at Bluejack National. I was eager to kick and punch my way around a Tiger Woods layout; I figured the future golf landscape would be full of them, and was curious to see if his design chops matched his on-course artistry. What he had created with design partner Beau Welling surprised me: I expected a Tiger course to be Pete Dye penal, a humbling grind for folks who wanted to suffer a Tiger-caliber test. But Beau explained to me that Tiger wanted his courses to be fun; he wanted people to go around them without losing or looking for balls, so while Bluejack wasn't an easy or simple design, it was pure playability, with land that moved in photogenic ways.

They spared zero expense on Tiger's first build in the US. Bluejack was a big ballpark, befitting the outrageous gated community built around it. I passed a kids' play zone with waterslides, a pro-style football field, and a replica of Fenway Park. The halfway house was like the food hall at Harrods: a soup and grilled cheese station, a candy wall, tacos and mac 'n' cheese and a hot dog hub, with signed Tiger tournament bags lining the walls—and in case you were still hungry, they were making carnitas out on the course, beside another shack for sweets and ice cream. In the evening, there were virtual hitting bays by the bar, just a few steps from an illuminated pitch 'n' putt where a bag of glistening wedges tempted me to grab one and have a go. Canvas-bag-toting purists might loathe all the amenities, preferring a simpler, purer golf experience, but their kids would tell them to get over themselves and take them to Bluejack.

True to Tiger's vision, we didn't lose a ball that day, not even on the holes where ponds forced us to tighten our belts and execute. There was more room around them than we thought, and Tiger and Beau had employed a savvy strategy of showing you a scary hazard, then giving you plenty of room to avoid it. I played Bluejack with another unknown Instagram contact, but social media had a knack for picking the right partners: Tim Gaestel, it turned out, had been awarded the Purple Heart after a roadside bomb blew up his convoy south of Baghdad in 2003. He would recover after shrapnel was removed from his back, and was now a high school golf coach in Cedar Park,

Texas. He had an infectiously upbeat attitude, and as we went around Blue-jack in our rain gear, it was obvious that he was loving every yard of the place. The next day, he emailed the team at Bluejack to thank them for his round and tell them how much he enjoyed their course. I was shocked a few weeks later when Tim texted me a picture of a full-page letter from Tiger Woods; his note had somehow reached Tiger, and he thanked Tim for his service and his kind words about Bluejack, and wished his high school team well.

My adventures as a half-assed tourist continued in San Antonio, when I parked my car without bothering to feed the meter—I wasn't staying long—and took a selfie in front of the Alamo, arriving for my tee time at Bracken-ridge with minutes to spare. It was another Tillinghast and the pride of the Alamo City Golf Trail, where I was stunned to meet my vocational doppel-gänger on a golf course. It was another spot where I'd put out a call to come join me on Twitter, and by the slimmest odds, one of the takers happened to be a young English professor at Abilene Christian. He put my pedagogy to shame by showing off the Junot Díaz novel he had stuffed in his bag; the guy actually did his reading for class as he walked between shots, whereas I did my reading for class as I walked into class. I did have tenure, though, which stirred his pre-tenure envy, and he said I'd given him hope the way Billy Collins had done for me, proving there was space for golf junkies within the ivory towers.

I pushed west toward the Mexican border and a town called Del Rio, where an emailer named Sam had messaged me early and often about visit-ing the course on which he'd grown up. It was twilight when I pulled into town, and with an hour to spare before the barbecue dinner he'd planned for me, I called to ask if he knew where I might procure my first pair of cowboy boots. It was the lone non-golf souvenir on my list, and I doubted whether I could say I'd really done America if I returned home in loafers. Sam sent me an address and said he'd meet me there; a Yankee wasn't to be left alone for such a purchase.

We met at a small shop that let us in just before closing; Sam introduced me as a Philadelphian looking for his first boots, which created a buzz among

the Mexican staff. There were plenty of boots to look at, but only two options, Sam said: Lucchese and Ariat. The former label was the Jimmy Choo
of men's high-heeled leather, with ornate stitching and price tags to match.
Sam was an Ariat man—sturdy and comfortable, I'd wear them for twenty
years, he claimed. I wondered if I'd wear them for ten minutes after the flight
home, but I chose a modest square-toed Ariat pair and headed off to dinner
with a long Texas strut, brandishing all the confidence of three extra heeled
inches.

I had passed two border stations on the road to Del Rio and was stopped
at only one of them, where the guard took a quick look and waved me
through. Very unlike my hopscotching experience at Aroostook Valley in
Maine, the border patrol SUVs were highly conspicuous down here. Sam
said the crossings crackdown might have been useful for folks in DC, but
for people who actually lived on the border, it was less than convenient; the
proposed walls were cutting farmers off from chunks of their property that
existed past the build sites, and fewer Mexicans were willing to come over
into Del Rio to work or do their daily shopping. The anxiety was hurting
local businesses and had diminished a long partnership between Del Rio and
its sister city across the Rio Grande, Ciudad Acuña.

At our barbecue buffet, Sam told me how the Del Rio fire department
used to ride over into Mexico when help was needed, and an annual parade
of friendship would crisscross the border, with Americans and Mexicans
celebrating in one another's neighborhoods. That didn't happen anymore,
though the Fiesta de Amistad still took place every year, when politicians,
dignitaries, and police from both sides met on the Amistad Dam for hugs to
commemorate President Eisenhower's actual embrace of Mexican president
Mateos after they signed the treaty for the cross-border dam. Times were
different now, at least for our presidents, but one thing that hadn't changed—
and never would—was the town golf course.

Built on rare freshwater springs, the San Felipe Springs Golf Course's
archaeological record stretched back thousands of years, when West Texas
water made it a coveted site for Native Americans, then European explorers,
then the US Army stationed at Camp Robert E. L. Michie to defend the rail
lines during the Mexican Revolution. Digs around the course had unearthed

troves of artifacts—arrowheads, hammers, ceramics, bones—and the state's Antiquities Code deemed all such finds off-limits to golfers hunting for their balls. No fundraising was needed to save this muni; geology and history had conspired to protect it from ever being anything but a golf course.

The course was the first design by John Bredemus, a Princeton grad who had dabbled in course architecture before moving to San Antonio in 1919 to become a school principal. He was a golf nut in search of places to play, so, as detailed in Dan Utley's *Links to the Past*, he started building them himself. Bredemus designed Colonial and several other layouts across the Lone Star State, and in the process became the little-known godfather of Texas golf. He helped start the Texas Open and founded the Texas PGA; Harvey Penick himself credited Bredemus with being one of the first golf instructors in the state. It was far more history than I'd bargained for when Sam messaged me about an out-of-the-way course I'd never heard of, but as we went around its nine holes twice and drank straight from its springs, this fifteen-dollar muni of short, crafty holes was an education in things beyond our game. It would take a dozen lifetimes to find the end of all these roads, which frustrated me as a searcher, but as an American I was brimming with awe. I used to think I had to travel to Europe to find unexpected history. I had been wrong.

I felt awe again when the ranger at the toll booth leaned into my car and asked for thirty dollars. I protested that I wasn't here to visit Big Bend National Park but was just passing through on my way to a golf course at Lajitas—I promised I wouldn't look at any of the scenery—but my GPS had stuck me with an expensive direct route. Frankly, I would have paid triple the park fee to shorten the dusty drive. The rocks were golden and grand, but you had to be in a golden and grand mood to appreciate them. I wanted food and bed, and the route to Lajitas, stuck down in Texas's little toe, wasn't giving either up easily. Its golf course deserved the detour, if for nothing else than the chance to drive from a canyon tee so high in the clouds that we counted the seconds between our balls landing and the sound of the thud reaching our ears—but when I arrived that evening, I was a grumpy guest in stiff cowboy boots who banged the bell at reception, then set off for the restaurant. A father and son I'd met on the Internet were waiting there already; they were energized and ready to hear tales of the road. I slumped in my chair, using body language to ward off the chat, and when the dad asked me what the book I was writing was about, I wanted to plant my face in the gravy of my chicken fried steak.

I skipped dessert and walked back to my room, where across from my balcony I spotted a long, clean driving range stacked with pyramids of gleaming golf balls. A huge statue of Robert E. Lee on horseback stood guard nearby (in case you wondered where removed Confederate monuments ended up, the answer is Texas driving ranges, apparently). For all the golf I was playing, I hadn't practiced in months—and it showed. So I grabbed a few clubs from my room and walked down to the practice tee. I hit balls in the twilight, clipping neat divots until dark, and the direct relationship between quality of mood and ball-striking was again revealed. The next morning, I was a glad-handing raconteur, laughing it up with my two dinner buddies, who I found to be both genuine guys and good golfers.

The bright mood lasted through Marfa, where I was unfazed to find its community eighteen was closed on Mondays. It just gave me more time to investigate the distant artisan outpost known for edgy creatives and good food, and the mysterious lights that popped up on its horizon every evening. I was too tired, and too comfortable, in the James Dean room at the Hotel Paisano (the actor had actually stayed there while filming *Giant*) to drive nine miles into the desert and stare at the dark, waiting for something to twinkle, but plenty of tourists did flock to see the ghost lights, even though science deemed they were likely refracted high beams. I went to bed early to make my rescheduled six a.m. tee time. I knew it would be frigid before sunrise on the Marfa links, and the next morning I was heavy with layers as I crossed its hardpan fairways. It was as firm as any links I'd played, and the rough was tougher than that at Oakmont—not in height, but in composition. Marfa's edges were all asphalt nuggets and chunks and gravel—leftovers, I assumed, from the abandoned Marfa army airfield. Wherever it came from, I imagined the flat and windswept holes had produced some straight drivers. I finished eighteen in less than two hours, and the pro shop was still dark when I pulled out of the parking lot.

I felt as if I'd spent months in Texas as I crossed into New Mexico, where at Red Hawk I was disappointed to not see any hot-air balloons above the holes (my small Eastern imagination envisioned the bright balls as the state's primary mode of transport) but enjoyed the company of Cody and Mike, who worked at the nearby air force base on a program that shot down incoming ballistic missiles. I thought back to Ryan, my missileer friend from Montana, and wondered if I should put them in touch; Mike and Cody would be handy guys to know if he ever accidentally set one loose. Prior to this trip, my active military contacts had totaled one buddy in the coast guard, but now I had dozens of uniformed friends to text or email. Dad would appreciate that—and now I could appreciate that American military might wasn't just about bombs and planes but about American livelihoods and food on the table.

The following afternoon I landed in Arizona like a retiree seeking refuge from the November chill, and found it in golf-rich Phoenix and Scottsdale, where I warmed my bones before finding the cold again in the Sedona hills. I met up with longtime painting pal Lee Wybranski, who had gotten his golf start designing scorecards and painting yardage books back in Philadelphia before moving his studio out to Flagstaff. Now he did the official posters for the US Open, the Open Championship, and the PGA. If you've been to a major, you've probably seen skinny Lee in a stylishly rumpled blazer signing his artwork—or maybe you have his flawless signature on your wall. He credited the nuns from his parochial education for his handwriting (though I had the same teachers and can't read my own).

Lee took me up into the red rocks for two of his visitor-friendly favorites—Oakcreek and Sedona Golf Resort—and I quickly understood why he'd come out here to paint. The stone walls that framed our drives turned to fire at sunset, and I could feel the magic for which Sedona was popular. Its vortexes (vortices) attracted yoga types from around the world, hungry for its rare earth energy. Lee warned me that the phenomenon also made putts difficult to read, which I went ahead and proved via a string of three-putts that I blamed on the yoga people and their crystals. Still, there was a good spirit here, a Sedona vibe that said *Come chill with me and the pines and the rock piles.* Maybe it was catching up with an old friend that had me feeling a new zing, or maybe it was getting away from the previous day's downer. Either way, I'd take it.

• • •

Over the past seven months, I'd visited most of the country, including every southern state, with little evidence of the old attitudes that beset the game when I was a kid.

As a caddie in the 1980s and '90s, I heard jokes and words you wouldn't share in a foursome today, back when a Black player at your club was fast-spreading news, when "faggot" was a common admonishment after a weak putt, and when the unspoken consensus at establishment clubs was that Jewish golfers would be better off elsewhere. That all felt like a century ago, but I'm not that old; while golf remained largely a white-dude pursuit, I'd found proof that it had shed so much of its tired baggage. Still, I knew there might be some more to go, and I wondered if I was enjoying my straight white self too much to notice, denying an undeniable American issue in my American journey. Had golf's bigotry really been exorcised in so few years? I wasn't going to invent bad if it wasn't there, and if I golfed my way across America without a crude moment of intolerance, I'd be proud to celebrate that progress. But somewhere in the greater Phoenix area, I was woken from my fairy tale by a guy—let's call him DB—who didn't know how to order a latte.

The club was private. That's as specific as I'll get, and before you go searching, its name won't be on the final course list in the back of this book. I'm not afraid to throw shade, but I'm not one for painting an entire club, or game for that matter, with one ugly brush—but when DB sat down at our breakfast table and yelled, "Hey, can I get one of those gay coffees?" across the grillroom and nobody raised an eyebrow, it was a reminder that the assholes, though diminished in number, were still playing through.

He was a guest like me, invited to fill out our foursome by the two members with whom I'd been enjoying breakfast. The waitress approached, and he couldn't help himself. "Yeah, one of those gay coffees. You know what I mean?"

"Do you mean a latte?" she asked, unamused.

"Yeah. That sounds gay enough," he said. Apparently, he was hungover from a nine-hundred-dollar dinner the night before—most of which he said they'd drank—and needed something easy on his stomach. He was around sixty years old, and an old friend of my hosts. As I'd been invited here via a mutual contact, I was quickly the outsider. He bragged some more about his bar tab before even getting my name, then asked his friends about the sign he'd seen on the drive in advertising the Arizona Gay Rodeo. The idea would probably make most of my gay friends chuckle, I thought, but DB found it disgusting. "What the hell is happening to this state?" he complained. "I swear, it's all the people coming in from California."

The rest of the breakfast conversation bounced from American Express raising the annual fee on its Black Card—the horror—to the scrambled state of Joe Biden's mind. I didn't talk politics on the golf course, a rule handed down to me by Dad from his time in the navy—in social settings, you didn't discuss God, politics, or the opposite sex—and yet here we were not even *on* the course yet and I was already getting the highlights of what the liberal scumbags were doing to undermine our president. He thanked the waiter for his gay coffee, then asked me where I was from.

"Philadelphia. Wow," he said after I answered. "Maybe it's changed, but that city was a dump when I was there. I was staying at the Four Seasons, and I called down for extra pillows. Someone knocks on the door, and I open it, and there are these two *big Black* guys standing there! I threw my hands up. 'Hey, take anything you want!'" He laughed. "They said, 'No, no, we're housekeeping.' Jesus Christ, I thought they were going to rob me. It was too funny."

The rest of the table chuckled. I looked down at my napkin, a cowardly guest. It was all very strange; in Mississippi, I'd learned how they were celebrating the life of a Union General who had fought to emancipate the slaves, but in Arizona, I was listening to the hateful musings of a bigot with a Porsche. The grossest part was that he knew nothing about me, other than that I was white and had been invited to an exclusive golf club, two things that, in his mind, meant I was on his team. Later, out on the course, the subject turned to a spiced bourbon that had become one of the members' go-to nightcap.

"Sounds like firewater to me," DB said. "Sounds like what the Indians were drinking. That's why they're stuck on the reservation. If they were drinking wine, they'd be fine!"

I'd been pissed at DB for lumping me in with the rest of the wankers; now, I was pissed at myself for lowering my head and staying quiet. Part of me was honestly curious about what he'd say next. It was a credit to golf that I'd traveled so far and played so much and identified only one unabashed ass-face, and now that I'd found him, I felt compelled to keep listening like a diligent journalist, documenting this cliché come to life. Another part of me wanted to tell him he was a crap golfer and awful company, but I didn't know anyone here for longer than this morning, and I feared spoiling a business relationship for the mutual friend who'd hustled to win me this invitation. *I'll have to be sure to thank him*, I thought, as I counted down the holes until I no longer felt like I was carrying golf bags in 1989, listening to an old man tell me a joke he just *knew* I was going to love.

I recounted it all later to Lee, to help clean it out of my head, and he said that Arizona had a little bit of everything; good and bad, but mostly good. I knew I had to believe him. Every state, every county, every course had its shortcomings; if we weren't afraid to see them, they had every chance of getting better. In the meantime, you took the good parts with you. Lee showed me some of Arizona's very good parts in Sedona, but it was tomorrow I was most looking forward to, when I suspected we might be seeing its best.

THE NAVAJO NATION

The only way to contact them was a through a Facebook page with three hundred followers and infrequent updates. I threw messages at it tirelessly, until finally a kind reply came back, telling me I was welcome to visit their course and should call Donald for directions. So, on the evening before Lee and I were set to head east for new territory, I dialed the number and heard a voice, soft and slow, like I had just joined him in a dream. "Oh, yah, you can come play the golf course," Donald said, then described a list of place markers for me to follow. They didn't have road signs or street names, he explained, but I'd eventually see a big white sign that said REZ GOLF.

I crossed my fingers and pulled out of Flagstaff. In a few hours, Lee and I had only missed the sign once before circling back and pulling down a dirt lane, parking beside a square two-story building that could have been either Donald's home or the clubhouse. It turned out to be the latter, with one room upstairs and one down, and some golf clubs and scorecards scattered about. Donald lived just over the ridge, I was told, and Lee and I poked around as he and two buddies walked in off the course to meet us.

It was an easy-enough place to miss; if you were waiting for green grass to identify the golf course, you would have been driving until Oklahoma. There were some lawn chairs outside, and a list of rules posted on a score-board: "No spikes allowed!!! No smoking—fire hazard. Alcohol and drugs prohibited!!! Keep hydrated and drink plenty of fluids." Donald was wearing a bright orange hoodie and a camo fishing cap, with round-rimmed glasses and cheeks weathered from the sun. He introduced us to his brother Larry, who wore jeans and sneakers—we soon learned the course was sneakers only, to protect the crusty earthen putting surfaces—and their buddy Freddie wore a black vest patched with a school bus on the back.

Freddie was a literal champion school bus driver; he'd been the Arizona state champ twice and qualified for nationals on two occasions, though his daily contributions, he explained, were more meaningful. He called his bus the Legacy of Excellence, and he covered its ceiling with photographs and news clippings of local youth who had gone on to excel at sports or in col-lege, reminding the kids on his bus of the possibilities available to them. We learned quickly that our three hosts were givers—Donald worked as a project manager for the nearby Steamboat community, and Larry was a medical driver, a taxing, vital job in such a thinly populated setting. The course they'd created was nine holes without greens fees, a gift from them to the community.

"My nephews were playing golf on top of the hill back there, just going back and forth, back and forth with a tin can in the ground for them," Don-ald recalled. "They were out there all day, and we didn't want them to grow up playing like that, so we threw in a little idea: What if we designed a little three-hole golf course for them? That's how number one, number six, and number seven originated. Then it grew from there. The community mem-bers, some of them as far as maybe twenty-five miles west, they started com-ing out. Pretty soon, we had ten or twelve players on the weekends, and the question we got off that was, 'Are you guys going to sponsor a tournament?' I mean, just imagine us sponsoring a three-hole tournament. It doesn't make any sense. So we kind of added two holes per year, and pretty soon we end up with nine holes. And that's how the annual tournament began ten years ago."

The hand-painted sign out front read REZ GOLF, probably because the full course name wouldn't fit. They called it Wagon Trail to Lonesome Pine, named for the rogue pine tree in the distance—Freddie said you wouldn't find another one for miles—beside the spot where the Navajo used to drive their wagons up over a hill. Its yearly two-man scramble drew in over a hundred players from the community and beyond. "A nine-hole golf course can only handle so many players, so we're thinking about putting the cap on it next year, where we can just go with ninety-six players," Donald said. As I studied the property, I wondered if he fully understood what he had accomplished here among the dirt and sage. To build a golf course with no budget, no grass, and no revenue and turn it into a place where you had to turn golfers away—to me, Lonesome Pine was a miracle. To its creators, however, it was just something good to give the people here, which was what you tried to do every day.

The Navajo Nation occupied an area larger than ten of the states I'd visited, and while the relocation of Native Americans was among America's darkest chapters, there was more pride and partnership in these acres than any I'd visited elsewhere. One might imagine the reservations as dusty wastelands confined to the West, but there were 310 within America's borders, in places like Maine and Michigan and Long Island (the Shinnecock Nation wasn't far from the golf course). Reservation horror stories had prepared me for scenes of stumbling derelicts drunk on rubbing alcohol, but here was a playground where booze was banned and a family next door was playing in their field after church. Life didn't look easy here—nothing looked very new or close by—but Freddie and Donald and Larry talked of all the things they had, and nothing they lacked. This wasn't blight; this was hard work and honest living, and some gratifying golf.

Local rules said we could move our balls from the hardpan onto whatever tufts of grass we could find. The holes were mostly par 3s, with a few chances to watch your drives split the sage and kick up dust. Aside from one intricate dogleg, they were straightforward holes where scores ballooned around the greens. The islands of watered and sunbaked soil rolled true, but our hosts laughed as we begged our balls to bite. The mud flats were immune to backspin; you had to scoot your ball up to the pins without getting greedy and facing a comeback chip off hardpan, and aiming short of the greens was a Scottish flashback in the Navajo Nation.

There were patio chairs and benches and perched viewing platforms around the tees; you got the sense that when a neighbor had extra furniture or some spare lumber, they came out here and found a use for it. Above all, Lonesome Pine's most sublime feature was the pack of dogs escorting us around the holes—Donald's sheepdogs would sit under our feet on the benches, then dart out into the brush after we hit, weaving between bushes and dodging rattlesnakes and then reappearing at the green, where they sat along the edge, tongues wagging like a gallery of thirsty fans.

They didn't charge any of the visiting golfers, Donald explained. There were other Rez Golf courses in Arizona and New Mexico, but this was one of the longer ones, and people traveled here for the good conditions. As long as they used the cans for their trash, they were welcome to go around as many times as they liked. One golden rule, and I'd broken it—I apologized and told Donald I'd left my can of seltzer on the second tee.

"I know," he said, and I was simultaneously embarrassed and pleased he had noticed. He said he would throw out the can on his next loop that afternoon. Just because the course was homemade didn't mean you treated it with any less care; it meant you treated it with more. It was a small moment, but within it was a respect for the land that transcended its latest role as a golf course.

Before we left, I gave the guys one of my US Open posters for their club-house, and Donald presented me with a handmade necklace. It had a beaded crucifix hanging from it, and he told me it would bless my travels.

I had thus far been collecting ball markers and pencils on my travels—I had Ziploc bags stuffed with them—plus logo balls from the Open venues. My hat collection had multiplied into teetering stacks in my closet, where 90 percent of the hangers were now occupied by golf shirts. T-shirts, belts, sweatshirts, and even spice rub from Sand Hills; the reminders of this trip would last well into the winter of my life. I'm not a particularly religious person, but of all the souvenirs and garb from my travels, there's only one that I haven't taken off since receiving it. And my travels have been abundantly blessed.

SAN FRANCISCO, CALIFORNIA

HOLE #1

Shane had pinpointed all the Starbucks between our hotel and the Olympic Club, so l let his phone guide us to a nonnegotiable pit stop before our seven a.m. tee time. He seemed offended that I didn't drink coffee, and explained that this would be a good day for me to start. I stuck to hydrating with water, prepping for a golf day with no discernible end.

Shane Bacon was a smooth-toned broadcaster and a member of Fox Golf's television team. He was also a plus-handicap who had scraped around the mini-tours before pursuing an announcing career, an experience that, in my opinion, elevated him above golf's other play-by-play presenters who could only guess at what it felt like to drive it 330. Shane had that shot in his bag; his arms and shoulders were protein-packed, and every time I texted, he seemed to be in the gym. He wouldn't need his driver today, though; we'd signed up for a fundraiser supporting Youth on Course, an organization that underwrote junior greens fees, allowing kids to play almost any public track for five dollars. Together we were on pace to raise over $8,000 for the cause, provided we fulfilled the promise we made to our sponsors by playing one hundred golf holes in a single day.

The Olympic Club had lent its Cliffs Course to the Youth on Course hikers for the day—there were about twelve of us playing in San Francisco, with other 100 Hole sites spread around the country. We didn't choose a nine-hole par 3 course because we were soft, though we didn't protest too much when the Cliffs ended up being the only site that would fit both our schedules. Set directly on the Pacific, it was a hilly enough walk, and as we unloaded our bags in the parking lot beside veteran 100 Holers, it was clear we were the new guys. We walked over to the short course with 7 iron through putter in the sacks over our shoulders, while the pros around us had no bags at all. Most of them carried one club with a suction cup stuck to the end—those back-saver things your grandfather used to pick his ball out of the hole—and when the clock struck seven, they dashed off to different tee boxes while Shane and I looked at each other, a little worried about all the running.

"I think they're going to finish before we do," he said, and I agreed. The sun was just breaching the cliffs as we hit to a green we both missed, but we would have many, many more opportunities to do better.

I had been in California since spending Thanksgiving weekend at home, during which I was able to console my wife that the long stretches were over; two more weeks and I'd be back for good, ready to hang the Christmas lights. I'd arrived home just in time to eat turkey and lay around for two days—I was really testing the elasticity of our marital bond, while I think Allyson had forgotten she was even married—recovering from a New Orleans–to–Nevada haul that I'd finished off with a swing into Utah (Sand Hollow's back-nine mountain edges were knee-wobbling) and a final afternoon at Royal Links in Las Vegas. There were plenty of Vegas courses to choose from, but Royal Links had chosen me—it advertised its holes as replicas of famous British Open offerings, and for someone who'd played all the real ones, I felt compelled to investigate an American interpretation. Plus, the place had been created by Billy Walters, the legendary sports bettor who'd become famous for his thirty-year winning streak against the Vegas bookmakers, and maybe some of that luck would bless my scorecard (he'd been less lucky of late, after an insider-trading conviction in 2017). The holes felt more like Nevada than Scotland, despite a storybook by each tee explaining their foreign inspiration, but I embraced the Vegas kitsch and the faux-castle clubhouse and the ten-foot Claret Jug out front. That evening, I lost $200 playing blackjack and ate a lonely bowl of wonton soup at Mandalay Bay; Thanksgiving couldn't come quickly enough. I flew to Philadelphia the next morning, and after my brief holiday layover, I boarded my penultimate westward flight, this one to Los Angeles.

I was distracted from my tour of Hollywood homes by some exceptional golf holes at Los Angeles Country Club and Riviera; from the basin holes at the latter, our caddie pointed to patios up above that belonged to Larry David and Tom Werner, the Red Sox and Liverpool F.C. boss. While they famously maintained a non-Hollywood membership at LACC (denying Bing Crosby made that policy famous), I could still see Aaron Spelling's palace from its fairways, peek into Lionel Richie's backyard—*Hello?*—and hear the parrots at the Playboy Mansion squawking from the other side of the fence. George Thomas had designed both of these US Open courses (LACC's North was hosting in 2023), and these sunny superstar layouts were a long way from that rainy Thomas nine-holer we'd played on Cape Cod.

Riviera seemed the meaner test of the two; with head-high bunkers guarding greens set at such nervy angles, you had to place your tee balls oh so deliberately. You also had to hit the hell out of them, because Riv played long and offered an up-close introduction to my new unfavorite word: *barranca*, Spanish for gulley or ravine. At home we called them ditches, and somebody usually filled them in, but the courses out here embraced their trenches, and I found plenty at Riviera and at Los Angeles Country Club. Both had Thomas's angles, but a recent reno by Gil Hanse had opened up LACC in a way that made it feel like a grander spread; a richer variety of holes and an unpredict-able topography made it the easy pick for which course I would want to play every day. It was also the course you'd play if you wanted to forget you were in Los Angeles. It felt strange to be in the heart of America's second-largest city (if you considered LA a city instead of a confederacy of strip malls linked by highways) and not see any urban hints on the horizon. It was a bubbled enclave, and not by accident, it seemed. California was such a blue state that one wondered if conservatives bothered living here at all, but I was quick to learn that they did, and most of them belonged to LACC, where Ronald Reagan's locker remained a celebrated artifact. As I changed my shoes near the former president's locker, I overheard a member correcting a guest for greeting him with *happy holidays*. "We say *Merry Christmas* here," he replied. Maybe it was less a political statement and more about how much they loved Christmas; the LACC gingerbread display was museum-quality, though I was unable to bring home pictures of it for my kids. My host apologized—even when it came to Santa's workshop, no cameras was strict LACC code.

It seemed a strange protocol for a club every golfer on the planet was going to see on a US Open broadcast in three years' time (a big deal for a club so reclusive that it had previously rejected US Open and US Amateur propositions from the USGA), but the no-pictures and no-guest-money-in-the-pro-shop policies had less to do with being inhospitable to visitors and more to do with *Warfield v. Peninsula Golf & Country Club*, a 1995 Califor-nia Supreme Court ruling that stated any private club receiving income from nonmembers (such as greens fees or merchandise sales) was not entirely pri-vate, and was therefore subject to state business laws and regulation. For a club to remain truly exclusive, you basically had to Venmo your host if you wanted to buy a hat at places like the Cal Club or LACC. Photography got lumped in as a potential nonmember enterprise, should the photos be used in a commercial capacity. Some clubs were more careful than others in keep-ing to their *Warfield* standards, while some of the California courses I visited wouldn't know *Warfield* from waffles.

HOLE #37

I was down three to Shane, but if ever there was a match with enough time left for a comeback, this was it. Energy levels had been high through our first and second nines as we acquainted ourselves with Cliffs Course tee boxes vaulted high above the ocean and tucked up into the woods. We bashed 8 irons over rocky gulches (probably a wedge for Shane), then stepped aside as the one-clubbers came racing through. The holes might have played short, but they didn't walk short, and by our fourth nine, resentful of the speedsters lapping us again, we decided to change the rules of our endeavor. Forget playing the ninth hole—you had to cross the street to get there—we'd keep the loops interesting by inventing our own holes and hitting to the wrong greens, not too unlike what I'd accidentally done down in LA.

Around the corner from LACC sat eighteen golf holes packed into 832 yards of a public park, but what an 832 yards they were. Rarely in the course of human events have two adjacent golf properties held so little in common. The Armand Hammer Golf Course, or the Pony Course as its infrequent guests called it, resided in semi-secluded Holmby Park, an oasis of public tranquility amid the Beverly Hills buzz of accruing interest and reinvesting dividends. The park wasn't immune to the glamour and shine—BMWs and Maseratis circled the leafy plot in search of parking, and stepping forth from said conveyances were women in white leggings carrying loaf-sized dogs. By the dozens, they circled the park with heads down, studying their phones as their dogs nosed one another's poopers. But within that asphalt ring, golf holes that stretched to fifty and sometimes fifty-five yards called to us from a distant cosmos, where for four dollars we played in basketball shorts and T-shirts, lost in our golf as Beverly Hills receded from our imaginations.

Discovering that Armand Hammer was not a baking soda tycoon shook me deeply, and as I dug into his story, I wondered what other deceits the universe had in store. I found that he was an oilman and philanthropist who did eventually acquire a partner's share in Arm & Hammer, if for no better reason than to stop feeling like such a fraud in the supermarket. His money had saved the golf course on which we were playing, and God save Armand Hammer for that. He passed away in 1990, but save him anyway, because his course possessed one of the higher grins-to-yards ratios in California golf. The greens were the size of tires, but their shaggy tops were ideal for a skins game with some new Internet buddies where so much more was at stake than five bucks. With parked Porsches for backstops, every flop shot off the dead sod was a butt-clenching venture. The guy at the starter's shack told us he didn't have enough pins for all eighteen cups, so we'd have to find a few holes on our own. Our fun would not be thwarted; we were up to the task.

There was little doubt that we'd discovered the fourteenth tee beside some untended vegetation, and we proceeded to rip the earth with our wedges. Our balls showed little interest in the flag ahead of us, but as we bent to pick up our putters, I noticed a small, dark notch in the earth. I explored it with my finger and found a hard rim. Eureka! A golf hole. We had found not the fourteenth tee but the fifteenth green. We cheered like climbers at the summit, then went hunting for the dark chunks we'd just torn out of the putting surface. The world around us might have been Rodeo Drive, but within our bubble of bad golf, we were skins-chasing bastards, the kings of 832, and a troop of slobs who all forgot to pay Max his skins in the end. There was hope for Los Angeles yet.

HOLE #52

Shane was adamant that we play our way past the halfway point before we stopped for lunch, and so we did. We laid in the grass and ate donated sandwiches, watching the sprinters wander back across the street to their cars, having finished their hundred holes before one o'clock. Shane changed into his second pair of socks—he had packed wisely—while I dropped trou in the middle of the course and pulled on some shorts. Who cared; the day was getting warm, and there was only one other hiker left on property, and she was nowhere in sight. We had yet to be properly introduced, but I had a feeling we were about to join forces, if for no other reason than that she had a small gallery with her—a caddie and friends trailing her with provisions— that might energize us for our back forty-eight.

We finished our lunches and sat silently in the grass. The course was quiet now, and with just three of us remaining, I felt the loneliness of the left-behind. My thoughts drifted back to a recent afternoon in LA when I'd never felt less lonely on a golf course.

I'd been greeted at a public called Penmar by an eclectic assembly of twenty players whose enthusiasm for nine holes of golf reminded me to savor them as my itinerary neared its end. Their willingness to offer me some company proved how the trip had changed from a one-man show headed for Connecticut to a circus train where the locals were happy to come out and help me hoist the tent. It had happened at the resplendent Keney Park muni in Hartford, where the pro was kind enough to make space for thirty golfers on a Saturday morning, and at Mountain Shadows in Arizona, where a small crowd showed up for some short-course delight. One of them was carrying the storied Traveling Sunday Bag, and I played a hole with its worn canvas over my shoulder. A diary in its pocket revealed the hundreds of places it had visited, and I was proud to add my own note and join the Sisterhood of the Traveling Sunday Bag.

There had been a few members of the Sisterhood in the crowd at Penmar, a nine-holer made semi-famous when Harrison Ford crash-landed his vintage prop plane on one of its fairways in 2015. I'd dropped back every few holes to make sure I met each golfer who'd come out, not so they could say they golfed with me—in Los Angeles, I had less celebrity cachet than the grassy dent from Ford's plane—but so I could say I had golfed with them. The positivity and spontaneity of the online and public golf community was inspiring stuff (one guy was in town from Seattle for the Seahawks game and thought he'd bring his sticks and meet some golfers he followed on the web). I'd sampled every brand and mode of the golf life, and the folks living the muni life were the most dedicated, the most knowledgeable, and unquestionably the most fun. There was something about not taking your next tee time for granted that engendered a passion and appreciation for the hole you were on. The holes at Penmar were straightforward, and we relished each one. They were well kept for such a busy track, and on the eighth I threw down a closest-to-the-pin challenge where the winner would get one of the US Open venue posters (on Twitter, folks were offering me hundreds of dollars for them, but as the artwork included about ninety-seven trademark infringements, they remained giveaway-only).

A new buddy named Michael had stepped up large and flagged it in front of a small crowd. When I went to my car to get his prize, I heard people shouting in the parking lot. A man with a bicycle was banging on the rusty hood of a woman's car, repeatedly exclaiming that she was a prostitute who plied her trade as a means of procuring narcotics (his diction was less pleasant—unrepeatably so). She stumbled out of the car and took a swing at him, which he returned, and suddenly he had a handful of her hair and used it to knock her into a trash can on the sidewalk. I shouted "Hey!" a few times and started jogging toward them, not sure if the poster tube in my hand would be enough to encourage him to stop, but he jumped on his bike and sped off across the street.

The woman lifted herself back into her car and sat with a half-there look on her face. Words dribbled from the corner of her mouth—she was thoroughly stoned and waved me away. I told the starter about what had happened in case he wanted to call someone, but he said such encounters weren't uncommon. The third hole at Penmar was lined with tarps sheltering the homeless and the addicted. The LA shelters and rehabs were overrun, so the city was allowing people to live on the sidewalks; there was simply nowhere else to put them, and tent cities had popped up across Los Angeles. As someone who might once have imagined a tent with a bottle as a decent way to hide from the day, I viewed the scene with uncomfortable empathy. Later that afternoon, I traveled north from LA to San Francisco, grateful for whatever grace had decided I should have the choice to do so.

HOLE #70-ISH

We had lost clubs (Shane and I were both down to wedge and putter), lost our place on the course (one of us was supposed to be counting the holes, but we forgot who), lost complete track of our match (I was getting smoked), and probably lost some weight, too—but all was truly lost as Shane kicked around the rough, mourning his golden Titleist. His lone goal of completing our hundred holes with one golf ball was sunk when, on one of our improvised tee shots over trees to a blind green around the corner, his yellow ball disappeared, kidnapped by hubris. Our arches ached, and with low shoulders we tossed yet another tee ball toward another flag. Then we crossed paths with Lynda, and she pulled our mission out of the murk.

She couldn't have been more than five feet tall, but Lynda led a steady moving convoy as she approached her eightieth green. Her husband was caddying for her, and friends had visited throughout the day to cheer or reward her with snacks. Her pace was all purpose—she didn't rush, but she didn't pause, either, and we decided to join up for a few holes. She looked too young to be retired, though she said she was, and that she did this hike every year to support Youth on Course. As an African American woman who loved her golf, she wished more diverse young people would find the game, and wasn't one for sitting around waiting for that to happen. Even though she already had her PhD, she had recently gone back to school at a junior college to help a young woman live a golf dream.

Napa Valley College didn't have enough female golfers to field a team that season, and when Lynda heard about a girl who was therefore losing out on her dream of playing collegiate golf, she and some of her other golf girlfriends enrolled ("We took the classes that involved drinking wine," she said). Lynda didn't have any more degrees to pursue, but she had plenty of athletic eligibility left, and not only did Napa Valley field a team that year but Lynda made all-conference, and at age sixty-one played in the California Community College state championship.

Listening to Lynda's moxie and her accomplishments, I felt like lint beside a golfing rock. I'd been whining about whether any sandwiches would be left when we finished, and here was this benevolent luminary, still grinding for birdies (she set a goal of making eighteen that day, and reached it). Shane and I stiffened our backs and picked up our pace. We decided we were on hole seventy-four, and I was charged with announcing the tally like a town crier: "Seventy-five!" I called, then "Seventy-six!" loud enough to shake the lockers over in the Olympic clubhouse. We were those last-place marathoners with the trash crews close on our heels, but our feet were still moving, and our three-digit number was just around the bend.

I kept thinking about how far away yesterday's golf felt—I recalled playing Sharp Park, but it seemed as if it might have happened back in high school. I'd arrived in the morning at the San Francisco muni and met two of the forces behind the Save Sharp Park initiative—architect Jay Blasi and course historian Richard Harris—which aimed to preserve and restore Alister MacKenzie's only other seaside course after Cypress. The map said Sharp Park would be near the ocean, but I didn't believe a muni would ever be set so close to the waves; it was, and those waves had reclaimed a handful of MacKenzie's holes. Twelve of his originals remained on a course that had once held two versions of his legendary Lido hole (a two-shot template with a safe bogie route right and a bold birdie left) that GCA folks mourned like a vanished relic after the Lido Club in New York went under in the Great Depression. As a city course, Sharp Park had no equal when it came to location, and holding on to those acres had proved an arduous task—an eight-year legal battle saved the grounds from being closed off as habitat for a garter snake and a rare frog, yet another example of conservationists failing to embrace golf's protective capacities.

It was a subject Scotsman David McLay Kidd had stamped into my psyche: Lay out some golf holes and fragile terrain is instantly preserved and protected, because it now has purpose, both commercially and recreationally. Leave those lands to the whims of absent government agencies or to the wishful benevolence of neighbors and dunes quickly became cut-throughs to the beach or spots for bonfires and keggers. Done right, golf development could be a great green shield for protecting those rare spaces, with course superintendents serving as caretakers who were more efficient and knowledgeable than overstretched municipal agencies. Jay Blasi explained that this argument was lost on the forces prohibiting the restoration of Sharp Park; golf was still considered classist, unnecessary, and unequal to the noble intentions of conservationists who didn't understand that a course thrived only when its setting thrived, and that a conscientious golf architect was really offering to do the environmentalists' work for them. Jay was prohibited from aligning the holes to MacKenzie's vision as closely as he had hoped, but every year they did a few small projects to improve conditions, and they would keep pushing to keep Sharp Park solvent—and thus protected—by returning it to its former glory.

I'd driven north that afternoon through San Francisco, across the Golden Gate, and up to Northwood Golf Club, where a rainy mist fell between the redwoods. It wasn't a long detour for the chance to play a MacKenzie nine-holer, and for NorCal golfers looking for a low-budget weekend, the place was prime. There were three businesses attached to Northwood's parking lot: a pro shop, a pub/restaurant, and a motel, and each one looked camping cozy. The golf holes were pretty simple, but who cared—they were bordered by trees that touched the clouds, where tree stumps were carved into bears and where, in the summertime, you could listen for sounds of the curious rituals at Bohemian Grove across the river. The Northwood holes were as close as any of us were getting to that unseen enclave of American power; Bohemian Grove dated back to 1872, and conspiracy theorists considered it to be a secret society of robed politicians and capitalists who plotted the world's path beside bonfires. Others saw it as summer camp for elites with odd but harmless traditions. I would have liked to wade over and eavesdrop for stock tips, but Shane was about to land at SFO, and tomorrow was as full as our golf days got.

HOLE #100

At the end of my days, as the lights dim and the periphery fades and all that's left is a lone image lingering at the end of a tunnel, I won't need a blinding light to know I'm home; rather, I'd like to see a white ball resting at the bottom of a cup (I'd be happy to see Allyson and the kids, too, but they're going to outlive me). A holed ball was beautiful and final. All it left you were the stories of how it arrived there, powerless to change that plot. It was a poignant vision in any setting, but on my life's first (and likely only) hole one hundred, a buried ball was, in the words of golfing poet Sir John Betjeman, *splendour, splendour, everywhere.*

We laid in the grass as the sun touched the cliffs, trying to not move for at least a little while. The pedometer clocked us in at around fifteen miles, and while that wasn't a distance record for either of us, for sheer continuity of golf, it was a treadmill our minds would be stuck on for weeks. Our efforts had underwritten 1,200 rounds of youth golf, but as Shane and I sat there waiting for someone to carry us back to my car, we decided it would have been easier to teach kids how to sneak onto golf courses instead. As

Maimonides professed: Give a man a tee time, and he golfs for one day; teach a man to trespass, and he golfs for a lifetime.

We helped each other stand and hobbled back to the car, and I dropped Shane at the hotel before heading south for Monterey. My legs would be sore at Pebble tomorrow, I thought, but sore legs were better than the shaking ones Mike had brought from New York.

PEBBLE BEACH, CALIFORNIA

Dripping socks were hung by the chimney with care. There were headcovers and gloves and rain pants draped from the mantel as well; it looked like a desperate golf flea market instead of a five-star room at the Inn at Spanish Bay. Mike and Fairway Joe had spent $550 to go through a carwash at Pebble Beach that morning, and Mike regretted not bringing some of his firefighting coveralls with him to California. His golf waterproofs had been compromised by the third hole, and though I had teed off at Pebble three hours after they had, my room down the hall looked much the same. None of our rain gear would be dry in time for Cypress tomorrow, and I shot up a string of foxhole prayers, beseeching some morning sunshine from any and all qualified deities.

I wished our reunion had come under dryer circumstances, but it was still poignant to see Mike and his dad all the way out here and recall how a chance eighteen holes on the other side of America had turned strangers into cross-country companions. Mike had come out a few days early to play all the other Monterey prize courses with his dad.

"I figured we were doing this trip once, so might as well do it together and do it right," he said.

Fairway Joe sat in the corner drinking his last free Diet Coke. The room came with two per day, while everything else on its shelf of Pebble Beach items—golf balls, snacks, souvenirs—was tagged with shameless prices.

"You can take a picture of this room now," Mike joked, "and take another when we leave, and all that's going to be left are the things on that price list. For what this room cost, it's going to be a Pebble Beach Christmas at our house. Shampoo for the wife; towels for the boy."

Advance tee times at Pebble were still available only to guests staying at the resort, which helped maintain Pebble Beach's status as the priciest public tee time in golf by a healthy margin. Plenty of would-be visitors took umbrage at the perceived golf gouging, but until Pebble had empty spots on their tee sheet, it was hard to argue with the price point. The cost hadn't kept us away, and at dinner we debated whether it was worth the splurge. We agreed that it was. I'd prepared myself to be underwhelmed—some pundits knocked Pebble for turning ordinary as it veered away from the sea, but anything was ordinary compared to the routing's waterside offerings. The greens were delightfully petite, and each hole sounded its own entertaining notes, with or without waves to catch your slices. The boardwalk horseshoe of shops and lodging that surrounded the first tee and practice green created a charming village that buzzed with golf anticipation. Mike and I would both be paying off our Pebble Beach charges for a while, but neither of us would send those checks and think, "Damn, I wish I hadn't played Pebble Beach."

We might have wished for more time at Pasatiempo and Pacific Grove, though, where a Monterey golf trip offered some friendlier values—extremely friendly at Pacific Grove, dubbed "the poor man's Pebble Beach," where a sleepy front nine led you to nine oceanside holes through the dunes. Pasatiempo was on the other side of the bay in Santa Cruz, and it wasn't cheap at $295, but it felt reasonable for the chance to play MacKenzie's greatest daily-fee course and the one he considered his favorite design, a partiality proven by his choosing to spend his final years in a home along its sixth fairway. Pasatiempo gave you your greens-fee's worth on every shot, from *barrancas* to ravines to audaciously shaped bunkers by the former camouflage artist (recently restored by Tom Doak and Jim Urbina). MacKenzie used every idiosyncrasy the land gave him, and molded them into golf shots you'd never quite considered before. Mike and FJ had played there yesterday in good weather, and it was their favorite stop of the trip so far.

"I've been trying to read everything I can find about Cypress," Mike told me at dinner that evening. "I read *The Match*, but there's nothing else out there about the place. It's like a ghost course. I bought a pamphlet some guy wrote about going there, but you can't find it on Instagram, and there's basically no pictures online." Then Mike pushed Cypress Point's actual existence into the realm of doubt and conspiracy theory: "Nobody on Facebook has ever checked in there!"

Our conversation was interrupted by a friendly voice. "Look at these losers," Brendan said, dropping his carry-on beside our table. It was their first time meeting in person, but he and Mike hugged like old friends. They'd become pals over a text thread where they'd discovered they were each impossible to offend. I hadn't seen Brendan since Ohoopee, and he looked different here in California. His hair was short now—not as a result of our match but because his wife, Trish, had finally had enough—and he looked like my buddy again. I'd forgotten how much fun he was to be around, but I remembered as I listened to him gently break the news to Mike that it was unlikely the small pro shop at Cypress was going to have a belt that fit him. We talked and laughed for close to an hour before the yawns went around the table, and on our way back to our rooms, Mike grilled me for pointers on how not to screw up tomorrow in front of the well-known member who was hosting us.

"Obviously I'm not changing my shoes in the parking lot," he said. "Are shorts okay? Do I need a jacket? How much cash do you think I need? I don't want to stiff anybody."

I told him to stop worrying; it was just a golf club, I said, without actually believing that myself. But the next day, that's sort of what it was—to my shock and relief, Cypress was kind of chill. As we pulled into the lot, a pro was milling about some empty parking spaces. He welcomed us and pointed us to the locker room to change our shoes. There was no gate or valet, no secret handshakes or primers on Cypress etiquette—Monterey's 17 Mile Drive actually went right through the golf course, quite unlike the guard post at Pine Valley where I always expected them to tell me to turn around. We relaxed and realized that this was still California, bro, and we didn't have to be afraid of a golf course. It took Mike a little while longer to get that message—he sweated through his shirt before we reached the first tee, and his eyes looked like he'd come here to have an organ removed.

The clubhouse was small and efficient—Scottish in nature, with a minimal pro shop where my search for a souvenir ball marker led me to a box of shiny pennies. The pro said that a club president had figured out that the coins were cheaper than ball markers, so pennies were the Cypress tradition. I scooped up three dollars' worth and met Brendan and Mike by the lockers, where we could tell the room had recently been updated, but not the benches—ninety years of spike marks remained, stamped into the wood. I ran my fingers over them, considering the owners of the shoes that had once leaned here, and felt convinced there was no more beautiful finish than the rippled sheen of steel-pressed dots.

Mike sat in front of a locker, catching his breath. "I can't believe I'm here, man," he said, and though I didn't need a paper bag to breathe into, I felt the same way. He picked up one of the long Cypress Point shoehorns set in front of each locker. "You think they would miss this?" He was joking, but in case he wasn't, I told him they probably would, especially since we were the only guests on the property, and the shoehorns were placed in careful arrangement. Instead, we paid for our souvenirs while we waited for our host to arrive. Headcovers, shirts, belts, hats, and rolled-up prints of the sixteenth hole—it was suddenly Black Friday at Cypress, and we clogged my trunk with our bags before heading off to the first tee with a host that Mike's research had revealed worked in banking.

"I don't think he was a teller, if you know what I mean," Mike whispered to me.

"I think you're right," I replied. Our anxieties about matching his standards dissipated quickly; he was easy company and a generous guide, maybe sixty years old, with a swing that looked like he'd been around these holes a few thousand times. I thought I would break the ice by telling him we shared a course in common: His sweater had a St. Andrews cross on it, which I identified as the logo of the St. Andrews Golf Club in Scotland, a not terribly exclusive club that I'd joined that past winter. He politely corrected me: "This is actually the Royal and Ancient," he said, which was a terribly exclusive club that I had not joined that past winter. I told him I'd heard of it, while Brendan turned his face to hide his smile. Mike walked somewhere behind us, counting his steps and still looking like he might pass out.

His legs lost their wobble by the fourth hole. Mike's big turn loosened up, and he was soon knocking his drives alongside ours as he looked around and shook his head.

"This is insane. There's nobody else here," he said. I was told a busy day at Cypress was forty golfers, and with a small membership of mostly nonlocals, the empty fairways and silent clubhouse were a reminder of our good fortune, and a suggestion to savor every last swing.

Our caddies helped us relax into the round. They weren't dressed in white jumpsuits to impress or intimidate guests—mine was wearing a hoodie and a fishing cap, with the grinning demeanor of a Deadhead who'd left the tour for a little while to read some greens. He read them well and pulled clubs like a savant, and I didn't mind at all when he put my bag down next to a white mushroom, thinking he'd found my drive. I was surprisingly comfortable at Cypress, cracking jokes with Mike and Brendan and even holing the odd birdie, a bonus I wasn't expecting. The holes were challenging but not I'll-just-drop-one-here hard. They did tighten up toward the close, making it an ideal match-play routing, though Brendan and I had decided we weren't going to play a match; this was too fine an opportunity to spend it resenting each other.

Golf had been brought to Monterey by Samuel Finley Brown Morse (cousin of the inventor of Morse Code), a real estate visionary who fell in love with the area and bought up most of it in 1919. Known as "The Duke of Del Monte," he had purchased the Hotel Del Monte and the surrounding Del Monte Forest and set aside most of the acres for preservation, with plans to develop portions as golf courses and home sites. Marion Hollins, the 1921 US Women's Amateur Champion, happened to work for Morse selling his real estate, and she became the force behind bringing Cypress to life (Pasatiempo, too). Seth Raynor was initially commissioned to design three courses on the peninsula (Morse was a Yalie, where Macdonald and Raynor had designed the university's golf course), but he passed away before the work on Cypress commenced, and Hollins recommended MacKenzie for the job.

I had only seen pictures of Cypress's backside beach-hugging holes, so I assumed we'd be working our balls off the waves all afternoon long, but the course was more like three layouts in one: There were holes that snuck back into the woods, others that worked their way across a sandy stretch of dunes, and then those portrait pieces that hung off the cliffs. In all my rounds, I had never had to carry a blind drive over the corner of a dune after cutting a 3 wood off a line of pines and then begging my ball to carry two hundred yards of ocean breakers. When it came to variety of holes and shots, Cypress had no peer, and the fact that it was all so damn beautiful—we went into the day knowing it could never match our expectations. We were right, because our expectations had not been grand enough.

None of our balls found terra firma on sixteen, Cypress's celebrated 230-yard par 3 set on an ocean outcropping, and it was the best time any of us had ever had making double. Brendan and I actually giggled when we hoisted 7 irons over the island of timber that interrupted the seventeenth fairway, finding the green and snatching pars. Even its maligned eighteenth hole was a funfest, where my caddie gave me 4 iron and told me to hit it at the tree trunks (if you come off Cypress complaining that its closing dogleg—a blind, twisting, climbing tunnel of cypresses—is a weak finisher, then I mourn for the golfer who could have had your spot).

We thanked our host as if he'd plucked us from the abyss, then said goodbye to the spike marks in the locker room. Ours was the only car in the parking lot as we loaded up and headed for dinner. We cruised along 17 Mile Drive and stopped at the Lone Cypress for some pictures, catching the miraculous conifer at golden hour, its roots clinging to a rocky ledge and its branches reaching out over the waves. Finally we retired to Clint Eastwood's Mission

Ranch restaurant, an old Carmel hang where we polished off steaks beside a meadow of grazing sheep. Fairway Joe was waiting for us in the piano bar when we arrived, and we had a hard time recounting the day to him. Mike showed him the painting of sixteen he'd bought—"I'll look at this and remember the time I didn't come anywhere close to that green"—and Brendan added that the belt he'd bought would motivate him to stay in good-enough shape to keep wearing it. By the time dessert came—it was a day that called for ice cream—I thought we'd shown off all the souvenirs in our bags, but Mike had one more, and like a knight presenting his sword, he laid it down across our table: the Cypress shoehorn.

"I couldn't help myself," he said, confessing with red face. "It somehow found its way down my shorts."

I flinched, ready to smack his hand with it. We'd come so close to getting through Cypress Day without revealing ourselves as common louts who'd have stolen the toilet paper if it had a logo on it. Instead, I laughed with the rest of the table. If I ever got invited back to Cypress, I'd be happy to repay the debt—and if a shoehorn barred my return, so be it. It would be a small price for that kind of golf with these kinds of friends. Plus, it gave us something to bust Mike's balls about the next time we played, and as we said our goodbyes in the parking lot, there was no doubt we would have that chance soon.

Brendan and I were still talking about our approach shots on seventeen as we drove back up to San Francisco that night. He had a red-eye the next evening, but not before we fit in one more match. He wouldn't come all the way out here and miss a chance to remind me, yet again, that I couldn't beat him. And I couldn't put away the suitcase and call this trip done until I got my chance to exorcise Ohoopee.

Maybe it was returning to the Olympic Club and having to play only eighteen holes that made the air feel lighter (I averted my gaze from the Cliffs Course across the street, where just a few days before I'd golfed like Sisyphus), or maybe it was the prospect of crossing the final meal off my cuisine checklist—Olympic's halfway house burgerdog—that greased up my swing. Maybe it was my impending flight to Hawaii that had me unworried about my match; whatever the reason, I had Brendan two-down at the turn, where the burgerdog met the hype head-on. You know you've played a lot of courses when you're at the home of five US Opens and the primary attraction in your golf-weary mind is a tube of ground beef. Back in the 1950s, Hot Dog Bills had decided they could save on buns if their burgers fit into hot dog rolls when they set up shop next to Olympic. They were soon invited to move their food stand onto the Lake Course, where Brendan and I got the last burgerdogs of the day and discovered they were a savory blend of fat, spices, and fried onions. I could have remained there piping beef down my gullet all afternoon, but I'd been up two at the turn at Ohoopee as well, and Brendan was happy to remind me: "Lots of golf left."

The Olympic Club boasted three courses and an enormous membership, most of which joined for access to its Athletic Club downtown, where Olympic had gotten its start as the oldest athletic club in America. Dating to 1860, it had cranked out champion runners and swimmers and cyclists, along with water polo Olympians and elite football, rugby, and basketball squads. It added golf in 1918 when it acquired the Lakeside Golf Club and turned it into a country campus with two eighteen-hole courses (the par 3 Cliffs Course was added in 1994). The Lake Course hosted the Opens, and its tree-lined fairways stepped down the side of a hill like the terraces at Machu Picchu, a gradual descent from a capstone clubhouse to the edge of Lake Merced. It was a long, tight test where par could win a hole—at least in our match.

I was still ahead as we played the lower holes of thirteen, fourteen, and fifteen, and when I picked up Brendan's ball marker on sixteen to concede a halve (the gimme mind-games were finally behind us), he did me more good than he might have liked. *The more relaxed you are, the better you are at everything.* I read the words, and believed them, even as he won the seventeenth to square the match. Both our approaches on the short eighteenth landed in greenside rough; Brendan pitched his to eight feet, while I rolled mine up to five. I didn't smile or needle or react at all as his par putt slid past. I just relaxed. I relaxed and picked my par out of the bottom of the cup, because the more relaxed you are, the better you are at beating your best friend.

Brendan's face was a tangle of emotions; it would be hard for him to abandon *You cannot beat me*, but somewhere in his eyes was a begrudging satisfaction in seeing me finally close one out. He was grinding for that halve, but he knew I deserved a day, and golf knew it, too. It didn't give it up easily, but it handed me a moment when the Brendans went quiet and I was finally as good as I wanted to be. It took me ten thousand miles and three thousand swings to grab it, and I wouldn't have asked for a trial of one single step less.

Brendan texted me that night as he was waiting to board his flight: *I'm in the airport wearing a Cypress hat, Olympic sweater, and Ohoopee belt. I look like a golf asshole.* I smiled and wrote back that he was, but before I could hit send, another note from him popped up on my screen: *Thanks, man. This has been the greatest golf year of my life. Thanks for making it happen.*

I felt a strange tingle in my nose, and it inched upward toward my eyes. Ours was supposed to be a shoulder-to-shoulder friendship, but even though I was staring at a phone, Brendan was looking right at me, and I back at him.

I wasn't sure if my golf travels across America had made me a better golfer, better traveler, or better American, but so much roaming had proven that the things that matter are the things that stick. The road had made me want to be one of those things, and being a genuine friend was primary among them.

I wrote back: *Best year ever. I just played golf. You made it great. Thanks for being there.* I hit send and boarded my plane. The engines roared to life, and I drifted off in my seat, dreaming of a Mele Kalikimaka.

KUKIO, HAWAII

Once upon a time, there was a boy who believed in fairways. He believed in greens, too, where he often found a ball resting within arm's length of a hole. Golf was easy for him, and he couldn't imagine a time when it might be otherwise. He wielded his club without fear, and the ball followed the pictures in his mind, heard the intentions in his heart. He didn't send it very far—not yet—but distance was dispensable when you slung your rock like David. His club was indeed a weapon, a bow from which he launched steady bolts of courage that felled men who dreamed they could go back and play like a boy again.

That boy's name wasn't Tom. When I was a kid, I just wanted to hit it far, with little idea or concern for where, eschewing the prudent shot and willing to suffer a string of 8s for one roll at eagle. The boy in this story was named Blake, or Blakey, and as I watched him carve up the holes at Kukio where his dad, Kiley, looped on the weekends, I wept for my misspent golfing youth. Blake wasn't quite four feet tall yet, but at eight years old, he didn't meet too many holes he couldn't par, and drove it so straight that it looked as if he might play the same ball until high school. Blakey was golf-obsessed, his dad told me. He had read all my books and wanted to golf the links of Europe soon. When we met in person on the Big Island of Hawaii, I apologized for the awful words I'd added to his son's vocabulary and thanked him for emailing me and bringing me out to Kukio to meet Blakey. I'd met celebrities and pros and architects on this journey, but watching a kid play was a lucky way to finish. It reminded me why I was here. It reminded me of a lot of things.

Blake rode in my golf cart, where his feet didn't come close to touching the floorboards. I loved that he called me Uncle Tom—a Hawaiian label of respect for an elder—and on his way to beating me one-up, he asked me the perfect questions as we drove: *What is your favorite fruit? Which club is your favorite? What was your favorite subject in school? Do you want a cocktail?*

I laughed and told him that no, I didn't need a Mai Tai as we perused the halfway drink selections—Kiley was a liquor salesman when he wasn't working as the only caddie at Kukio, so his boy Blakey was precociously versed in mixology. We took our time at the comfort stations; the course was an immaculate Hawaiian beauty, but Blake and I were most interested in the unmanned snack shacks, where everything from smoothies to ice cream sandwiches to jars of wrapped candies awaited our fingers. I still had candy in my pockets that evening as I sat on my hotel balcony watching waves roll over the rocks and wondering how I'd arrived here. The thing that had gotten me to the finish line, I decided, wasn't golf, or writing, or resolve—it was that I'd somehow learned to stop forcing life and just start following it. It had bigger plans than my mind could accept. I'd doubted my itinerary every month and every mile, but life, it turned out, had a pretty high tolerance for wild ideas.

Blake and Kiley joined me the following morning for my final round. I'd decided to cap things off at Nanea, a David McLay Kidd masterwork that he'd stretched across black lava slopes for clients Charles Schwab and

George Roberts. They didn't ask for an easy course, David told me, and so he'd covered the lava mantle with unforgiving slopes and greens guarded by deep run-offs. As we played, Kiley shared some Hawaiian pidgin dialect—he knocked one into the stones and asked, "Where do I stay?" which seemed off topic and a tad existential for a round of golf, but he explained it meant *Where am I?* or *Where did it go?* I just waved a shaka with my hand—thumb and pinky extended—and pretended to understand before being told to never shake a shaka. I had expected Hawaiian golf to be a tropical rain forest adventure, with tees obscured by waterfalls and a lei dropped onto my neck by a hula-dancing starter, but this western side of the Big Island was mostly patches of blond grass poking through dark lava fields. Kiley explained that, in local mythology, the volcano goddess Pele and the rainmaking demigod Kamapua'a had battled until they agreed to divvy up the island between them. Pele got the western half and Kamapua'a the eastern portion—thus the Big Island's split between a rocky west coast and a lush eastern side.

I was glad I'd come to Pele's share, as the conditions were linksy; the goddess's breath blew strong across the black moonscapes, and the lava-top fairways played as firm as any Scottish fields. The sheer beauty of treeless green strips snaking through dark rocks softened the mess I was making on my last scorecard, and while it was visited by precious few, I knew I was ending at a course that captured Hawaii. Its clubhouse consisted of five hut-like structures to mimic the island's five volcanoes, and the best of them was the locker room, where outdoor showers were open to a bright Hawaiian sky.

I bounced back from my defeat at Kukio to close out Blakey on the sixteenth hole. For the record, I wasn't playing him for money or insisting we compete—it was Blakey who wanted to rumble, and who kept reminding me of the score. He begged Uncle Tom for a new match on the final two holes, which we pushed, and before I headed in to take the greatest shower of my life, we said our goodbyes in the parking lot, and Kiley said it was too bad my flight was leaving that afternoon. They were heading back to Kukio for eighteen more, and not at Dad's request. Kiley wasn't pushing his son; rather, his son was pulling him along, and it reminded me of my own dad, who'd left me to my golf to take it or leave it. I certainly took it, and though I didn't swing like Blakey at that age, I'd begged Dad to keep playing, too, and as I left Nanea for the airport, I wondered if it might be possible to talk him into going around again.

The in-between was the puzzle, but this journey's start and end had existed the moment I'd imagined America. I would kick off at the first spot to host a US Open and finish where golf in America—golf anywhere—started for me: a round with my father at his former club.

I didn't tell Dad about my plans. His erstwhile Saturday partners at Rolling Green weren't around or alive anymore to invite him back, so I wanted our return to remain a surprise. The new head pro had been generous enough to offer me a tee time, but then Dad's back went, and out came the walker. He rehabbed through the winter and was using a cane by Christmas, and in a few months, Dad was getting around on two feet, though I'd still catch him steadying himself on a chair or table.

I'd been home for a few months when I called to check in, and Mom told me he was out playing nine holes at LuLu. I wasn't sure she had her story straight—Dad playing golf again seemed a too-wishful update—but I was wrong: he was back on the course, rusty and cart-bound, but he was playing. I fired off a happy note to tell the pro at Rolling Green we were coming just as soon as the days warmed up, but when they did, golf disappeared. The courses closed and the tee sheets went offline. I taught my girls math in the morning and chipped balls around my backyard in the afternoon, and with each passing day, all the golf and the miles and the flights and the handshakes felt more and more like a dream than a life I'd actually lived.

Lost golf doesn't even rank on the register of Covid-19 tragedies, and I quarantined with gratitude for my family's health and for having completed my travels just a few months before travel ceased to exist. I counted the days until our governor declared we could golf again, and when he finally did, the pro at Rolling Green said the invitation still stood, and the tee sheet on Dad's June birthday had an open slot.

As I pulled up the winding drive that passed the third hole and ended at a Tudor clubhouse, I saw Dad off to my left, already talking with someone on the tee. I was glad he'd recognized a friend so quickly. The place had been our home for years, and after Dad made the hard choice to leave, I wasn't sure how eager he would be to return. Memories can be hard for us Irish types—we excel at putting things behind us without a backward glance—but Mom had said he could hardly sleep after I told him we were going to Rolling Green for his birthday. He'd already been there for a half hour by the time I arrived, catching up with pals and holding court around the golf carts, the same way I'd found him on a thousand summer afternoons. There was no limp in his step, and when he caught sight of me, he said, "Tom boy, we're waiting for you." No matter how early I arrived for golf with Dad, I was always late. "Looks like you didn't stand too close to your razor this morning," he said. "Let's go. Tee's open."

And with that, his months stuck in bed, the weeks stuck in their apartment, my year on the road, my children and marriage and every single thing that had happened in thirty years—whole decades stepped aside, and on the day my dad turned eighty-six, I went back to being fourteen. The land on which this game is played holds memories for a very long time, and once in a while, it lets us come back and walk around in them.

I was sure he'd have to skip the occasional hole to steady his legs; Rolling Green was as rolling a course as you could find in Philadelphia, and all I wanted was for him to finish, fearing that the hills he used to walk with ease would now be too much. Not only did Dad play every hole but he didn't pick up once, refusing to invoke the quitter's refrain of *Give me a seven*. He had a few good looks at par, and didn't take any gimmes. He seemed determined to experience every shot, and while he didn't bring the club back much farther than shoulder height, he advanced through the holes 120 yards at a time, straight and steady as ever.

I hadn't wished for this round to be extraordinary—rather, my hope was that it would feel regular, uneventful, familiar, just another eighteen holes with Dad. Same as yesterday, same as tomorrow. Not a last hurrah or some sort of victory lap for my father but just golf, because just golf had always been plenty, and just golf was what I would miss the most. I knew there was going to be a time, hopefully far into the future, when I would be willing to trade all my rounds for one ordinary eighteen with my dad. An eighteen like this one, where the only thing that was different was how he talked about the course.

I never remembered him mentioning how great a golf course this was, but now I caught him stopping to look around. "This is beautiful," he said, as if noticing for the first time. He thanked me for bringing him back here, which hit me in an unguarded spot. I didn't bring him here; it was the other way around, and I should have been thanking him for giving me this golf life, for giving me golf dreams, for bringing me here when I didn't want to try golf because it was a grown-up, stupid waste of time. I didn't have those words at the ready, or the guts to say them, so instead I smiled and wished Dad a happy birthday.

EPILOGUE

Dad held his golf club with ten fingers, a baseball grip he'd brought to golf from the Scranton playgrounds. Nobody had ever suggested he do it differently when he picked up his first driver on the naval base, and his partners were probably holding their clubs the same way, a lunchtime gang of self-taught golfers looking to break the monotony of military office work.

I had played Torrey Pines in the morning—lovely to look at, and damn difficult—where Dad and his beginner buddies would splurge for a forty-dollar foursome on Saturdays. I had Los Angeles and Monterey and Hawaii still on my schedule, but I'd left the afternoon empty for a course I wasn't sure existed. I couldn't find it on any map, and when I asked the pro at Torrey about it, he took me upstairs to see the manager, who took me down the hall to see another man who oversaw Torrey Pines for the city. They'd lived in San Diego most of their lives and were eager to help, but I'd stumped them with my questions about a nine-hole course on the navy base. They knew of other navy courses nearby—Sea 'N Air, Admiral Baker—but they were eighteen-hole layouts beyond the main gates. The course I was hunting was definitely a nine-holer within the base—"across the street from the navy office buildings" was the best hint Dad had given me. San Diego's naval presence was huge and always had been, so my clues were uselessly vague. They wished me well on my search, and I found a spot in the clubhouse where I could scroll through satellite images on my phone.

It didn't occur to me that spying on a military base from above might land my IP address on any number of undesirable lists; I was distracted by the nobility of my cause, and searched until I spotted a lone green space amid the base's roofs and parking lots. I zoomed in to see the outline of what might have been a green, and Google identified my find as the Naval Base Golf Performance Center. It looked like more of a driving range than a golf course, but it was definitely within the base, and near what looked like office buildings. I gave it a shot and dialed the number.

I'd never called up a military base before, and I was nervous that the phone might be answered by an angry officer demanding to know where I'd gotten this number. Instead, a friendly voice picked up, and a guy who introduced himself as Bill indulged me as I rattled off my story: "My dad was stationed here after Korea, he said he first played golf on a nine-hole course on the base. I'm a golf writer and I've been playing all fifty states, and I really want to find the place where he learned to play."

Bill said I had called the right number. The facility used to have nine holes, long before he was there, but navy housing and parking lots had now taken over most of the property. They had four greens left, with three sets of tees for each, so it was now twelve short par 3s, plus a driving range where you hit into a net, all of it squeezed into two or three acres. "This was the only nine-hole course that was ever on the base, as far as I know," he said. "You're welcome to come check it out. Are you military?"

I told him I wasn't, and he paused. "Yeah, you gotta have military ID to get through the gates. I'm sorry about that."

I told him I understood. I thanked him for his time, and asked if there was anyone I might call for some sort of special clearance. Dad was a lieutenant commander, I said, and maybe there were some records somewhere that could help me make a case for a visit.

"Where are you right now?" he asked.

"I'm at Torrey Pines."

"Okay," he replied. "Here's what we'll do." He gave me directions to a gas station across the street from the base. He told me to call back when I got there, and he would come pick me up and bring me through as his visitor. The navy allowed Department of Defense employees to bring in guests, he explained, as long as they took responsibility for them while on property. I told him it all sounded great to me, and I promised my stay would be brief and uneventful.

I found the gas station and called Bill. Within a few minutes, I spotted a man in a red shirt walking across the parking lot. "You Tom?" We shook hands, and I thanked him repeatedly for going out of his way like this.

"Happy to help. It's a cool story," he said. "I'm glad some holes are still left for you to play."

It was a quick drive across the street, and the guards waved us through the gates. Bill said there wasn't much to the Golf Center, but it was enough space to let the sailors blow off some steam and knock it around. He was retired military and said he enjoyed the chance to still hang around the troops, and since his job was considered an essential service, he didn't get furloughed when the government shut down.

"So the military considers golf an essential activity?" I asked, a new patriotism bubbling up within me.

"Well, the troops' morale and well-being are, so recs and activities keep going."

When we parked in front of a cinder-block building with an ad for a new driver on the door, I turned around to see the hitting bays and a few flags in the small field across the street. Bill brought me into his pro shop, where a Marine in fatigues was waiting at the counter. He asked if he could play a few holes before his shift; he didn't have any cash with him, but Bill just waved him on and told him to get in as many holes as he could. It was a simple room with used clubs for sale and good deals on golf balls, and Bill gave me a Naval Base Golf Performance Center ball marker and told me to give it to my dad.

He walked me across the street to show me the driving range, where a few men in camouflage uniforms were working their way through buckets of balls. Hitters had about fifty yards before their shots found the net, but it was enough room for Bill to give lessons to the men and women stationed here. We went to the first tee, and he explained how the course worked—you went around its four greens three times, and each tee would bring me to the green from a different angle. I wouldn't need more than a wedge, he said, so I left the rest of my bag there in the grass, confident it might be the most secure spot in golf to leave your clubs unattended.

I asked Bill to take a picture of me with the holes in the background so I could send it to my dad, proof that I'd found his first course, or at least some of it. Dad had a picture of us standing together on the Swilcan Bridge in St. Andrews, where they say the game began, but for us, it started here. This was our home of golf, and while it might not have been as pretty as Scotland, it held more meaning than any course I'd ever touched.

"So, what do you think?" Bill said. "Is this the place you were looking for?"

I dropped my ball onto the tee, holding my wedge lightly in my fingers, and told him that it was.

He said I was welcome to go around as many times as I liked. I think I played all twelve holes—it got a little confusing with so many more tees than greens, but the walk was effortless, and they'd squeezed every shot out of the space they had. I made some birdies and bogies and pars; I wasn't thinking much about the shots. I was looking around at the other sailors on the course and imagining my dad out here among them. He'd be in short sleeves, probably in his service khakis, and, like the shipmen around me, he'd be trying to figure out how to get his ball off the ground. He'd be in his twenties with a full head of hair and thick-rimmed glasses, with no kids or career yet, living on the other side of the country with my mother, both of them just having seen America for the first time on their drive out here.

I wondered what his hopes were back then, or what he expected for his future. I doubt he was guessing he'd have a golf-wandering son who would walk this ground sixty years later, or that this game he was learning would come to fill so much of his life. His American journey was just beginning. There were miles and miles to go, and the road could take him anywhere.

APPENDIX A: THE SCORES

COURSE	STATE	SCORE	BURGERDOGS
Chena Bend GC (p)	AK	74	3
Fairbanks GC* (p)	AK	77	1½
The Judge (p)	AL	77	2
Alotian Club	AR	87	3½
Mystic Creek (p)	AR	76	2½
Pine Valley (p)	AR	68	1½
Mountain Shadows** (p)	AZ	55	3
Oakcreek (p)	AZ	80	3
Papago GC (p)	AZ	78	3
Sedona Golf Resort (p)	AZ	71	3
Unidentified GC	AZ	75	2
Wagon Trail to Lonesome Pine* (p)	AZ	32	4
Ben Brown's GC* (p)	CA	34	3½
Cal Club	CA	74	3½
Cypress Point	CA	78	4
Goat Hill Park (p)	CA	66	3
Hacienda	CA	77	3
Holmby Park** (p)	CA	58	3
Los Angeles CC North	CA	76	3½
Naval Base Golf Performance Center	CA	34	4
Northwood GC (p)	CA	73	3½
Pacific Grove (p)	CA	71	3½
Pasatiempo (p)	CA	83	3½
Pebble Beach (p)	CA	81	3½
Penmar (p)	CA	35	3
Riviera	CA	78	3

COURSE	STATE	SCORE	BURGERDOGS
Roosevelt* (p)	CA	35	🍔🍔🍔
Rustic Canyon (p)	CA	77	🍔🍔🍔
Sharp Park GC (p)	CA	75	🍔🍔🍔
The Olympic Club Cliffs**	CA	347	🍔🍔🍔
The Olympic Club Lake	CA	80	🍔🍔🍔
Torrey Pines South (p)	CA	82	🍔🍔🍔🍔
TPC Harding Park (p)	CA	79	🍔🍔🍔
Ballyneal	CO	75	🍔🍔🍔🍔
Cherry Hills	CO	78	🍔🍔🍔
CommonGround (p)	CO	76	🍔🍔🍔
Fossil Trace (p)	CO	75	🍔🍔🍔
Fenwick* (p)	CT	74	🍔🍔🍔🍔
Keney Park (p)	CT	75	🍔🍔🍔🍔
Shennecossett CC (p)	CT	75	🍔🍔🍔
Yale	CT	76	🍔🍔🍔🍔
East Potomac (p)	DC	75	🍔🍔🍔
Langston (p)	DC	75	🍔🍔🍔
Bidermann	DE	77	🍔🍔🍔🍔
Capital City	FL	78	🍔🍔🍔
Dubsdread (p)	FL	79	🍔🍔
Golden Bear at Keene's Pointe	FL	79	🍔🍔
Havana GC* (p)	FL	76	🍔🍔🍔
Jacksonville Beach GC (p)	FL	80	🍔🍔🍔
McArthur	FL	87	🍔🍔🍔
Ocala GC (p)	FL	73	🍔🍔🍔
Ocala National (p)	FL	82	🍔🍔
Palatka GC (p)	FL	77	🍔🍔🍔
Palm Beach GC (p)	FL	60	🍔🍔🍔
Seminole	FL	86	🍔🍔🍔🍔
Streamsong Black (p)	FL	79	🍔🍔🍔🍔
Streamsong Blue (p)	FL	80	🍔🍔🍔
Streamsong Red (p)	FL	75	🍔🍔🍔🍔
Streamsong Roundabout** (p)	FL	44	🍔🍔🍔
The Villages Nancy Lopez	FL	72	🍔🍔
Winter Park* (p)	FL	75	🍔🍔🍔🍔
Atlanta Athletic Club	GA	76	🍔🍔🍔
Bobby Jones* (p)	GA	73	🍔🍔🍔
Candler Park* (p)	GA	39	🍔🍔🍔

COURSE	STATE	SCORE	BURGERDOGS
East Lake	GA	81	3
Lookout Mountain	GA	76	3½
Ohoopee	GA	78	3½
Ohoopee Whiskey Routing	GA	70	3½
Peachtree	GA	74	4
Savannah GC	GA	86	2½
The Landings Deer Creek	GA	76	2½
Hualālai GC (p)	HI	82	2½
Kukio	HI	84	3½
Mauna Lani (p)	HI	78	3
Nanea GC	HI	80	4
Rice Lake (p)	IA	70	2½
Waveland (p)	IA	75	3½
Circling Raven (p)	ID	81	3
Coeur d'Alene (p)	ID	82	3
Canal Shores (p)	IL	69	3½
Chicago GC	IL	77	3½
Downers Grove* (p)	IL	37	3
Glen View GC	IL	77	3½
Medinah #3	IL	81	3
Midlothian	IL	75	3
North Shore CC	IL	79	3
Olympia Fields North	IL	76	3
Onwentsia	IL	76	3½
Skokie	IL	83	3
Culver Academies*	IN	74	4
Notre Dame Warren (p)	IN	80	3
Brough Creek National* (p)	KS	23	4
Prairie Dunes	KS	87	4
Heritage Hill (p)	KY	74	2½
Audubon Park (p)	LA	63	3
LSU Alexandria* (p)	LA	35	2½
Blue Rock** (p)	MA	56	2½
Brae Burn	MA	76	3
Chequessett* (p)	MA	36	2½
Eastward Ho!	MA	84	3½
Essex CC	MA	77	3½
Highland Links* (p)	MA	39	4

COURSE	STATE	SCORE	BURGERDOGS
Hyannisport	MA	77	🍔🍔🍔
Kittansett	MA	72	🍔🍔🍔🍔
Marion GC* (p)	MA	35	🍔🍔🍔
Myopia Hunt Club	MA	77	🍔🍔🍔🍔
Old Sandwich	MA	76	🍔🍔🍔🍔
Plymouth GC	MA	79	🍔🍔🍔
The Country Club	MA	76	🍔🍔🍔
Thorny Lea	MA	75	🍔🍔🍔
Worcester	MA	76	🍔🍔🍔
Baltimore CC East	MD	83	🍔🍔🍔🍔
Columbia CC	MD	80	🍔🍔🍔
Congressional Blue	MD	78	🍔🍔🍔
Congressional Gold	MD	76	🍔🍔🍔
Gibson Island*	MD	75	🍔🍔🍔
Aroostook Valley (p)	ME	72	🍔🍔🍔
Belgrade Lakes (p)	ME	74	🍔🍔🍔
Cape Arundel (p)	ME	71	🍔🍔🍔🍔
Kebo Valley (p)	ME	67	🍔🍔🍔
Northeast Harbor	ME	76	🍔🍔🍔🍔
Arcadia Bluffs (p)	MI	82	🍔🍔🍔
Crystal Downs	MI	78	🍔🍔🍔🍔
Dunes Club*	MI	77	🍔🍔🍔🍔
Forest Dunes (p)	MI	83	🍔🍔🍔
Leslie Park (p)	MI	76	🍔🍔🍔
Oakland Hills	MI	79	🍔🍔🍔
The Loop Black (p)	MI	73	🍔🍔🍔🍔
The Loop Red (p)	MI	72	🍔🍔🍔🍔
Wawashkamo*	MI	73	🍔🍔🍔🍔
Birnamwood** (p)	MN	28	🍔🍔🍔
Fox Hollow (p)	MN	75	🍔🍔🍔
Hazeltine	MN	85	🍔🍔🍔
Interlachen	MN	79	🍔🍔🍔🍔
Minikahda	MN	80	🍔🍔🍔
Spring Hill GC	MN	80	🍔🍔🍔🍔
White Bear Yacht Club	MN	79	🍔🍔🍔🍔
Bellerive	MO	81	🍔🍔🍔
Big Bass** (p)	MO	28	🍔🍔
Buffalo Ridge (p)	MO	79	🍔🍔🍔

COURSE	STATE	SCORE	BURGERDOGS
Harrisonville GC* (p)	MO	36	2
Heart of America* (p)	MO	36	2
Mountain Top** (p)	MO	43	3
Ozarks National (p)	MO	80	3½
St. Louis CC	MO	75	4
Swope Memorial (p)	MO	82	3½
Top of the Rock** (p)	MO	59	3
Mossy Oak (p)	MS	74	3½
Old Waverly (p)	MS	77	3½
Lakeview CC* (p)	MT	36	2
Old Works (p)	MT	77	3
Dormie Club	NC	77	3
Pine Needles (p)	NC	74	3½
Pinehurst #2 (p)	NC	79	3
Pinehurst #2 (p)	NC	84	3
Pinehurst #4 (p)	NC	80	3½
The Cradle** (p)	NC	30	3½
Tobacco Road (p)	NC	72	4
Bully Pulpit (p)	ND	77	3
Hawktree GC (p)	ND	78	3
Prairie Club Dunes (p)	NE	74	3
Prairie Club Pines (p)	NE	76	3½
Sand Hills	NE	72	4
Sand Hills	NE	75	4
Mount Washington (p)	NH	74	2½
Red Hawk (p)	NM	78	3
Ballyowen (p)	NJ	74	3
Baltusrol Lower	NJ	77	3½
Baltusrol Upper	NJ	81	3
Crystal Springs (p)	NJ	80	2
Skyway* (p)	NJ	38	3½
Royal Links (p)	NV	76	2½
Amsterdam Municipal (p)	NY	74	3
Apawamis	NY	82	3½
Bellport GC	NY	72	3
Bethpage Black (p)	NY	80	3
Country Club of Buffalo	NY	82	3
Fishers Island	NY	85	4

COURSE	STATE	SCORE	BURGERDOGS
Fresh Meadow	NY	83	●●●◗
Friar's Head	NY	77	●●●●
Garden City	NY	80	●●●◗
Grover Cleveland (p)	NY	74	●●
Hay Harbor*	NY	35	●●●◗
Inwood	NY	79	●●●
Maidstone	NY	76	●●●●
Monroe GC	NY	75	●●●
Montauk Downs (p)	NY	78	●●●
National Golf Links of America	NY	77	●●●●
Oak Hill	NY	81	●●●
Poxabogue* (p)	NY	29	●●●
Quogue Field Club*	NY	40	●●●
Sebonack	NY	77	●●●◗
Shelter Island CC* (p)	NY	36	●●●
Shinnecock Hills	NY	74	●●●●
Sleepy Hollow	NY	81	●●●●
Sleepy Hollow	NY	75	●●●●
Southampton GC	NY	79	●●●◗
Southward Ho	NY	82	●●●
Split Rock (p)	NY	81	●●
Saint Andrew's GC	NY	81	●●●
St. George's	NY	77	●●●●
The Bridge	NY	81	●●●
Van Cortlandt Park (p)	NY	77	●●●
Winged Foot East	NY	82	●●●
Winged Foot West	NY	77	●●●◗
Canterbury	OH	83	●●●◗
Inverness	OH	74	●●●
Muirfield Village	OH	81	●●●
Ohio State Scarlet (p)	OH	72	●●●◗
Scioto	OH	73	●●●◗
Scioto	OH	71	●●●◗
Southern Hills	OK	88	●●●◗
Bandon Crossings (p)	OR	73	●●●◗
Bandon Dunes (p)	OR	76	●●●●
Bandon Preserve** (p)	OR	42	●●●◗
Bandon Trails (p)	OR	84	●●●◗

COURSE	STATE	SCORE	BURGERDOGS
Gearhart Golf Links (p)	OR	72	🍔🍔🍔🍔
Highlands GC (p)	OR	36	🍔🍔🍔🍔
Old Macdonald (p)	OR	77	🍔🍔
Pacific Dunes (p)	OR	78	🍔🍔🍔🍔
Silvies McVeigh's Gauntlet** (p)	OR	24	🍔🍔🍔🍔
Silvies Chief Egan Course** (p)	OR	27	🍔🍔🍔
Silvies Craddock Course (p)	OR	73	🍔🍔🍔🍔
Silvies Hankins Course (p)	OR	73	🍔🍔🍔🍔
Tetherow (p)	OR	77	🍔🍔🍔
The Pub Course at McMenamins (p)	OR	14	🍔🍔🍔
Carlisle CC	PA	81	🍔🍔🍔
Cobbs Creek (p)	PA	72	🍔🍔
Fox Chapel	PA	85	🍔🍔🍔🍔
French Creek	PA	77	🍔🍔🍔
Hershey's Mill GC	PA	85	🍔🍔
Lookaway	PA	76	🍔🍔🍔
LuLu CC (p)	PA	75	🍔🍔🍔
Merion East	PA	84	🍔🍔🍔🍔
Oakmont	PA	80	🍔🍔🍔🍔
Philadelphia CC	PA	74	🍔🍔🍔
Philadelphia CC	PA	78	🍔🍔🍔
Philadelphia Cricket Militia Hill	PA	76	🍔🍔🍔
Philadelphia Cricket St. Martins*	PA	36	🍔🍔🍔🍔
Philadelphia Cricket Wissahickon	PA	74	🍔🍔🍔🍔
Philadelphia Cricket Wissahickon	PA	74	🍔🍔🍔🍔
Rolling Green GC	PA	73	🍔🍔🍔🍔
Sunnybrook	PA	74	🍔🍔🍔
Waynesborough CC	PA	76	🍔🍔🍔
Waynesborough CC	PA	78	🍔🍔🍔
Waynesborough CC	PA	90	🍔🍔🍔
Newport CC	RI	78	🍔🍔🍔
Sakonnet	RI	76	🍔🍔🍔
Aiken GC (p)	SC	73	🍔🍔🍔🍔
Bulls Bay	SC	73	🍔🍔🍔🍔
Charleston Muni (p)	SC	75	🍔🍔🍔
Columbia CC	SC	78	🍔🍔🍔
Country Club of Charleston	SC	83	🍔🍔🍔
May River	SC	82	🍔🍔🍔

COURSE	STATE	SCORE	BURGERDOGS
McNair Memorial** (p)	SC	20	3
Palmetto GC	SC	78	4
Yeamans Hall	SC	78	3½
Prairie Green (p)	SD	83	2½
Red Rock (p)	SD	74	3
Sutton Bay	SD	75	3½
The Honors Course	TN	82	3
Sewanee* (p)	TN	38	3½
Sweetens Cove* (p)	TN	79	3½
Sweetens Cove* (p)	TN	73	3½
Austin CC	TX	82	3
Black Jack's Crossing (p)	TX	75	3
Bluejack National	TX	77	3½
Brackenridge Park (p)	TX	74	3½
Buttterfield Trail (p)	TX	75	3
Champions GC	TX	75	3
Colonial CC	TX	74	3
Lions Municipal (p)	TX	71	3
Marfa Municipal* (p)	TX	72	2
Northwood Club	TX	77	3
San Felipe Springs (p)	TX	78	3
Texas Star (p)	TX	75	2½
Sand Hollow (p)	UT	74	3
Ballyhack Goat Trak**	VA	53	3½
Ballyhack GC	VA	83	3½
Laurel Hill (p)	VA	76	3
Schoolhouse Nine** (p)	VA	28	3
Dorset Field Club	VT	73	3½
Ekwanok CC	VT	76	4
Chambers Bay (p)	WA	82	3½
Gamble Sands (p)	WA	77	4
Gold Mountain Olympic (p)	WA	79	3
McCormick Woods (p)	WA	82	2½
Meadow Park (p)	WA	82	3
Wine Valley (p)	WA	75	3½
Erin Hills (p)	WI	79	4
Kenosha	WI	74	3
Lawsonia Links (p)	WI	80	4

COURSE	STATE	SCORE	BURGERDOGS
Lawsonia Woodlands (p)	WI	73	▯▯▯
Sand Valley (p)	WI	77	▯▯▯◖
Sand Valley Mammoth Dunes (p)	WI	74	▯▯▯▯
Sand Valley Sandbox** (p)	WI	53	▯▯▯◖
Troy Burne (p)	WI	80	▯▯◖
Whistling Straits Irish (p)	WI	76	▯▯▯◖
Whistling Straits Straits (p)	WI	77	▯▯▯
Unfortunate WV GC (p)	WV	72	▯
Devils Tower (p)	WY	77	▯▯◖

*Nine-hole layout
**Par 3 course
(p) Denotes public, semiprivate, or resort accessible

Holes: 5,182	Score: 21,727 (+1,712)
Courses: 295	Round average to par: +6
Rounds: 301	Birdies: 424
Yards: 1,748,777	Eagles: 13

A note on the Burgerdog Scale: An unempirical, impulsive metric that compares the excitement of playing a particular course to the anticipation of devouring a burgerdog at the Olympic Club.

APPENDIX B: THE LISTS

FAVORITES, NOT FACTS

Rounds to Revisit Before I Die

1. Cypress Point (CA)
2. Oakmont (PA)
3. Tobacco Road (NC)
4. Wagon Trail to Lonesome Pine (AZ)
5. Silvies Valley (OR)
6. Culver Academies (IN)
7. Gamble Sands (WA)
8. Gearhart (OR)
9. White Bear Yacht Club (MN)
10. Rolling Green (PA)

US Open Venues

1. Oakmont (PA)
2. St. Louis CC (MO)
3. Shinnecock (NY)
4. Merion GC (PA)
5. Erin Hills (WI)
6. Pebble Beach (CA)
7. Myopia Hunt Club (MA)
8. Garden City (NY)
9. Chicago GC (IL)
10. Chambers Bay (WA)

Resort/Destination Courses (visitors welcome)

1. Gamble Sands (WA)
2. Bandon Dunes (OR)
3. Bandon Trails (OR)
4. Mammoth Dunes (WI)
5. Pebble Beach (CA)
6. Streamsong Red (FL)
7. The Loop Red/Black (MI)
8. Old Waverly (MS)
9. Arcadia Bluffs (MI)
10. Ozarks National (MO)

Publics (not previously mentioned)

1. Pasatiempo (CA)
2. Lawsonia Links (WI)
3. Cape Arundel (ME)
4. Keney Park (CT)

5. Waveland (IA)
6. Swope Memorial (MO)
7. Lions Municipal (TX)
8. CommonGround (CO)
9. Pacific Grove (CA)
10. Amsterdam Municipal (NY)

Nine-holers

1. Culver Academies (IN)
2. Sweetens Cove (TN)
3. Dunes Club (MI)
4. Fenwick (CT)
5. Sewanee (TN)
6. Highland Links (MA)
7. Wawashkamo (MI)
8. Winter Park (FL)
9. Highlands GC (OR)
10. Skyway (NJ)

Shorties

1. Bandon Preserve (OR)
2. The Cradle (NC)
3. Canal Shores (IL)
4. Silvies, McVeigh's Gauntlet (OR)
5. Schoolhouse Nine (VA)
6. Sand Valley Sandbox (WI)
7. Ballyhack Goat Trak (VA)
8. Mountain Shadows (AZ)
9. Palm Beach Par Three (FL)
10. Top of the Rock (MO)

Inconspicuous Treasures

1. Aiken GC (SC)
2. Downers Grove (IL)
3. Northeast Harbor (ME)
4. Gibson Island (MD)
5. Apawamis (NY)
6. Fox Hollow (MN)
7. Hawktree (ND)
8. Bandon Crossings (OR)
9. San Felipe Springs (TX)
10. Havana GC (FL)

Best Values

1. Waveland (IA): $26
2. Aiken GC (SC): $22
3. Swope Memorial (MO): $32
4. Roosevelt (CA): $24
5. Marion GC (MA): $23
6. Candler Park (GA): $28
7. Ben Brown's (CA): $25
8. Northwood (CA): $41
9. Pasatiempo (CA): $295
10. Holmby Park (CA): $4

Best Golf States

1. New York
2. California
3. Oregon
4. Pennsylvania
5. Wisconsin
6. Massachusetts
7. Georgia
8. Michigan
9. North Carolina
10. Minnesota

APPENDIX C:
GOLF ARCHITECTS GLOSSARY

DONALD ROSS (1872-1948): Scottish. Pinehurst. Genius. Influential for both quality and quantity. Grew up in Dornoch; learned from Old Tom Morris. Designed or reworked more than four hundred courses in America. His upturned-saucer greens at Pinehurst have left a too-permanent impression on golf mythology, inaccurately branding him "the saucer guy."

CHARLES BLAIR MACDONALD (1855-1939): Refer to him as C. B. or Charlie to show off your chops. Golf's first architect, because he called himself that. Built first American eighteen-holer at Chicago GC, and complained the USGA into existence. Cribbed from the best holes in Britain, re-creating these "ideal" template holes in his own designs. National Golf Links is his opus. If his name comes up in conversation, just say "The Lido" and walk away.

SETH RAYNOR (1874-1926): Macdonald's man. Not a golfer but an engineer hired to survey National Golf Links, and then stayed on as Macdonald's partner/builder for life. Middle name Jagger; like the other Jagger, struck out on solo projects for cash. Died young, but not before crafting heavyweights like Fishers Island and Yeamans Hall. Took on protégé Charles Banks, who finished Raynor's work after his death. Banks designed more than a dozen of his own classics, thus completing the design triumvirate of Macdonald-Raynor-Banks. Banks also passed away at an early age.

DEVEREUX EMMET (1861-1934): A free-spirited hunting-dog salesman who learned the links while peddling pooches abroad. He married well and got a gig from his wife's uncle to take a crack at designing Garden City Golf Club, followed by St. George's (both masterworks). Close pal of Macdonald who sketched British holes for C. B. Chipped in at National; built the original version of Congressional's Blue.

A. W. TILLINGHAST (1876-1942): Born Albert Warren, known as Tilly. Philly boy who took inspiration from the courses of the British Isles, where he bumped elbows with Old Tom. The trauma of a childhood void of Super Bowls clearly engendered a mean streak expressed via merciless cross-bunkering. Not as prolific as Ross, but overall résumé may be unmatched: Baltusrol, Philly Cricket, Winged Foot, Newport, Baltimore CC, San Francisco, Bethpage Black (maybe).

ALISTER MACKENZIE (1870-1934): Englishman, trained as an MD, learned the science of camouflage in the Royal Army, which influenced his course designs. Liked the sauce. Worked around the globe, specializing in bucket-list rankings-toppers: Royal Melbourne, Augusta National, Cypress Point. A designer so beloved that his devotees maintain an online MacKenzie chronology aimed at tracing his whereabouts for every single day of his life.

MARION HOLLINS (1892-1944): Women's Am champ turned driving force behind Pasatiempo and Cypress Point. More developer than designer. Projects included the Women's National on Long Island by Devereux Emmet. Confidante of Alister MacKenzie. Sent by MacKenzie to Augusta for site visit, which ruffled Georgian feathers. MacKenzie responded: "I do not know of any man who has sounder ideas." Responsible for the greatest par 3 in golf, sixteen at Cypress Point. Original designer Raynor lamented not being able to build the hole due to its impossible ocean carry. Hollins teed one up and fired it safely across the waves, convincing him otherwise.

GEORGE CRUMP (1871-1918): Pine Valley's tragic hero. Golf's great one-hit wonder, Pine Valley in south Jersey was both Crump's obsession and demise, labeled Crump's Folly for its numerous setbacks and runaway costs. Crump committed suicide (initially reported as a tooth infection) prior to its completion, never seeing his life's only design ascend to the top spot in the world rankings.

WALTER TRAVIS (1862-1927): Aussie born, the Grandma Moses of golf. Took his first swing at age thirty-five; won three US Ams within the next seven years. Notable design credits: Ekwanok, West Chester, Country Club of Scranton. Reworked

Emmet's Garden City to great acclaim; founded the *American Golfer*, golf's most influential publication of the day.

WILLE PARK JR. (1864-1925): Scotsman born into one of golf's greatest families, with a brother and uncle both named Mungo. (Seriously.) Two-time Open champion; split design work between America and the UK. Designed Olympia Fields North, then Maidstone before succumbing to mental illness shortly after its completion. Passed away in a mental hospital in Scotland.

GEORGE THOMAS (1873-1932): Philly guy; went to Episcopal Academy, which is now part of the campus of St. Joseph's University, where I teach. He did other stuff, too, like design Riviera and Bel-Air and LACC, but most significantly walked the hallways where I now get lost on the way to class.

TOM BENDELOW (1868-1936): Scottish transplant who built America's first public eighteen-holer, Van Cortlandt Park in the Bronx. Worked for Spalding and Wilson golf divisions, laying out courses across the country. Medinah in Chicago is his standout achievement.

WILLIAM FLYNN (1890-1945): Cut his design teeth assisting at Merion. Helped out at Pine Valley. Partnered with engineer Howard Toomey for work at Shinnecock, Philadelphia CC, Rolling Green, Cherry Hills, The Country Club. Sleeper pick for best architect of the Golden Age (the era of golf design between end of World War I and the Depression).

HUGH WILSON (1879-1925): Philadelphian and first club champ at Aronimink. Credited with Merion, though historians debate how much of the design should in fact be credited to Macdonald and Merion superintendent William Flynn. Worked on Pine Valley. His only complete design outside Merion is Cobbs Creek, a Philadelphia public treasure currently undergoing a philanthropic restoration.

PERRY MAXWELL (1879-1952): Kentucky man who joined with MacKenzie for U of Michigan, Crystal Downs, Ohio State. Partnered with his son, Press, for later designs. Worked widely through the central US and extensively in Oklahoma. Best known for Prairie Dunes in Kansas.

JOSEPH BARTHOLOMEW (1885-1971): African American caddie turned golf superintendent and course designer. Learned from Seth Raynor; helped build Metairie

Country Club in Louisiana and became its first head pro, though he was prohibited from playing the course. Was denied playing most of his designs, until he built New Orleans's first municipal course for African Americans. Founded a construction company and invested wisely. Started life earning three dollars a day caddying for white members; retired with a fortune from ventures in insurance, real estate, and ice cream.

ROBERT TRENT JONES SR. (1906–2000): Rochester raised, studied at Cornell (no Big Red degree, but left his mark on the agriculture program). Adept self-promoter who changed his middle name to Trent after another Bobby T. Jones achieved golf's only Grand Slam in 1930. Became the "Open Doctor," pinching fairways for the USGA in a style he called "Heroic Golf." The rest of us call it Hard Golf. Designed over five hundred courses. Best known for the RTJ Trail in Alabama, a 378-hole (expanded to 468) string of courses throughout the state; American golf's most ambitiously scaled project, controversially funded and maintained by the Alabama state retirement system. Sons RTJ Jr. and Rees Jones have notable design careers; occasionally critiqued by GCA gurus for overwrought designs. Rees took up his father's mantle as Open Doctor deux.

PETE DYE (1925–2020): Ohioan who met Donald Ross at Pinehurst while stationed at Fort Bragg. Influenced by MacKenzie and RTJ Sr. and the courses of Scotland, where he found the idea for using sleepers (railway ties) on his courses. Noted for both his hands-on approach to course construction and his family tree of architects: helped launch the careers of Tom Doak, Jim Urbina, Bill Coore, Bobby Weed, and Rod Whitman. Patron saint of punitive golf. Layouts known for being both demanding and visually stunning, evidenced by Whistling Straits, Casa de Campo, TPC Sawgrass, and Kiawah Ocean Course. Quoted as saying, "Golf is not a fair game. So why build a course fair?" Wife Alice Dye was a noted player and designer who contributed significantly to his most celebrated layouts.

TOM FAZIO (1945–): The Faz. Another Philadelphia guy; grew up working on his uncle George's designs, one of which is my home course, Waynesborough. Known for big-budget projects that move big earth and achieve big results. Bankable Fazio builds are regular award winners.

MIKE STRANTZ (1955–2005): Apprentice of Tom Fazio who struck out on his own to sculpt some of golf's most audacious layouts. Originally a fine artist, his courses—most notably Tobacco Road—are appreciated like fine art: beloved by some, dismissed as confusing by others. A visionary of unfulfilled genius. Golf's Kurt Cobain. Cancer took his life in his prime.

GIL HANSE, BILL COORE & BEN CRENSHAW, TOM DOAK, DAVID MCLAY KIDD: The pillars of America's current, second Golden Age of golf design. Philosophies generally involve a degree of earth-moving minimalism, stressing rugged naturalism, focusing on player experience and strategic options instead of manufactured difficulty.

ROB COLLINS, TAD KING, KEITH RHEBB, RILEY JOHNS: American designers to watch; builders of paradigm-shifting short courses, shaking up perceptions about what a golf course can be.

ACKNOWLEDGMENTS

For every round of the three hundred I played in 2019, there is a name—often a few—to thank for the company, the hospitality, or the effort expended in helping a near-stranger find a tee time. Their numbers are far too large to list here, or to print on the cover of this book where they belong, because this course called America was designed by their generosity and friendship.

The longstanding support of my editor, Jofie Ferrari-Adler, and my agent, Dan Mandel, continue to allow me to live my golf and writing dreams. My gratitude to both of them is profound. Thanks also to Julianna Haubner for her invaluable and painstaking edits, as well as Carolyn Kelly, Morgan Hoit, Jordan Rodman, Allie Lawrence, Samantha Hoback, and Ben Holmes at Avid Reader/Simon & Schuster. And thank you to the friends and partners who helped spread word of my wanderings: Jeffrey Stewart, Zac O'Bryan, Thomas Young, Chandler Withington, Mike DePaolo, Eric Soderstrom, Alicia Madden, Joe Gomes, Tom Casey, Billy Draddy, Zak Kozuchowski, Abby Liebenthal, Erin Gregory, and Seth McWhorter.

To my wife, Allyson, and my girls, Maggie and Caroline—your love, patience, and support are in every word here. The only way to try and thank you is to stick to my word—yes, this was indeed the final odyssey.

Unless, of course, you'd like to go walkabout down under. . . .

ABOUT THE AUTHOR

TOM COYNE is the author of the *New York Times* bestsellers *A Course Called Ireland* and *A Course Called Scotland*; *Paper Tiger*; and the novel *A Gentleman's Game*, named one of the best twenty-five sports books of all time by the *Philadelphia Daily News* and adapted into a motion picture starring Gary Sinise. He is podcast host and senior editor for the *Golfer's Journal* and has written for *GOLF Magazine*, *Golfweek*, *Sports Illustrated*, the *New York Times*, and numerous other publications. He earned an MFA in fiction writing from the University of Notre Dame, where he won the William Mitchell Award for distinguished achievement. He lives outside Philadelphia with his wife and two daughters.